THE 'CHARACTERS'
OF JEAN DE LA BRUYÈRE

LECTOR HOUSE PUBLIC DOMAIN WORKS

THE 'CHARACTERS' OF JEAN DE LA BRUYÈRE

JEAN DE LA BRUYÈRE,
HENRI VAN LAUN

ISBN: 978-93-89509-26-7

Published: 1885

LECTOR HOUSE LLP
E-MAIL: lectorpublishing@gmail.com

JEAN DE LA BRUYÈRE

THE "CHARACTERS"
OF JEAN DE LA BRUYÈRE

NEWLY RENDERED INTO ENGLISH
BY HENRI VAN LAUN

With an Introduction, a Biographical Memoir and Notes

ILLUSTRATED WITH TWENTY-FOUR ETCHINGS
BY B. DAMMAN AND V. FOULQUIER

1885

CONTENTS

LIST OF ILLUSTRATIONS

INTRODUCTION.

T is a common practice for translators to state to the public that the author they are going to introduce, and whom they sometimes traduce, is one of the greatest men of the age, and that already for a long time a general desire has been felt to make the acquaintance of such a master-mind. It would be an insult to French scholars to speak thus of La Bruyère, for the merits of his "Characters" are known; but, for the benefit of those who are not so well acquainted with our author, I may state that he is neither so terse, epigrammatic, sublime, nor profound as either Pascal or La Rochefoucauld are, but that he is infinitely more readable, as he is always trying to please his readers, and now and then sacrifices even a certain depth of thought to attain his object.

La Bruyère takes good care to tell us that he has not imitated any one; Pascal "makes metaphysics subservient to religion, explains the nature of the soul, its passions and vices; treats of the great and serious motives which lead to virtue, and endeavours to make a man a Christian;" La Rochefoucauld's "mind, instructed by his knowledge of society, and with a delicacy equal to his penetration, observed that self-love in man was the cause of all his errors, and attacked it without intermission, wherever it was found; and this one thought, multiplied as it were in a thousand different ways by a choice of words and a variety of expression, has always the charm of novelty."[1] Our author, on the contrary, openly declares: "I did not wish to write any maxims, for they are like moral laws, and I acknowledge that I possess neither sufficient authority nor genius for a legislator."[2]

What is the plan and idea of the book of "Characters?" Let La Bruyère himself answer this: "Of the sixteen chapters which compose it, there are fifteen wholly employed in detecting the fallacy and ridicule to be found in the objects of human passions and inclinations, and in demolishing such obstacles as at first weaken, and afterwards extinguish, any knowledge of God in mankind; therefore, these chapters are merely preparatory to the sixteenth and last, wherein atheism is attacked, and perhaps routed, wherein the proofs of a God, such at least as weak

[1] Pascal's Pensées were published in 1670, six years after their author's death; La Rochefoucauld's Maximes appeared in 1665, and of both works from five to six editions had been sold before the "Characters" saw the light. I have borrowed the definition of these authors' labours from La Bruyère's "Prefatory Discourse concerning Theophrastus," which came out at the same time as the "Characters," and served as an introduction.

[2] Preface to La Bruyère's "Characters," page v.

man is capable of receiving, are produced; wherein the providence of God is defended against the insults and complaints of freethinkers."[3]

La Bruyère is not a speculative moralist, but an observer of the manners of men, or, as he likes to call himself a philosopher, and above all a Christian philosopher, such as a friend of Bossuet ought to be. He was the first to make morality attractive, and to paint characters in a literary and delicate manner; he does not dogmatise, and above all shows neither personal hatred nor venom; in other words, to use his own expressions, he "gives back to the public what it lent"[4] him.

Underneath the literary man people often look for the man, with all his passion, his likes and dislikes; hence the many "Keys" of the "Characters," published during the author's lifetime and after his death, in which all kinds of allusions were attempted, and all sorts of hypothetical explanations ventured on.

Of the concocters of the "Keys" La Bruyère speaks as follows:

"They make it their business, if possible, to discover to which of their friends or enemies these portraits can apply; they neglect everything that seems like a sound remark or a serious reflection, though almost the whole book consists of them; they dwell upon nothing but the portraits or characters, and after having explained them in their own way, and after they imagine they have found out the originals, they publish to the world long lists, or, as they call them, 'Keys,' but which are indeed 'false keys,' and as useless to them as they are injurious to the persons whose names are deciphered, and to the writer who is the cause of it, though an involuntary one."[5]

And yet some of these "Keys" have been of great use to modern commentators, and served to elucidate several traits in the "Characters" which otherwise would not have been discovered.

It would be ridiculous to deny that La Bruyère never had any particular personage in view in delineating a certain character, but, as he himself says: "If I might be allowed to be a little vain, I should be apt to believe that my "Characters" have pretty well portrayed men in general, since they resemble so many in particular; and since every one thinks he finds there his neighbour or his countryman. I did indeed paint after the life, but did not always mean to paint, in my book of "Characters," one individual or another. I did not hire myself out to the public to draw only such portraits as should be true and like the originals, for fear that sometimes they would be thought incredible, and appear feigned or imaginary ones. Becoming yet more difficult I went farther, and took one lineament from one person and one from another, and from these several lineaments, which might be found in one and the same person, I drew some likely portraits, studying not so much to please the reader by describing the characters of certain people, or, as

[3] Preface to La Bruyère's "Speech upon his Admission as a Member of the French Academy, June 15, 1693," which preface was published for the first time with the eighth edition of the "Characters," in 1694.

[4] Preface to La Bruyère's "Characters," page i.

[5] Preface to La Bruyère's "Speech upon his Admission as a Member of the French Academy, June 15, 1693."

the malcontents would say, by satirising them, as to lay before him what faults he ought to avoid, and what examples to follow."[6]

Our author, therefore, did not wish to depict individuals, but men in general; for man is the same in all seasons and at all times, and is swayed by the same motives and passions, though they exercise a different influence in various ages, produce different results amongst many races, and do not even act in precisely the same manner in divers centuries, climates, and under heterogeneous circumstances. He had no intention of presenting a series of historical events,[7] but of depicting Frenchmen at the end of the seventeenth century as they lived, breathed, and moved; not animated by violent likes and dislikes, as those of the Ligue or the Fronde were, nor filled by the importance of their own overweening individualities. When we read him, we behold in our mind's eye the subdued subjects of Louis XIV., slavishly obeying the "Roi Soleil," admitting the King can do no wrong, becoming devout to please His Majesty and Madame de Maintenon, inaugurating the reign of courtly hypocrisy, embracing the principle of one religion in one state, and seeing the royal sun gradually decline, and the star of William III. in its ascendancy.

The notes of the present edition are necessary, I imagine, to assist in illustrating the life of a past age, for "no usages or customs are perennial, but they vary with the times.... Nothing can be more opposed to our manners than all these things; but the distance of time makes us relish them." The "Characters" themselves, as well as the notes, represent a "history of ... times," when the usual custom was "the selling of offices; that is to say, the power of protecting innocence, punishing guilt, and doing justice to the world, bought with ready money like a farm." They will also make my readers acquainted with "a great city," which at the end of the seventeenth century was "without any public places, baths, fountains, amphitheatres, galleries, porticoes, or public walks, and this the capital of a powerful kingdom; they will be told of persons whose whole life was spent in going from one house to another; of decent women who kept neither shops nor inns, yet had their houses open for those who would pay for their admission,[8] and where they could choose between dice, cards, and other games, where feasting was going on, and which were very convenient for all kinds of intercourse. They will be informed that people crowded the street only to be thought in a hurry; that there was no conversation nor cordiality, but that they were confused, and, as it were, alarmed by the rattle of coaches which they had to avoid, and which drove through the streets as if for a prize at some race. People will learn, without being greatly astonished, that in times of public peace and tranquillity, the inhabitants went to church and visited ladies and their friends, whilst wearing offensive weapons; and that there was

---

[6] Preface to La Bruyère's "Speech upon his Admission as a Member of the French Academy, June 15, 1693."

[7] Sir Walter Scott, in his introduction to Dryden's "Absalom and Achitophel," says: "He who collects a gallery of portraits disclaims, by the very act of doing so, any intention of presenting a series of historical events."

[8] It was the custom in Paris, at the time La Bruyère wrote, for any gentleman or lady to leave part of their gains on the table, to pay, as it were, for the cards; hence the allusion.

hardly any one who did not have dangling at his side wherewith to kill another person with one thrust."[9]

La Bruyère, though a shrewd observer, has the daring of an innovator, but always remains very guarded in his language. When now and then his feelings get the better of him, he expresses his opinions like a man, and attacks the vices of his age with a boldness which none of his contemporaries has surpassed. Nearly the whole of his chapter "Of the Gifts of Fortune" is an attack on the financiers; in the chapter "Of the Great," he certainly does not flatter the courtiers, whilst he himself never pretends to be anything else but "a plebeian,"[10] and almost always sides with his own class. If he flatters the king, it is because he thinks him necessary to the state, and, perhaps, also because he wishes to have a defender against the many enemies his book had raised up. He was, moreover, very cautious, and in the endless alterations he made in the various editions of the "Characters,"[11] published during his lifetime, he but seldom envenomed the barb he had shot, or boasted of it if he did so.[12] Though he touched on all the passions of men, he did not set one class against another, a task which was left to the so-called philosophical authors of the eighteenth century.

The style of La Bruyère has been praised by competent judges for its conciseness and picturesqueness; he always employs the right word in the right place, is correct in his expressions, varied in his thoughts, highly imaginative, and, therefore, maybe called a perfect literary artist.[13] A few words and expressions, which I have noticed, have become antiquated, or have changed their meaning, but the "Characters" will still, I think, be read for many ages, be found very entertaining, and, what cannot be said of the works of every classical French author, will be better liked the more they are read. If sometimes one of the characters is portrayed with too many details, it is because it is taken not from one man, but composed of a series of shrewd and clever observations made on different personages; and hence our author calls them "Characters," and not "portraits."

Since La Bruyère's death many editions of the "Characters" have appeared; I have collated and compared the best of them, amongst which those edited by

[9] All the passages on pages 15 and 16 between inverted commas (" ") have been taken from La Bruyère's "Prefatory Discourse concerning Theophrastus."

[10] See the Chapter "Of the Great," page 230, § 25. When, in the Chapter "Of Certain Customs," page 408, § 14, he speaks of his "descent from a certain Godfrey de la Bruyère," he does so jocularly.

[11] Compare "Preface," page iv., "I did not hesitate," till page v., "and more regular."

[12] In his "Introduction to the Reader," printed before "Absalom and Achitophel," and published in 1681, Dryden openly admits: "I have laid in for those, by rebating the satire, where justice would allow it, from carrying too sharp an edge. They who can criticise so weakly as to imagine I have done my worst, may be convinced at their own cost that I can write severely with more ease than I can write gently." La Bruyère would never have ventured to speak so plainly, and this difference between the French and English author seems very characteristic of the two nations. Compare also Dryden's poetic delineation of Buckingham as Zimri to La Bruyère's portrait of Lauzun as Straton.

[13] Perhaps no author is more quoted in Littré's Dictionnaire de la langue française than La Bruyère is.

Mons. G. Servois and Mons. A. Chassang have laid me under great obligations. I am indebted to these two editions for many of the notes, and for a few to those of MM. Destailleur and Hémardinquer.

Several imitations of the "Characters" have also been published, amongst others a *Petit la Bruyère, ou Caractères et mœurs des enfants de ce siècle*, and a *Le la Bruyère des domestiques, précédé de considérations sur Pétat de domesticité en général*, both by that voluminous author, Madame de Genlis, a *Le la Bruyère des jeunes gens*, and a similar work for *jeunes demoiselles*, which attract the attention by the oddity of their titles.

La Bruyère's "Characters" have also been translated several times into English.

1. A translation seems to have been published in London as early as 1698.[14]

2. The "Characters of Theophrastus," translated from M. Bruyère's French version by Eustace Budgell, Esq., London, 1699; and another edition of the same work published in 1702.[15]

3. The "Characters of Theophrastus," together with the Characters of the Age, by La Bruyère, with a prefatory discourse and key: London, 1700.[16]

4. The "Characters, or the Manners of the Age," by Monsieur de la Bruyère of the French Academy, made English by several hands, with the "Characters of Theophrastus," translated from the Greek, and a prefatory discourse to them, by Monsieur de la Bruyère, the third edition, corrected throughout, and enlarged, with the Key inserted in the margin: London, Leach, 1702.

5. The Works of Monsieur de la Bruyère, containing: I. The Moral Characters of Theophrastus; II. The Characters, or the Manners of the Present Age; III. M. Bruyère's Speech upon his Admission into the French Academy; IV. An Account of the Life and Writings of M. Bruyère, by Monsieur Coste, with an original Chapter of the Manner of Living with Great Men, written after the method of M. Bruyère, by N. Rowe, Esq. This translation seems to have been very successful, for the sixth edition, the only one I have seen, was published in two volumes in 1713: London, E. Curll.

6. The Moral Characters of Theophrastus, by H. Gaily: London, 1725.

7. The Works of M. de la Bruyère, in two volumes, to which is added the Characters of Theophrastus, also The Manner of Living with Great Men, written after the manner of Bruyère, by N. Rowe, Esq.: London, J. Bell, 1776.

I have consulted the edition mentioned in No. 2, and printed in 1702, in which the attacks of La Bruyère on William III. in the Chapter "Of Opinions," §§ 118 and <u>119, are omitted</u>; the sixth edition of the "Characters," given in No. 5, and pub-

[14] M. G. Servois, in his bibliographic Notice of La Bruyère's works, &c., vol. iii., first part, quotes a passage from the London correspondent of the Histoire des Ouvrages des savants (see page 19, note 68) in affirmation of this statement, and seems to think this translation to have been the first edition of the one mentioned in No. 4.

[15] Watt's "Bibliotheca Britannica."

[16] According to M. Servois, this edition is mentioned in Lowndes' "The Bibliographer's Manual," but I have not been able to find it there.

lished in 1713; and the edition referred to in No. 7.

In the "Advertisement concerning the new edition" of 1713, printed with the "Characters," it is stated, "We procured the last English edition to be compared verbatim with the last Paris edition (which is the ninth), and ... all the Supplemental Reflections ... we got translated, and added to this present edition; and that it might be as complete as possible, we have not scrupled to translate even those parts which at first sight may perhaps disoblige some who have a just veneration for the memory of our Glorious Deliverer, the late King William." La Bruyère's speech upon his admission into the French Academy was in this edition "made English by M. Ozell."

In the edition of 1776, the "parts" reflecting on William III. are again omitted. It greatly differs from the one of 1713, and is dedicated to the Right Honourable Henry, Earl of Lincoln, Auditor of the Exchequer, Knight of the most noble order of the Garter, &c. &c.

Many faults may be found in the old translations, but I have endeavoured to amend them; and I never scrupled to adopt any expressions, turn of thought, or even page of any or every translation of my predecessors, whenever I found I could not improve upon them.

Translations of the "Characters" have appeared in several other languages; four of these were published in German, the last one printed in 1872, whilst already the final chapter of La Bruyère's book "Of Freethinkers" had come out in a German dress in 1739; moreover, La Bruyère's book has been translated twice into Italian, once into Spanish, and once into Russian.

The imitations of the "Characters" into English are—

1. "The English Theophrastus, or the Manners of the Age, being the modern Characters of the Court, the Town, and the City," by Boyer: London, 1692 and 1702.

2. The Chapter "Of the Manner of Living with Great Men," written after the method of M. Bruyère, by N. Rowe, mentioned already.

3. Imitations of the Characters of Theophrastus: London, 1774.

I imagine that the author of the "English Theophrastus" was M. Abel Boyer, the compiler of the well-known dictionary, born at Castres in 1664, who fled to England at the revocation of the Edict of Nantes, and died at Chelsea in 1729.

The direct influence of La Bruyère's writings on English literature is not easily to be traced. Swift may, possibly, have studied him, though he never mentions him,[17] and so may, perhaps, Anthony Cooper, third earl of Shaftesbury,[18] "who spoke French so fluently, and with so perfect an accent, that in France he was often mistaken for a native."[19] I venture to think that Addison and Steele were also acquainted with our Frenchman;[20] but the English author who in expression,

---

[17] I imagine I can observe slight traces of La Bruyère in Swift's "Account of the Empire of Japan, written in 1728," beginning with the words: "Regoge was the 34th emperor of Japan;" in nearly all he wrote for the Tatler; in many of the portraits to be found in the Examiner, for example in the portrait of "Laurence Hyde, late earl of Rochester," beginning with the words: "The person who now presides at the Council, etc." Compare also "A Short Character of Thomas, Earl of Wharton;" the "Narrative of Guiscard's Examination;" and in the "True Relation of the Intended Riot," the passage beginning with "the surprising generosity, and fit of housekeeping the German princess has been guilty of this summer." Swift, moreover, possesses a far more trenchant style than the French author, but I imagine the latter did as much execution, though he used a rapier, whilst Swift employed a bludgeon.

[18] There are few portraits in Shaftesbury's "Characteristics;" one of the few exceptions being the portrait of "a notable enthusiast of the itinerant kind," supposed to be Van Helmont; now and then, however, he seems to have borrowed a few ideas of La Bruyère, as for example, in the second section of "A Letter concerning Enthusiasm," his remarks on criticism and ridicule. Compare also Shaftesbury in section 2, saying: "The vulgar, indeed, may swallow any sordid jest, any mere drollery or buffoonery; but it must be a finer and truer wit which takes the men of sense and breeding," to La Bruyère's Chapter "Of Works of the Mind," §§ 51, 52; the whole of this "Letter" is somewhat like La Bruyère, as in section iv. the crafty beggars, addressing some one they meet in a coach, and of whose quality they are ignorant. In Shaftesbury's "Sensus Communis, an Essay on the Freedom of Wit and Humour," part 1, section 3, his remarks about true raillery; and the opening of the second part, section 1: "If a native of Ethiopia were of a sudden transported into Europe," etc., as well as in the "Soliloquy," the allegory of the love-spent nobleman, and in the "Moralists" the portraits of Palemon, Philocles, and Theocles, and the opening of the third part, "it was yet deep night," appear somewhat like reminiscences of the French author.

[19] "English Philosophers:" Shaftesbury and Hutcheson. By Thomas Fowler, President of Corpus Christi College: London, 1882.

[20] It will, of course, be impossible to give "chapter and verse" for every passage of the "Spectator" which is faintly like one of La Bruyère's observations, nor do I mean to say that Addison, Steele, and the other contributors to the English paper borrowed literally, and without acknowledgment, from the French author. But what I intended to convey was that, though the humour of the Spectator and its Sir Roger de Coverley, Sir Andrew Freeport, Will Honeycomb, Captain Sentry, &c., are preeminently English, several of the remarks and portraits to be found there are more or less inspired by a careful study of La Bruyère. Compare for example Addison's paper about the opera, Spectator No. 5, to § 47 of La Bruyère's Chapter "Of Works of the Mind;" and the remarks in No. 10 of the Spectator, about the occupations of the female world, and Nos. 144, 156, and No. 265 of the same paper, with some paragraphs of La Bruyère's Chapter "Of Women." Nos. 45, 57, 77, 88, 98, 100, 129, 193, 236, 238, and 494, appear to me somewhat like several of La Bruyère's paragraphs. The "fair youth" in No. 104 of the "Spectator" is not unlike a reverse picture of La Bruyère's portrait of Iphis in the Chapter "Of Fashion," page 389, § 14; whilst the remark in No. 226, "Who is the better man for beholding the most beautiful Venus," &c., reminds one of La Bruyère's remark on obscene "pictures painted for certain princes of the Church," in his Chapter "Of Certain Customs," page 409, § 17. Steele's opinions about corporal punishments (Spectator, No. 157) are very much in advance of those of La Bruyère on the same subject; the English author remarks about Louis XIV. (Spectator, No. 180 and 200) should be compared with La

turn of thought, art of delineating character, and in his mixture of seriousness and familiarity, is most like him, is a doctor of divinity, R. South, Prebendary of Westminster, and Canon of Christ Church, and yet he wrote before La Bruyère, and therefore cannot have imitated him.[21]

I am not aware La Bruyère knew English, though his successor at the French Academy states that he spoke several foreign languages;[22] he was well acquainted with German, Italian, and I think also Spanish; nor do I know if any of Dr. South's sermons were published separately before La Bruyère wrote, and if he, therefore, could have seen them. I should imagine he never read any of them.

Six portraits, which adorn these volumes, have been specially etched for this edition by M. B. Damman, whilst the portrait of La Bruyère, and the vignettes at the head of each chapter, have been drawn and etched by M. V. Foulquier.

In the biographical memoir of La Bruyère, I have only stated what is known of him, which is very little.

HENRI VAN LAUN.

Bruyère's glorification of the same monarch.

[21] I have consulted the edition of Dr. R. South's sermons, eleven vols., the first six published by H. Lintot, 1732; the last five by Charles Bathurst, 1744. In the sermon preached at Westminster Abbey, February 22, 1684-85, on Prov. xvi. 33: "The lot is cast into the lap," &c., the passage about Alexander the Great, in his famed expedition against Darius, the remarks about Hannibal and Cæsar, Agathocles, the potter who became King, Masaniello, and finally what the Doctor says about Cromwell: "and who, that had beheld such a bankrupt beggarly fellow as Cromwell first entering the Parliament House, with a threadbare, torn cloak, and a greasy hat (and perhaps neither of them paid for), could have suspected that in the space of so few years, he should, by the murder of one king, and the banishment of another, ascend the throne, be invested in the royal robes, and want nothing of the state of a king, but the changing of his hat into a crown," seem like some expressions of La Bruyère. Compare also sermon x.: "Good Intentions no Excuse for Bad Actions," full of pithy characteristics in word-painting, and his sermons: "The Fatal Imposture and Force of Words," Isaiah v. 20, "Woe unto them that call evil good and good evil," which are very La Bruyèresque, and somewhat like several paragraphs of the Chapter "Of Certain Customs." See also in "The Nature and Measures of Conscience," a sermon preached Nov. 1, 1691, the portrait of the "potent sinner upon earth," and a sermon on "Pretence of Conscience no Excuse for Rebellion," preached before Charles II., 13th January, 1662-63, the anniversary of the "execrable murder" of Charles I., in which South says, "I wonder where the blasphemy lies which some charge upon those who make the king's suffering something to resemble our Saviour's." Compare finally the portrait of the "cozening, lying, perjured shop-keeper" in the second sermon, "On Avarice as contradictory to Religion," with La Bruyère's tradesman in his Chapter "Of the Gifts of Fortune," § 43.

[22] The Abbé Claude Fleury, the learned author of the Histoire Ecclésiastique, who succeeded La Bruyère as a member of the French Academy, said of his predecessor in his opening speech: "Il savait les langues mortes et les vivantes."

A BIOGRAPHICAL MEMOIR
OF
JEAN DE LA BRUYÈRE.

OR a long time it has generally been taken for granted that our author first saw the light at Dourdan, a small town in the department of Seine-et-Oise, but it has only lately been discovered that he was born in Paris in the month of August 1645. His father, Louis de la Bruyère, was *contrôleur des rentes de la ville*, a sort of town-tax collector, whilst his mother, Elizabeth Hamonin, belonged to a respectable family of Parisian burgesses. His grandfather and great-grandfather on the father's side, declared partisans of the Ligue, were both exiled from France when Henri IV. came to the throne. Perhaps, therefore, the feelings our author entertained for the people may be explained by atavism. A younger brother of his father and our author's godfather, a very wealthy man, and most likely a money-lender, as well as interested in the farming of certain taxes, seems to have produced no favourable impression on his god-son, for the latter always attacks the farmers of the revenue.

Jean de la Bruyère was educated at the Oratorians in Paris, and two years before his father died, in the month of June 1664, took his degree of licentiate at law at the University of Orléans. He became an advocate, but in 1673, when twenty-eight years old, he forsook the bar, and bought for about 24,000 *livres* the post of *trésorier des finances* in the Caen district, in Normandy. There were fifteen *trésoriers* at Caen, of whom only some were obliged to reside there, but all became ennobled by virtue of their office, and received as non-residents a yearly salary of about 2500 *livres*. La Bruyère had bought this treasurership of a certain Joseph Metezeau, said to have been a relative by marriage of Bossuet, but this is not at all proved; and in 1686, about two years before he was going to publish the "Characters," and when already he had been for some time one of the teachers of the Duke de Bourbon, a grandson of the Prince Louis de Condé, he sold again his post for 18,000 *livres* to Charles-François de la Bonde, Seigneur d'Iberville.

On the recommendation of Bossuet, La Bruyère, in 1684, had been appointed teacher of history to the Duke de Bourbon; and remained with the Condés for twelve years, until the day of his death. He instructed his pupil not only in history, but also in geography, literature, and philosophy; yet his lessons appear to have produced no great impression, and moreover, they did not last very long, for the youthful duke married in 1685 a daughter of Madame de Montespan and Louis XIV.,[23] and La Bruyère received then the appointment of *écuyer gentilhomme* to Henri Jules, Duke of Bourbon, the father of his former pupil.

Why La Bruyère ever accepted the post of teacher, and afterwards of "gentleman in waiting," cannot be elucidated at the present time; he may have suffered reverses of fortune, which compelled him to gain a livelihood, but in any case he made the best use of his residence with a noble family, by studying the personages whose vices and ridicules he so admirably portrayed. Living with the Condés at their hotel at Paris, at their country seats at Chantilly and Saint Maur, or when they were visiting the Court, at Versailles, Marly, Fontainebleau, or Chambord, amidst the noble and high-born of the land, without being considered one of them, he had the best opportunity of penetrating the characters of those men who strutted about in gaudy trappings, and lorded it over the common herd, whilst soliciting offices or dignities; and for observing that these men were neither superior in feelings nor intellect to the "common people."[24]

All his reflections and observations he arranged under a certain number of headings, called the whole of them "Characters," and read some passages to a few of his friends, who seem not to have been greatly smitten by them. But this did not discourage La Bruyère; he translated into French the "Characters" of Theophrastus, a Greek philosopher of the peripatetic school, the successor of Aristotle as the head of the Academy, who seems to have lived until about the year 285 B.C., wrote a prefatory discourse to them, in which he displayed more satirical power than in any of his other works,[25] and resolved to publish his translation, and to print as a kind of appendix his own "Characters" at the end of it. One day,[26] whilst La Bruyère was sitting in the shop of a certain bookseller, named Michallet, which he visited almost daily, and was playing with the shopkeeper's little daughter, he took the manuscript of the "Characters" out of his pocket, and told Michallet he might print it if he liked, and keep the profits, if there were any, as a dowry for his child. The bookseller hesitated for some time, but finally published it, and the sale of it was so large that he brought out one edition after another as quick as he could.

It is certain that the publication of the "Characters" in 1688 made its author many enemies, but he calmly pursued the even tenor of his way, and increased the number of his paragraphs during the remaining portion of his life.[27]

In 1691 he endeavoured to be elected a member of the French Academy, and

[23] See the Chapter "Of Mankind," page 289, note 553.

[24] See the Chapter "Of the Great," page 242, § 53.

[25] Some of the passages of this "Prefatory Discourse" will be found in the Introduction.

[26] In a lecture read before the Academy of Sciences and Literature of Berlin, the 23d of August 1787, and printed in the memoirs of that Academy, Formey told this story on the authority of M. de Maupertuis, who is said to have heard it from the lady herself, the wife of the financier, Charles Rémy de July, to whom she brought a dowry of more than 100,000 livres.

[27] See note 3, page 4.?

to become the successor of Benserade,[28] but failed, thanks to the number of his enemies, amongst whom probably Fontenelle and Thomas Corneille, the nephew and brother of the great poet Pierre Corneille, were the most active; yet in 1693 he was elected without having made the usual visits to the Academicians to solicit their votes,[29] though his friends, Racine, Boileau, the secretary of state, de Pontchartrain,[30] and others, used all their influence to ensure his nomination.

The speech he delivered at his reception seems not to have given general satisfaction, for La Bruyère defended the partisans of the classical and attacked those of the modern school, proclaimed Boileau a judicious critic, and hardly admitted Corneille to be the equal of Racine. This speech, preceded by a very satirical preface,[31] in which he ridiculed his enemies under the name of "Theobalds," was published with the eighth edition of the "Characters."

But if he had bitter enemies he had also warm friends, amongst whom, besides the illustrious men I have already named, must be reckoned: Phélypeaux, the son of de Pontchartrain; the Marquis de Termes; Bossuet, and his nephew the Abbé Bossuet; Fénelon; de Malesieu; Renaudot; de Valincourt; Regnier-Desmarais; La Loubère, and Bouhier, nearly all present or future members of the French Academy; the poet Santeuil, and the historian Caton de Court.

We hardly know anything for certain of the character of La Bruyère except by the glimpses we get now and then in his book, or by what is told of him in some of the letters and writings of his friends and enemies. He was unmarried, and seems to have been a man of a modest disposition, fond of his books and his friends, polite in his manners, and willing to oblige. I imagine he must have felt it sometimes hard to be dependent on so fantastic, suspicious, half-demented a man as was the father of his former pupil, above all, after the death of the great Condé, which took place on the 8th of December 1686,[32] and also to have disliked being made now and then the butt of courtiers[33] his mental inferiors, but aristocratic superiors; hence he was often silent for fear of being laughed at.[34]

[28] See the Chapter "Of Society and Conversation," page 122, § 66, and note 228; about Fontenelle, see in the same Chapter the character of Cydias, page 127, § 75.

[29] This he stated openly in the speech he delivered at his reception at the Academy, the 15th of June 1693; his enemies would certainly have contradicted him if it had not been the truth.

[30] See the Chapter "Of the Court," page 201, note 413.

[31] In the Introduction are to be found some extracts from this preface.

[32] La Bruyère's bitter feelings appear in such paragraphs as § 43, page 56; in the Chapter "Of the Town," page 166, § 4; in that "Of the Great," pages 223 and 224, §§ 11 and 12; page 232, § 33; and in the Chapter "Of Opinions," page 334, § 19. Molière felt a somewhat similar bitterness; at least in the dedication of les Fâcheux he says to Louis XIV.: "Those that are born in an elevated rank may propose to themselves the honour of serving your Majesty in great employments; but, for my part, all the glory I can aspire to, is to amuse you." Compare also Shakespeare's hundred and eleventh Sonnet beginning—"Oh! for my sake do you with Fortune chide."

[33] See the Chapter "Of Society and of Conversation," page 120, §§ 56, 57.

[34] See in the Chapter "Of the Great," page 230, § 26, which seems to me to prove this fear.

He was scarcely fifty when, according to some reports, he became suddenly deaf; a few days afterwards, during the night of the 10th of May 1696, he died of an attack of apoplexy at the hotel of the Condés at Versailles.

In 1699 were published some *Dialogues sur le Quiétisme*, attributed to La Bruyère; but as the editor, the Abbé du Pin, admitted he had partly altered them, as well as added some of his own, it is difficult to judge what was the original share of our author in their composition.

Only twenty-one authenticated letters of La Bruyère are in existence, of which seventeen are in the collection of the Duke d'Aumale, at Twickenham.

THE AUTHOR

PREFACE.

"Admonere voluimus, non mordere; prodesse, non lædere;
consulere moribus hominum, non officere."[35]

T HE subject-matter of this work being borrowed from the public, I now give back to it what it lent me; it is but right that having finished the whole work throughout with the utmost regard to truth I am capable of, and which it deserves from me, I should make restitution of it. The world may view at leisure its picture drawn from life, and may correct any of the faults I have touched upon, if conscious of them. This is the only goal a man ought to propose to himself in writing, though he must not in the least expect to be successful; however, as long as men are not disgusted with vice we should also never tire of admonishing them; they would perhaps grow worse were it not for censure or reproof, and hence the need of preaching and writing. Neither orators nor authors can conceal the joy they

---

[35] "We have wished to warn and not to bite; to be useful and not to wound; to benefit the morals of men, and not to be detrimental to them." This quotation is taken from one of the letters of Erasmus to Martin Dorpius, in which the former replies to some criticisms on his "Praise of Folly." The preface to the "Characters," altered and augmented several times by the author himself, is found for the first time, in its present form, in the eighth edition of his work.

feel on being applauded, whereas they ought to blush if they aim at nothing more than praise in their speeches or writings; besides, the surest and least doubtful approbation is a change and regeneration in the morals of their readers and hearers. We should neither write nor speak but to instruct; yet, if we happen to please, we should not be sorry for it, since by those means we render those instructive truths more palatable and acceptable. When, therefore, any thoughts or reflections have slipped into a book which are neither so spirited, well written, nor vivid as others, though they seem to have been inserted for the sake of variety, as a relaxation to the mind, or to draw its attention to what is to follow, the reader should reject and the author delete them, unless they are attractive, familiar, instructive, and adapted to the capacity of ordinary people, whom we must by no means neglect.

This is one way of settling things; there is another which my own interest trusts may be adopted; and that is, not to lose sight of my title, and always to bear in mind, as often as this book is read, that I describe "The Characters or Manners of the Age;" for though I frequently take them from the court of France and from men of my own nation, yet they cannot be confined to any one court or country, without greatly impairing the compass and utility of my book, and departing from the design of the work, which is to paint mankind in general, as well as from the reasons for the order of my chapters, and even from a certain gradual connection between the reflections in each of those chapters. After this so necessary precaution, the consequences of which are obvious enough, I think I may protest against all resentment, complaint, malicious interpretation, false application and censure, against insipid railers and cantankerous readers. People ought to know how to read and then hold their tongues, unless able to relate what they have read, and neither more nor less than what they have read, which they sometimes can do; but this is not sufficient—they must also be willing to do it. Without these conditions, which a careful and scrupulous author has a right to demand from some people, as the sole reward of his labour, I question whether he ought to continue writing, if at least he prefers his private satisfaction to the public good and to his zeal for truth. I confess, moreover, that since the year MDCLXXXX, and before publishing the fifth edition, I was divided between an impatience to cast my book into a fuller and better shape by adding new Characters, and a fear lest some people should say: "Will there never be an end to these Characters, and shall we never see anything else from this author?" On the one hand several persons of sound common-sense told me: "The subject-matter is solid, useful, pleasant, inexhaustible; may you live for a long time, and treat it without interruption as long as you live! what can you do better? The follies of mankind will ensure you a volume every year." Others, again, with a good deal of reason, made me dread the fickleness of the multitude and the instability of the public, with whom, however, I have good cause to be satisfied; they were always suggesting to me that for the last thirty years, few persons read except for the pleasure of reading, and not to improve themselves, and that, to amuse mankind, fresh chapters and a new title were needed; that this sluggishness had filled the shops and crowded the world with dull and tedious books, written in a bad style and without any intelligence, order, or the least correctness, against all morality or decency, written in a hurry, and read in the same way, and then only for the sake of novelty; and that if I could do nothing else but enlarge a sensible book, it would be much better for me to take a rest. I adopted something of both those advices, though they were at variance with one another, and observed an impartiality which clashed with neither. I did not hesitate to add some fresh remarks to those which already had doubled the bulk of the first edition of my book;[36] but, in order not to oblige the public to read again what had been printed before, to get at new material, and to let them immediately find out what they only desired to read, I took care to distinguish those second additions by a peculiar mark ((¶));[37] I also thought it would not be useless to distinguish the first augmentations by another and simpler mark (¶), to show the progress of my "Characters," as well as to guide the reader in the choice he might be willing to make. And lest he be afraid I should never have done with those additions, I added to all this care a sincere promise to venture on nothing more of the kind. If any one accuses me of breaking my word, because I inserted in the three last editions[38] a goodly number of new remarks, he may perceive at least that by adding new ones to old, and by completely suppressing those differences pointed out in the margin, I did not so much endeavour to entertain the world with novelties, as perhaps to leave to posterity a book of morals more complete, more finished, and more regular. To conclude, I did not wish to write any maxims, for they are like moral laws, and I acknowledge that I possess neither sufficient authority nor genius for a legislator. I also know I have transgressed the ordinary standard of maxims, which, like oracles, should be short and concise.[39] Some of my remarks are so, others are more diffuse; we do not always think of things in the same way, and we describe them in as different a manner by a sentence, an argument, a metaphor, or some other figure; by a parallel or a simple comparison; by a story, by a single feature, by a description, or a picture; which is the cause of the length or brevity of my reflections. Finally, those who write maxims would be thought infallible; I, on the contrary, allow any one to say that my remarks are not always correct, provided he himself will make better ones.

---

[36] The first edition of the "Characters," published in 1688, contained 420 characters, the fourth edition 771.

[37] This mark, a ((¶)) between double parentheses, as well as the same mark between single parentheses, was first employed in the fifth edition (1690) of the "Characters," and in all the following ones. But the mere ¶ without any parentheses was used by La Bruyère in all editions to denote the beginning of a paragraph.

[38] This refers to the sixth (1691), seventh (1692), and eighth (1694) editions. The fifth edition contained 923 characters, the sixth 997, the seventh 1073, and the eighth 1120. The ninth edition (1696) was published about a month after the death of La Bruyère.

[39] This seems to allude to La Rochefoucauld's "Maxims."

STUDY

I.

OF WORKS OF THE MIND.

(1.) AFTER above seven thousand years,[40] during which there have been men who have thought we come too late to say anything that has not been said already, the finest and most beautiful ideas on morals and manners have been swept away before our times, and nothing is left for us but to glean after the ancients and the ablest[41] amongst the moderns.

(2.) We should only endeavour to think and speak correctly ourselves, without wishing to bring others over to our taste and opinions;[42] this would be too great an undertaking.

---

[40] M. de La Bruyère adopts the chronology of Suidas, a Greek lexicographer who flourished during the latter end of the eleventh century; according to the Hebrew chronology the world had only existed 5692 years when the "Characters" were first published in 1688.

[41] Abile in the original, in the sense of the English word "able," and used as a noun, was already then considered antiquated.

[42] Sentiment, in the original, was during the seventeenth century not seldom employed in French for "opinion," as "sentiments" are at present in English.

(3.) To make a book is as much a trade as to make a clock; something more than intelligence is required to become an author. A certain magistrate was going to be raised by his merit to the highest legal dignity; he was a man of subtle mind and of experience, but must needs print a treatise of morality, which was quickly bought up on account of its absurdity.[43]

(4.) It is not so easy to obtain a reputation by a perfect work as to enhance the value of an indifferent one by a reputation already acquired.

(5.) A satirical work or a book of anecdotes[44] handed about privately in manuscript from one to another, passes for a masterpiece, even when it is but middling; the printing ruins its reputation.

(6.) Take away from most of our works on morality the "Advertisement to the reader," the "Epistle dedicatory," the "Preface," the "Table of contents," and the "Permission to print," and there will scarcely be pages enough left to deserve the name of a book.

(7.) In certain things mediocrity is unbearable, as in poetry, music, painting, and eloquence. How we are tortured when we hear a dull soliloquy delivered in a pompous tone, or indifferent verses read with all the emphasis of a wretched poet!

(8.) Some poets in their tragedies employ a goodly number of big sounding verses, which seem strong, elevated, and filled with lofty sentiments.[45] They are listened to anxiously, with eyes raised and gaping mouths, and are thought to please the public; and where they are understood the least, are admired the most; people have no time to breathe, they have hardly time to exclaim and to applaud. Formerly, when I was quite young, I imagined those passages were clear and intelligible to the actors, the pit, and the galleries; that the authors themselves understood them, and that I must have been very dull not to understand what it was all about. But now I am undeceived.

(9.) Up to the present time there exists hardly any literary masterpiece which is

---

[43] This magistrate is said to have been Pierre Poncet de la Rivière, Count d'Ablys (1600-1681), a barrister, a councillor of state, and member of the royal council of finances, whose absurd moral treatise, Considérations sur les avantages de la vieillesse dans la vie chrétienne, politique, civile, économique et solitaire, was published under the pseudonym of the Baron de Prelle, in the month of August 1677, about one month before the death of the Lord Chancellor d'Aligre, and more than three months before President Lamoignon's decease.

[44] At that time so-called collections of anecdotes, such as Boléana, Ménagiana, and Segraisiana, were greatly in vogue.

[45] It is said that the great dramatic poet Pierre Corneille (1606-1684) is alluded to as one of those poets.

the joint labour of several men.[46] Homer wrote the Iliad,[47] Virgil the Æneid, Livy the Decades, and the Roman orator[48] his Orations.

(10.) There is in art an acme of perfection, as there is in Nature one of goodness and completeness. Any one who feels this and loves art possesses a perfect taste; but he who is not sensible of it, and loves what is below or above that point, is wanting in taste. Thus there exists a good and a bad taste, and we are right in discussing the difference between them.

(11.) Men have generally more vivacity than judgment; or, to speak more accurately, few men exist whose intelligence is combined with a correct taste and a judicious criticism.

(12.) The lives of heroes have enriched history, and history has adorned the actions of heroes; and thus I cannot say whether the historians are more indebted to those who provided them with such noble materials, or those great men to their historians.

(13.) A heap of epithets is but a sorry commendation. Actions alone, and the manner of relating them, speak a man's praise.

(14.) The whole genius of an author consists in giving accurate definitions and in painting well. Only Moses,[49] Homer, Plato, Virgil, Horace, excel all other writers in their expressions and their imagery: to express truth is to write naturally, forcibly, and delicately.

(15.) People have been obliged to do with style what they have done with architecture; they wholly abandoned the Gothic style, which the barbarians introduced in their palaces and temples,[50] and brought back the Doric, Ionic, and Corinthian orders. That which was only seen amongst the ruins of ancient Rome and time-honoured Greece has become modernised, and now shines forth in our porticoes and colonnades. So, in writing, we can never arrive at perfection, and, if possible, surpass the ancients, but by imitating them.

How many centuries have elapsed before men were able to come back to the taste of the ancients in arts and sciences, and, finally, took up again a simple and natural style.

---

[46] All the "Keys" pretend this is a hit at the "Dictionary of the Academy," and they may be right; for the Dictionary, only published in 1694, six years after the "Characters" first saw the light, had been expected for more than forty years. But most likely La Bruyère was thinking of the tragedy-ballet of Psyché (1671), words by Pierre Corneille and Molière, music by Quinault and Lulli; of the opera which in 1680 Racine and Boileau, joint historiographes of Louis XIV., began, and which never saw the light; and of the newly-acted Idylle sur la Paix and the Eglogue de Versailles (1685), written by Quinault, Racine, and Molière.

[47] Even in La Bruyère's lifetime doubts were already expressed about the Iliad being written by Homer.

[48] This Roman orator was Cicero.

[49] La Bruyère adds in a footnote: "Even merely considered as an author."

[50] Almost every one felt during the seventeenth century a dislike for Gothic architecture.

A man[51] feeds on the ancients and intelligent moderns; he squeezes and drains them as much as possible; he stuffs his works with them; and when at last he becomes an author and thinks he can walk alone, he lifts up his voice against them, and ill-treats them, like those lusty children, grown strong through the healthy milk on which they have been fed, and who beat their nurses.

An author of modern times usually proves the ancients inferior to us in two ways: by reason and examples. The reason is his own opinion, and the examples are his own writings.[52]

He confesses that the ancients, though they are unequal and incorrect, have a great many beautiful passages; he quotes them, and they are so fine, that his criticism is read only for their sake.

Some able men declare in favour of the ancients against the moderns; but we doubt them, as they seem to be judges in their own cause, for their works are so exactly written after the model of antiquity, that we cannot accept their authority.[53]

(16.) We ought to like to read our works to those who know how to correct and appreciate them.

He who will not listen to any advice, nor be corrected in his writings, is a rank pedant.

An author ought to receive with the same moderation all praises and all criticisms on his productions.

(17.) Amongst all the various expressions which can render our thoughts, there is but one which is correct. We are not always so fortunate as to hit upon it in writing or speaking, but, nevertheless, such a one undoubtedly exists, and all others are weak, and do not satisfy a man of culture who wishes to make himself understood.

A good author, who writes carefully, often finds that the expression he has been looking for for some time, and which he did not know, proves, when found at last, to be the most simple, the most natural, and the one which was most likely to present itself to him spontaneously at first.

Fanciful authors often touch up their works. As their temper is not always the same, and as it varies on every occasion, they soon grow indifferent about those very expressions and terms they liked so much at first.

(18.) The same common-sense which makes an author write good things,

---

[51] Probably Bernard le Bovier de Fontenelle (1657-1757) is meant here. This author had made excellent classical studies in a Jesuit college, but attacked the ancients in his Discours sur L'Eglogue and in his Digression sur les anciens et les modernes, published together with his Poésies Pastorales in 1688. The paragraph beginning "A man feeds" and ending "nurses" was only printed for the first time in the fourth edition of the "Characters," published in 1689.

[52] It is generally thought that Charles Perrault (1628-1703), a member of the French Academy, is alluded to, but this seems more than doubtful.

[53] Those "able men" were the dramatist Jean Racine (1639-1699) and the satirist Nicolas Boileau Despréaux (1636-1711).

makes him dread they are not good enough to deserve reading.

A shallow mind thinks his writings divine; a man of sense imagines he writes tolerably well.

(19.) Aristus says, "I was prevailed upon to read my works to Zoilus,[54] and I did so. At first he liked them, before he had leisure to disapprove of them; he commended them coldly in my presence, and since then, has not said one word in their favour to any one. I excuse him, and desire no more from any author; I even pity him for listening to so many fine things which were not his own."

Those men who through their rank are exempt from an author's jealousy, have either other passions or necessities to distract them, and to make them indifferent towards other men's conceptions. Almost no one, whether through disposition, inclination, or fortune, is willing to relish the delight that a perfect piece of work can give.

(20.) The pleasure of criticism takes away from us the pleasure of being deeply moved by very fine things.

(21.) Many people perceive the merit of a manuscript which is read to them, but will not declare themselves in its favour until they see what success it has in the world when printed, or what intelligent men will say about it. They do not like to risk their opinion, and they want to be carried away by the crowd, and dragged along by the multitude. Then they say that they were amongst the first who approved of that work, and the general public shares their opinion.[55]

Such men lose the best opportunities of convincing us that they are intelligent, clever, and first-rate critics, and can really discover what is good and what is better. A fine work falls into their hands; it is an author's first book, before he has got any great name; there is nothing to prepossess any one in his favour, and by applauding his writings one does not court or flatter the great. Zelotes,[56] you are not required to cry out: "This is a masterpiece; human intelligence never went farther; the human speech cannot soar higher; henceforward we will judge of no one's taste but by what he thinks of this book." Such exaggerated and offensive expressions are only employed by postulants for pensions or benefices, and are even injurious to what is really commendable and what one wishes to praise. Why not merely say—"That's a good book?" It is true you say it when the whole of France has approved of it, and foreigners as well as your own countrymen, when it is printed all over Europe, and has been translated into several languages, but then it is too late.

(22.) Some people, after having read a book, quote certain passages which they do not thoroughly understand, and moreover completely change their character

[54] Zoilus, a Greek grammarian, flourished about 356-336 B.C., and assailed Homer, Plato, Isocrates, and other Greek authors with merciless severity.

[55] According to all the "Keys," this is said to be an allusion to the Abbé de Dangeau (1643-1723), a member of the French Academy, and a brother of the better known marquis. But why and wherefore this Abbé has been singled out, has not reached posterity. Some say the President Cousin, the editor of the Journal des Savants, was meant.

[56] Ζηλωτής means "envious."

by what they put in of their own. Those passages, so mutilated and disfigured that they are nothing else but their own expressions and thoughts, they expose to censure, maintain them to be bad, and the world agrees with them; but the passage such critics think they quote, and in reality do not, is not a bit the worse for it.[57]

(23.) "What is your opinion about Hermodorus' book?" — "That it is wretchedly written," replies Anthymus. — "Wretchedly written! what do you mean, sir?" — "Just what I say," he continues; "it is not a book, at least it does not deserve to be talked about" — "Have you read it?" — "No," replies Anthymus. Why does he not add that Fulvia and Melania have condemned it without reading, and that he is a friend of those two ladies?

(24.) Arsène,[58] from the height of his own wisdom, contemplates men, and from the eminence he beholds them seems frightened as it were at their littleness. Commended, extolled, and raised to the skies by certain persons who have reciprocally promised to admire one another, he fancies, though he has some merit, that he has as much as any man can have, which he never will; his mind being occupied and filled with sublime ideas, he scarcely finds time to pronounce certain oracles; raised by his character above human judgments, he leaves to vulgar souls the merit of leading a regular and uniform life, being answerable for his variations to none but to a circle of friends who worship them. They alone know how to judge, to think, to write, and they only ought to write; there is no literary work, though ever so well received by the world and universally liked by men of culture, which he does approve of, nay, which he would condescend to read; he is incapable of being corrected by this picture, which will not even be read by him.

(25.) Theocrines[59] knows a good many useless things; he is singular in his sentiments, and less profound than methodical; he only exercises his memory, is absent-minded, scornful, and seems continually laughing to himself at those whom he thinks his inferiors. By chance I one day read him something of mine: he heard it out, and then spoke about some of his own writings. "But what said he of yours?" you'll ask me. "I have told you already; he spoke to me only of his own."

(26.) The most accomplished literary work would be reduced to nothing by carping criticism, if the author would listen to all critics and allow every one to erase the passage which pleases him the least.

(27.) Experience tells us, that if there are ten persons who would strike a thought or an expression out of a book, we could easily find a like number who would insist upon its being put back again. The latter will exclaim: "Why should

[57] In his Recueil de divers ouvrages en prose et en vers, 1676, Charles Perrault defended the Alceste of Quinault and attacked the Alcestis of Euripides. Unfortunately his criticism contained several errors, which Racine noticed in the preface of Iphigénie, accusing Perrault at the same time of having carelessly read the work he was censuring.

[58] This was meant for Henri-Joseph de Peyre, Count de Troisvilles (1642-1708), pronounced Tréville, a very intelligent and highly-cultivated nobleman, brought up in his youth with Louis XIV., whose talents he rather undervalued. He was on intimate terms with the Port-Royalists, and after several alternate fits of devotion and dissipation, ended his days devoutly and penitently.

[59] The Abbé de Dangeau, a pedantical purist mentioned already, page 13, note.

such a thought be suppressed? it is new, fine, and wonderfully well expressed." The former, on the contrary, will maintain, "that they would have omitted such an idea, or have expressed it in another way." "In your work," say the first, "there is a very happy phrase which depicts most naturally what you meant to say." The second maintain "that a certain word is venturesome, and moreover does not give the precise meaning you perhaps desired to give." It is about the same thought and the same word those people argue; and yet they are all critics, or pass for such. What then can an author do but venture, in such a perplexity, to follow the advice of those who approve of the passage.

(28.) A serious-minded author is not obliged to trouble his head about all the foolish sayings, the obscene remarks, and bad words that are uttered, or about the stupid constructions which some men put on certain passages of his writings; much less ought he to suppress them. He is convinced that let a man be never so careful in his writings, the insipid jokes of wretched buffoons are an unavoidable evil, since they often only turn the best things into ridicule.

(29.) If certain men of quick and resolute mind are to be believed, words would even be superfluous to express feelings; signs would be sufficient to address them, or we could make ourselves be understood without speaking. However careful you may be to write closely and concisely, and whatever reputation you may have as such, they will think you diffuse. You must allow them to supply everything and write for them alone. They understand a whole phrase by reading the first word, and an entire chapter by a single phrase. It is sufficient for them to have heard only a bit of your work, they know it all and understand the whole. A great many riddles would be amusing reading to them; they regret that the wretched style which delights them becomes rare, and that so few authors employ it. Comparisons of a river flowing rapidly, though calmly and uniformly, or of a conflagration which, fanned by the winds, spreads afar in a forest, where it devours oaks and pine-trees, gives to them not the smallest idea of eloquence. Show them some fireworks[60] to astonish them, or a flash of lightning to dazzle them, and they will dispense with anything fine or beautiful.

(30.) What a prodigious difference is there between a fine work and one that is perfect or regular. I am not aware whether a single one of the latter kind still exists. It is perhaps less difficult for uncommon minds to hit upon the grand and the sublime than to avoid all kinds of errors. The *Cid*, at its first appearance, was universally admired; it rose in spite of power and politics, which attempted in vain to crush it. People of rank and the general public, though always divided in their opinions and feelings, were in favour of it; they learned it by heart so as to anticipate the actors who were performing it. The *Cid*, in short, is one of the finest poems ever written, and one of the best criticisms on any subject is that on the *Cid*.[61]

---

[60] In the seventeenth century fireworks were in French feu grécois, literally "Greek fire."

[61] The Cid, the dramatic masterpiece of Pierre Corneille, was first performed in 1636. Cardinal Richelieu tried to get up a cabal to crush it, but was unsuccessful; he also persuaded the Academy to publish a severe criticism on it, which is too favourably spoken of by La Bruyère. Boileau says in his ninth satire: —

(31.) When, after having read a work, loftier thoughts arise in your mind and noble and heartfelt feelings animate you, do not look for any other rule to judge it by; it is fine and written in a masterly manner.[62]

(32.) Capys,[63] who sets up for a judge of style and fancies he writes like Bouhours[64] and Rabutin,[65] disagrees with public opinion, and is the only person who says that Damis[66] is not a good author. Damis is of the same opinion as a large number of people, and says artlessly, as well as the public, that Capys is a dull writer.

(33.) It is the business of a newsmonger to inform us when any book is published; if it is printed by Cramoisy,[67] and with what type; if it is well bound, and on what paper, and at what price it is sold; he ought even to know what the bookseller's sign is; but it is foolish in him to pretend to criticise it.

The highest point a newsmonger can reach is to reason in a vague manner on politics.

A newsmonger lies down at night quietly, after having received some information, but it is spoiled overnight, and he is obliged to throw it away when he wakes in the morning.[68]

"En vain contre le Cid un ministre se ligue,
Tout Paris pour Chimère a les yeux de Rodrigue.
L'Académie en corps a beau le censurer,
Le public révolté s'obstine à l'admirer."

[62] Courageux and courage were not seldom used in the seventeenth century for "heartfelt" and "heart," whilst main d'ouvrier, "hand of a workman," was sometimes employed instead of main de maître, "hand of a master."

[63] The dramatist Edme Boursault (1638-1701) had had a literary quarrel with Boileau, who attacked him in his ninth Satire, to which Boursault replied by his comedy La Satire des Satires. But they had been reconciled more than a year before the "Characters" were published.

[64] Father Bouhours (1628-1702), a literary Jesuit of some reputation and talent, published in 1689 his Pensées ingénieuses des anciens et des modernes, in which he several times praised the "Characters." La Bruyère, not to be behind-hand, inserted the learned father's name in his fifth edition, published in 1690.

[65] Roger de Rabutin, Count de Bussy (1618-1693), a friend of our author, enjoyed a certain literary reputation in the seventeenth century, now completely lost. He is only remembered by his licentious and satirical Histoire amoureuse des Gaules, for which he was banished from the court for more than twenty years.

[66] Damis was meant for Boileau.

[67] There had been a whole family of printers of that name, though only André was alive when the "Characters" appeared. At that time books in France and in England were almost always sold bound.

[68] By "newsmonger" our author alludes to the manufacturers of manuscript newspapers, containing all kinds of social and political scandal, eagerly sought for, and who were severely punished when caught. The English translator of 1702 gives for nouvelliste "journalist," and says in his "Key:" "The author of the Works of the Learned of Paris," etc. The Histoire des Savants, edited by H. Basnage (1656-1710), was published in Holland. Mr. N. Rowe, in his translation published in 1713, also uses the word "journalist," and says in the

(34.) A philosopher[69] wastes his life in observing men, and wears himself out in exposing vice and folly. If he shapes his thoughts into words, it is not so much from his vanity as an author as to place entirely in its proper light some truth he has discovered, that it may make the desired impression. Yet some readers think they repay him with interest if they say, with a magisterial air, "that they have read his book, and that there is some sense in it;" but he does not mind their praise, for he has not laboured and passed many sleepless nights to obtain it: he has higher aims, and acts from nobler motives: he demands from mankind greater and more uncommon results than empty praise, and even than rewards; he expects them to lead better lives.

(35.) A fool reads a book and does not understand it; a man of ordinary mind reads it and fancies he perfectly understands it; a man of intelligence sometimes does not wholly understand it; he perceives what is really obscure and what is really clear, whilst witlings[70] imagine those passages obscure which are not so, and think they do not understand what is really intelligible.

(36.) In vain an author endeavours to obtain admiration by his works. A fool may sometimes admire him, but then he is only a fool; an intelligent man has within him the germs of all truth and of all sentiments; nothing is new to him; he admires few things, but he finds that many things deserve some praise.

(37.) I question if it be possible to write more clever letters in a more agreeable manner and in a better style than those of Balzac[71] or Voiture;[72] but they are void of those sentiments which have swayed us since their time and originated with the ladies. That sex excels ours in this kind of writing; from their pens flow naturally those turns and expressions which often are with us the effects of tedious labour and troublesome research; they are fortunate in the selection of their wordings, which they employ so cleverly, that though they are not new, they have all the charm of novelty, and seem only designed for the use they put them to; they alone can express an entire sentiment in a single word, and render a delicate thought as delicately; their arguments are connected in an inimitable manner, follow one another naturally, and are only linked together by the sense. If the ladies wrote always correctly, I might affirm that perhaps the letters of some of them would be

---

"Key:" "On the authors of Journals, or accounts of books and News, published in France, Holland," etc.

[69] La Bruyère speaks here of himself.

[70] In the seventeenth century, bel esprit, plural beaux esprits, in the original, meant a man of intelligence, but began already in La Bruyère's time to have the meaning of "witling."

[71] Jean Guez de Balzac (1594-1655), one of the first members of the French Academy, wrote, besides his over-praised "Letters," a Socrate Chrétien, the Prince, a panegyric on Louis XIII., and Entretiens ou Dissertations littéraires.

[72] Voiture (1598-1648), also a member of the French Academy, is chiefly known by his "Letters" and some namby-pamby poetry, amongst which is the well-known sonnet on "Uranie," which was by many preferred to the sonnet on "Job" by Benserade, and gave rise to a pretty literary quarrel in the seventeenth century. Voiture and Balzac are now deservedly buried in oblivion.

among the best in our language.[73]

(38.) Terentius[74] wanted nothing but to be less cold. What purity! what preciseness! what polish! what elegance! what characters! Molière wanted nothing but to avoid the vulgar tongue and barbarisms and to write elegantly.[75] What fire! what artlessness! what original and good jokes! how well he imitates manners! what imagery! and how he lashes what is ridiculous! But what an author might have been formed of these two comic writers!

(39.) I have read Malherbe and Théophile.[76] They both understood nature, with this difference: the first, in a nervous and uniform style, displays at one and the same time whatever is beautiful, noble, ingenuous and simple, and depicts or describes it; the other, without choice or accuracy, with a loose and uneven pen, some times overloads his descriptions, goes into too many details, and analyses too much; sometimes he imagines certain things,[77] exaggerates, outstrips what is true in nature, and becomes a romancer.

(40.) In both Ronsard[78] and Balzac, each in their kind, are found a sufficient number of good and bad things to form after them very great men either in verse or prose.

(41.) Marot,[79] by his phraseology and style, seems to have written after Ronsard wrote; there is very little difference, except in a few words, between the style of the former and our present style.

(42.) Ronsard and his contemporaries have done more harm than good to style; they delayed its progress towards perfection, and exposed it to the danger of being always defective and of never becoming perfect again. It is astonishing that Marot's works, which are so natural and easy, have not made of Ronsard, so full of rapture and enthusiasm, a greater poet than he or Marot ever were; and that, on the contrary, Belleau, Jodelle, and du Bartas[80] were soon followed by a

[73] The letters of Madame de Sévigné (1626-1696) were not published until 1726, or thirty years after La Bruyère's death, though perhaps he might have seen some of them in manuscript. Among the ladies celebrated for their epistolary style in the seventeenth century were Madame de Maintenon, Mademoiselle de Scudéry, Madame de Bussy-Lameth, and above all Madame de Boislandry. See the Chapter "Of Opinions," § 28, "A Fragment."

[74] Publius Terentius Afer (194-158 B.C.), a celebrated Latin comic dramatist.

[75] Some commentators on La Bruyère think that the words "vulgar tongue (jargon) and barbarisms" refer to Molière having put peasants on the stage, and letting them speak their dialect. See § 52.

[76] Malherbe (1555-1628) was one of the greatest purists amongst the authors of his time. Théophile de Viau (1591-1626), a writer of tragedies and a poet, was by some of his contemporaries thought to be a rival of Malherbe.

[77] In the original il feint, the Latin fingit, he shapes, imagines.

[78] Ronsard (1524-1585), the chief of the "Pleiad" or constellation of seven authors, was the most celebrated poet of his time, and the author of the Franciade.

[79] Clément Marot (1495-1544), the favourite poet of Francis I., was born twenty-nine years before Ronsard, who lived about forty years longer than Marot.

[80] Rémy Belleau (1528-1577), Jodelle (1532-1573), and du Bartas (1544-1590), were all poets of the school of Ronsard and belonging to the "Pleiad." Du Bartas›s chief work has

Racan[81] and a Malherbe, and that the French language was no sooner vitiated than it recovered.

MICHEL DE MONTAIGNE

been translated into English by "silver-tongued" Joshua Sylvester (1563-1618), under the title of "The Divine Week and Works;" and Spenser speaks of "his heavenly muse," and of his filling "the world with never-dying fame."

[81] Honorat de Bueil, Marquis de Racan (1589-1670), the favourite pupil of Malherbe, is chiefly known by his pastoral dialogue, Les Bergeries. La Bruyère praises Malherbe and Racan for their pure style, but the fabulist Jean de la Fontaine says of them:—

> "Malherbe avec Racan parmi le chœur des anges,
> Là-haut de l'Eternel célébrant les louanges
> Ont emporté leur lyre."

(43.) Marot and Rabelais[82] are inexcusable for scattering so much filth in their writings: they both had genius and originality enough to be able to do without it, even for those who seek rather what is comical than what is admirable in an author. Rabelais above all is incomprehensible: his book is a mystery, a mere chimera; it has a lovely woman's face, with the feet and tail of a serpent or of some more hideous animal; it is a monstrous jumble of delicate and ingenious morality and of filthy depravation. Where it is bad, it excels by far the worst, and is fit only to delight the rabble; and where it is good, it is exquisite and excellent, and may entertain the most delicate.

(44.) Two writers have condemned Montaigne[83] in their works. I am of their opinion, and believe him not always free from blame; but it seems that none of these two can see anything good in him. One of these thinks too little to enjoy an author who thinks a great deal; the other thinks with too much subtlety to be pleased with thoughts that are natural.[84]

(45.) A grave, solemn, and correct style will go a long way. Amyot and Coëffeteau[85] are read, but who else of their contemporaries? The phraseology and the expression of Balzac have become less antiquated than those of Voiture; but if the style, the intelligence, and originality of the latter are not modern nor in anything resemble our present writers, it is because it is easier not to pay any attention to him than to imitate him, and because the few who follow him could never overtake him.

(46.) The H ... G ...[86] is distinctly less than nothing, and there are a good many works like it. There is as much trickery required to grow rich by a stupid book as there is folly in buying it; a man would never know the people's taste if he did not venture sometimes on some great piece of silliness.

(47.) We perceive that an opera is an outline of a magnificent spectacle, of which it serves to give an idea.

I cannot understand how the opera, with such perfect music and quite a regal expenditure, has been able to tire me.[87]

---

[82] François Rabelais (1459-1553), author of the Chroniques de Gargantua et de Pantagruel.

[83] La Bruyère writes "Montagne," and so it is even now pronounced. Montaigne's (1533-1592) "Essays" are known everywhere.

[84] The author who "thinks too little" is said to have been the Port-Royalist, Pierre Nicole (1625-1695), though some imagine Balzac was meant; the author who thought "with too much subtlety" seems to have been Father Malebranche (1638-1715), who attacked Montaigne in his Recherche de la Vérité (1674).

[85] Jacques Amyot (1513-1593), the translator of Plutarch. Nicolas Coëffeteau (1574-1623), bishop of Marseille, is best known by his translation of the Roman historian, Florus.

[86] The letters H. G. stand for Hermes Galant, "Hermes" being the Greek for Mercury, and there existing since 1672 a kind of monthly review, called the Mercure Galant, edited by Donneau de Visé, Thomas Corneille, and Fontenelle, and printing some news from the court and the army, a few literary articles, and as many advertisements as possible. Since 1677 its title changed to Mercure de France.

[87] Boileau, La Fontaine, and Saint Evremond were, like La Bruyère, no lovers of the

There are some passages in an opera which make us long for others; it some-times happens we wish it was all over: this is the fault of the decorations, or of a want of action or interest.

An opera is not even to this day a poem, for it contains nought but verses; nor is it a spectacle, since machinery has disappeared through the dexterous man-agement of Amphion and his kindred;[88] it is a concert of voices assisted by in-struments. We deceive ourselves and acquire a bad taste when we state, as has been done, that machinery is only an amusement fit for children and suitable for puppet-shows.[89] Machines increase and embellish poetical fiction and maintain among the spectators that gentle illusion in which the entire pleasure of a theatre consists, to which it also adds a feeling of wonder. There is no need of flights, or cars, or changes when *Bérénice* or *Pénélope*[90] are represented, but they are neces-sary in an opera, as the characteristic of such a spectacle is to enchant the mind as well as the ear and the eye.

(48.) Some busybodies[91] have erected a theatre and machinery, composed ballets, verses, and music; theirs is the whole spectacle, even to the room where the performance was held, from the roof to the very foundation of the four walls. Who has any doubt that the hunt on the water,[92] the delights of "La Table,"[93] the marvels of the Labyrinth[94] were also invented by them? I think so, at least, by the agitation they are in and by the self-satisfied air with which they applaud their success. Unless I am deceived, they have not contributed anything to a festival so opera.

[88] The Abbé Perrin and his brother-in-law, the Marquis de Sourdéac, the first reg-ular directors of opera in France, ruined themselves in less than three years through their expensive decorations and machinery. In 1672 Lulli and his son-in-law Francine obtained permission to manage another opera-house, but spent far less money on decorations than their predecessors had done. Our author calls Lulli "Amphion," a Greek musician who is said to have built Thebes by the music of his lute.

[89] At that time there was a regular theatre for puppet-shows, founded by Pierre d'At-telin, better known as Brioché.

[90] In 1670 Corneille and Racine had each a tragedy, Bérénice, represented; Pénélope, a tragedy of the Abbé Genest, was played in 1684.

[91] One of those busybodies is said to have been a certain M. Manse, engineer of the waterworks of Chantilly, the seat of the Condés; and he pretended to have chiefly organ-ised the festival given by the Prince de Condé, a son of the great Condé and the father of La Bruyère's pupil, the Duke de Bourbon, to the Dauphin, the son of Louis XIV., at Chantilly during the month of August 1688. This entertainment lasted eight days; hence the necessity of a theatre.

[92] The "hunt on the water" took place on the sixth day of the festival, when some living deer and other animals were thrown alive into a large lake, which the ladies, in boats, tried to catch by means of ropes, and which, when caught, were set at liberty.

[93] On the first day of the feast a splendid "collation" was given by the Prince to the Dauphin, at the cross-way of "La Table," amidst a temple of verdure erected for the occa-sion. Any meal taken between the dinner and supper hours, or any festive repast, was called in Louis XIV.'s time a collation.

[94] "Another wonderful collation given in the Labyrinth of Chantilly," says a note of La Bruyère. An engraving still exists of the table, its decorations and ornaments.

splendid, so magnificent, and so long kept up, and which one person planned and paid for; so that I admire two things: the ease and quietness of him who directed everything, and the fuss and gesticulations of those who did nothing.[95]

(49.) The critics, or those who, thinking themselves so, decide deliberately and decisively about all public representations, group and divide themselves into different parties, each of whom admires a certain poem or a certain music and damns all others, urged on by a wholly different motive than public interest or justice. The ardour with which they defend their prejudices damages the opposite party as well as their own set. These men discourage poets and musicians by a thousand contradictions, and delay the progress of arts and sciences, by depriving them of the advantages to be obtained by that emulation and freedom which many excellent masters, each in their own way and according to their own genius, might display in the execution of some very fine works.[96]

(50.) What is the reason that we laugh so freely in a theatre but are ashamed to weep? Is it less natural to be melted by what excites pity than to burst into laughter at what is comical? Is it the alteration of our features that checks us? It is more visible in immoderate laughter than in the most passionate grief; and we avert our faces when we laugh or weep in the presence of people of rank, or of all those whom we respect. Is it because we are reluctant to let it be seen we are tender-hearted, or to show any emotion, especially at an imaginary subject, and by which it seems we are imposed upon? But without quoting those austere men, or those who do not care for the opinions of the world,[97] who think that excessive laughter or tears betray weakness, and who forbid both, what is it that we look for in tragedy? Is it to laugh? Is truth not depicted there as vividly as in comedy? And have we not to feel that those things are realities in either case before we are moved? Or is it so easily to be pleased, and is no verisimilitude needed? It is not thought odd to hear a whole theatre ring with laughter at some passage of a comedy, but, on the contrary, it implies that it was funny, and very naturally performed; therefore the extreme restraint every one puts on himself not to shed tears and the affected laughter with which one tries to disguise them, clearly prove that the natural result of lofty tragedy should be to make us all weep without concealment and publicly, and without any other hindrance than wiping our eyes; moreover, after we have agreed to indulge in our passion, it will be found there is often less room to fear we should weep in a theatre than that we should be tired out there.

(51.) Tragedy, from its very beginning, oppresses the spectator's feelings, and, whilst being acted, scarcely allows him liberty to breathe and leisure to recover, or if it leaves him some respite, it is only to be plunged again into fresh abysses and new alarms. Through pity he is led to terror, or reciprocally through terror to pity;

---

[95] This compliment to the Prince de Condé only appeared for the first time in the fourth edition of the "Characters," published in 1689, when the whole court was still talking about the entertainment.

[96] This is said to be a hit at the partisans of Quinault, who could see no charms in anything except in his operas.

[97] In the original, esprit fort, which sometimes meant "a man who does not care for the opinions of the world," and sometimes "a freethinker."

it leads him through tears, sobs, uncertainty, expectation, fear, surprises and horror to a catastrophe. It should not, therefore, be a collection of pretty sentiments, tender declarations, gallant conversations, agreeable pictures, soft words, or something comical enough to produce laughter, followed, in truth, by a final scene in which the "mutineers" do not listen to reason,[98] and in which for decency's sake there is at last some blood spilled, and some unfortunate man's life taken.[99]

(52.) It is not sufficient for the manners of the stage not to be bad; they should be decent and instructive. Some comical subjects are so low, so mean, or even so dull and so insignificant, that a poet should not be permitted to write about them, nor could an audience by any possibility be diverted by them. A peasant or an intoxicated man may furnish some scenes for a farce writer; but they can scarcely be personages of true comedy; for how can they be the basis of the main action of a comedy? Perhaps it may be said that "such characters are natural." Then, according to a similar rule, the attention of an entire audience may be occupied by a lackey whistling, or a sick person on his bed-chair, or by a drunken man snoring and being sick; for can anything be more natural?[100] An effeminate dandy rises late, spends part of the day at his toilet, looks at himself in the glass, perfumes himself, puts patches on his face, receives his letters and answers them. But such a character brought on the stage, made to stop for any length of time, during one or two acts, and depicted as natural and as like the original as possible, will be as dull and as tedious as it well can be.[101]

(53.) Plays and novels, in my opinion, may be made as useful as they are pernicious. They exhibit so many grand examples of constancy, virtue, tenderness and disinterestedness; so many fine and perfect characters, that when young people cast their eyes on what they see around them and find nothing but unworthy objects, very much inferior to those they just admired, it is not to be wondered at that they cannot have the least inclination for them.

(54.) Corneille cannot be equalled where he is excellent; he shows then original and inimitable characteristics, but he is unequal. His first plays[102] are uninteresting and heavy, and did not lead us to expect that he would afterwards soar to such a height, just as his last plays make us wonder at his fall from such a pinnacle. In some of his best pieces there are unpardonable errors in the characters of the dra-

---

[98] La Bruyère puts in a note: "A rebellion was the ordinary ending of tragedies."

[99] Some commentators think this is an allusion to the tragedies of Quinault, but they were already buried in oblivion when he died in 1688: it seems rather to refer to those of Jean Galbert de Campistron (1656-1713), who, during ten years, from 1683 to 1693, produced almost yearly a tragedy, none of which have come down to posterity.

[100] Molière often put peasants on the stage; but he never made of them, nor of intoxicated persons, his principal characters: the "sick person" is said to be a hit at Argan in Molière's Le Malade imaginaire. See also page 21, § 38.

[101] This is an allusion to the actor Baron's L'Homme à bonnes fortunes (1686) and the Débauché (1690); this latter comedy, acted before the court the very year the above paragraph first appeared, was a complete failure, and has never been printed. Intoxicated people were often represented on the stage in La Bruyère's time.

[102] In the original comédies, a word employed for tragedies as well as for comedies.

ma[103]—a declamatory style which arrests the action and delays it, and such negligence in his versification and in his expressions that we can hardly understand how so great a man could be guilty of them. His highest individual quality is his sublime genius, to which he is beholden for some of the most beautiful verses ever read; for the plots of his plays, in which he sometimes ventures to transgress the rules of the ancients; and finally, for his catastrophes. In this he does not always follow the taste of the Greeks and their grand simplicity; on the contrary, he delights in crowding the stage with events, which he almost always disentangles successfully; and is above all to be admired for his great variety and the little similarity of his plots in the large number of dramas he has written. It seems that Racine's plays are more like one another, and that they lead up a little more to the same ending; but he is uniform, lofty in style, and everywhere the same, as well in the plots and incidents of his plays, which are sound, regular, rational and natural, as in his versification, which is correct, rich in its rhythm, elegant, melodious,[104] and harmonious. He is an exact imitator of the ancients, whom he carefully follows in their distinctness and simplicity of action, and like Corneille, not lacking the sublime and marvellous, the moving and the pathetic. Where can we find greater tenderness diffused than in *Le Cid, Polyeucte,* and *Les Horaces?*[105] What grandeur do we not observe in Mithridates, l'orus, and Burrhus![106] Both poets were well acquainted with terror and pity, those favourite passions of the ancients, which the dramatic authors were fond of producing on the stage; as Orestes in the *Andromaque* of Racine, *Phèdre* of the same author, as well as *Œdipus* and the *Horatii* of Corneille clearly prove. If, however, it is allowable to draw some comparison between them, and distinguish what are the peculiarities of each of them, as is generally discovered in their writings, I should probablyŒ say: Corneille enthralls us by his characters and ideas; Racine's coincide with ours; the one represents men as they ought to be, the other as they are. There is in the first more of what we admire and what we ought even to imitate; and in the second more of what we perceive in others or feel within ourselves. Corneille elevates, surprises, controls and instructs us; Racine pleases, affects, moves and penetrates us. The former employs the most beautiful, the most noble, and the most commanding arguments; the latter depicts the most praiseworthy and the most refined passions. One is full of maxims, rules, and precepts; the other of taste and feeling. Our mind is kept more occupied by Corneille's tragedies, but by Racine's we are more softened and moved. Corneille is more moral, Racine more natural.[107] The one seems to imitate Sophocles, the

---

[103] Cinna in the tragedy of that name, Felix in Polyeucte, and Rodogune in Rodogune are examples of this.

[104] The original has nombreux, the Latin numerosus.

[105] Three tragedies by Corneille. Though he himself calls the last tragedy by the name given above, its real title is Horace.

[106] Mithridates, the hero of Racine's tragedy of that name; Porus, a character in the Alexandre, and Burrhus in the Britannicus of the same author.

[107] In the comparison between Corneille and Racine there are some reminiscences of a Parallèle de M. Corneille et de M. Racine, published in 1686 by a certain author, de Requeleyne, Baron de Longepierre.

other Euripides.[108]

(55.) What the people call eloquence is the facility some persons have of speaking alone and for a long time, aided by extravagant gestures, a loud voice, and powerful lungs. Pedants also will not recognise eloquence except in public orations, and can see no distinction between it and a heap of figures, the use of big words and flowing periods.

It seems that logic is the art of making some truth prevail, and that eloquence is a gift of the soul which renders us master of the hearts and minds of other men, so that we suggest to them, or persuade them, to do whatever we please.

Eloquence may be found in conversations and in all kind of writings; it is rarely found when looked for, and sometimes discovered where it is least expected.

Eloquence is to the sublime what the whole is to its part.

What is the sublime? It does not appear to have been defined. Is it a figure of speech? Does it spring from figures, or at least from some figures of speech?[109] Does the sublime enter into all kinds of writings, or are grand subjects only fit for it?[110] Can an eclogue display anything but fine simplicity, and familiar letters as well as conversation anything but great delicacy? Are simplicity and delicacy not the sublime of those works of which they are the perfection? What is this sublime? Where does it begin?[111]

Synonyms are several words or various phrases which are the precise equivalents of each other. An antithesis is an opposition of two truths which throw light on one another. A metaphor or a comparison borrows from a foreign matter a sensible and natural image of a truth.[112] A hyperbole exaggerates truth to enable the mind to understand it better. The sublime paints nothing but the truth, and that only in noble subjects; it depicts all its causes and effects; it is the most meritorious expression or image of this truth. Ordinary minds cannot find the only right expression, and, therefore, use synonyms. Young men are dazzled by the lustre of an antithesis, and employ it. Sensible people, who delight in exact imagery, of course, are led away by comparisons and metaphors. Sharp people, full of fire, and carried away by a lively imagination beyond all bounds and accuracy, cannot be satiated

[108] Sophocles (495-406 B.C.), Euripides (480-406 B.C.)

[109] Cassius Longinus (213-273), a Greek orator, philosopher, and author, is chiefly known by his "Treatise on the Sublime," which is generally attributed to him. In it he states that there are five principal sources of the sublime, and that the third is nought but the figures of speech turned about in a certain manner. Boileau's translation of this "Treatise" appeared in 1674, and in his preface he described but did not define the sublime, a definition also not found in Longinus.

[110] The original has capable, in the sense of the Latin capax.

[111] According to Boileau, Longinus does not understand by "sublime" a sublime style, but something extraordinary and marvellously striking, which causes a work to enrapture, delight, and transport us. A sublime style always requires grand, eloquent words; but the sublime may be found in a single thought, a single figure of speech, a single phrase. Longinus himself says that anything which leaves us food for thought, which almost carries us away, and of which the remembrance is lasting, is sublime.

[112] In rhetoric there is a difference between a metaphor and a comparison.

with hyperboles. As for the sublime, even among the greatest geniuses, only the highest can reach it.

(56.) Every author who wishes to write clearly should put himself in the place of his readers, examine his own work as something new to him, which he reads for the first time, is not at all concerned in, and which has been submitted to his criticism; and then be convinced that no one will understand what is written merely because the author understands it himself, but because it is really intelligible.

(57.) People write only to be understood, but they should, at least, in their writings produce very beautiful things. They ought to have a pure style, and, in truth, employ a suitable phraseology; moreover, their phrases should express noble, intense, and solid thoughts, and contain a very fine meaning. A pure and clear style is thrown away on a dry, barren subject, without either spirit, use, or novelty. What avails it to any reader to understand easily and without any difficulty some frivolous and puerile subject, not seldom dull and common, when he is less in doubt about the meaning of the author than tired with his work?

If we aim at being profound in certain writings, if we affect a polite turn, and sometimes too much delicacy, it is merely because we have a good opinion of our readers.

(58.) The disadvantage of reading books written by people belonging to a certain party or a certain set is that they do not always contain the truth. Facts are disguised, the arguments on both sides are not brought forward in all their strength, nor are they quite accurate; and what wears out the greatest patience is that we must read a large number of harsh and scurrilous reflections, tossed to and fro by serious-minded men, who consider themselves personally insulted when any point of doctrine or any doubtful matter is controverted. Such works possess this peculiarity, that they neither deserve the prodigious success they have for a certain time, nor the profound oblivion into which they fall afterwards, when the rage and contention have ceased, and they become like almanacks out of date.[113]

(59.) It is the glory and the merit of some men to write well, and of others not to write at all.

(60.) Some persons have been writing regularly for the last twenty years; they have faithfully observed all rules of composition, enriched the language with new words, thrown off the yoke of Latinism, and given to style a pure French phraseology; they have almost recovered that harmony which Malherbe and Balzac first discovered, and which since then so many authors allowed to be lost; they have, in short, given to our style all the clearness it is capable of, and this will gradually lead to it becoming easily understood.[114]

(61.) There are some artists[115] or men of ability whose intelligence is as ex-

[113] The above paragraph is said to refer to the polemical writings interchanged between the Jesuits and Jansenists, and seems not quite fair to Pascal's Lettres Provinciales.

[114] Some "Keys" mention the names of Bouhours and Bourdaloue, whilst more modern commentators think that La Bruyère only wished to give a paragraph on the French prose of his time.

[115] The original has artisan, which even in La Bruyère's time meant an artisan, when

tensive as the art or science they profess; they repay with interest, through their genius and inventive powers, what they borrowed from it and from its first principles; they stray from art to ennoble it, and deviate from its rules if they do not make use of them to attain the grand and the sublime; they walk alone and unaccompanied, but they soar very high and are very penetrating, always certain of the advantages sometimes to be obtained by irregularity, and assured of their success. Careful, timorous, and sedate minds not alone never obtain those advantages, but they do not admire them nor even understand them, and are much less likely to imitate them; they dwell peaceably within the compass of their sphere, go up to a certain point, which is the limit of their capacity and knowledge, but penetrate no farther, because they see nothing beyond it; they are at best but the first of a second class and excel in mediocrity.

(62.) If I may venture to say so, there are certain inferior or second-rate minds, who seem only fit to become the receptacle, register, or storehouse of all the productions of other talents;[116] they are plagiarists, translators, compilers; they never think, but tell you what other authors have thought; and as a selection of thoughts requires some inventive powers, theirs is ill-made and inaccurate, which induces them rather to make it large than excellent. They have no originality, and possess nothing of their own; they only know what they have learned, and only learn what the rest of the world does not wish to know; a useless and dry science, without any charm or profit, unfit for conversation, nor suitable to intercourse, like a coin which has no currency. We are astonished when we read them, as well as tired out by their conversation or their works. The nobility and the common herd mistake them for men of learning, but intelligent men rank them with pedants.

(63.) Criticism is often not a science but a trade, requiring more health than intelligence, more industry than capacity, more practice than genius. If it is exercised by a person of less discernment than culture, and treats of certain subjects, it will spoil the reader's judgment as well as that of the author criticised.

(64.) I would advise an author who can only imitate,[117] and who is modest enough to tread in the footsteps of other men, to choose for his models writings

---

used without being qualified; our author employs it, however, for "artist."

[116] Some annotators say a certain Abbé Bourdelon (1653-1730), a completely forgotten critic, was meant; others think it was a hit at Ménage (1613-1692), who had the good sense not to recognise himself in this portrait, and is said to have been also the original of Vadius in Molière's Femmes Savantes.

[117] This author was the Abbé de Villiers, who published in 1682 a poem in four cantos, L'Art de Prêcher, in which he tried to imitate L'Art poétique of Boileau, and in 1690 Réflexions sur les défauts d'autrui, which were very successful; some suppose Father Bouhours' Pensées ingénieuses des anciens et des modernes (1689) hinted at; whilst M. G. Servois, the able editor of La Bruyère in the Grands Ecrivains de la France (1865-1878), thinks that possibly the "author" was Jacques Brillon, a lawyer and indefatigable imitator, who in his youth may have been presumptuous enough to have asked La Bruyère's advice on some of his literary works, the Portraits sérieux, etc., the L'Ouvrage nouveau dans le goût des Caractères de Théophraste et des Pensées de Pascal, the Théophraste moderne, etc., which three books appeared, however, after La Bruyère's death, from 1696 to 1700. Adrien Baillet, an erudite scholar and fertile author, is also mentioned by some "Keys."

that are full of intelligence, imagination, or even learning: if he does not come up to his originals, he may at least come somewhat near them, and be read. He ought, on the contrary, to avoid, as a rock ahead, the imitation of those authors who have a natural inclination for writing, employ phrases and figures of speech which spring from the heart, and who draw, if I may say so, from their inmost feelings all they express on paper. They are dangerous models, and induce those who endeavour to follow them to adopt a cold, vulgar, and ridiculous style. Indeed, I should laugh at a man who would seriously imitate my tone of voice, or endeavour to be like me in the face.

(65.) A man born a Christian and a Frenchman is constrained when he uses satire, for he is forbidden to exercise it on great subjects; sometimes he commences to write about them, but then turns to trifling topics, which he enhances by the splendour of his genius and style.[118]

(66.) The turgid and puerile style of Dorilas and Handburg[119] should always be avoided. In certain writings, on the contrary, a man sometimes may be bold in his expressions, and use metaphorical phrases which depict his subject vividly, whilst pitying those who do not feel the pleasure there is in employing and understanding them.

(67.) He who only writes to suit the taste of the age, considers himself more than his writings. We should always aim at perfection, and then posterity will do us that justice which sometimes our contemporaries refuse us.

(68.) We ought never to turn into ridicule a subject that does not lend itself to it; it spoils our taste, vitiates our judgment as well as other men's; but we should perceive ridicule where it does exist, show it up delicately, and in a manner which both pleases and instructs.

(69.) "Horace or Boileau have said such a thing before you." — "I take your word for it, but I have used it as my own. May I not have the same correct thought after them, as others may have after me?"

------

[118] It is now generally supposed that by the satirist described Boileau is meant, for he sometimes commences grand subjects, as in his satires Sur l'Homme or Sur la Noblesse, but he never enters deeply into the matter, and treats of Les Embarras de Paris or Le Repas ridicule.

[119] Those names stand for Varillas (1624-1695) and Maimbourg (1610-1686), two voluminous historians, the first of whom is known for the inaccuracy of his facts, the second by his pretentious style, though Madame de Sévigné and Voltaire do not entirely condemn the latter, and Bayle, in his Dictionnaire, praises his knowledge and accuracy. "Handburg" is the German for "Maimbourg."

TIRED OUT

II.

OF PERSONAL MERIT.

(1.) WHAT man is not convinced of his inefficiency, though endowed with the rarest talents and the most extraordinary merit, when he considers that at his death he leaves a world that will not feel his loss, and where so many people are ready to supply his place?

(2.) All the worth of some people lies in their name; upon a closer inspection it dwindles to nothing, but from a distance it deceives us.

(3.) Though I am convinced that those who are selected to fill various offices, every man according to his talents and his profession, perform their duties well, yet I venture to say that perhaps there are many men in this world, known or unknown, who are not employed, and would perform those duties also very well. I am inclined to think so from the marvellous success of certain people, who through chance alone obtained a place, and from whom until then no great things were expected.

How many admirable men, of very great talent, die without ever being talked about! And how many are there living yet of whom one does not speak, nor ever will speak!

(4.) A man without eulogists and without a set of friends, who is unconnected with any clique, stands alone, and has no other recommendations but a good deal of merit, has very great difficulty in emerging from his obscurity and in rising as high as a conceited noodle who has a good deal of influence!

(5.) No one hardly ever thinks of the merit of others, unless it is pointed out to him. Men are too engrossed by themselves to have the leisure of penetrating or discerning character, so that a person of great merit and of greater modesty may languish a long time in obscurity.

(6.) Genius and great talents are often wanting, but sometimes only opportunities. Some people deserve praise for what they have done, and others for what they would have done.

(7.) It is not so uncommon to meet with intelligence as with people who make use of it, or who praise other persons' intelligence and employ it.

(8.) There are more tools than workmen, and of the latter more bad than good ones. What would you think of a man who would use a plane to saw, and his saw to plane?

(9.) There is no business in this world so troublesome as the pursuit of fame: life is over before you have hardly begun your work.

(10.) What is to be done with Egesippus who solicits some employment? Shall he have a post in the finances or in the army? It does not matter much, and interest alone can decide it, for he is as able to handle money or to make up accounts as to be a soldier. "He is fit for anything," say his friends, which always means that he has no more talent for one thing than for another, or, in other words, that he is fit for nothing. Thus it is with most men; in their youth they are only occupied with themselves, are spoiled by idleness or pleasure, and then wrongly imagine, when more advanced in years, that it is sufficient for them to be useless or poor for the commonwealth to be obliged to give them a place or to relieve them. They seldom profit by that important maxim, that men ought to employ the first years of their lives in so qualifying themselves by their studies and labour, that the commonwealth itself, needing their industry and their knowledge as necessary materials for its building up, might be induced, for its own benefit, to make their fortune or improve it.

It is our duty to labour in order to make ourselves worthy of filling some office: the rest does not concern us, but is other people's business.

(11.) To make the most of ourselves through things which do not depend on others but on ourselves alone, or to abandon all ideas of making the most of ourselves, is an inestimable maxim and of infinite advantage when brought into practice, useful to the weak, the virtuous, and the intelligent, whom it renders masters of their fortune or their ease; hurtful to the great, as it would diminish the number of their attendants, or rather of their slaves, would abate their pride, and partly their authority, and would almost reduce them to the pleasures of the table and the splendour of their carriages; it would deprive them of the pleasure they feel in being entreated, courted, solicited; of allowing people to dance attendance on them, or of refusing any request; of promising and not performing; it would thwart the disposition they sometimes have of bringing fools forward and of depressing merit when they chance to discern it; it would banish from courts plots, parties, trickery, baseness, flattery, and deceit; it would make a court, full of agitation, bustle, and intrigue, resemble a comedy, or even a tragedy, where the wise are only spectators; it would restore dignity to the several conditions of men, serenity to their looks, enlarge their liberty, and awaken in them their natural talents as well as a habit for work and for exercise; it would excite them to emulation, to a desire for renown, a love for virtue; and instead of vile, restless, useless courtiers, often burdensome to the commonwealth, would make them clever administrators, exemplary heads of families, upright judges or good financiers, great commanders, orators, or philosophers; and all the inconvenience any of them would suffer through this would be, perhaps, to leave to their heirs less treasures, but excellent examples.

(12.) In France a great deal of resolution, as well as a widely cultivated intellect, are required to decline posts and offices, and thus consent to remain in retirement and to do nothing. Almost no one has merit enough to play this part in a dignified manner, or solidity enough to pass their leisure hours without what is vulgarly called "business." There is, however, nothing wanting to the idleness of a philosopher but a better name, and that meditation, conversation, and reading should be called "work."

(13.) A man of merit, and in office, is never troublesome through vanity. The post he fills does not elate him much, because he thinks that he deserves a more important one, which he does not occupy, and this mortifies him. He is more inclined to be restless than to be haughty or disdainful; he is only uncomfortable to himself.

(14.) It goes against the grain of a man of merit continually to dance attendance, but for a reason quite the opposite of what some might imagine. His very merits make him modest, so that he is far from thinking that he gives the smallest pleasure by showing himself when the prince passes, by placing himself just before him, and by letting him look at his face; he is more apt to fear being importunate, and he needs many arguments based on custom and duty to persuade himself to make his appearance; while, on the contrary, a man who has a good opinion of himself, and who is usually called a conceited man,[120] likes to show himself, and pays his court with the more confidence as it never enters into his head that the great people by whom he is seen may think otherwise of him than he thinks of himself.

(15.) A gentleman[121] repays himself for the zeal with which he performs his duty by the pleasure he enjoys in acting thus, and does not regret the praise, esteem, and gratitude which he sometimes does not receive.

---

[120] Glorieux in the original, which in La Bruyère's time, and even later, had the meaning "conceited." One of N. Destouches' (1680-1754) best comedies is called Le Glorieux.

[121] The original has un honnête homme, which meant, in La Bruyère's time, "a gentleman, a well-mannered man," but never "an honest man," which is in French un homme de bien.

(16.) If I dared to make a comparison between two conditions of life vastly different, I would say that a courageous soldier applies himself to perform his duty almost in the same manner as a tyler goes about his work; neither the one nor the other seeks to expose his life, nor are diverted by danger, for to them death is an accident of their callings, but never an obstacle. Thus the first is scarcely more proud of having appeared in the trenches, carried some advanced works or forced some intrenchment, than the other of having climbed on some high roof, or on the top of a steeple. Both have but endeavoured to act well, whilst an ostentatious man gives himself endless trouble to have it said that he has acted well.

(17.) Modesty is to merit what shade is to figures in a picture; it gives it strength and makes it stand out. A plain appearance is to ordinary men their proper garb; it suits them and fits them, but it adorns those persons whose lives have been distinguished by grand deeds; I compare them to a beauty who is most charming in *négligé*.

Some men, satisfied with themselves because their actions or works have been tolerably successful, and having heard that modesty becomes great men, affect the simplicity and the natural air of truly modest people, like those persons of middling size who stoop, when under a doorway, for fear of hurting their heads.

(18.) Your son stammers; do not think of letting him make speeches; your daughter, too, looks as if she were made for the world, so never immure her among the vestals.[122] Xanthus, your freedman, is feeble and timorous; therefore do not delay, but let him instantly leave the army and the soldiers.[123] You say you would promote him, heap wealth on him, overwhelm him with lands, titles, and possessions: make the most of your time, for in the present age they will do him far more credit than virtue. "But this will cost me too much," you reply. "Ah, Crassus, do you speak seriously? Why, for you to enrich Xanthus, whom you love, is no more than taking a drop of water from the Tiber; and thus you prevent the bad consequences of his having entered a profession for which he was not fit."

(19.) It is virtue alone which should guide us in the choice of our friends, without any inquiry into their poverty or riches; and as we are resolved not to abandon them in adversity, we may boldly and freely cultivate their friendship even in their greatest prosperity.

(20.) If it be usual to be strongly impressed by things that are scarce, why are we so little impressed by virtue?

(21.) If it be a happiness to be of noble parentage, it is no less so to possess so

[122] "The stammerer" was meant for the son of Achille de Harlay (1639-1712), chief president of the parliament of Paris, and is said not to have stammered, but to have been very idle, and without any oratorical talents. Yet, in 1691, at the age of twenty-three, he was appointed advocate-general, through the influence of his father. Hence his appearance in the sixth edition of the "Characters," also published in 1691. Mdlle. de Harlay, a daughter of the first president, was sent to a convent in 1686 on account of her affection for Dumesnil, a singer at the Opera.

[123] Xanthus was M. de Courtenvaux, the eldest son of the Minister for War, M. de Louvois, and is said not to have excelled either in good looks or bravery.

much merit that nobody inquires whether we are noble or plebeian.

(22.) From time to time have appeared in the world some extraordinary and admirable men, refulgent by their virtues, and whose eminent qualities have shone with prodigious brilliancy, like those uncommon stars of which we do not know why they appear, and know still less what becomes of them after they have disappeared. These men have neither ancestors nor posterity; they alone are their whole race.

(23.) A sensible mind shows us our duty and the obligation we lie under to perform it, and if attended with danger, to perform it in spite of danger; it inspires us with courage or supplies the want of it.

(24.) He who excels in his art, so as to carry it to the utmost height of perfection, goes in some measure beyond it, and becomes the equal of whatever is most noble and most transcendental: thus V ... is an artist, C ... a musician, and the author of *Pyrame* a poet; but Mignard is Mignard, Lulli is Lulli, and Corneille is Corneille.[124]

(25). A man who is single and independent, and who has some intelligence, may rise above his fortune, mix with the world, and be considered the equal of the best society, which is not so easily done if encumbered. Marriage seems to place everybody in their proper station of life.

(26.) Next to personal merit, it must be owned that from eminent dignities and lofty titles men derive the greatest distinction and lustre; and thus a man who will never make an Erasmus[125] is right when he thinks of becoming a bishop.[126] Some, to spread their fame, heap up dignities, decorations,[127] bishoprics, become cardinals, and may want the tiara; but what need for Trophime[128] to become a cardinal.

----

[124] V ... stands for Claude François Vignon (1634-1703), a son of an artist of the same name; C ... is Pascal Colasse, a pupil of Lulli, whose opera, Achille et Polyxène, was played a short time before the "Characters" were first published (1687); Pyrame, written by Pradon (1632-1698), was acted in 1674; he had brought out several other tragedies before the first appearance of La Bruyère's book. At that time Pierre Mignard (1635-1695), the celebrated artist, and Pierre Corneille (1606-1694) were still alive, and Lulli (1633-1687), the great musician, had only been dead a few months.

[125] Desiderius Erasmus (1467-1536), one of the most celebrated scholars and learned men of his time.

[126] By this bishop some say was meant M. de Harlay (1625-1695), archbishop of Paris; others think the archbishop of Rheims, Le Tellier (1642-1710), the brother of Louvois, was designated. See also page 141, note 282.

[127] The original has collier d'ordre, the collar of the order of the Holy Ghost.

[128] Trophime, it was supposed, stood for our author's friend Bénigne Bossuet (1627-1704), the eminent theologian, preacher, and bishop of Meaux, but he never became a cardinal. So general was this supposition, that in all editions of the "Characters" published after the author's death the name of "Bénigne" was put instead of "Trophime." Some "Keys," however, mention the name of Etienne le Camus (1632-1707), bishop of Grenoble, who became a cardinal in 1686.

(27.) You tell me that Philemon's[129] clothes blaze with gold, but that metal also shone when they were in the tailor's shop. His clothes are made of the finest materials; but are those same materials less fine in the warehouse or in the whole piece? But then the embroidery and trimmings make them still more magnificent. I praise, therefore, the skill of his tailor. Ask him what o'clock it is, and he pulls out a watch, a masterpiece of workmanship; the handle of his sword is an onyx,[130] and on his finger he wears a large diamond which dazzles our eyes and has no flaw. He wants none of all those curious nicknacks which are worn more for show than service, and is as profuse[131] with all kinds of ornaments as a young fellow who has married a wealthy old lady. Well, at last you have excited my curiosity: I should, at least, like to see all this finery: send me Philemon's clothes and jewels; but I do not wish to see him.

You are mistaken, Philemon, if you think you will be esteemed a whit the more for your showy coach, the large number of rogues who follow you, and those six horses that draw you along; we mentally remove all splendour which is not properly yours, to reach you personally, and find you to be a mere conceited noodle.

Not but that a man is sometimes to be forgiven who, on account of his splendid retinue, his rich clothes, and his magnificent carriage, thinks himself of more noble descent and more intelligent than he really is; for he sees this opinion expressed on the countenances and in the eyes of those who speak to him.[132]

(28.) At court, and often in the city, a man in a long silken cassock or one of very fine cloth,[133] with a broad cincture tied high upon his stomach, shoes of the finest morocco leather, and a little skull-cap of the same material, with well-made and well-starched bands, his hair smoothed down, and with a ruddy complexion; who, besides, remembers some metaphysical distinctions, explains what is the *lumen gloriæ*, and what it is to behold God face to face,[134] is called a doctor.[135] A man of humble mind, who is immured in his study, who has meditated, searched,

[129] Lord Stafford is meant here; he was a relative to the Duke of Norfolk, very rich and very eccentric, and married in 1694 a daughter of the Count de Gramont. Some think the Count d'Aubigné, the brother of Mdlle. de Maintenon, is spoken of.

[130] La Bruyère adds in a footnote, "an agate."

[131] In the original il ne se plaint non plus. Plaindre had sometimes the meaning of "to be sparing," and Le Sage employs it in Gil Blas in that sense.

[132] This is said to apply to a certain M. de Mennevillette, receveur-général of the clergy, whose son married Mdlle. de Harlay.

[133] In the original drap de Hollande, because the best cloth came from Holland. Colbert induced some Dutch and Flemish weavers to settle in France, where they made a cloth called Toile Colbertine, of which Molière wore a doublet as the Marquis in les Fâcheux. Colberteen is also mentioned in "The Fop's Dictionary" (1690), and in Congreve's "The Way of the World."

[134] The lumen gloriæ is, according to Roman Catholic theologians, "The help God affords to the souls of the blessed, to strengthen them that they may be able to see God 'face to face,' as St. Paul says (1 Cor. xiii. 12), or by intuition; as they say in the schools; for without such a help they could not bear the immediate presence of God."

[135] A certain preacher, Charles Boileau, was meant; others think it was a canon of Notre-Dame, called Robert.

compared, collated, read or written all his lifetime, is a man of learning.[136]

(29.) With us a soldier is brave, a lawyer learned; we proceed no farther. Among the Romans a lawyer was brave and a soldier learned; a Roman was a soldier and a lawyer.

(30.) A hero seems to have but one profession, namely, to be a soldier, whilst a great man is of all professions—a lawyer, a soldier, a politician or a courtier; put them both together and they are not worth an honest man.[137]

(31.) In war it is very difficult to make a distinction between a hero and a great man, for both possess military virtues. It seems, however, that the first should be young, daring, unmoved amidst dangers and dauntless, whilst the other should have extraordinary sense, great sagacity, lofty capacities, and a long experience. Perhaps Alexander was but a hero, and Cæsar a great man.[138]

(32.) Æmilius[139] was born with those qualities which the greatest men do not acquire without guidance, long study, and practice. He had nothing to do in his early years but to show himself worthy of his innate talents, and to give himself up to the bent of his genius. He has done and performed deeds before he knew anything; or rather, he knew what was never taught him. I dare say it: many victories were the sport of his childhood. A life attended by great good fortune as well as by long experience, would have gained renown by the mere actions of his youth.[140] He embraced all opportunities of conquest which presented themselves, whilst his courage and his good fortune created those which did not exist; he was admired for what he has done, as well as for what he could have done. He has been looked upon as a man incapable of yielding to an enemy, or giving way to numbers or difficulties; as a superior mind, never wanting in expediency or knowledge, and seeing things which no one else could see; as one who was sure to lead to victory when at the head of an army; and who singly was more valuable than many battalions; as one who was great in prosperity, greater when fortune was against him,—the being compelled to raise a siege[141] or to beat a retreat have gained him more honour than a victory, and they rank before his gaining battles or taking of towns,—as one full of glory and modesty. He has been heard to say, "I fled," as calmly as he said, "We beat the enemy;" he was a man devoted to the State,[142] to

[136] The man of learning is Mabillon (1632-1707), a scholarly Benedictine, and author of De Re diplomatica, De Vetera analecta, and other works.

[137] The original has homme de bien. See page 43, note 121.

[138] Montaigne, Saint-Evremond, and the latest French writer on Alexander, M. Jurien de la Gravière, happily still alive, and formerly Minister for the French Navy, think more favourably than La Bruyère did of the talents of the youthful king of Macedonia.

[139] Æmilius is the Prince de Condé (1621-1686). The whole of the above paragraph is filled with reminiscences from Bossuet's Oraison funèbre du Prince de Condé, delivered in the year 1687.

[140] The battle of Rocroi was won in 1643, when Condé was only twenty-two years old, whilst those of Freiburg, Nordlingen, and Lens were gained, respectively, in 1644, 1645, and 1648.

[141] An allusion to the siege of Lerida, raised by Condé in 1647.

[142] La Bruyère forgets the wars of the Fronde (1648-1653) and the part Condé took in

his family, to the head of that family;[143] sincere towards God and men, as great an admirer of merit as if he had not been so well acquainted with it himself; a true, unaffected, and magnanimous man, in whom none but virtues of an inferior kind were wanting.[144]

(33.) The offspring of the gods,[145] if I may express myself so, are beyond the laws of nature, and, as it were, an exception to them. They expect almost nothing from time or age; for merit, in them, precedes years.[146] They are born well informed, and reach manhood before ordinary men abandon infancy.

(34.) Short-sighted men, I mean those whose minds are limited and never extend beyond their own little sphere, cannot understand that universality of talent one sometimes observes in the same person. They allow no one to possess solid qualities when he is agreeable; or, when they think they have perceived in a person some bodily attractions, such as agility, elasticity, and skill, they will not credit him with the possession of those gifts of the mind, perspicacity, judgment, and wisdom; they will not believe what is told in the history of Socrates, that he ever danced.

(35.) There exists scarcely any man so accomplished, or so necessary to his own family, but he has some failing which will diminish their regret at his loss.

(36.) An intelligent man, of a simple and straightforward character, may fall into some snare, for he does not think that anybody would spread one for him or select him in order to deceive him. This assurance makes him less cautious, and he is caught by some rogues through this failing. But the latter will not be so successful when they attempt it a second time; such a man can only be deceived once.

If I am a just man, I will be careful not to offend any one, but above all not to offend an intelligent man, if I have the smallest regard for my own interests.

(37.) There exists nothing so subtle, so simple, and so imperceptible which is not revealed to us by a something in its composition. A blockhead cannot enter a room, nor leave it, nor sit down, nor rise, nor be silent, nor stand on his legs like an intelligent man.

(38.) I made the acquaintance of Mopsus[147] through a visit he made me without knowing me previously; he asks people whom he does not know to present him to others to whom he is equally unknown; he writes to ladies whom he only

---

them, as well as in the wars of Spain against France, from 1652 till 1659.

[143] His grandson and his nephew married illegitimate daughters of Louis XIV.

[144] An allusion to his bad and hasty temper.

[145] La Bruyère adds in a note, "Sons and grandsons, descendants of kings." This seems a reminiscence of the Homeric Διογενεῖς, Διοτρεφεῖς, Βασιλεῖς.

[146] This compliment was addressed to the princes of the Condé family, of whom one, the Prince de Conti (1629-1661), was in command of the army in Catalonia, though he had never served. Compare the saying of Mascarille in Molière's Les Précieuses Ridicules: "People of quality know everything without ever having learned anything."

[147] Charles Castel, Abbé de Saint Pierre (1658-1743), a member of the French Academy, whence he was ejected in 1718 on account of his Discours sur la Polysynodie, a work in which he proposed a kind of Constitution for the French nation.

knows by sight. He introduces himself into a company of highly respectable people, though he is a perfect stranger to them, and without waiting till they address him, or feeling that he interrupts them, he often speaks, and that in an absurd manner. Another time he enters a public meeting, sits down anywhere, without paying any regard to others or to himself; and if removed from a place destined for a Minister of State, he goes and seats himself in the seat of a duke and peer of the realm; he is the laughing-stock of the whole company, yet the only person who keeps his countenance. He is like a dog that is driven out of the king's chair and jumps into the pulpit. He looks with indifference, without any embarrassment or without any shame, upon the world's opinion; he and a blockhead have the same feelings of modesty.

(39.) Celsus[148] is not of a very high birth, but he is allowed to visit the greatest men in the land; he is not learned, but he is acquainted with some learned men; he has not much merit, but he knows people who have a great deal of it; he has no abilities, but he has a tongue that serves him to be understood, and feet that carry him from one place to another. He is a man made to run backwards and forwards, to listen to proposals and to talk about them, to do this officially, to exceed the duties of his post, and even to be disowned; to reconcile people who fall out the first time they see one another; to succeed in one affair and fail in a thousand; to arrogate all the honour of success to himself, and cast all the blame of a failure on others. He knows all the scandal and the tittle-tattle of the town; he does nothing but only repeats and hears what others do; he is a newsmonger, he is even acquainted with family secrets, and busies himself about the greatest mysteries; he tells you the reason why a certain person was banished and another has been recalled; he knows why and wherefore two brothers have quarrelled,[149] and why two ministers have fallen out.[150] Did he not predict to the former the sad consequences of their misunderstanding? Did he not tell the latter their union would not last long? Was he not present when certain words were spoken? Did he not enter into some kind of negotiation? Would they believe him? Did they mind what he said? To whom do you talk about those things? Who has had a greater share in all court intrigues than Celsus? And if it were not so, or if he had not dreamed or imagined it to be so, would he think of making you believe it? Would he put on the grave and mysterious look of a man newly returned from an embassy?

(40.) Menippus[151] is a bird decked in various feathers which are not his. He

[148] Celsus is the Baron de Breteuil, who was sent in 1682 on a diplomatic mission to the dukes of Parma and Modena, but failed, and was disowned.

[149] The "two brothers" are said to have been the counsellors of the parliament, Claude and Michel le Peletier, and the quarrel was about a question of precedence.

[150] The "two ministers" were Louvois and de Seignelay, a son of Colbert, and the chief cause of their falling out seems to have been the more or less assistance which should be given to James II. against England.

[151] Menippus is the Marshal François de Villeroy (1644-1730), the favourite of the king and of Mademoiselle de Maintenon, only known as a perfect courtier when La Bruyère published his book, but who later on proved himself an incapable general. In the Mémoires of the Duke de Saint-Simon, he is called glorieux à l'excès par nature. See also page 43, note 120. Some commentators say Menippus was the Marquis de Cavoye (1640-1716), one of the

neither says nor feels anything, but repeats the feelings and sayings of others; it is so natural for him to make use of other people's minds that he is the first deceived by it, and often believes he speaks his own mind or expresses his own thoughts when he is but the echo of some man he just parted with. He is bearable[152] for a quarter of an hour, but a moment after he flags, degenerates, loses the little polish his shallow memory gives him, and shows he has nothing more left.[153] He alone ignores how very far he is from the sublime and the heroic; and having no idea of the extent of his intelligence, ingenuously believes that he possesses as much as it is possible for any man to have, and accordingly assumes the air and manners of one who has nothing more to wish for nor to envy any one. He often soliloquises, and so little conceals it, that the passers-by see him and think he is always making up his mind, or is finally deciding some matter or other. If you bow to him at a certain time, you perplex him as to whether he has to return the bow or not; and, whilst he is deliberating, you are already out of his sight. His vanity, which has made him a gentleman, has raised him above himself, and made him what naturally he is not. When you behold him, you can judge he has nothing to do but to survey himself, so that he may perceive everything he wears suits him, and that his dress is not incongruous; he fancies all men's eyes are upon him, and that people come to look on him one after another.

(41.) A man who has a palace of his own, with apartments for the summer and the winter season, and yet sleeps in an *entresol* in the Louvre,[154] does not act thus through modesty; another, who, to preserve his elegant shape, abstains from wine and eats but one meal a day, is neither sober nor temperate; whilst it may be said of a third, who, importuned by some poor friend, finally renders him some assistance, that he buys his tranquillity, but by no means that he is liberal. It is the motive alone that gives merit to human actions, and disinterestedness perfects them.

(42.) False greatness is unsociable and inaccessible; as it is sensible of its weakness, it conceals itself, or at least does not show itself openly, and only allows just so much to be seen as will carry on the deceit, so as not to appear what it really is, namely, undoubtedly mean. True greatness, on the contrary, is free, gentle, familiar, and popular; it allows itself to be touched and handled, loses nothing by being seen closely, and is the more admired the better it is known. Out of kindness it stoops to inferiors, and recovers, without effort, its true character; sometimes it unbends, becomes negligent, lays aside all its superiority, yet never loses the power of resuming it and of maintaining it; amidst laughter, gambols, and jocularity it preserves its dignity, and we approach it freely, and yet with some diffidence. It is noble, yet sympathetic, whilst inspiring respect and confidence, and makes us view princes as of lofty, nay, of very lofty rank, without making us feel that we are

---

handsomest men and one of the greatest duellists of the court.

[152] The original has de mise, which was also used by Voltaire and Rousseau, but seems now to have become antiquated.

[153] Montre la corde in the original.

[154] When the "Characters" first made their appearance in 1689, Louis XIV. no longer resided in the Louvre, but at Versailles. The greatest nobles, in order to pay their court to the king, lodged in some wretched rooms in the palace.

of inferior condition.[155]

(43.) A wise man is cured of ambition by ambition itself; his aim is so exalted that riches, office, fortune, and favour cannot satisfy him. He sees nothing good and sufficiently efficient in such a poor superiority to engage his affections and to render it deserving of his cares and his desires; he has to use some effort not to despise it too much. The only thing that might tempt him is that kind of honour which should attend a wholly pure and unaffected virtue; but men but rarely grant it, so he does without it.

(44.) A man is good who benefits others: if he suffers for the good he does, he is still better; and if he suffers through those to whom he did good, he has arrived at such a height of perfection that nothing but an increase of his sufferings can add to it; if he dies through them, his virtue cannot stand higher; it is heroic, it is complete.

---

[155] The first part of this paragraph, referring to "false greatness," is said to apply to the Marshal de Villeroy; the second, alluding to "true greatness," to Marshal Turenne (1611-1675).

THE TOILETTE

III.

OF WOMEN.

(1.) THE male and female sex seldom agree about the merits of a woman, as their interests vary too much. Women do not like those same charms in one another which render them agreeable to men: many ways and means which kindle in the latter the greatest passions, raise among them aversion and antipathy.

(2.) There exists among some women an artificial grandeur depending on a certain way of moving their eyes, tossing their heads, and on their manner of walking, which does not go farther; it is like a dazzling wit which is deceptive, and is only admired because it is superficial. In a few others is to be found an ingenuous, natural greatness, not beholden to gestures and motion, which springs from the heart, and is, as it were, the result of their noble birth; their merit, as unruffled as it is efficient, is accompanied by a thousand virtues, which, in spite of all their modesty, break out and display themselves to all who can discern them.

(3.) I have heard some people say they should like to be a girl, and a handsome girl, too, from thirteen to two-and-twenty, and after that age again to become a man.

(4.) Some young ladies are not sensible of the advantages of a happy disposition, and how beneficial it would be to them to give themselves up to it; they enfeeble these rare and fragile gifts which Heaven has given them by affectation and by bad imitation; their very voice and gait are affected; they fashion their looks, adorn themselves, consult their looking-glasses to see whether they have sufficiently changed their own natural appearance, and take some trouble to make themselves less agreeable.

(5.) For a woman to paint herself red or white is, I admit, a smaller crime than to say one thing and think another; it is also something less innocent than to disguise herself or to go masquerading, if she does not pretend to pass for what she seems to be, but only thinks of concealing her personality and of remaining unknown; it is an endeavour to deceive the eyes, to wish to appear outwardly what she is not; it is a kind of "white lie."

We should judge of a woman without taking into account her shoes and head-dress, and, almost as we measure a fish, from head to tail.[156]

(6.) If it be the ambition of women only to appear handsome in their own eyes and to please themselves, they are, no doubt, right in following their own tastes and fancies as to how they should beautify themselves, as well as in choosing their dress and ornaments; but if they desire to please men, if it is for them they paint and besmear themselves, I can tell them that all men, or nearly all, have agreed that white and red paint makes them look hideous and frightful; that red paint alone ages and disguises them, and that these men hate as much to see white lead on their countenances as to see false teeth in their mouths or balls of wax to plump out their cheeks;[157] that they solemnly protest against all artifices women employ to make themselves look ugly; that they are not responsible for it to Heaven, but, on the contrary, that it seems the last and infallible means to reclaim men from loving them.

If women were by nature what they make themselves by art; if they were to lose suddenly all the freshness of their complexion, and their faces to become as fiery and as leaden as they make them with the red and the paint they besmear themselves with, they would consider themselves the most wretched creatures on earth.

(7.) A coquette is a woman who never yields to the passion she has for pleasing, nor to the good opinion she entertains of her own beauty; she regards time and years only as things that wrinkle and disfigure other women, and forgets that age is written on her face. The same dress, which formerly enhanced her beauty when she was young, now disfigures her, and shows the more the defects of old age; winning manners and affectation cling to her even in sorrow and sickness; she

[156] An allusion to a fashion of the time La Bruyère wrote, when the ladies wore shoes with very high heels and enormous head-dresses, called Fontanges; the latter were invented by Marie-Angélique Scoraille de Roussille, Duchesse de Fontanges (1661-1681), who was one of the mistresses of Louis XIV. Our author refers to them in his chapter "Of Fashion," § 12.

[157] Some of the ladies at court, in order to hide the hollowness of their cheeks, used, it is said, to hold small balls of wax in their mouths.

dies dressed in her best, and adorned with gay-coloured ribbons.

(8.) Lise[158] hears that people make fun of some coquette for pretending to be young and for wearing dresses which no longer suit a woman of forty. Lise is as old as that, but years for her have less than twelve months; nor do they add to her age; she thinks so, and whilst she looks in the glass, lays the red on her face and sticks on the patches, confesses there is a time of life when it is not decent to affect a youthful appearance, and, indeed, that Clarissa with her paint and patches is ridiculous.

(9.) Women make preparations to receive their lovers, but if they are surprised by them, they forget in what sort of dress they are, and no longer think of themselves. They are in no such confusion with people for whom they do not care; they perceive that they are not well dressed, bedizen themselves in their presence, or else disappear for a moment and return beautifully arrayed.

(10.) A handsome face is the finest of all sights, and the sweetest music is the sound of the voice of the woman we love.

(11.) Fascination is despotic; beauty is something more tangible and independent of opinion.

(12.) A man can feel his heart touched by certain women of such perfect beauty and such transcendent merit that he is satisfied with only seeing them and conversing with them.

(13.) A handsome woman, who possesses also the qualities of a man of culture, is the most agreeable acquaintance a man can have, for she unites the merits of both sexes.

(14.) A young lady accidentally says many little things which are clearly convincing, and greatly flatter those to whom they are addressed. Men say almost nothing accidentally; their endearments are premeditated; they speak, act, and are eager to please, but convince less.

(15.) Handsome women are more or less whimsical; those whims serve as an antidote, so that their beauty may do less harm to men, who, without such a remedy, would never be cured of their love.

(16.) Women become attached to men through the favours they grant them, but men are cured of their love through those same favours.

(17.) When a woman no longer loves a man, she forgets the very favours she has granted him.

(18.) A woman with one gallant thinks she is no coquette; she who has several thinks herself but a coquette.

A woman avoids being a coquette if she steadfastly loves a certain person, but she is not thought sane if she persists in a bad choice.

[158] Lise is generally supposed to have been Catherine-Henriette d'Angennes de la Loupe, Countess d'Olonne, one of the most dissolute ladies of the court of Louis XIV., who was fifty-five years old when this paragraph appeared (1692), and died in 1714. Many particulars about her are related in Bussy-Rabutin's Histoire amoureuse des Gaules.

(19.) A former gallant is of so little consideration that he must give way to a new husband; and the latter lasts so short a time that a fresh gallant turns him out.

A former gallant either fears or despises a new rival, according to the character of the lady to whom he pays his addresses.

Often a former gallant wants nothing but the name to be the husband of the woman he loves; if it was not for this circumstance he would have been dismissed a thousand times.

(20.) Gallantry in a woman seems to add to coquetry. A male coquette, on the contrary, is something worse than a gallant. A male coquette and a woman of gallantry are pretty much on a level.

(21.) Few intrigues are secret; many women are not better known by their husbands' names than they are by the names of their gallants.

(22.) A woman of gallantry strongly desires to be loved; it is enough for a coquette to be thought amiable and to be considered handsome. This one seeks to form an engagement; that one is satisfied with pleasing. The first passes successively from one engagement to another; the second has at one and the same time a great many amusements on her hands. Passion and pleasure are predominant in the first; vanity and levity in the second. Gallantry is a weakness of the heart, or perhaps a constitutional defect; coquetry is an irregularity of the mind. A woman of gallantry is feared; a coquette is hated. From two such characters might be formed a third worse than any.

(23.) A weak woman is one who is blamed for a fault for which she blames herself; whose feelings are struggling with reason, and who should like to be cured of her folly, but is never cured, or not till very late in life.

(24.) An inconstant woman is one who is no longer in love; a giddy woman is one who is already in love with another person; a flighty woman neither knows if she loves or whom she loves; and an indifferent woman is one who loves nobody.

(25.) Treachery, if I may say so, is a falsehood told by the whole body; in a woman it is the art of arranging words or actions for the purpose of deceiving us, and sometimes of making use of vows and promises which it costs her no more to break than it did to make.

A faithless woman, if known to be such by the person concerned, is but faithless; if she is believed faithful, she is treacherous.

The benefit we obtain from the perfidy of women is that it cures us of jealousy.

(26.) Some women in their lifetime have a double engagement to keep, which it is as difficult to violate as to conceal; in the one nothing is wanting but a legal consecration, and in the other nothing but the heart.

(27.) If we were to judge of a certain woman by her beauty, her youth, her pride, and her haughtiness, we could almost assert that none but a hero would one day win her. She has chosen to fall in love with a little monster deficient in intelligence.[159]

[159] This is said to allude to a certain Mademoiselle de Loines, who fell in love with a

(28.) There are some women past their prime, who, on account of their constitution or bad disposition, are naturally the resource of young men not possessing sufficient wealth. I do not know who is more to be pitied, either a woman in years who needs a young man, or a young man who needs an old woman.[160]

(29.) A man who is looked upon with contempt at court, is received amongst fashionable people[161] in the city, where he triumphs over a magistrate in all his finery,[162] as well as over a citizen wearing a sword; he beats them all out of the field and becomes master of the situation; he is treated with consideration and is beloved; there is no resisting for long a man wearing a gold-embroidered scarf[163] and white plumes; a man who talks to the king and visits the ministers. He kindles jealousy amongst men as well as amongst women; he is admired and envied; but in Versailles, four leagues from Paris, he is despised.[164]

(30.) A citizen is to a woman who has never left her native province what a courtier is to a woman born and bred in town.

(31.) A man who is vain, indiscreet, a great talker and a mischievous wag, who speaks arrogantly of himself and contemptuously of others, who is boisterous, haughty, forward, without morality, honesty, or commonsense, and who draws for facts on his imagination, wants nothing else, to be adored by many women, but handsome features and a good shape.

(32.) Is it for the sake of secrecy, or from some eccentricity, that a certain lady loves her footman and Dorinna her physician?[165]

(33.) Roscius treads the stage with admirable grace: yes, Lelia, so he does; and I will allow you, too, that his limbs are well shaped, that he acts well, and very long parts, and that to recite perfectly he wants nothing else, as they say, but to open his mouth. But is he the only actor who is charming in everything he does? or is his

---

crooked, ill-looking, dwarfish limb of the law.

[160] The memoirs of the time of Louis XIV. teem with examples of young men of the highest families who considered it no disgrace to live at the expense of rich and amorous old crones, and even to receive money from young ladies.

[161] The original has dans une ruelle. Ruelle means literally "a small street," hence the narrow opening between the wall and the bed, on which bed superfine ladies, gaily dressed, were lying when they received their friends, and thus ruelle came to mean "any fashionable assembly." In Dr. Ash's "Dictionary of the English Language," London, 1755, ruelle is still defined "a little street, a circle, an assembly at a private house."

[162] En cravate et en habit gris, says the French, which was the usual dress of dandified magistrates, although they were strictly forbidden to wear any other clothes but black ones.

[163] Only officers of the king's household were allowed to wear gold-embroidered scarfs.

[164] This alludes to the Count d'Aubigné, a brother of Madame de Maintenon, who was no favourite at court. See also the portrait of "Theodectes" in the chapter "Of Society and Conversation," § 12, page 106.

[165] The "lady" is said to have been Madame de la Ferrière, the wife of a maître des requêtes, and Dorinna a certain Mdlle. Foucault, a relative of some well-known conseiller au parlement, who was in love with a Doctor Moreau.

profession the noblest and most honourable in the world? Moreover, Roscius cannot be yours; he is another's, or, if he were not, he is pre-engaged. Claudia waits
for him till he is satiated with Messalina. Take Bathyllus, then, Lelia. Where will
you find, I do not say among the knights you despise, but among the very players,
one to compare with him in rising so high whilst dancing or in cutting capers? Or
what do you think of Cobus, the tumbler, who, throwing his feet forward, whirls
himself quite round in the air before he lights on the ground? But, perhaps, you
know that he is no longer young? As for Bathyllus, you will say, the crowd round
him is still too great, and he refuses more ladies than he gratifies. Well, you can
have Draco, the flute-player; none of all his profession swells his cheeks with so
much decency as he does whilst playing on the hautboy or the flageolet; for he can
play on a great number of instruments; and he is so comical that he makes even
children and young women laugh. Who eats or drinks more at a meal than Draco?
He makes the whole company intoxicated, and is the last to remain comparatively
sober. You sigh, Lelia. Is it because Draco has already made his choice, or because,
unfortunately, you have been forestalled? Is he at last engaged to Cesonia, who
has so long pursued him, and who has sacrificed for him such a large number of
lovers, I might even say, the entire flower of Rome? to Cesonia, herself belonging
to a patrician family, so young, so handsome, and of so noble a mien? I pity you,
Lelia, if you have been infected with this new fancy which possesses so many
Roman ladies for what are called public men, whose calling exposes them to the
public gaze. What course will you pursue, then, since the best of their kind are
already engaged? However, Brontes, the executioner,[166] is still left; everybody
speaks of his strength and his skill; he is young, broad-shouldered and brawny,
and, moreover, a negro, a black man.[167]

(34.) A woman of fashion looks on a gardener as a gardener, and on a mason
as a mason; but other women, who live more secluded, look upon a mason and a
gardener as men. Anything is a temptation to those who dread it.[168]

(35.) Some ladies are[169] liberal to the Church as well as to their lovers; and
being both gallant and charitable, are provided with seats and oratories within the

[166] The original has questionnaire, a word then already antiquated, and which meant
a man applying the question or rack.

[167] Roscius seems to have been intended for a portrait of the celebrated actor Michael
Baron (1653-1729), whilst the names of Lelia, Cesonia, Claudia, and Messalina probably
allude to some of the ladies of the court who intrigued with actors. During the eighteenth
century the names of the Maréchale de la Ferté, and of her sister the Countess d'Olonne
(see page 61, note 158), both of very dissolute manners, were mentioned as having been the
originals of Claudia and Messalina, whilst Claudia was also, according to some, a portrait
of Marie-Anne Mancini, Duchesse de Bouillon, though it is not probable that La Bruyère intended to allude to her. Bathyllus and Cobus stand for Le Basque, Pécourt, or Beauchamps,
dancers at the Opera; Draco is Philibert, a German flute-player of those times; Lelia or Cesonia are supposed to have been a certain widow of the Marquis de Constantin.

[168] Is this not an allusion of our author to some nunneries not in very good repute
at the time?

[169] This applies, it is said, to the Maréchale de la Ferté, mentioned on page 67, note 2,
and to the Duke d'Aumont's second wife, who died in 1711, sixty-one years old.

rails of the altar, where they can read their love-letters, and where no one can see whether they are saying their prayers or not.

(36.) What kind of a woman is one who is "spiritually directed"? Is she more obliging to her husband, kinder to her servants, more careful of her family and her household, more zealous and sincere for her friends? is she less swayed by whims, less governed by interest, and less fond of her ease? I do not ask if she makes presents to her children who already are opulent, but if, having wealth enough and to spare, she provides them with the necessaries of life, and, at least, gives them what is their due? Is she more exempt from egotism, does she dislike others less, and has she fewer worldly affections? "No," say you, "none of all those things." I repeat my question again: "What kind of a woman is one who is 'spiritually directed'?" "Oh! I understand you now; she is a woman who has a spiritual director."[170]

(37.) If a father-confessor and a spiritual director cannot agree about their line of conduct, what third person shall a woman take to be arbitrator?

(38.) It is not essential that a woman should provide herself with a spiritual director, but she should lead such a regular life as not to need one.

(39.) If a woman should tell her father-confessor, among her other weaknesses, those which she has for her director, and the times she wastes in his company, perhaps she might be enjoined as a penance to leave him.

(40.) Would I had the liberty of shouting, as loud as I could, to those holy men who formerly suffered by women: "Flee from women; do not become their spiritual directors, but let others take care of their salvation!"

(41.) It is too much for a husband to have a wife who is a coquette and sanctimonious as well; she should select only one of those qualities.

(42.) I have deferred it for a long time, but after all I have suffered it must come out at last; and I hope my frankness may be of some service to those ladies who, not deeming one confessor sufficient to guide them, show no discrimination in the choice of their directors. I cannot help admiring and being amazed on beholding some people who shall be nameless; I open my eyes wide when I see them; I gaze on them; they speak and I listen; then I inquire, and am told certain things, which I do not forget. I cannot understand how people, who appear to me the very reverse of intelligent, sensible, or experienced, and without any knowledge of mankind, or any study of religion and morality, can presume that Heaven, at the present time, should renew the marvels of an apostolate, and perform a miracle on them, in rendering such simple and little minds fit for the ministry of souls, the most difficult and most sublime of all vocations. It is to me still more incomprehensible if, on the contrary, they fancy themselves predestined to fill a function so noble and so difficult, and for which but few people are qualified, and persuade themselves that in undertaking it they do but exercise their natural talents and follow an ordinary

[170] At the time La Bruyère wrote, nearly every fashionable lady had, besides her father-confessor, a spiritual director, who was her "guide, philosopher, and friend." Boileau, in his tenth satire, says:—

"Mais de tous les mortels, grâce aux dévotes âmes,
Nul n'est si bien soigné qu'un directeur de femmes."

vocation.

I perceive that an inclination of being intrusted with family secrets, of being useful in bringing about reconciliations, of obtaining various appointments, or of procuring places to people,[171] of finding all doors of noblemen's houses open, of eating frequently at good tables, of driving about the town in private carriages, of making pleasant excursions to charming country-seats, of seeing several persons of rank and quality concern themselves about our life and health, and of employing for others and ourselves every worldly interest,—I perceive, I say so again, that for the sake of those things solely has been invented the specious and inoffensive pretence of the care of souls, and an inexhaustible nursery of spiritual directors planted in this world.

(43.) Devotion[172] with some people, but especially with women, is either a passion, or an infirmity of age, or a fashion which must be followed. Formerly such women divided the week in days for gambling, for going to a theatre, a concert, a fancy-dress ball, or a nice sermon. On Mondays they went and lost their money at Ismena's; on Tuesdays their time at Climène's, and on Wednesday their reputation at Célimène's; they knew overnight what amusements were going on the next day, and the day after that; they thus enjoyed the present, and knew what pleasures were in store for them; they wished it were possible to unite them all in one day, for this was then the sole cause of their uneasiness and all they had to think about; and if they sometimes went to the Opera, they regretted they had not gone to any other theatre. But with other times came other manners; now, they exaggerate their austerity and their solitude; they no longer open their eyes, which were given them to see; they do not make any use of their senses, and what is almost incredible, but little of their tongues; and yet they think, and that pretty well of themselves and ill enough of others; they compete with each other in virtue and reformation in a jealous kind of way; they do not dislike being first in their new course of life, as they were in the career they lately abandoned out of policy or disgust. They used gaily to damn themselves through their intrigues, their luxury and sloth, and now their presumption and envy will damn them, though not so merrily.[173]

(44.) Hermas, were I to marry a stingy woman, she will be sure not to ruin me; if a woman fond of gambling, she may enrich me; if a woman fond of learning, she may teach me; or if prim and precise, she will not fly into a rage; if a passionate one, she will exercise my patience; if a coquette, she will endeavour to please me; if a woman of gallantry, she will perhaps be so gallant as to love me; but tell me, Hermas, what can I expect if I were to marry a devout woman[174] who would de-

---

[171] Placer des domestiques, in the original; domestique was used for any person belonging to the household of some great nobleman, even if he were himself a noble; it also meant "a household."

[172] A note of La Bruyère says that this refers to "assumed piety."

[173] Those ladies are supposed to have been the Duchesse d'Aumont, already mentioned; the Countess de Lyonne, the wife of a minister of state; the Duchess de Lesdiguières, and the Countess de Roucy.

[174] Our author's note says, "A pretended pious woman."

ceive Heaven, and who really deceives herself?

(45.) A woman is easily managed if a man will only give himself the trouble. One man often manages a great many; he cultivates their understanding and their memory, settles and determines their religious feelings, and undertakes even to regulate their very affections. They neither approve nor disapprove, commend or condemn, till they have consulted his looks and his countenance. He is the confidant of their joys and of their sorrows, of their desires, jealousies, hatred, and love; he makes them break with their gallants, embroils and reconciles them with their husbands, and is useful during the intervals. He looks after their business, solicits for them when they have lawsuits, and goes and sees the judges;[175] he recommends them his physician, his tradesmen, his workmen; he tries to find them a residence, to furnish it, and he orders also their carriages. He is seen with them when they drive about in the streets, and during their walks, as well as in their pew at church and their box at the theatre; he goes the same round of visits as they do, and attends on them when they go to the baths, to watering-places, and on their travels; he has the most comfortable apartment at their country-seat. He grows old, but his authority does not decline; a small amount of intelligence and the spending of a good deal of leisure time suffice to preserve it; the children, the heirs, the daughter-in-law, the niece, and the servants, are all dependent on him. He began by making himself esteemed, and ends by making himself feared. This old and necessary friend dies at last without being regretted, and about half a score of women he tyrannised over recover their liberty at his death.

(46.) Some women have endeavoured to conceal their conduct under a modest exterior; but the most any one of them has obtained by the closest and most constant dissimulation has been to have it said, "One would have taken her for a Vestal virgin."

(47.) It is a proof positive that a woman has an unstained and established reputation if it is not even sullied by the familiar intercourse with some ladies who are unlike her, and if, with all the inclination people have to make slanderous observations, they ascribe a totally different reason to this intimacy than similarity of morals.

(48.) An actor overdoes his part when on the stage; a poet amplifies his descriptions; an artist who draws from life heightens and exaggerates passions, contrasts, and attitudes; and he who copies him, unless he measures with a pair of compasses the dimensions and the proportions, will make his figures too big, and all parts of the composition of his picture by far larger than they were in the original. Thus an imitation of sagacity becomes pretentious affectation.

There is a pretended modesty which is vanity, a pretended glory which is levity, a pretended grandeur which is meanness, a pretended virtue which is hypocrisy, and a pretended wisdom which is affectation.

An affected and pretentious woman is all deportment and words; a sensible woman shows her sense by her behaviour. This one follows her inclination and

---

[175] It was then the custom for people who had a lawsuit to go and solicit their judges in person.

disposition, that one her reason and her affections; the one is formal and austere, the other is on all occasions exactly what she ought to be. The first hides her weaknesses underneath a plausible outside; the second conceals a rich store of virtue underneath a free and natural air. Affectation and pretension shackle the mind, yet do not veil age or ugliness, but often imply them; common-sense, on the contrary, palliates the imperfections of the body, ennobles the mind, gives fresh charms to youth, and makes beauty more dangerous.

(49.) Why should men be blamed because women are not learned? What laws, edicts, or regulations prohibit them from opening their eyes, from reading and remembering what they have read, and from introducing this in their conversation and in their writings? Is their ignorance, on the contrary, not owing to a custom introduced by themselves; or to the weakness of their constitution, or to the indolence of their mind, or the care of their beauty, or to a certain flightiness which will not allow them to prosecute any continuous studies, or to a talent and aptitude they only have for needlework, or to an inattention caused by domestic avocations, or to a natural aversion for all serious and difficult things, or to a curiosity quite distinct from that which gratifies the mind, or to a wholly different pleasure from that of exercising the memory? But to whatever cause men may ascribe this ignorance of women, they may consider themselves happy that women, who rule them in so many things, are inferior to them in this respect.

We look on a learned woman as we do on a fine piece of armour, artistically chiselled, admirably polished, and of exquisite workmanship, which is only fit to be shown to connoisseurs, of no use whatever, and no more apt to be used for war or hunting than a horse out of a riding-school is, though it may be trained to perfection.

Whenever I find learning and sagacity united in one and the same person, I do not care what the sex may be, I admire; and if you tell me that a sensible woman hardly thinks of becoming learned, or that a learned woman is hardly ever a sensible woman, you have already forgotten what you have just read, namely, that women are prevented from studying science by certain imperfections. Now you can draw your own conclusions, namely, that those who have the fewest imperfections are most likely to have the greatest amount of common-sense, and that thus a sensible woman bids fairest to become learned; and that a learned woman could never be such without having overcome a great many imperfections, and this is the very best proof of her sense.[176]

(50.) It is very difficult to remain neutral when two women, who are both our friends, fall out through some cause or other in which we are not at all concerned; we must often side with one or lose both.

(51.) There are certain women who love their money better than their friends, and their lovers better than their money.

[176] In La Bruyère's time many ladies had a great reputation for learning, such as Madame de Sévigné, and her daughter, Madame de Grignan, who greatly admired Descartes' philosophy; Madame de la Fayette; and a sister of Madame de Montespan, who was Abbess of Fontévrault. Montaigne was of opinion that women had no need of learning, and Molière, in his Femmes Savantes, holds the golden mean.

(52.) We are amazed to observe in some women stronger and more violent passions than their love for men, I mean ambition and gambling. Such women render men chaste, and have nothing of their own sex but the dress.[177]

(53.) Women run to extremes; they are either better or worse than men.

(54.) Most women have hardly any principles;[178] they are led by their passions, and form their morals and manners after those whom they love.

(55.) Women exceed the generality of men in love; but men are their superiors in friendship. Men are the cause that women do not love one another.

(56.) There is some danger in making fun of people. Lise, who is more or less in years, in trying to render a young woman ridiculous, has changed so much as to become frightful. She made so many grimaces and contortions in imitating her, and now has grown so ugly, that the person she mimicked cannot have a better foil.

(57.) In the city many male and female nincompoops have the reputation of being intelligent; at court many men who are very intelligent are considered dolts; and a beautiful woman who has some intelligence will hardly escape being called "foolish" by other women.

(58.) A man keeps another person's secret better than his own; a woman, on the contrary, keeps her own secrets better than any other person's.

(59.) There is no love, however violent, raging in the heart of a young woman, but there is still some room left for interest and ambition.

(60.) There comes a time when the wealthiest women ought to marry; they seldom let slip the first opportunity without repenting it for many a day; it seems that the reputation of their wealth diminishes in the same proportion as their beauty does. On the contrary, every thing is favourable to young girls, even men's opinions, for they attribute to them every accomplishment, to render them still more desirable.

(61.) To how many girls has a great beauty been of no other use but to make them expect a large fortune!

(62.) Handsome girls are apt to gratify the revenge of the lovers they have ill-treated, by giving their hand to ugly, old, or unworthy husbands.

(63.) Most women judge of the merits and good looks of a man by the impression he makes on them, and very rarely allow either of those qualities to a person who is indifferent to them.

---

[177] Such were, for example, the heroines of the Fronde, who only cared for ambition. Saint Simon in his Mémoires speaks of the Maréchale de Ciérambault, "who only left off gambling whilst at meals;" the Princess de Harcourt, who took usually the sacrament after having gambled until four in the morning; and the Duchesse d›Aumont, whom we have already mentioned.

[178] "Most women have no characters at all," says Pope in the Second Epistle "Of the Characters of Women." The late Rev. Whitwell Elwin thinks this "a literal rendering" of La Bruyère's § 65 "Of Men." I imagine it inspired by the above paragraph.

(64.) A man who is anxious to know whether his appearance is changed, and if he begins to grow old, needs only to consult the eyes of any fair one he addresses, and the tone of her voice as she converses with him, and he will then learn what he dreads to know. But it will be a severe lesson to him!

(65.) A woman who always stares at one and the same person, or who is for ever avoiding to look at him, makes us conclude but one and the same thing of her.

(66.) Women are at little trouble to express what they do not feel; but men are still at less to express what they do feel.

(67.) It sometimes happens that a woman conceals from a man the love she feels for him, while he only feigns a passion he does not feel.

(68.) Suppose a man indifferent, but intending to declare to a woman a passion he does not feel, it may be doubted whether it would not be easier for him to deceive[179] a woman who loves him than one to whom he is indifferent.

(69.) A man may deceive a woman by a pretended inclination, but then he must not have a real one elsewhere.

(70.) A man storms and rails at a woman who no longer cares for him, but he finds consolation; a woman is not so vociferous when she is forsaken, but she remains unconsolable for a longer time.

(71.) Sloth in women is cured either by vanity or love; though, in vivacious women, it is an omen of love.

(72.) It is certain that a woman who writes letters full of passion is agitated, though it is not so sure that she is in love. A deep and tender passion is more likely to become dejected and silent; and the greatest and most stirring interest a woman can feel whose heart is no longer free, is less to convince her lover of her own affection than to be assured of his love for her.

(73.) Glycera[180] does not love her own sex; she hates their conversation and their visits; she gives orders to be denied to them, and often to her male friends, who are not many, whom she treats very abruptly, keeps within limits, and whom she never allows to transgress the bounds of friendship. She is absent-minded when they are present, answers them in monosyllables, and seems to seek every opportunity of getting rid of them; she dwells alone, and leads a very retired life in her own house; her gates are better guarded and her rooms are more inaccessible than those of Montauron or d'Esmery.[181]

Only Corinna is expected and admitted at all hours, embraced several times, caressed, and addressed with bated breath, though they are alone in a small room;

[179] To deceive some one is now in French en imposer à quelqu'un, but until the last hundred years imposer was used, which meant "to deceive" and "to impose respect."

[180] Glycera is said to have been Madame de la Ferrière, whom we have already mentioned. See page 66, note 165.

[181] Pierre du Puget, lord of Montauron, who died in 1664, first president of the bureau des finances at Montauban, was celebrated for his riches and vanity. P. Corneille dedicated his tragedy Cinna to him. Michael Particelli, lord of Esmery, became, through the patronage of Cardinal Mazarin, surintendant des finances, and died in 1650.

whatever she says is attentively listened to; complaints are poured into Corinna's ears about another person; everything is told her, though nothing is new to her, for she possesses the confidence of that other person as well. Glycera is seen with another lady and two gentlemen at a ball, in the theatre, in the public gardens, on the road to Venouse,[182] where people eat fruit early in the season; sometimes alone in a sedan-chair on the way to the grand suburb,[183] where she has a splendid fruit-garden, or else at Canidia's[184] door, who possesses so many rare secrets, promises second husbands to young wives, and tells them also when and under what circumstances they will obtain them. Glycera appears commonly in a low and unpretentious head-dress, in a plain morning gown, without any stays, and in slippers; she is charming in this dress, and wants nothing but a little colour. People remark, nevertheless, that she wears a splendid brooch, which she takes special care to conceal from her husband's eyes. She cajoles and caresses him, and every day invents some new pretty names for him; the "dear husband" and his wife have but one bedroom, and would not sleep in any other room. The morning she spends at her toilet and in writing some urgent letters; a servant[185] enters, and speaks to her in private; it is Parmenion, her favourite, whom she upholds against his master's dislike and his fellow-servants' jealousy. Who, indeed, delivers a message or brings back an answer better than Parmenion? who speaks less of what should not be mentioned? who opens a private door with less noise? who is a more skilful guide up the back-stairs? or more cleverly leads a person out again the same way?

(74.) I cannot understand how a husband who gives way to his freaks and his temper, who, far from concealing his bad qualities, shows, on the contrary, only his worst, who is covetous, slovenly in his dress, abrupt in his answers, impolite, dull and taciturn, can expect to defend successfully the heart of a young wife against the attacks of a gallant who makes the most of dress, magnificence, complaisance, politeness, assiduity, presents, and flattery.[186]

(75.) A husband seldom has a rival who is not of his own making, and whom he has not introduced himself to his wife at one time or other; he is always praising him before her for his fine teeth and his handsome countenance; he encourages his civilities and allows him to visit at his house; and next to the produce of his own estate, he relishes nothing better than the game and the truffles his friend sends him. He gives a supper, and says to his guests: "Let me recommend this to you; it

---

[182] Venouse is not Venuzia, the native town of the Roman lyric poet Horace, but Vincennes; the road from Paris to Vincennes was a favourite spot for walking.

[183] The Faubourg Saint-Germain is meant by the "grand suburb."

[184] Canidia, a Neapolitan lady, is said to have been loved by Horace, and to have deserted him. Out of revenge the poet, in his Epodes v. and xvii., depicted her as an old sorceress who could unsphere the moon. Canidia is supposed to allude to La Voisin, who was burned at the stake in Paris, in 1680, for having poisoned several people.

[185] In the original affranchi, freedman.

[186] All the "Keys" say that "the husband" of this paragraph and the following one was a certain Nicolas de Bauquemare, président de la deuxième chambre des requêtes au palais.

is sent by Leander and costs me nothing but thanks."

(76.) A certain wife seems to have annihilated or buried her husband, for he is not so much as mentioned in this world;[187] it is doubted whether such a man be alive or dead. In his family his only use is to be a pattern of timid silence and of implicit submission. He has nothing to do with jointure or settlement; if it were not for that, and his not lying-in, one would almost take him for the wife and her for the husband. They are for months in the house together without any danger of meeting one another; in reality they are only neighbours. The master of the house pays the cook and his assistants, but the supper is always served in my lady's apartment. Often they have nothing in common, neither bed, board, nor even the same name; they live in the Greek or Roman fashion; she keeps her name, and he has his; and it is only after some time, and when a man has been initiated in the tittle-tattle of the town, that at last he comes to know that Mr. B ... and Madam L ... have been man and wife these twenty years.[188]

(77.) Another wife, who does not give her husband any uneasiness on account of her disorderly behaviour, repays herself for it by worrying him about her high birth, her connections, the dowry she has brought him, her enchanting beauty, her merits, and by what some people call "her virtue."

(78.) There are few wives so perfect as not to give their husbands at least once a day good reason to repent of ever having married, or at least of envying those who are unmarried.

(79.) Dumb and stupefied grief[189] is out of fashion; women weep, are garrulous, and so concerned about their husbands' death that they do not forget to harp on every one of the details.

(80.) Is it impossible for a husband to discover the art of making his wife love him?

(81.) An insensible woman is one who has not yet met the person whom she is to love. In Smyrna there lived a very handsome young lady, named Emira, yet better known throughout the town for her strict conduct than for her beauty, and above all, for the indifference she showed for all men, whom, as she said, she beheld without any danger, and without any greater emotions than when in the company of her female friends and her brothers. She could not believe a thousandth part of all the follies ascribed to love at all times; and those which she saw herself, seemed to her unaccountable. Friendship was the only feeling she knew, and her first experience of it was through a youthful and charming maiden, who pleased her so much that she only thought how to continue it, never imagining that any other inclination could ever abate that feeling of esteem and confidence

[187] Wives of a similar kind seem to have been Madame de Montespan, Madame de Sévigné, and Madame de la Fayette.

[188] This paragraph refers again to the président, mentioned on page 80, note 2, and to his wife, who was always called "D'Ons-en-Bray," pronounced "D'Osembray," after a property belonging to her husband.

[189] Stupide had, in La Bruyères time, the meaning of "stupefied" as well as of "stupid."

in which she now exulted. All her conversation was about Euphrosyne, for this was the name of her faithful friend, and the whole town talked about nothing else but about her and Euphrosyne; their friendship became a proverb. Emira had two brothers, both young, and so handsome that all the ladies of the city were in love with them, whilst she herself loved them as a true sister. One of the priests of Jupiter, who visited at her father's house, fell in love with her, and dared to declare his passion, but was repelled with scorn. A man of a certain age, who, relying on his noble birth and large estates, had the same assurance, met with the same repulse. She boasted of this, however; and even when in the company of her brothers, the priest, and the old noble, declared she was insensible to love. It seemed that Heaven reserved severer trials for her; yet these had no other effect but to render her more vain and to enhance her reputation as a maiden superior to love. Of three lovers smitten by her charms in succession, and whose affections she did not dread, the first, in a fit of passion, stabbed himself at her feet; the second, despairing of ever succeeding in his suit, went to seek his death in the wars of Crete; and the third ended his days in languor and passed his nights without sleep. The man who was to avenge them had not yet made his appearance. The aged noble, who had not been fortunate in his suit, was cured of his love by reflecting on his age and on the character of the young lady to whom he paid his addresses; however, he wished to visit her sometimes, and received her permission so to do. One day he introduced to her his youthful son, who united to a charming countenance manners full of dignity. Emira beheld him with some interest; but as he remained silent in the presence of his father, she thought he was wanting in intelligence, and could have wished him more. He saw her afterwards alone, and conversed long enough and intelligently; but as he did not look at her much, and talked still less about her and her beauty, she was surprised and somewhat indignant that such a nice-looking and clever young man should be so void of gallantry. She spoke of him to her friend, who expressed a desire to see him. He, then, only looked at Euphrosyne, and praised her beauty. At this the unfeeling Emira became jealous; she perceived that Ctesiphon spoke what he really felt, and that he was not only capable of gallantry, but even of tenderness. From that time she cooled towards her friend; yet she wished to see the couple together once more, to make quite sure that her suspicions were well-founded. The second interview showed her more than she dreaded to see, and changed her suspicions into certainty. She now avoided Euphrosyne; she no longer perceived in her that merit which charmed her before; she lost all pleasure in her conversation; she loved her no longer; and this alteration made her aware that love had driven friendship from her heart. Ctesiphon and Euphrosyne saw each other every day, loved one another, agreed to marry, and, finally, were married. The news spread through the town, and was talked about the more as it is not often that two persons who love one another are married. Emira heard of it, and became desperate; she now felt all the power of love; she again visited Euphrosyne only for the pleasure of anew beholding Ctesiphon; but that young husband still remained a lover, and in his new wife found all the charms of a mistress; he looked on Emira but as a friend of her who was dear to him. This unfortunate girl could no longer rest, and refused to take any nourishment; she got weaker and weaker, and at last her mind became affected;

she mistook her brother for Ctesiphon, and spoke to him as a lover; she recollected herself, and blushed for her error, yet soon relapsed into greater errors, for which she did not blush, for she was no longer aware of them. Now she dreads men, but it is too late; that is the cause of her madness. She has lucid intervals, but these are the most painful to her. The youth of Smyrna, who saw her formerly so proud and so void of feeling, now think that the gods have punished her too severely.[190]

[190] It might have been expected that some of the "Keys" would have told us who Emira was, but this anecdote is either invented by La Bruyère or founded on a fact only known to him.

IV.

OF THE AFFECTIONS.

(1.) PURE friendship is something which men of an inferior intellect can never taste.

(2.) Friendship can exist between persons of different sexes, without any coarse or sensual feelings; yet a woman always looks upon a man as a man, and so a man will look upon a woman as a woman. Such a connection is neither love nor pure friendship, but something out of the common.

(3.) Love arises suddenly, without any warning, through a natural disposition or through weakness; one glance of the fair transfixes us, determines us. Friendship, on the contrary, is formed gradually, in time, through familiarity and long acquaintance. How much intelligence, kindness of heart and affection; how many good offices and civilities are required among friends to accomplish in several years what a lovely face or a fine hand does in a minute.

(4.) Time, which strengthens friendship, weakens love.

(5.) As long as love lasts, it feeds on itself, and sometimes by those very means which seem rather likely to extinguish it, such as caprice, severity, absence, jealousy. Friendship, on the contrary, needs every assistance, and dies from want of attention, confidence, and kindness.

(6.) It is not so difficult to meet with excessive love as with perfect friendship.

(7.) Love and friendship exclude each other.

(8.) A man who is passionately in love neglects friendship, and one whose whole feelings are for friendship has none to give to love.

(9.) Love begins with love; and the warmest friendship cannot change even to the coldest love.

(10.) Nothing is more like the most ardent friendship than those acquaintances which we cultivate for the sake of our love.

(11.) We never love with all our heart and all our soul but once, and that is the first time we love. Subsequent inclinations are less instinctive.

(12.) Sudden love takes the longest time to be cured.

(13.) Love, slow and gradual in its growth, is too much like friendship ever to be a violent passion.

(14.) A man who loves so ardently that he wishes he were able to love ever so many thousand times more than he does, yields in love to none but to a man who loves more intensely than he could wish.

(15.) If I were to admit that in the ebullitions of a violent passion one may love another person better than oneself, whom should I please most—those who love or those who are beloved?

(16.) Men are not seldom inclined to fall in love, but cannot succeed in their desire; they seek every opportunity of being conquered, but fail to meet it, and, if I may say so, are compelled to remain at liberty.

(17.) Those who love too violently at first, soon contribute individually to their loving one another less, and, finally, to their not loving one another any longer. It is not so easy to decide who is most to blame for this rupture, the man or the woman. Women accuse men of being inconstant, and men retort that women are fickle.

(18.) However particular we may be in love, we pardon more faults in love than in friendship.

(19.) It is a sweet revenge to a man who loves passionately to make an ungrateful mistress appear still more so, by his very actions.

(20.) It is a sorry circumstance to love when we have not a fortune large enough to render those whom we love so happy that there is nothing more they can wish for.

(21.) If a woman with whom we have been violently in love, and who has not returned our passion, afterwards renders us some important services, she will hardly meet with anything but ingratitude.

(22.) A lively gratitude denotes a great esteem and affection for the person who lays us under some obligation.

(23.) To be in the company of those whom we love satisfies us; it does not signify whether we dream of them, speak or not speak to them, think of them or think of indifferent things, as long as we are near them.

(24.) Hatred is nearer to friendship than antipathy is.

(25.) It seems that antipathy changes oftener into love than into friendship.

(26.) We confide our secret to a friend, but in love it escapes us.

It is possible to enjoy some people's confidence, and yet not their affections; he who possesses these needs no trusting, no confidence; everything is open to him.

(27.) In friendship we only see those faults which may be prejudicial to our friends; in those whom we love we discern no faults but those by which we suffer ourselves.

(28.) The first tiff in love, as the first fault in friendship, is the only one of which we are able to make good use.

(29.) Methinks that if an unjust, eccentric, and groundless suspicion has been called jealousy, that other jealousy which is just, natural, founded on reason and on experience, deserves some other name.

Our natural disposition has no small share in jealousy which does not always spring from a great passion. Yet it is a paradox for a violent love not to be esoteric.

Our idiosyncrasy often causes no suffering to any one but to ourselves; but in jealousy we suffer ourselves and give pain to others.

Those women who do not respect any of our feelings and give us so many opportunities of becoming jealous, should not be worthy of our jealousy if we were guided rather by their sentiments and conduct than by our affections.

(30.) Coolness in friendship and the slackening of its ties, arise not without cause; in love there is hardly any other cause for our ceasing to love but that of having loved to excess.

(31.) It is no more in our power to love always than it was not to love at all.

(32.) Love receives its death-wound from aversion, and forgetfulness buries it.

(33.) We perceive when love begins and when it declines by our perplexity when alone.

(34.) To cease from loving is a distinct proof that the powers of man are limited and his affections as well.

It is a weakness to love; it is sometimes another weakness to attempt the cure of it.

We are cured in the same way as we are comforted, for we cannot always weep nor love with all our heart.

(35.) There should be within the heart inexhaustible sources of grief for certain losses. It is seldom that either by our virtue or strength of mind we overcome a great affliction; we weep bitterly and are deeply moved, but afterwards we are either so weak or so flighty that we console ourselves.[191]

(36.) When a plain-looking woman is loved, it is certain to be very passionately; for either her influence on her lover is irresistible, or she has some secret and more irresistible charms than those of beauty.

(37.) For a long time visits among lovers and professions of love are kept up through habit, after their behaviour has plainly proved that love no longer exists.

(38.) To endeavour to forget any one is a certain way of thinking of nothing else. Love has this in common with scruples, that it becomes embittered by the reflections and the thoughts that beset us to free ourselves. If we could do it, the only way to extinguish our passion would be never to think of it.

(39.) We should like those whom we love to receive all their happiness, or, if this were impossible, all their unhappiness from our hands.

(40.) To bewail the loss of a person we love is a happiness compared with the necessity of living with one we hate.

(41.) However disinterested we may be with regard to those we love, we must sometimes constrain ourselves for their sake, and have the generosity to accept gifts.

A man may freely accept a gift if he feels as great a pleasure in receiving it as his friend felt in giving it him.

(42.) To give is to act; we do not suffer any pains by our liberality, nor by yielding to the importunity or necessity of postulants.

(43.) If at any time we have been liberal to those we loved, whatever happens afterwards, there is no occasion to think of what we have given.

(44.) It has been said in Latin[192] that it costs less to hate than to love; or, in other words, that friendship is more expensive than hatred. It is true that we need not be liberal towards our enemies; but does revenge cost nothing? Or, if it be so pleasing and natural to harm those we hate, is it less so to do good to those we love? Would it not be disagreeable and painful for us not to do so?

(45.) There is a pleasure in meeting the glance of a person whom we have lately laid under some obligations.

(46.) I do not know whether a benefit conferred upon an ungrateful person, and thus on a person unworthy of it, does not change its name, and whether it deserves any gratitude.[193]

(47.) Liberality consists not so much in giving a great deal as in giving season-

[191] La Rouchefoucauld, in the Maximes (1665), makes almost the same remarks, and so does Pascal in the Pensées (1670). It often happens that those two authors agree in their expressions and thoughts with La Bruyère, who carefully studied them before publishing his Caractères.

[192] Discordia fit carior concordia is a saying of the Latin poet Publius Syrus (104-41 B.C.)

[193] In the chapter "Of the Affections," La Bruyère has borrowed a goodly number of ideas of Seneca's treatise De beneficiis; this is one of them.

ably.

(48.) If it be true that in showing pity and compassion we think of ourselves, because we fear to be one day or another in the same circumstances as those unfortunate people for whom we feel, why are the latter so sparingly relieved by us in their wretchedness?

It is better to expose ourselves to ingratitude than to neglect our duty to the distressed.

(49.) Experience proves us that if we are effeminate, and indulgent towards ourselves, and obdurate towards others, we show but one and the same vice.

(50.) A moiling, toiling man, who shows no mercy to himself, is only lenient to others by excess of reason.

(51.) Though the charge of maintaining a poor person may be very burdensome to us, yet a change of fortune, which makes him no longer our dependent, gives us no great pleasure, in the same way as our joy at the preferment of a friend is somewhat tempered by the small grudge we bear him for having become our superior or our equal. Thus we agree but ill with ourselves, for we should like to have others dependent on us, but, it must cost us nothing; and we should like to see our friends prosperous, yet when good fortune comes to them, the first thing we do is not always to be glad about it.

(52.) People send you invitations, ask you to come to their house, offer you even board and lodging, nay, their very fortune and their services; all this costs them nothing; but will they be as good as their word?

(53.) One faithful friend is enough for a man, and he is very fortunate to meet with one; yet he cannot have too many which may be of use to others.

(54.) When we have done all that we can do for certain people in order to acquire their friendship, and we find we have been unsuccessful, there is still one resource left to us, which is, not to do anything more.

(55.) To live with our enemies as if they might one day become our friends,[194] and to live with our friends as if they might some time or other become our enemies, is equally opposed to the very nature of hatred, as well as to the rules of friendship. It may be a political maxim, it is certainly not a moral one.

(56.) We ought not to make those people our enemies who might have become our friends, if we had only known them better. We ought to choose friends of such a high and honourable character that, even after having ceased to remain our friends, they should not abuse our confidence, nor make us dread them as our enemies.

(57.) It is pleasant to visit our friends because we like and esteem them; it is a torture to frequent them because we want them; then we become applicants.

(58.) We should try and gain the affections of those to whom we wish to do

---

[194] An imitation of another line of Publius Syrus: Ita amicum habeas, posse inimicum fieri ut putes.

good rather than of those who could do us some good.[195]

(59.) We do not employ the same means for bettering our position as we do in pursuing frivolous and fanciful things. We feel a certain kind of freedom in acting according to our fancy, and, on the contrary, a certain kind of thraldom in labouring for obtaining a place. It is natural to desire it ardently and to take little pains to obtain it, for we think that we deserve it without seeking for it.

(60.) He who knows how to wait for what he desires does not feel very desperate if he fails in obtaining it; and he, on the contrary, who is very impatient in procuring a certain thing, takes so much pains about it, that, even when he is successful, he does not think himself sufficiently rewarded.

(61.) There are certain people who so ardently and so passionately[196] desire a thing, that from dread of losing it they leave nothing undone to make them lose it.

(62.) Those things which we desire most never happen at all, or do not happen at the right time, and under those circumstances when they would have given us the greatest pleasure.

(63.) We must laugh before we are happy, or else we may die before ever having laughed at all.

(64.) Life is short, if we are only said to live when we enjoy ourselves; and if we were merely to count up the hours we spent agreeably, a great number of years would hardly make up a life of a few months.

(65.) How difficult is it to be pleased with any one!

(66.) We imagine that it would be impossible to prevent our feeling some pleasure if we were present at the death of a wicked man, for then we could reap the harvest of our hatred, and get from him all that we could ever hope to get from him, namely, the delight his death causes us. But when at last this man really dies, and at a time when our interest will not permit us to rejoice, he dies either too soon or too late for us.

(67.) It is difficult for a proud man ever to forgive a person who has found him at fault, and who has good grounds for complaining of him; his pride is not assuaged till he has regained the advantages he lost and put the other person in the wrong.

(68.) As our affection increases towards those whom we wish to assist, so we violently hate those whom we have greatly offended.

(69.) It is as difficult at first to stifle the resentment of a wrong done to us as to retain it after many years.

(70.) It is weakness which makes us hate an enemy and seek revenge, and it is idleness that pacifies us and causes us to neglect it.

(71.) It is as much from idleness as from weakness that we allow ourselves to

[195] This paragraph was not very clear in the original. We have followed M. Destailleur's explanation.

[196] In the original déterminément, an adverb employed by the best authors of the seventeenth century, but now antiquated.

be controlled.

No man should think of controlling another person all at once, and without some preliminaries, in some important matter of business which might be of great consequence to him and to his family; such a person would at once become aware of the sway and ascendency intended to be obtained over him, and would throw off the yoke out of shame or inconsistency. He should be tried first with trifling things, and then success is certain when attempting greater ones. Some people, who, at first, scarcely ventured to make a man leave for the country or to let him return to town, obtained such an influence over him at last, that he made his will, as they told him, and only left his own son what he was obliged to leave him.[197]

In order to control a man for any length of time and completely, a light hand is necessary, so as to let him feel his dependence as little as possible.

Some people allow themselves to be controlled up to a certain point, but beyond that they are intractable and ungovernable; suddenly all influence is lost over their feelings and mind, and neither rough nor gentle means, force nor address, can reduce them: yet, with this difference, that some act thus moved by reasoning and conclusive evidence, and others through inclination and constitution.

There are some men who turn a deaf ear to reason and good advice, and wilfully go wrong for fear of being controlled.

There are others who allow their friends to control them in trifling things, and thence presume to control them in things of weight and consequence.

Drance[198] would fain pass for a man who rules his master, though his master and the world know better. For a man in office to talk incessantly to his employer, a man of high rank, at improper times and places, to be always whispering or using certain words with mysterious intent, to laugh boisterously in his presence, to interrupt him when he speaks, to interfere when others address him, to treat with contempt those who come to pay their court to his master, or express impatience till they are gone, to stand near him in too unconstrained an attitude, to lean with his back against the chimney-mantel as his master does, to pluck him by his coat, to tread upon his heels, to affect a certain familiarity and to take such liberties, are signs of a coxcomb rather than of a favourite.

An intelligent man neither allows himself to be controlled nor attempts to control others; he wishes reason alone to rule, and that always.

Had I a friend, a man of sense, I should not object to confide in him, and to be controlled by him in everything, completely and for ever. I should then be sure of acting rightly without the trouble of thinking about it, whilst enjoying all the calm of a man swayed by common-sense.

(72.) All passions are deceptive; they conceal themselves as much as possible from others and from themselves as well. No vice exists which does not pretend to be more or less like some virtue, and which does not take advantage of this

[197] This is called la légitime in French.

[198] All commentators are agreed that by Drance the Count de Clermont-Tonnerre, first gentleman-in-waiting of the Duke of Orléans, brother of Louis XIV., is meant.

assumed resemblance.

(73.) We open a book of devotion, and it affects us; we open a book of gallantry, and that, too, impresses us. If I may say so, it is the heart alone which reconciles things so opposed to one another, and allows incompatibilities.

(74.) Men are less ashamed of their crimes than of their weaknesses and their vanity. The same man who is openly unjust, violent, treacherous, and a slanderer, will conceal his love or his ambition for no other reason but to conceal it.

(75.) It rarely happens that a man can say he is ambitious, for if he has been so once, he remains so; but there comes a time when he admits he has been in love.

(76.) Men begin with love and end with ambition, and are seldom free from passion till they die.

(77.) Nothing is easier for passion than to overcome reason, but the greatest triumph is to conquer a man's own interests.

(78.) A man who is swayed by his feelings is more sociable and agreeable to converse with than one who is swayed by his intelligence.

(79.) There are certain sublime sentiments, certain noble and lofty actions, for which we are indebted rather to the kindness of our disposition than to the strength of our mind.

(80.) There is no excess in the world so commendable as excessive gratitude.

(81.) A man must be completely wanting in intelligence if he does not show it when actuated by love, malice, or necessity.

(82.) There are certain spots which we admire, others which we love, and where we long to pass our days.

It seems that our mind, our temper, passions, taste and feelings, are influenced by the places where we dwell.[199]

(83.) Benevolent persons should be the only ones to be envied, if there were not a better course open to us, which is, to excel them; thus we can avenge ourselves pleasantly on those whom we dislike.

(84.) Some people pretend they never were in love and never wrote poetry; two weaknesses which they dare not own—one of the heart, the other of the mind.

(85.) During the course of our life we now and then enjoy some pleasures so inviting, and have some encounters of so tender a nature, that though they are forbidden, it is but natural to wish that they were at least allowable. Nothing can be more delightful, except it be to abandon them for virtue's sake.

---

[199] Montesquieu has developed this idea of the influence of climate on the mind and race in his Esprit des Lois, as well as H. A. Taine in his "History of English Literature."

SOCIETY

V.

OF SOCIETY AND OF CONVERSATION.

(1.) A man must be very inert to have no character at all.

(2.) A fool is always troublesome, a man of sense perceives when he pleases or is tiresome; he goes away the very minute before it might have been thought he stayed too long.

(3.) Mischievous wags are a kind of insects which are in everybody's way and plentiful in all countries. Real wit is rarely to be met with, and even if it be innate in a man, it must be very difficult to maintain a reputation for it during any length of time; for, commonly, he that makes us laugh does not stand high in our estimation.

(4.) There are a great many obscene minds, yet more railing and satirical, but very few fastidious ones. A man must have good manners, be very polite, and even have a great deal of originality to be able to jest gracefully and be felicitous in his remarks about trifles; to jest in such a manner and to make something out of nothing is to create.

(5.) If in ordinary conversation we were to pay great attention to every dull, vain, and puerile remark, we should be ashamed to speak or even to listen, and we should perhaps condemn ourselves to a perpetual silence, which would be more injurious to society than idle talk. We must, therefore, accommodate ourselves to all intellects, bear as a necessary evil the spreading of false news, of vague reflections on the Government or on the interests of princes, listen to the enunciation of fine sentiments which are always the same, and even allow Arontius[200] to utter wise saws, and Melinda to speak of herself, her nerves, her headaches, and her want of rest.

(6.) We meet with persons who, in their conversation, or in the little intercourse we have with them, disgust us with their ridiculous expressions, the novelty, and, if I may say so, the impropriety of the phraseology they use, as well as by linking together certain words which never came together but in their mouths, and were never intended by their creators to have the meaning they give to them. In their conversation they neither follow reason nor custom, but only their own eccentricity; and their desire always to jest, and perhaps to shine, gradually changes it into a peculiar sort of dialect which at last becomes natural to them; they accompany this extraordinary language by affected gesticulations and a conceited kind of pronunciation. They are all highly delighted with themselves, and with their pleasant wit, of which, indeed, they are not entirely destitute; but we pity them for the little they have, and, what is worse, we suffer through it.

(7.) What do you say? What? I do not understand you. Will you be kind enough to say it again? I understand you still less. Oh, I guess your meaning at last; you wish to tell me, Acis, that it is cold! Why don't you say so? You wish to let me know that it rains or snows; say at once that it rains or snows. You think I am looking well, and you wish to congratulate me; say that you think I am looking well. But you'll reply that it is so plain and clear, anybody might have said it. What does that signify, Acis? Is it so very wrong to be intelligible in speaking, and to speak as everybody does? There is one thing, Acis, which you, and men like you, who utter *phébus*[201] want very much; you have not the smallest suspicion of it, and I know I am going to surprise you. Do you know what that thing is? It is wit. But that is not all. There is too much of something else in you, which is the opinion that you have more intelligence than other men; this is the cause of all your pompous nonsense, of your mixed-up phraseology, and of all those grand words without any meaning. The next time I find you addressing anybody, or entering a room, I shall pull your coat-tails and whisper to you: "Do not pretend to be witty; be natural, that is better suited to you; use, if you can, plain language, such as those persons speak whom you fancy are without wit; then, perhaps, we may think you have some yourself."

(8.) Who, that goes into society, can help meeting with certain vain, fickle,

---

[200] Arontius is said to be Perrault (see page 14, note 57.) Who Melinda was has never been discovered.

[201] Phébus is nonsensical and exaggerated language, so called after Phœbus, the sun-god, on account of his brilliancy. The poet M. Regnier (1573-1613) had already made use of this word; it was something like the language employed by the Englishman, John Lily, in his "Euphues, the Anatomy of Wit," etc., published 1578-1580.

familiar, and positive people who monopolise all conversation, and compel every one else to listen to them? They can be heard in the anteroom, and a person may boldly enter without fear of interrupting them; they continue their story without paying the smallest attention to any comers or goers, or to the rank and quality of their audience; they silence a man who begins to tell an anecdote, so that they may tell it themselves according to their fashion, which is the best; they heard it from Zamet, from Ruccellaï, or from Concini,[202] whom they do not know, to whom they never spoke in their lives, and whom they would address as "Your Excellency," if ever they spoke to any one of them. They sometimes will go up to a man of the highest rank among those who are present, and whisper in his ear some circumstance which nobody else knows, and which they would not have divulged to others for the world; they conceal some names to disguise the anecdote they relate and to prevent the real persons being found out; you ask them to let you have these names, you urge them in vain. There are some things they must not tell, and some persons whom they cannot name; they have given their word of honour not to do so; it is a secret, a mystery of the greatest importance; moreover, you ask an impossibility. You might wish to learn something from them, but they know neither the facts nor the persons.[203]

(9.) Arrias has read and seen everything, at least he would lead you to think so; he is a man of universal knowledge, or pretends to be, and would rather tell a falsehood than be silent or appear to ignore anything. Some person is talking at meal-time in the house of a man of rank of a northern court; he interrupts and prevents him telling what he knows; he goes hither and thither in that distant country as if he were a native of it; he discourses about the habits of its court, the native women, the laws and customs of the land; he tells many little stories which happened there, thinks them very entertaining, and is the first to laugh loudly at them. Somebody presumes to contradict him, and clearly proves to him that what he says is untrue. Arrias is not disconcerted; on the contrary, he grows angry at the interruption, and exclaims: "I aver and relate nothing but what I know on excellent authority; I had it from Sethon, the French ambassador at that court, who only a few days ago came back to Paris, and is a particular friend of mine; I asked him several questions, and he replied to them all without concealing anything." He continues his story with greater confidence than he began it, till one of the company informs him that the gentleman whom he has been contradicting was Sethon himself, but lately arrived from his embassy.[204]

(10.) In conversation there is a middle course between a certain backwardness in speaking or a kind of incogitancy which leads us to wander away from the

[202] La Bruyère says in a note, "They would call them 'Sir.'" He also, and on purpose, leads the reader astray by using the names of three courtiers who died some time ago: Zamet, a favourite of Catherine de Medici and Henri IV., who died in 1614; Ruccellaï, one of Concini's partisans, who lived till 1627; and Concini, Maréchal d'Ancre, assassinated in 1617.

[203] Some traits of this character apply to Saumery, a gentleman-in-waiting of the Duke of Burgundy, a grandson of Louis XIV.

[204] Such an adventure is said to have happened to a certain conseiller au châtelet, Robert de Châtillon. Montesquieu, in his Lettres Persanes, describes a similar character.

subject under discussion, so as to make us ask untimely questions or return silly answers, and between paying too great attention to the least word said, in order to improve upon it, to joke about it, to discover in it some mystery hidden to all others, to find something shrewd and subtle in it, only to have an opportunity of showing how clever we are.

(11.) Any one who is infatuated with himself and quite convinced he is very clever, only shows that he has but very little intelligence or none at all. It is a misfortune for a man to listen to the conversation of such a person. What a great many affected phrases he has to endure! How many of those fanciful words which appear of a sudden, live for a short time, and then are never heard again! If such a person relates some trifling event, it is not so much to give some information to his hearers, as merely for the honour of telling it and of telling it cleverly. He amplifies it till it becomes a romance; he makes the people connected with it think as he does; he puts his own trivial expressions in their mouths, and renders them, like himself, very talkative; he falls then into some parentheses which may pass for episodes, and by which speaker and hearers forget what the story really was about. It is difficult to say what might have become of them, had not somebody fortunately come in to break up the company and put an end to the narrative.

(12.) Theodectes[205] is heard in the anteroom; the nearer he comes the more he raises his voice; he enters, he laughs, he shouts, he vociferates; everybody stops his ears; he is a mere thunderer, and no less to be dreaded for what he says as for the loud tone in which he speaks. He becomes quiet and less boisterous only to stammer out some idle talk and some nonsense. So little regard has he for time, individuals, or decency, that he offends every one without intending it; before he has taken a seat he has already insulted the whole company. When dinner is served, he is the first to sit down, and always in the place of honour; the ladies are to the right and left of him, but he eats, drinks, talks, banters, and interrupts every one at the same time; he has no respect for any one, neither for master nor guests, and takes advantage of the foolish way they look up to him. Is it he or Euthydemes who is the host? He assumes all authority while at dinner; and it is better to give way to him than to quarrel with him about it. Neither eating nor drinking improve his temper. If some gambling is going on, and if he wins, he banters his antagonist and insults him; the laughers are on his side, and there is no sort of folly they do not overlook in him. At last I leave him and go away, unable to bear any longer with Theodectes and those who bear with him.

(13.) Troïlus is useful to those who have too much wealth; he eases them of their onerous superfluity, and saves them the trouble of hoarding up money, of making contracts, locking trunks, carrying keys about, and of dreading to be robbed by servants. He assists them in their pleasures, and afterwards is able to serve them in their passions; in a short time he regulates and dictates their conduct; he is the oracle of the house, whose decisions are anxiously expected, nay, even anticipated and surmised; he orders a slave to be punished, and he is flogged; another to be freed, and he is set at liberty. If a parasite does not make him laugh, he perhaps does not please him, and therefore must be dismissed. The master of

---

[205] Theodectes is the Count d'Aubigné. See page 65, note 164.

the house may consider himself lucky if Troïlus leaves him his wife and children. If at table he declares that a certain dish is excellent, the master and the guests, who did not pay much attention to it, find it also excellent, and cannot eat enough of it; if, on the contrary, he says of some other dish that it is insipid, those who were just beginning to enjoy it dare not swallow the piece they had in their mouths, but throw it on the floor;[206] every eye is on him, and every one observes his looks and his countenance before giving an opinion on the wine or the dishes before them. Do not look for him anywhere else but in the house of an opulent man, whose adviser he is; there he eats, sleeps, digests his food, quarrels with his servant, gives audience to those whom he employs, and puts off his creditors; he lays down the law in the drawing-room, and receives there the adulation and homage of those persons, who, more cunning than the rest, only wish to curry favour with the master through Troïlus' intercession. If any one enters who is unfortunate enough to have a countenance which Troïlus does not like, he frowns and turns away his head; if a stranger accosts him, he sits still, and if the latter sits down close to him, he leaves his seat; if he talks to him, he does not reply, and if he continues to speak, Troïlus stalks away into another chamber; if the stranger follows him, he makes for the stairs, and would rather climb from one storey to another or throw himself out of a window, than encounter a man whose face and voice he dislikes. Both are very charming in Troïlus, and he has turned them to good account to insinuate himself or to overcome a difficulty. At last he considers everything unworthy of his attention, and he scorns to keep his position[207] or to continue to please by exercising any of those talents by which he first brought himself into notice. It is a condescension if sometimes he leaves off his musings and his taciturnity to contradict, and deigns once a day to show his wit, though only to criticise. Do not expect him to listen to what you may have to say, to be courteous, or to commend you, for you are not even sure that he will permit you to approve him, or allow you to be polite.[208]

(14.) Do not interrupt a stranger whom you meet by chance in a stage-coach, at an entertainment, or at any public exhibition; and if you listen to him, it will not be long before you'll know who he is; he'll tell you his name, his residence, his native country, what his property is worth, his position, and his father's, his mother's family, his kindred, his family connections, and even his coat-of-arms; for he will soon let you know that he is nobly born, and that he has a castle beautifully furnished, a suitable retinue, and a carriage.[209]

(15.) Some men speak one moment before they think; others tediously study

---

[206] It was the custom in La Bruyère's time, even among the upper classes, to throw on the floor what was left on the plates or in the glasses. See also the character of Menalcas, chapter xi., "Of Mankind," § 7.

[207] Il est au-dessus de vouloir se soutenir, literally, he is above wishing to keep himself up. This expression seems to be peculiar to La Bruyère.

[208] No suggestion has ever been made as to what person is portrayed as Troïlus; still it seems to have been intended by our author for one of his contemporaries.

[209] A certain boasting Abbé de Vassé is meant, who refused the bishopric of Mans, and died in 1716 at the age of sixty-five.

everything they say, and in conversation bore us as painfully as was the travail of their mind; they are, as it were, made up of phrases and quaint expressions, whilst their gestures are as affected as their behaviour. They call themselves "purists,"[210] and do not venture to say the most trifling word not in use, however expressive it may be. Nothing comes from them worth remembering, nothing is spontaneous and unrestrained; they speak correctly,[211] but they are very tiresome.

(16.) The true spirit of conversation consists more in bringing out the cleverness of others than in showing a great deal of it yourself; he who goes away pleased with himself and his own wit is also greatly pleased with you. Most men rather please than admire you; they seek less to be instructed, and even to be amused, than to be praised and applauded; the most delicate of pleasures is to please another person.

(17.) Too much imagination is to be avoided in our conversation and in our writings, as it often gives rise to idle and puerile ideas, neither tending to perfect our taste nor to improve our conduct. Our thoughts should originate from sound sense and reasoning, and always be the result of our judgment.

(18.) It is a sad thing when men have neither enough intelligence to speak well nor enough sense to hold their tongues; this is the root of all impertinence.

(19.) To say simply that a certain thing is good or bad, and to state the reasons for its being so, requires some common-sense and power of expression, which is not so easily found. A much shorter way is to give one's opinion peremptorily, which is a convincing proof a man is right in his statement, namely, that the thing is execrable or wonderful.

(20.) Nothing is more displeasing to Heaven and to men than to confirm everything said in conversation, and even the most trifling subjects, with long and disgusting oaths. Whether a gentleman merely says "Yes" or "No," he deserves to be believed; his reputation swears for him, adds weight to his words, and obtains for him every confidence.[212]

(21.) He who continually affirms he is a man of honour and honest as well, that he wrongs no man but wishes the harm he has done to others to fall on himself, and raps out an oath to be believed, does not even know how to imitate an honest man.

An honest man, with all his modesty, cannot prevent people saying of him what a dishonest man says of himself.

(22.) Cléon[213] talks always rather rudely or inaccurately; he does either the

---

[210] The author's note says, "A kind of people who pretend to be very nice in their language."

[211] Proprement, in the original, was in La Bruyère's time generally used for "elegantly," "correctly."

[212] Oaths were more commonly used by the upper classes in the seventeenth century than they are now.

[213] Cléon is supposed to have been a certain financier Monnerot, who died in prison rather than pay a fine of two million francs, to which he had been condemned by a court

one or the other; but he says he cannot help it, and that it is his natural disposition to speak just as he thinks.

(23.) There are such things as to speak well, to speak easily, to speak correctly, and to speak seasonably. We offend against the last way of speaking if we mention a sumptuous entertainment we have just been present at before people who have not had enough to eat; if we boast of our good health before invalids; if we talk of our riches, our income, and our fine furniture to a man who has not so much as an income or a dwelling; in a word, if we speak of our prosperity before people who are wretched; such a conversation is too much for them, and the comparison which they then make between their condition and ours is very painful.

(24.) "As for you," says Euthyphron,[214] "you are rich, or ought to be so, for you have a yearly income of ten thousand *livres*,[215] all from land. I think that glorious! charming! and a man could be happy with much less." The person who talks in this fashion has fifty thousand *livres* a year, and thinks he has not half what he deserves. He settles what you'll have to pay, values what you are worth, determines what you have to spend; and if he thought you deserved a better fortune, and even such a one as he himself aspires to, he would be certain to wish it to you. He is not the only man who makes such wretched estimations or such odious comparisons; the world is full of Euthyphrons.

(25.) A person inclined to the usual flattery, and accustomed to praise and exaggeration, congratulates[216]

Theodemus on a sermon he did not hear, and of which no one had, as yet, given him an account. He extols his genius, his delivery, and, above all, his excellent memory, when, in truth, Theodemus had stopped short in the middle of his sermon, and had forgotten what he wished to say.[217]

(26.) Some abrupt, restless, conceited men, who are unemployed, and have no manner of business to call them away, will dismiss you from their presence in a few words, and only think to get rid of you; you are still speaking to them, and they are already gone and have disappeared. They are as impertinent as those people who stop you only to bore you; but the former are perhaps less irksome.

(27.) To speak and to offend is with some people but one and the same thing; they are biting and bitter; their words are steeped in gall and wormwood; sneers

---

of justice.

[214] This personage is said to stand for Constantin Heudebert du Buisson, appointed intendant des finances the same year (1690) the seventh edition of the "Characters" was published. See also page 153, § 63.

[215] The livre parisis, probably meant here, was equal in value to the franc, first coined in 1573, under Henri III. An income of ten thousand francs in La Bruyère's time would represent one of fifty thousand francs now.

[216] The original has congratuler, now only used with a ridiculous meaning attached to it.

[217] It is generally supposed Theodemus was a certain Abbé de Drubec, who stopped short in the middle of a sermon preached before the court of Louis XIV.; others imagine it was a hit at the Abbé Bertier, who became bishop of Blois in 1697.

as well as insolent and insulting remarks flow from their lips. It had been well for them had they been born mute or stupid; the little vivacity and intelligence they have prejudices them more than dulness does others; they are not always satisfied with giving sharp answers, they often attack arrogantly those who are present, and damage the reputation of those who are absent; they butt all round like rams, for rams, of course, must use their horns. We therefore do not expect, by our sketch of them, to change such coarse, restless, and stubborn individuals. The best thing a man can do is to take to his heels as soon as he perceives them, without even turning round to look behind him.[218]

(28.) There are persons of such a disposition or character that a man ought never to be compromised with them; of such persons he should complain as little as possible, and not even be permitted to vanquish them in arguments.

(29.) When two persons have had a violent quarrel, of whom one is in the right and the other is in the wrong, the bystanders, for fear of being appealed to, or through a certain frowardness which always seemed to me ill-timed, condemn both. This is an important lesson, and a weighty and necessary reason for going away, even when a coxcomb is seen in quite another direction, so as to avoid sharing in his disgrace.

(30.) I hate a man whom I cannot accost or salute before he bows to me, without debasing myself in his eyes, or sharing in the good opinion he has of himself. Montaigne would say:[219] "I will have elbow-room: I will be courteous and affable according to my fancy, without fear or remorse. I cannot strive against my inclination nor go contrary to my disposition, which leads me to address myself to every one whom I meet. If such a person is my equal and not my enemy, I anticipate his courtesy; I ask him about his temper and his health, I offer him my services without any haggling, and am not always on my guard, as some people say. That man displeases me who by my knowledge of his habits and behaviour deprives me of such liberty and freedom.

How should I remember, as soon as I see him afar off, to put on a grave and important look, and to let him know that I think I am as good as he, and better? To do this I must call to mind all my good qualities and points, and his bad ones, so as to compare them together. This is too much trouble for me, and I am not at all able of showing such an abrupt and sudden presence of mind; even if I had been successful at first, I am sure I should give way and lose my head a second time, for I cannot put any restraint on myself nor assume a certain haughtiness for any man."[220]

(31.) We may be virtuous, intelligent, and well-behaved, and yet be unbear-

---

[218] In this paragraph, as well as in the preceding one, some commentators imagine there is an allusion to the President Achille de Harlay, so bitterly attacked by St. Simon in his Mémoires. See also page 45, note 122.

[219] Our author says in a note, "Written in imitation of Montaigne."

[220] The principal antiquated words in this imitation are estriver, to strive, to quarrel; se ramentevoir, to call to mind, used by Molière in the Dépit amoureux (iii. 4); and succéder, to be successful, which, of course, is at present in French réussir.

able. By our manners, which we consider of no consequence, the world often forms either a good or a bad opinion of us; a little care to appear obliging and polite will prevent its condemning us. The least thing is enough to make people believe that we are proud, impolite, haughty, and disobliging; but, on the other hand, still less is needed to make them esteem us.

(32.) Politeness does not always produce kindness of heart, justice, complacency, or gratitude, but it gives to a man at least the appearance of it, and makes him seem externally what he really should be.

We may define all the essentials of politeness, but we cannot determine how and where they should be used; they depend on ordinary habits and customs, are connected with times and places, and are not the same in both sexes nor in different ranks of life; intelligence alone cannot find this out; politeness is acquired and perfected by imitation. Only some persons are naturally disposed to be polite, as others are in acquiring great talents and solid virtue. Politeness tends, undoubtedly, to advance merit and to render it agreeable; a man must have very eminent qualities to hold his own without being polite.

The very essence of politeness seems to be to take care that by our words and actions we make other people pleased with us as well as with themselves.

(33.) It is an offence against politeness to bestow excessive praise on a person's singing or playing before any other who has sung or played for you, or to commend another poet in the presence of those who have read you their verses.

(34.) A man may be giving entertainments and feasts to certain persons, may make them presents, and let them enjoy themselves, and he may do this well; but he will do much better by acting according to their inclinations.

(35.) It is more or less rude to scorn indiscriminately all kinds of praise; we ought to be proud of that which comes from honest men, who praise sincerely those things in us which are really commendable.

(36.) An intelligent man, who is naturally proud, abates nothing of his pride and haughtiness because he is poor; on the contrary, if anything will mollify him and make him more pliant and sociable, it is a little prosperity.

(37.) Not to be able to bear with all bad-tempered people with whom the world is crowded, shows that a man has not a good temper himself: small change is as necessary in business as golden coin.

(38.) To live with people who have been quarrelling and to whose complaints you have to listen, is like being in a court of justice from morning till night listening to pleadings and lawsuits.

(39.) Two persons had all their lives been very intimate with one another; their incomes were in common, they lived together, and were never out of one another's sight. After fourscore years they thought it was time to part and put an end to their intimacy; they had then but one day to live, and dared not attempt to pass it together: they hastened to break before death, as their complacency would hold out no longer. They would have been good models had they not lived so long, for had they died one moment sooner, they still would have been good friends and have left behind them a rare example of perseverance in friendship.[221]

(40.) Families are often disturbed by mistrust, jealousy, and antipathy, while outwardly they seem happy, peaceable, and cheerful, and we suppose they enjoy a tranquillity which does not exist; there are very few who can bear investigation. The visit you pay only interrupts a domestic quarrel which awaits but your departure to break out afresh.

(41.) In all societies common-sense always gives way first. The most sensible people often are swayed by a most foolish and eccentric personage; they study his weakness, his temper, his fancies, and put up with them; they avoid thwarting him, and everybody gives him his way; when his countenance betrays he is cheerful, he is commended; they are grateful to him for not being always insufferable; he is feared, considered, obeyed, and sometimes beloved.

(42.) None but those persons who have had aged relatives, or those who have them still, and whose heirs they may become, can tell what they had, or have now, to endure.

(43.) Cleantes[222] is a very worthy man; he has taken unto himself a wife, who is the best and most sensible person in the world; both, in their ways, are the life and soul of the company they keep; a more straightforward and more polite behaviour than theirs is nowhere to be met with. They are to part to-morrow, and the deed of separation is already drawn up at the lawyer's. Surely they must possess certain merits which do not harmonise together and certain virtues which are incompatible.

(44.) A man may be sure of the dowry, the jointure, and his marriage settlements, but scarcely of the contract the parents have entered upon to board and lodge the young couple for a certain time;[223] for that depends on the frail harmony between the mother-in-law and the daughter-in-law, which often ends the first year of the marriage.

(45.) A father-in-law loves both his son and daughter-in-law, a mother-in-law her son and not her daughter-in-law; the latter pays her back in her own coin.

(46.) What a step-mother loves the least in the wide world are her husband's children; the fonder she is of her husband the worse step-mother she shows herself.

Step-mothers make of towns and villages complete deserts, and stock the country with more beggars, vagrants, servants, and slaves, than poverty does.

(47.) G ... and H ... are neighbours, living in the country;[224] their lands are

<hr>

[221] According to all the "Keys," this paragraph refers to a separation of two old friends, Courtois and Saint-Romain, both councillors of state; but they were still friends when the "Characters" were published.

[222] Some persons, now totally unknown, have been supposed to represent Cleantes: such as a certain M. Loyseau, receveur général des finances in Brittany; a M. de l'Escalopier, conseiller au parlement, and others.

[223] Such a contract was called les nourritures in French legal phraseology.

[224] G ... is supposed to stand for François Vedeau de Grammont, conseiller au parle-

contiguous; they dwell in a secluded and solitary spot. Far from towns and all intercourse with men, we might have thought that the dread of being completely estranged from the world and from all society should have kept up their mutual intimacy; but it is difficult to say what trifling circumstance has caused their being at variance, renders them implacable, and transmits their hatred to their descendants. Relatives, or even brothers, never quarrelled about a thing of less consequence.

Suppose there were but two men on this habitable globe, the sole possessors of it, who should divide it between them, even then I am convinced that soon some cause of disagreement would spring up, though it were only about boundaries.

(48.) It is often easier as well as more advantageous to conform ourselves to other men's opinions than to bring them over to ours.

(49.) I am now approaching a little town, and I am already on a hill whence I discover it. It is built on a slope, a river washes its walls and then meanders through a lovely meadow; a dense forest shelters it from cold winds and northern blasts. The weather is so bright that I can count its towers and steeples, and it seems, as it were, painted on the slope of the hill. I exclaim: "How agreeable must it be to dwell underneath such a pure sky and in such a delightful abode!" I enter the town, and have not spent there above two or three nights when I feel I am just like its inhabitants; I long to get away from it.

(50.) There is a certain thing which has never yet been seen under the canopy of heaven, and, in all likelihood, never will be: it is a small town without various parties, where all the families are united and all relations visit one another without reserve, where a marriage does not engender a civil war, where there are no disputes about precedence at the offertory,[225] the carrying of the censer, or the giving of a cake to the church to be consecrated and distributed during mass, as well as about processions and funerals: whence gossiping, falsehoods, and slandering are banished; where the *bailli* and the president of the court, the *élus* and the *assesseurs*[226] are on speaking terms together; where the dean is well with the canons, the canons do not disdain the choristers, and the choristers bear with the singing-boys.

(51.) Country people and fools are apt to get angry, and to fancy you make fun of them or despise them. You should never venture on the most innocent and

---

ment, or for his father-in-law, Philippe Genoud de Guiberville, and H ... for Charles Hervé, doyen du parlement; and the quarrel arose about the right of fishing in a brook. Vedeau lost his case, and was convicted of having falsified certain legal documents. Only a few years before La Bruyère's death he fired at different times on a legal officer and some soldiers who were attempting to arrest him in his house in Paris, killed one and wounded another, was finally imprisoned, dismissed from his office, and banished from the kingdom.

[225] L'offrande, l'encens et le pain benit, in the original. In small Roman Catholic towns there were formerly always quarrels about the sum to be given to the vicar when kissing the "patena," about the carrying of the censer, and above all, whose turn it was to give a cake to be consecrated by the officiating clergyman.

[226] A bailli was a magistrate who judged certain cases, an élu a sort of assessor of various taxes, and an assesseur an assistant magistrate.

inoffensive joke, unless it be with people of culture or intelligence.

(52.) A man should not pretend to show his talents in the society of men of rank; their very rank forbids it; nor with people of inferior degree who repel you by being always on their guard.

(53.) Men of merit discover, discern, and find out each other reciprocally; he who would be esteemed should frequent persons who are themselves estimable.

(54.) He who is of so lofty a rank as to be above repartee, ought never to joke in a racy kind of way.

(55.) There are some little failings which we freely abandon to censure, and about which we do not dislike being bantered; when we banter others we should select failings of the same kind.

(56.) It is a fool's privilege to laugh at an intelligent man; he is in society what a jester is at court—of no consequence whatever.

(57.) Banter is often a proof of want of intelligence.

(58.) You fancy a man your dupe, but if he only pretends to be so, who is the greatest dupe, you or he?

(59.) If you observe carefully those people who praise nobody, who are always finding fault, and are never satisfied with any one, you will discover them to be persons with whom nobody is satisfied.

(60.) The proud and disdainful will find precisely in society the contrary of what they expect, which is to be esteemed.

(61.) The pleasure of social intercourse amongst friends is kept up by a similarity of morals and manners, and by slender differences in opinion about science; this confirms us in our sentiments, exercises our faculties or instructs us through arguments.

(62.) Two persons will not be friends long if they are not inclined to pardon each other's little failings.

(63.) How many fine and useless arguments are laid before a person in great affliction to attempt to soothe him! Things from without which we call events are sometimes too strong for arguments and nature. Eat, drink, do not kill yourself with grief, think only to live, are magnificent admonitions, and impracticable as well. If we say to a man that it is not wise to unsettle his mind so much, do we not tell him in reality that he is a fool for being so unfortunate?

(64.) Advice which is necessary in all matters of business, is sometimes hurtful in social affairs to those who give it, and useless to the persons to whom it is given. You observe, perhaps, faults in manners and morals which are either not acknowledged, or, perhaps, considered virtues; you blot out some passages in a composition which please the author the most, and in which he thinks he has surpassed himself. By those means you lose the confidence of your friend without making him better or wiser.

(65.) Not long since certain persons of both sexes formed a society for intellectual conversation and interchange of ideas.[227] They left to the vulgar herd the art of talking intelligibly; an expression used by them, and which was not very clear, was followed by another still more obscure, which was improved on by others still more enigmatic, which were always crowned with prolonged applause, so that at last, by what they were pleased to call refinements, sentiments, turn and delicacy of expression, they succeeded in becoming unintelligible to others and to themselves. Common-sense, judgment, memory, or the smallest capacity were unnecessary in their conversation; all that was wanted was a certain amount of intellect, and that not of the right sort, but of a spurious kind, and in which imagination was too predominant.

(66.) I know it, Theobaldus,[228] you have grown old; but would you have me think you decline, that you are no longer a poet nor a wit, that you are now as bad a critic of all kind of writings as you are a wretched author, and that your conversation is neither ingenuous nor refined? Your careless and conceited behaviour reassures me, and convinces me of my error. You are the same to-day as you ever were, and perhaps better; for if you are so brisk and vivacious at your age, what name, Theobaldus, did you deserve in your youth, when you were the pet and the caprice of certain ladies who only swore by you, believed every word you uttered, and then exclaimed, "It is delightful! What has he said?"

(67.) We frequently speak hastily in conversation, often through vanity and natural inclination, seldom with the necessary caution, and only anxious to reply to what we have not heard; we follow our own ideas, and explain them without the smallest deference for other men's arguments; we are very far from finding out the truth, as we are not yet agreed upon what we are looking for. If any man could hear such conversations and write them down, he would now and then find many good things said without the smallest result.

(68.) Some time ago a sort of insipid and puerile conversation was in fashion, which turned on trivial questions about the affections, and what people please to call passion or tenderness. The reading of some novels first introduced this talk amongst the most gentlemanly men in town and at court, but they soon discarded it, and then the citizens took it up, as well as puns and plays on words.[229]

(69.) Some city ladies are so refined that they do not know or dare not pronounce the names of streets, squares, and public places, which they think are not noble enough to be known. They speak of the *Louvre*, the *Place Royale*, but they

---

[227] This is an allusion to the society of the Hotel de Rambouillet and to the so-called précieuses.

[228] It is generally supposed that here Isaac de Benserade (1612-1691) is meant, who was pre-eminently a court poet, and wrote a great deal of namby-pamby poetry, now deservedly forgotten. His "Character" appeared for the first time in the sixth edition of La Bruyère's work, only a few months before his death, when he was seventy-eight years old.

[229] Our author draws a distinction between gentlemen in town and at court, though he mentions those in town first. The silly novels he attacks were those of Gomberville (1600-1647), of La Calprenède (1610-1663), and above all those of Mdlle. de Scudéri (1607-1701), one of the précieuses of the Hotel de Rambouillet, and author of the Grand Cyrus (1650), Clélie (1665), and of many other works.

use certain circumlocutions and phrases rather than mention some names; and if, by chance, such a word escapes them, it is not without some alteration, and after some changes which reassure them; they are less natural in this than the ladies at court, who, when they have occasion to speak of the *Halles*, the *Châtelet*, or the like, simply say the *Halles* or the *Châtelet*.[230]

(70.) If people pretend sometimes not to remember certain names which they think obscure, and affect to spoil them in the pronunciation, it is through the good opinion they have of their own names.

(71.) When we are in a good temper, and when we can talk as we like, we often say silly things, which, in truth, we do not pretend to be anything else, and which are considered very good, because they are very bad.[231] This inferior kind of joking, fit only for the mob, has already infected a great part of the youth at court. It is true we need not fear it will spread further, for it is really too insipid and coarse to thrive in a country which is the centre of good taste and politeness. However, it should be rendered distasteful to those who employ it, for though it is never used seriously, yet it continually takes the place of better things in their mind and in their ordinary conversation.

(72.) Between saying bad things or saying such good things which everybody knows, and pretending they are quite new, there is so little difference that I do not know which to choose.

(73.) "Lucanus[232] has said a pretty thing. There is a fine expression in Claudianus.[233] There is a certain passage in Seneca;"[234] and then follow a good many Latin words, often quoted before people who do not know what they mean, though they pretend to understand them. The right thing would be to have sense and intelligence ourselves, for then we might dispense with the ancients, or after having read them carefully, we might still select the best and quote them pertinently.

(74.) Hermagoras[235] knows not who is king of Hungary, and wonders that no one talks about the king of Bohemia.[236] Speak not to him of the wars in Flanders

[230] It seems to have escaped all commentators of La Bruyère that in his time it was the fashion for the ladies at court to call a spade a spade with a vengeance, and to use very plain and realistic language, whilst the "city ladies" were not quite so daring; moreover, some of the streets, squares, etc., of Paris had very peculiar names, quite unfit for the mouth of any modest woman.

[231] By "silly things," our author means "plays on words" called in his time équivoques or turlupinades.

[232] Marcus Annæus Lucanus, a Latin poet, who died in the year 65, was put to death for his share in Piso's conspiracy, at the early age of twenty-seven.

[233] Claudus Claudianus (365-408), a Latin poet.

[234] L. Annæus Seneca, a stoic philosopher, and tutor to Nero, was also put to death in the year 65 by order of his former pupil.

[235] Hermagoras is, according to all commentators, Paul Perron, a learned Benedictine, and author of L'Antiquité des temps rétablie, etc. The old English translations name, however, also Isaac Vossius (1618-1688), an able Dutch philologist, and a well-known French literary man, Urbain Chevreau (1613-1701).

[236] In 1687, when this paragraph was first published, there was no longer an inde-

or in Holland,[237] or, at least, you must excuse him from answering any questions about them; he mixes up all dates; he neither knows when they began nor ended; battles and sieges are all new to him; but he is very well read in the Titans' war, and can tell you its progress and the most trifling details; nothing has escaped him; he unravels in the same way the horrible chaos of the Babylonian and Assyrian monarchies; he knows intimately the Egyptians and their dynasties. He never saw Versailles, nor ever will; but he has almost seen the tower of Babel, and counted its steps; he has found out how many architects were employed about that building, and even has their names at his fingers' ends. He believes Henri IV. to be a son of Henri III.,[238] and neglects to know anything about the reigning houses of France, Austria, and Bavaria. He asks what is the use of studying such trifles; but he can quote to you all the kings of Media and Babylon, and the names of Apronal, Herigebal, Noesnemordach, and Mardokampad[239] are to him as familiar as those of Valois and Bourbon are to us. He has yet to learn that the Emperor[240] is married, but he can tell you that Ninus[241] had two wives. He hears the king enjoys perfect health, and this reminds him that Thetmosis, a king of Egypt, was a valetudinarian, and that he inherited this disposition from his grandfather, Alipharmutosis.[242] What does he not know? What in all venerable antiquity is hid from him? He will tell you that Semiramis, or, as some call her, Serimaris, spoke so much like her son Ninyas, that their voices could not be distinguished from one another; but he dare not decide whether the mother had a manly voice like her son, or the son an effeminate voice like his mother; he will confide to you that Nimrod

---

pendent kingdom of Hungary, for three years before the crown had been declared hereditary in the House of Austria, which had ruled Bohemia as well since 1525.

[237] These wars, interrupted by the peace of Nymeguen (1678), were going on whilst our author wrote.

[238] Henri IV. (1553-1610), or Henri le Grand, according to La Bruyère's own note, was not the son of the last of the Valois, Henri III. (1551-1589), but after the latter's death became heir to the French throne, because Henry IV.'s father, Antoine de Bourbon, was descended from the Count de Clermont, the fifth son of Louis IX.

[239] Those names La Bruyère found in the Histoire du Monde of Chevreau see page 124, note 235); and nearly all of them are so wrongly spelt that it is almost hopeless to discover whom they meant.

[240] In the month of December of the same year this paragraph had been published, Joseph I. (1678-1711), emperor of the Romans, was crowned king of Hungary, in virtue of his hereditary right. See page 215, note 444.

[241] Ninus was the husband of Semiramis, about 2182 B.C., and founded with her Nineveh, of which empire she became queen; she abdicated after a reign of forty-two years in favour of her son Ninyas. All these persons seem, however, to have been mythological, and to have had no foundation in history. The Semiramis of Herodotus lived 810-781 B.C.

[242] The passage in Josephus containing Manethos' tradition says, "Mesphratuthmosis drove the Hyksos [or shepherd kings] as far as Avaris [San in Egypt], and shut them up in it. His son Tuthmosis obliged them to evacuate it." Tuthmosis is really Aahmes, the founder of the 18th dynasty, who drove the shepherd kings out of Egypt. Misphratuthmosis, sometimes written Misphramuthosis, and Alisphragmuthosis, his relative or ancestor, is meant by this name Alipharmutosis, but he has not been recognised in Egyptian records.

was left-handed, and Sesostris[243] ambidexter; that it is an error to imagine one of the Artaxerxes was called Longimanus[244] because his arms reached down to his knees, and not because one of his hands was longer than the other; he adds that though some grave authors affirm that it was his right hand, he has good grounds to maintain it was the left hand.

(75.) Ascanius is a sculptor, Hegio an iron-founder, Æschines a fuller, and Cydias a wit,[245] for that is his trade. He has a signboard, a shop, work that is ordered,[246] and journeymen who work under him; he cannot possibly let you have those stanzas he has promised you in less than a month, unless he breaks his word with Dosithea, who has engaged him to write an elegy; he has also an idyl on the loom which is for Crantor, who presses him for it, and has promised him a liberal reward. You can have whatever you like—prose or verse, for he is just as good in one as in the other. If you want a letter of condolence, or one on some person's absence, he will write them; he has them even ready made; step into his warehouse, and you may pick and choose. Cydias has a friend who has nothing else to do but to promise to certain people a long time beforehand that he will come to them, and who, finally, introduces him in some society as a man seldom to be met with, and exquisite in conversation. Then, just as a vocalist sings or as a lute-player touches his instrument in a company where it has been expected, Cydias, after having coughed, puts back his ruffles, extends his hand, opens his fingers, and very gravely utters his over-refined thoughts and his sophisticated arguments. Unlike those persons whose principles agree, and who know that reason and truth are one and the same thing, and snatch the words out of one another's mouths to acquiesce in one another's sentiments, he never opens his mouth but to contradict: "I think," he says graciously, "it is just the opposite of what you say;" or, "I am not at all of your opinion," or else, "Formerly I was under the same delusion as you are now; but, …" and then he continues, "There are three things to be considered," to which he adds a fourth. He is an insipid chatterer; no sooner has he obtained a footing into any society, than he looks out for some ladies whom he can fascinate, before whom he can set forth his wit or his philosophy, and produce his rare conceptions; for, whether he speaks or writes, he ought never to be suspected of saying what is true or false, sensible or ridiculous; his only care is not to express the same sentiments as some one else, and to differ from everybody. Therefore, in conversation, he often waits till every one has given his opinion on some casual subject, or one which not seldom he has introduced himself, in order to utter dogmatically things which are perfectly new, but which he thinks decisive and unanswerable. "Lu-

[243] Sesostris is the Greek name of the conqueror Rameses II., the third king of the 19th Egyptian dynasty.

[244] Artaxerxes Longimanus, king of Persia, succeeded his father Xerxes I., 465 B.C., and died about 425 B. C.

[245] Cydias is Fontenelle (see page 11, note 51), who was only thirty-seven years old when this paragraph was first printed in the eighth edition of the "Characters," in 1694, and who became La Bruyère's enemy ever since.

[246] Fontenelle had written for his uncle Thos. Corneille (1625-1709) certain parts of two operas, Psyché (1678) and Bellérophon (1679); for Beauval, in prose, an eulogy on Perrault (1688), and for a certain Mdlle. Bernard, part of a tragedy of Brutus (1691).

cianus[247] and Seneca,"[248] says Cydias, "come pretty near me; but as for Plato,[249] Virgil,[250] and Theocritus[251] they are quite below me," and his flatterer takes care to confirm him every morning in this opinion. As Cydias has the same taste and interest as the revilers of Homer,[252] he quietly expects that mankind will be undeceived and prefer modern poets to the blind bard; then he will put himself at the head of these poets, and reserve the second place for a friend.[253] He is, in a word, a compound of pedantry and formality, to be admired by cits and rustics, in whom, nevertheless, there is nothing great except the opinion he has of himself.

(76.) Profound ignorance makes a man dogmatical; he who knows nothing thinks he can teach others what he just now has learned himself; whilst he who knows a great deal can scarcely imagine any one should be unacquainted with what he says, and, therefore, speaks with more indifference.

(77.) Great things only require to be simply told, for they are spoiled by emphasis; but little things should be clothed in lofty language, as they are only kept up by expression, tone of voice, and style of delivery.

(78.) I think we generally say things more delicately than we write them.

(79.) Hardly any other men but born gentlemen or men of culture are capable of keeping a secret.

(80.) All confidence placed in another is dangerous if it is not perfect, for on almost all occasions we ought to tell everything or to conceal everything. We have already told too much of our secret, if one single circumstance is to be kept back.

(81.) Some men promise to keep your secret and yet reveal it without knowing they are doing so; they do not wag their lips, and yet they are understood; it is read on their brow and in their eyes; it is seen through their breast; they are transparent. Other men do not exactly tell a thing that has been intrusted to them, but they talk and act in such a manner that people discover it for themselves. Lastly, there are some who despise your secret, of whatever importance it may be: "it is something mysterious which such-a-one has imparted to me and forbade me to mention it," and then out it comes.

If a secret is revealed, the person who has confided it to another is to be blamed.

(82.) Nicander converses with Eliza about the gentle and courteous way in which he lived with his wife from the day of their marriage to the hour of her death; he had already said how sorry he was he had no children by her, and he now repeats it; he talks of the houses he has in town, and then of an estate he has

[247] Lucianus of Samosata, a satirist and a rhetorician (120-200 A.D.)

[248] The author adds "a philosopher and a tragic poet." See page 124, note 235.

[249] Plato, the well-known Greek philosopher (430-347 B.C.)

[250] Publius Virgilius Maro, the Roman epic and bucolic poet (70-19 B.C.)

[251] Theocritus, a Greek bucolic poet, who flourished about 272 B.C. Fontenelle had written Dialogues of the dead, as Lucianus had done; philosophical works and tragedies like Seneca, philosophical dialogues in Plato's style, and pastoral poetry like Virgil and Theocritus.

[252] Perrault, La Motte (1672-1731), De Visé (1640-1710), and others.

[253] This friend is supposed to have been La Motte.

in the country; he calculates what it brings him in, draws a plan of the buildings, describes its situation, expatiates on the conveniency of the apartments as well as on the richness and elegance of the furniture; he assures her he loves good cheer and fine horses and carriages, and complains that his late wife did not care much for play and company. "You are so wealthy," said one of his friends to him, "why do you not buy some official post,[254] or why not a certain piece of ground which would enlarge your estate?" "People think I am richer than I really am," replies Nicander. He neither forgets his birth nor his relatives, and speaks of his cousin, the superintendent of finances, or of his kinswoman, the Lord Chancellor's wife. He informs

Eliza how discontented he has become with his nearest relatives, and even with his heirs. "Am I wrong, and have I any cause for doing them good?" he asks her, and desires her to give her opinion. He then intimates that he is in a weak and wretched state of health, and speaks of the vault where he wishes to be interred. He insinuates himself, and fawns on all those who visit the lady he courts. But Eliza has not courage enough to grow rich at the cost of being his wife. Whilst he is thus conversing with her a military man is introduced, and by his mere presence defeats all the plans of the worthy citizen, who gets up disappointed and vexed, and goes somewhere else to say that he wishes to marry for the second time.

(83.) Wise men sometimes avoid the world, that they may not be surfeited with it.

---

[254] The right of presentation to nearly all offices at court, or official positions, was publicly bought and sold in Louis XIV.'s time.

VI.

OF THE GIFTS OF FORTUNE.

(1.) A very rich man may eat of his side-dishes, have his walls and recesses painted, enjoy a palatial residence in the country and another in town, have a large retinue, even become connected with a duke through marriage,[255] and make of his son a great nobleman, and all this will be considered quite right and proper; but to live happy is perhaps the privilege of other men.

(2.) A lofty birth or a large fortune portend merit, and cause it to be the sooner noticed.

(3.) The ambition of a coxcomb is excusable, because, after he has made a large fortune, people will be careful to discover in him some merit which he never had before, and as great as it is in his own opinion.

(4.) As favour and riches forsake a man, we discover in him the foolishness

[255] Commentators, who see allusions everywhere, suppose the "very rich man" was Louvois, whose sons-in-law were the Dukes de la Rocheguyon and de Villeneuve; or Colbert, who became the father-in-law of the Dukes de Chevreuse, de Beauvilliers, and de Mortemart; or, finally, Frémont, keeper of the royal treasury, who married his daughter to the Duke de Lorges.

they concealed, and which no one perceived before.

(5.) We could never imagine what a strange disproportion a few or a great many pieces of money make between men, if we did not see it every day with our own eyes.

Those few or many pieces of money are what determine men to adopt the profession of arms, of the law, or of the church, for they have hardly any other vocation.

(6.) Two merchants were neighbours and in the same line of business, but their success in life was quite different. They each had a daughter; and these, brought up together, had been as intimate as girls of the same age and the same condition in life could have been; later, one of them, driven by want and misery, endeavoured to get a place, and entered the service of a great lady, one of the highest rank at court;[256] and this same lady had formerly been her bosom friend.

(7.) If a financier fails in making a lucky stroke, the courtiers say of him, "He is a mere citizen, a man sprung from nothing, a boor;" but if he succeeds, they become suitors for his daughter's hand.

(8.) Some men in their youth serve an apprenticeship to a certain trade, to follow a very different one the rest of their lives.[257]

(9.) A man is very plain-looking, dwarfish in size, and wanting in intelligence;[258] but some one whispers to me that he has an annual income of fifty thousand *livres*. That concerns him alone, and I shall never be the better or the worse for it; but people might well consider me mad if I were to look on such a man in a different light because he is wealthy, and were to do so involuntarily.

(10.) It is in vain to attempt to turn a very rich blockhead into ridicule, for the laughers will be on his side.

(11.) N ...[259] has a clownish, rude doorkeeper, who looks somewhat like a Swiss,[260] a big hall and an anteroom, where people are obliged to tire themselves out by dancing attendance; at last he makes his appearance with a serious mien and a solemn gait, hears only a few words of what is said, and sends people away without seeing them to the door. However inferior he may seem elsewhere, in his own house he will attract something very akin to respect.

---

[256] This lady is said to have been Madame Fleurion d'Armenonville, daughter of a clothier, whose husband was keeper of the seals and directeur des finances.

[257] Those men were the so-called "farmers of the revenue," nearly all of low birth, and who formerly had been in some trade or business. See page 136, note 266, and page 137, § 15.

[258] Little, silly, ugly rich men were not more rare in our author's time than they are at present; but the commentators will have it that the Marquis de Gouverney and the Duke de Ventadour were meant.

[259] M. de Saint-Pouange, a relative of the ministers Colbert, Le Tellier, and Louvois, and the latter's principal secretary, is meant.

[260] Nearly all the great lords had Swiss doorkeepers. Petit-Jean, in Racine's comedy Les Plaideurs, says also: "Il m'avait fait venir d'Amiens pour être Suisse."

(12.) I want you, Clitiphon,[261] and this has driven me early from my bed and room, and brought me to your door. Would to Heaven I had no occasion to ask you a favour or be troublesome to you! Your servants tell me you are in your own room, and that it will be at least an hour before you can see me; I return before that time, and they inform me you are gone out. What keeps you so deeply engaged, Clitiphon, in the innermost corner of your residence, that prevents you from seeing me? You file some papers, you collate some register, you sign your name or your initials to some documents. I had but one thing to ask you, and you had only to say "Yes" or "No." If you wish to become a curiosity, be of use to those who depend on you, and you will be a greater curiosity by such conduct than by remaining invisible.[262] You are a man of importance and overwhelmed with business, but if you in your turn have need of my services, come to the solitude of my study, where the philosopher is always to be found, and where you will not be put off till another day. You will find me turning over Plato's writings "On the spirituality of the soul and its difference with the body,"[263] or, pen in hand, calculating the distance between Saturn and Jupiter;[264] admiring the works of the Creator and endeavouring, by acquiring a knowledge of truth, to rectify my opinions and to improve my morals. You can enter; all my doors are open; you will not get tired in my anteroom with waiting for me; you have no need to let me know beforehand when you are coming; you bring me something more precious than silver or gold, if it is an opportunity of being of service to you. Only tell me what you wish me to do for you? Do you want me to leave my books, my studies, my writings, and the line I have just begun? I am glad to be interrupted when I can be of service to you. A moneyed man, a man of business, is like a bear not yet tamed; there is no seeing him in his den but with the utmost difficulty; or, rather, he is not to be seen at all, for in the beginning he is but dimly visible, and afterwards you see no more of him. A man of letters, on the contrary, is as perceptible[265] as a pillar in a cross-road; he is to be seen by everybody, at all times and in all conditions, at table, in bed, without clothes, dressed, in sickness or in health; he is not a man of importance, and does not wish to be one.

(13.) Let us not envy a certain class of men for their enormous riches; they have paid such an equivalent for them that it would not suit us; they have given for them their peace of mind, their health, their honour, and their conscience; this is rather too dear, and there is nothing to be made out of such a bargain.

---

[261] The "Keys" mention several people for Clitiphon, such as M. le Camus, lieutenant-civil, or his brother the cardinal, or another brother who was maître des requêtes.

[262] In the original there is a play on the word rare which cannot be rendered in English.

[263] This seems to refer to Plato's "Timæus" and his "Phædo."

[264] Jupiter is the largest and Saturn the second largest planet of our solar system. The celebrated Dutch natural philosopher Huyghens van Zuylichem (1629-1695), who discovered the fourth satellite of Saturn and proved the existence of its ring, lived in Paris from 1666 till 1681, and may have met La Bruyère.

[265] The original has trivial, from the Latin trivialis and trivium, hence the meaning of exposed to the public gaze, "perceptible."

(14.) The P.T.S.[266] give us all possible sensations one after another; we first despise them for their low origin, then we envy them, afterwards fear, hate, and sometimes esteem and respect them; we often live long enough to finish by pitying them.

(15.) Sosia[267] was first a footman, then an under-farmer of the revenue, and by extortion, violence, and malversation has now raised himself to a high post on the ruins of several families. He was ennobled by virtue of his office, and the only thing he wanted was to be an honest man;[268] this marvel has been effected by his becoming churchwarden.

(16.) Arfuria[269] used formerly to walk by herself, and go on foot towards the main entrance of a certain church, in which she heard from a distance the sermon of a Carmelite friar or of a doctor of divinity, of whom she saw but the side face, and could not hear many words he said.

Her virtue was not apparent and her piety as well known as she herself was. Her husband has become a farmer of the *huitième denier*,[270] and made a prodigious fortune in less than six years. Now she never comes to church but in a carriage, wearing a heavy train, which is borne up: the preacher stops while she seats herself opposite to him, so that not a single word nor the smallest gesture can escape her. The priests intrigue among themselves as to who shall be her father-confessor, for all wish to give her absolution, but the victory remains with the vicar of the parish.

---

[266] By these initials are meant partisans, a name given to the farmers-general of the revenue. Until 1726, these persons obtained in France, for a fixed money payment, the right of collecting one or more of the public taxes. This system was first inaugurated by Sully (1560-1641), the able finance-minister of Henri IV., out of necessity, in order to raise money; and was continued for more than two hundred years, and the cause of many arbitrary measures and great oppression. The number of these fermiers-généraux was first forty and afterwards sixty, but there were a goodly number of sous-fermiers and many other agents, who were all practically irresponsible. In 1726, a company of capitalists undertook the collection of the greater part of the king's taxes, which was called the fermes-générales or unies, and lasted till the first French Revolution. The ministre des finances, a name only first given in 1795, was, in the sixteenth and part of the seventeenth century, called surintendant des finances, and from 1661 till 1791 contrôleur-général des finances.

[267] Sosia in Greek is generally used as the name of a servant or a slave, and Molière gives that name to a servant in his Amphitryon; in Latin a farmer of the public revenue was called socius, because he was the associate of other similar farmers. It was not at all uncommon in Louis XIV.'s time for footmen to rise to the rank of financiers, and La Bazinière, de Gourville, and de Bourvalais, who were all three very rich, as well as many others, might be quoted as examples of this. Two fermiers-généraux, Révol and d'Apougny, became churchwardens.

[268] See page 43, note 121.

[269] The wives of a good many farmers of the revenue have been named by various commentators and "Keys."

[270] The huitième denier was a tax imposed in 1672 during the war with Holland on all purchasers of estates from the clergy.

(17.) Crœsus[271] is carried to the churchyard; and of all the immense wealth which he acquired by rapine and extortion, and which he has lavished in luxury and riotous living, there is not enough left for a decent burial; he died insolvent, without any property, and consequently without any attendance; neither medicines, nor cordials, nor physicians were seen about him, nor the most inferior priest to shrive him.

(18.) Champagne,[272] rising from a prolonged dinner, quite gorged, and his head full of the agreeable fumes of Avenay or Sillery,[273] signs an order for a tax to be levied which would have produced a famine in a whole province, if other means had not been taken. He is excusable; for how can a man whose digestion is just beginning understand that people could anywhere die of starvation.

(19.) Sylvanus[274] has with his money bought rank and another name; he is lord of the same manor where his forefathers had been paying the *taille*;[275] formerly he was not good enough to be Cleobulus' page, but now he is his son-in-law?

(20.) Dorus[276] is carried in a litter along the Appian Way;[277] his freedmen and slaves run before him to clear the way and to turn aside the people; he wants nothing but Lictors;[278] he enters Rome with quite a retinue, a triumphant foil to the meanness and poverty of his father Sanga.

(21.) No one makes a better use of his fortune than Periander;[279] it gives him a certain rank, influence, and authority; people no longer ask him to be their friend, but they implore his protection. In the beginning he spoke of himself as "such

[271] The "Keys" give several names of financiers, such as Aubert, who at one time was worth more than three millions of francs, and who died in a garret, Guénegaud, and Rémond. The Chambre de Justice, a name given to certain committees which were appointed from time to time to inquire into financial malversations and abuses condemned in 1661 the above-named three gentlemen to pay very heavy fines; hence their comparative poverty.

[272] "Champagne" stands for Monnerot. (See page 110, note 213.) It was not uncommon to give such names as Poitevin, Lorrain, Basque, Provençal, etc., to footmen, after their supposed native provinces.

[273] Two still Champagne wines. Sparkling Champagne was not drunk till the eighteenth century.

[274] All commentators agree that here the farmer-general George is meant, who bought the Marquisate d'Entragues and married a daughter of the Marquis de Valençay.

[275] The taille was a king's tax levied every year only on the people and the commoners.

[276] Who Dorus is has not been found out.

[277] The Appian Way, the oldest and best of all the Roman roads, leads from the Porta Cappena at Rome to Capua.

[278] The Lictors at Rome, with the fasces, always walked before the Consul or the Dictator.

[279] Some think that here a certain M. de Langlée, maréchal des camps et armées du roi, was meant. Others think it was an uncle of the minister Colbert, a M. Pussort, one of the king's counsel of state; but the first was unmarried and had a very wealthy father, and the second, who was also unmarried, and a miser to boot, owed his influence wholly to his position.

a man as I am," but soon he says "a man of my rank;" for he pretends to be one of these men, and there are none who borrow money of him, or eat his dinners, which are exquisite, who dare dispute it. His residence is splendid; the outside is Doric, and there is no gate but a portico. Is it a private house or a temple? People are at a loss to know which. He is lord paramount of the entire precincts; every one envies him, and would rejoice at his downfall; his wife's pearl necklace has made all the ladies of the neighbourhood her enemies. Everything in him is of a piece, and nothing yet belies that grandeur he has acquired, for which he has paid and does not owe anything. But why did his old and feeble father not die twenty years ago before Periander's name was ever mentioned? How can any man ever endure those odious invitations to a funeral[280] which always reveal the real origin of the deceased, and often put the widows or the heirs to the blush? How shall he hide them from the eyes of the envious, malicious, keen-sighted town, and offend a thousand people who will insist on taking their due places at all funerals? Besides, what would you have him do? Shall he style his father *Noble homme* and perhaps *Honorable homme*, whilst he himself is dubbed *Messire*?[281]

(22.) How many men are like trees, already strong and full grown, which are transplanted into some gardens, to the astonishment of those people who behold them in these fine spots, where they never saw them grow, and who neither know their beginning nor their progress!

(23.) If some dead were to rise again and saw who bore their illustrious names, and that their ancient lands, their castles, and their venerable seats were owned by the very men whose fathers had perhaps been their tenants, what would they think of our age?

(24.) Nothing makes us better understand what trifling things Providence thinks He bestows on men in granting them wealth, money, dignities, and other advantages, than the manner in which they are distributed and the kind of men who have the largest share.

(25.) If you were to enter a kitchen, where all that art and method can do is employed to gratify your palate, and make you eat more than you want; if you see how the viands are prepared which will be served up at the feast; if you observe how they are manipulated, and the various modifications they undergo before they become first-rate dishes, and are brought to that neatness and elegance which charm your eyes, puzzle your choice, and make you decide to taste them all; and then saw the ingredients of this feast anywhere else than on a well-spread table, how offended and disgusted you would be! If you were to go behind the scenes, and count the weights, the wheels, the ropes in "flights" and in the machinery; if you were to consider how many men are employed in executing these movements, and how they ply their arms and strain their nerves, you would ask if these are the prime motors and mainsprings of so handsome and natural a spectacle, which

[280] The original has pancartes, which our author in a note states were billets d'enter-rement.

[281] Noble homme was a title which citizens of importance took in all legal contracts, whilst men of less influence, tradesmen and artisans, were styled Honorable homme, and Messire was only reserved for persons of rank.

seems so full of life and so intuitive, and you would be greatly astonished at such efforts and such energy. In like manner inquire not too narrowly into the origin of the fortune of any farmer of the revenue.

(26.) This youth,[282] so ruddy, so florid, and so redolent of health, is lord of an abbey and of ten other benefices; they bring him in altogether one hundred and twenty thousand[283] *livres* a year, which are paid him in golden coin.[284] Elsewhere there are a hundred and twenty indigent families who have no fire to warm themselves during winter, no clothes to cover themselves, and who are often wanting bread; they are in a wretched and piteous state of poverty. What an inequality? And does this not clearly prove that there must be a future state?

(27.) Chrysippus,[285] an upstart, and the first nobleman of his lineage, thirty years ago limited his aims to two thousand *livres* a year; this was the height of his desires and the summit of his ambition; at least he said so, as many still remember. Some time after, I do not know by what means, he was able to give to one of his daughters as her dowry as much money as he thought formerly an ample competency for his whole lifetime. A like sum is put away for each of his other children, and he has a good many of them; and this is only an advance of their share in his estate, for a good deal of wealth may be expected at his death. He is still alive, and though advanced in years, employs the few days which still remain to him in labouring to become richer.

(28.) Let Ergastus alone, and he will demand a duty from all who drink some water from the river or who walk on *terra firma*; he knows how to convert reeds, rushes, and nettles into gold;[286] he listens to all projects, and proposes everything he hears. The prince gives nothing to any one but at Ergastus' expense, and bestows no favours but what are his due, for his desire to have and to possess is never appeased. He would even deal in arts and sciences, and farm out harmony; were his advice to be taken, the people, for the pleasure of seeing him wealthy, and with a pack of hounds and a stable, would forget the music of Orpheus and be satisfied with his.

[282] This youth was M. le Tellier, who became Archbishop of Rheims in 1671, when he was only twenty-nine years old, but who already, before that time, received the revenues of six abbeys. (See also page 47, note 126.)

[283] Formerly six vingts, hundred and twenty—thus in the original—was as commonly used as quatre-vingt.

[284] The first two editions contained a note of La Bruyère, to say that by médailles d'or he meant louis d'or. This he thought no longer necessary in the other editions; he only wanted to draw attention to the fact that the "youth" received his clerical dues in golden coin, and not by a cheque on some fermier-général, who would have taken a discount for cash payment.

[285] This paragraph seems to be a hit at the fermier-général Langeois, whose daughter married the Marshal de Tourville, and whose son was married to a niece of de Pontchartrain, the contrôleur-général of the finances.

[286] Although this remark seems to refer to the Baron de Beauvais, capitaine des chasses, to whom the king had given the right of selling the briars and brambles growing on the road to Versailles, the portrait of Ergastus alludes to those men who were for ever advising to tax articles not already imposed, and by whom France became finally ruined.

(29.) Have no dealings with Crito,[287] who only looks after his own advantages; the snare is always ready spread for those who wish to acquire his office, his estate, or anything he possesses, for his conditions will be exorbitant. There is no consideration or arrangement to be expected from one so wrapt up in his own interest and so inimical to yours; he will always take a man in if he can.

(30.) Brontin,[288] according to common report, retires from the busy world, and during a whole week sees none but priests; they enjoy their meditations, and he enjoys his.

(31.) The people very often have the pleasure of seeing a tragedy acted, and of beholding expire on the world's stage the most hateful personages, who did as much harm as they could whenever they appeared, and whom they heartily detested.

(32.) If we divide the lives of the P.T.S.[289] into two parts, the first, brisk and active, is wholly occupied in trying to oppress the people, and the second, bordering on death, is spent in betraying and ruining one another.

(33.) The man[290] who made your fortune and that of several others was unable to keep his own, or secure a maintenance for his wife and children after his death; they live in obscurity and in wretchedness. You are informed of their miserable condition, but you do not think of alleviating it; indeed you cannot do so, for you give a good many dinners, you build a good deal; but out of gratitude you have kept the portrait of your benefactor, which, it is true, has been removed from your own private room to the anteroom. You have at least shown him some respect, for it might have gone to the lumber-room.

(34.) There exists a stubbornness of temper, and another of rank and condition, which both harden our hearts against the misfortunes of others, and, I should even say, prevent us from pitying the evils which befall our own family. A true financier grieves neither for the loss of friends, wife, nor children.

(35.) "Away, fly; you are not far enough." "Here," say you, "I am under another tropic." "Pass under the pole and into another hemisphere; ascend to the stars, if possible." "I am there." "Very well; then you are pretty safe." I look down and discover on this earth a rapacious, insatiable, and inexorable man, who, in spite of everything he meets on his way or may encounter, and at whatever cost to others, will provide for himself, enlarge his fortune, and wallow in wealth.

(36.) To make one's fortune is so fine a phrase, and of such charming import, that it is universally used; it is to be met with in all languages, is pleasing to strangers and to barbarians, is to be found at court and in the city, has made its way into

[287] Berrier, one of the secretaries of Colbert, is said to have been the original of Crito.

[288] This is generally believed to refer to de Pontchartrain, mentioned before, who, for some time, was very pious.

[289] See page 136, note 266.

[290] The old English translations of the "Characters" say this is an allusion to M. Fouquet (1615-1680), surintendant des finances, who, kept in prison by Louis XIV. for more than twenty years, had a great many friends and partisans when in prosperity, but they nearly all turned against him in his adversity.

cloisters and scaled the walls of convents for both sexes; there is no place so sacred where it has not penetrated, no desert or solitude where it is unknown.[291]

(37.) A man who knows how to make good bargains or finds his money increase in his coffers, thinks presently that he has a good deal of brains and is almost fit to be a statesman.

(38.) A man must have a certain sort of intelligence to make a fortune, and above all a large fortune; but it is neither a good nor a fine, a grand nor a sublime, a strong nor a delicate intellect. I am at a loss to tell exactly what it is, and shall be glad if some one will let me know.

Custom or experience are of more avail in making our fortune than intelligence; we think of it too late, and when at last we have made up our mind to make it, we begin by committing some errors which we have not always the time to repair; and this, perhaps, is the reason why fortunes are far from common.

A man of small intellect wishes to get on in life; he neglects everything, but from morning till evening he only thinks of one thing, and dreams of it at night, namely, to get on in the world. He begins early and from his very youth the chase after wealth; if a barrier in front of him stops the way, he naturally hesitates, and goes to the right or left, according as he sees an opening or thinks it most convenient; and if fresh obstacles arise, he returns to the path he just left, and determines, according to the nature of the difficulties, sometimes to overcome them, sometimes to avoid them, or to take other measures as his own interest, custom, and opportunity may direct him. Does any traveller need such a good head and such great talents to set out at first on a main road, and if that be crowded or impracticable, to cross the fields, jump over hedges and ditches, come back into the former road, and follow it until his journey's end? Does he require so much intelligence to attain the goal? Is it, then, so wonderful for a fool ever to become rich or of repute?

There are some stupid, and I may even say weak-minded men, who occupy handsome posts, and who die rich without any one ever supposing that they contributed to it in any way whatever by the smallest industry or their own labour. Somebody directed them to the fountainhead, or, perhaps, chance alone has led them to it; then they have been asked if they should like to have some water, and if so, to draw it; and they have drawn it.[292]

---

[291] The desire to make one's fortune was so great, that at that time, even at court, it was customary to take money from forgers and scoundrels; thus the Count de Grammont drew about fifty thousand livres from a peculator, and the wife of the son of the king of France received as a present from Louis XIV. the estate of a prisoner who had committed suicide in the Bastile, which was thought to be worth a great deal of money. A similar custom existed also at the courts of Charles II. and James II.; and William Penn was even accused of having become an agent for the maids-of-honour of the court, and of obtaining pardons for a pecuniary consideration, but it is now generally admitted it was another Penn who acted thus.

[292] The "Keys" think that either Nicholas d'Orville, the confidant of Louis XIV. and Mdlle. de la Vallière, and royal treasurer at Orléans, or Boucherat, chancelier de France, and a perfect noodle, according to St. Simon's Mémoires, were alluded to as the "weak-minded

(39.) When we are young we are often poor; either we have not yet acquired nor inherited anything. We become rich and old at the same moment; for seldom do men obtain every advantage at one and the same time. But even if some persons are so fortunate, we ought not to envy them, since they lose by their death sufficiently to deserve our compassion.

(40.) A man is thirty years old before he thinks of making his fortune, but it is not completed at fifty; he begins to build in his old age, and dies by the time his house is in a condition to be painted and glazed.

(41.) What is the advantage of having a large fortune, unless it be to enjoy the vanity, industry, labour and outlay of those who came before us, and to labour ourselves in planting, building, and hoarding for our posterity?

(42.) Men open their shops and set out their wares every morning to deceive their customers; and they close them at night after having cheated all day.

(43.) A tradesman turns over all his goods, that he may sell you the worst; he has a certain preparation to give them a lustre, or else holds these goods in a peculiar light, to conceal their faults and to make them appear sound; he asks too large a price for them, so as to sell them for more than they are worth; he has forged mysterious trade-marks, so that people may believe they get the full value for their hard cash; he employs a short yard measure, so that the buyer may obtain as little for his money as possible, and has a pair of scales to try whether the gold he receives be of full weight.

(44.) In all conditions of life a poor man is a near neighbour to an honest one,[293] and a rich man is as little removed from a knave; tact and ability alone seldom procure great riches.

A show of a certain amount of honesty is in any profession or business the surest way of growing rich.

(45.) The shortest and best way of making your fortune is to let people clearly see that it is their interest to promote yours.

(46.) Some men,[294] stimulated by the necessities of life, and sometimes by a desire to gain money or glory, improve their secular talents or adopt a profession far from reputable, and overlook its danger and consequences for a considerable time; they leave it afterwards from secret and devout reasons, which never stirred them before they had reaped their harvest and enjoyed a comfortable income.

(47.) There exist miseries in this world which wring the very heart; some people want even food; they dread the winter and are afraid to live; others eat hot-house fruits; the earth and the seasons are compelled to furnish forth delicacies; and mere citizens, simply because they have grown rich, dare to swallow in one morsel what would nourish a hundred families. Whatever may be brought for-

men."

[293] See page 43, note 121.

[294] A few of the "Keys" give Racine the poet as the original of such a man, but this is very unlikely, for Racine was a friend of our author, and, moreover, had acquired more glory than riches.

ward against such extremes, let me be neither unhappy or happy if I can help it; I take refuge in mediocrity.

(48.) It is well known that the poor are sad because they want everything and nobody comforts them; but if it be true that the rich are irascible, it is because they may want the smallest thing, or that some one might oppose them.

(49.) A man is rich whose income is larger than his expenses, and he is poor if his expenses are greater than his income.

There are some men[295] who with an annual revenue of two millions are yearly still five hundred thousand *livres* in arrears.

Nothing keeps longer than a middling fortune, and nothing melts away sooner than a large one.

Great riches are a temptation for poverty.

If it be true that a man is rich who wants nothing, a wise man is a very rich man.[296]

If a man be poor who wishes to have everything, then an ambitious and a miserly man languish in extreme poverty.

(50.) Passions tyrannise over mankind, but ambition keeps the others in abeyance, and makes for a while a man appear to possess every virtue.

I once believed that Tryphon, whom I now know to practise every vice, was sober, chaste, liberal, modest, and even pious; I might have believed so still if he had not made his fortune.

(51.) All that a man wishes for is riches and grandeur; he falls very ill, and death draws near, and though his face be shrivelled and his legs totter, yet he is still talking of his fortune and his post.

(52.) There are but two ways of rising in the world, either by your own industry or by the folly of others.

(53.) The features may indicate the natural disposition, habits, and morals of a man, but it is the expression of the whole countenance that discovers his wealth; it is written in a man's face whether he has more or less than a thousand *livres* a year.

(54.) Chrysantes, a wealthy and impertinent man, would think it a disgrace to be seen with Eugenius, who is a man of merit but poor; Eugenius entertains the same feelings towards Chrysantes; so there is no chance of their ever quarrelling together.

(55.) When I see some persons, who formerly were the first to bow to me, wait, on the contrary, till I salute them, and stand on ceremony with me, I say to myself, "All this is mighty fine, and I am very glad things go so well with them; it is quite

---

[295] Some commentators think that the Marquis de Seignelay, the eldest son of Colbert, is meant here; for after his death, which took place when he was only thirty-nine years old, he is said to have left five millions livres debts; others pretend he left a capital large enough to yield a yearly income of four hundred thousand francs.

[296] Boileau, in his fifth Epître, says also: "Qui vit content de rien possède toute chose."

certain that those gentlemen live in larger houses, have handsomer furniture and better repasts than formerly, and that for the last few months they have had a share in a business by which they have already made some very good profit. Pray Heaven they may in a short time come even to despise me!"

DESCARTES

(56.) If thoughts, books, and their authors were depending on the rich and on those who have made a large fortune, they would all be exiled, and that without appeal. Such men act superciliously and lord it over the learned! They keep their dignity with those poor wretches whose merit has not advanced or enriched them, and who still think and write sensibly! We must confess that at present the rich predominate, but the future will be for the virtuous and ingenious. Homer lives still and will ever flourish, whilst the tax-gatherers and publicans are no more and are utterly forgotten, and their native country and their very names are unknown at present. Were there any farmers of the revenue in Greece? What has become of all those important personages who despised Homer, who were careful to avoid him, who never bowed to him, or, if they did so, never called him "Sir," who did not think him worthy of being admitted to their tables, who looked on him as a man who was not rich and had written a book? What will become of the Fauconnets?[297] Will their names be transmitted to posterity as the name of Descartes was, who, though born a Frenchman, died in Sweden?[298]

(57.) The same amount of pride which makes a man treat haughtily his inferiors, makes him cringe servilely to those above him. It is the very nature of this vice, which is neither based on personal merit nor on virtue, but on riches, posts, influence, and useless knowledge, to render a man as supercilious to those who are below him as to over-value those who are of a loftier rank than they themselves are.

(58.) There are some sordid minds, formed of slime and filth, to whom interest and gain are what glory and virtue are to superior souls; they feel no other pleasure but to acquire money and never to lose it; they are covetous and are always wanting ten per cent.;[299] they only occupy themselves with their creditors; always dread the lowering or calling in of certain monies;[300] and are absorbed and immerged in contracts, deeds, and parchments. Such people are neither relatives, friends, citizens, Christians, nor perhaps men; they have money.

(59.) Let us first except those noble and courageous minds, if there are any yet on this earth, who assist those who are in want, contrive to do good, whom no necessities, nor inequality of rank or fortune, nor intrigues can separate from those they have once chosen for their friends; and after having made this remark, let us boldly state a lamentable truth, which makes us miserable to think about, namely, that there is not a person in this world, however intimately connected with us by social ties or by friendship, who likes us, enjoys our society, has a great many times offered us his services, and sometimes even rendered us one, who, when swayed by his own interests, would not feel inwardly disposed to break with us and become our enemy.

(60.) Whilst Orontes[301] is increasing in years, in wealth, and in income, a girl

---

[297] Jean Fauconnet, fermier-général des domaines de France, became also receiver-general of two other taxes, which was very unusual. Our author speaks of "Fauconnets," to indicate farmers of the revenues in general, though there was only one Fauconnet. In La Bruyère's time the financiers seem to have despised men of letters; but later on, during the Regency and the reign of Louis XV. and Louis XVI., it became the fashion to invite literary men on every festive occasion, and to lionise them—a custom not unknown, even at the present time, and in other countries than France.

[298] Our author had René Descartes' (1596-1650) name printed in small capitals, to remind his readers of the persecutions this philosopher had suffered.

[299] Au denier dix in the original.

[300] In former times French Governments often suppressed certain monies or diminished their legal value, and a law to this effect had been passed by Louis XIV. as late as 1679.

[301] Orontes is supposed to be a certain M. Neyret de la Ravoye, who became later trésorier-général de la marine, and who married a Mademoiselle Valière.

born in a certain family flourishes, grows up, becomes very handsome, and enters on her sixteenth year. Orontes, who is then fifty, of inferior birth, without intelligence and the smallest merit, has to be entreated to marry that young, handsome, and witty girl, and is preferred to all his rivals.

(61.) Marriage, which ought to be a source of all felicity, is often to a man a heavy burden which crushes him through want of fortune. For his wife's and children's sake he is sorely tempted to commit fraud, to tell falsehoods, and obtain illicit gains. It must be a dreadful situation for any man to have to choose between roguery and indigence.

To marry a widow means, in plain language,[302] to make one's fortune, though this is not always the case.[303]

(62.) A man who has only inherited sufficient money to live comfortably as a lawyer wishes presently to become an official, then a magistrate, and finally a judge.[304] Thus it is with all ranks and conditions of men straitened or limited in their means, who, after having attempted several things beyond their power, force, if I may say so, their destiny; they have neither sense enough to forbear being rich nor to continue rich.

(63.) Dine comfortably, Clearchus,[305] make a good supper, put some wood on the fire, buy a cloak, put hangings all round your room, for you have no love for your heir; you even do not know him; you have not got any.

(64.) When we are young we lay up for old age; when we are old we save for death; a prodigal heir first gives us a splendid funeral, and then lavishes whatever money is left to him.

(65.) After his death a miser spends more money in one day than he spent in ten years when he was alive; and his heir more in ten months than the miser could find in his heart to part with during his whole lifetime.[306]

(66.) When we lavish our money we rob our heir; when we merely save it we rob ourselves. The middle course is to be just to ourselves and to others.

(67.) Children, perhaps, would be dearer to their parents and parents to their children, were it not for the latter being their heirs.

(68.) How wretched is man's estate, and how it makes one sick of life! We have to moil and toil, to watch, to yield, and to be dependent, to acquire a little money, or else we get it at the last gasp of our nearest relations. He who can master his

[302] En bon français in the original; just as we say "in plain English."

[303] A certain Count de Marsan seems to have made his fortune by marrying first one rich widow and then another.

[304] These different degrees of legal dignity were formerly in French praticien, officier, magistrat, président.

[305] Without any proof whatever, the "Keys" pretend that a certain intendant des finances, M. du Buisson, was meant.

[306] The miser is supposed to have been a M. Morstein, formerly chief treasurer of Poland, who went to reside in Paris, where he died in 1693; two years later his only son was killed at the siege of Namur.

feelings so far as not to wish for his father's death is an honest man.

(69.) A person who expects to inherit something becomes over-polite; we are never better flattered, better obeyed, followed, courted, attended, and caressed than by those who hope to gain by our death, and wish it may happen soon.

(70.) As far as different places, titles, and inheritances are concerned, all men look upon themselves as one another's heirs, and, therefore, quietly and stealthily wish all their lives for one another's death. The happiest man, under such circumstances, is he who has most to lose by his death, and most to leave to his successor.

(71.) It is said of gambling that it makes all ranks equal; but there is often such a strange disparity and such a vast, immense, and profound chasm between this and that condition, that it pains us to see such extremes meet together.[307] It is like discord in music, like colours which do not harmonise, like words that clash and jar on our ears, like those sounds and noises which make us shudder. In a word, it is a subversion of all order and decency. If any one tells me gambling is the custom throughout the whole western hemisphere, I reply that perhaps it is one of the reasons why we are considered barbarians in another part of the globe, and what the Eastern nations who travel this way particularly remark of us in their journals. I have not the smallest doubt that such an excessive familiarity appears to them as disgusting as their *zombay*[308] and their other prostrations seem to us incongruous.

(72.) An assembly of the provincial states or a parliament[309] meeting to discuss a very important matter of business, presents nothing so grave and serious as a table crowded with gamblers who play very high; a melancholic severity is depicted on every countenance; implacable towards one another, and irreconcilable enemies as long as they are together, they neither regard relationship, connections, birth, or social distinctions. Chance alone, that blind and stern divinity, presides over the assembly, and pronounces her opinions like a sovereign; people show their respect for her by remaining very silent, and by being more attentive than

---

[307] Thus M. Langlée, a "man sprung from nothing," as St. Simon calls him, but a first-rate gambler, played for several years every day with the king. See also page 139, note 279. Gourville (see page 137, note 267) gambled with noblemen of the highest rank; and a certain Morin, after having lost large sums of money, was obliged to fly to London, where he managed the gambling table of the Duchess de Mazarin, and is often mentioned by St. Evremond.

[308] Our author says in a footnote: "See the narratives about the kingdom of Siam." The zombay seems to have been a very profound inclination and prostration of the body. In "A New Historical Relation of Siam by M. de Loubère, envoy extraordinary from the French king to the king of Siam in the years 1687 and 1688, done out of French," and printed in London in 1693, we find "they (the Siamese) kept themselves prostrated on their knees and elbows, with their hands joined at the top of their forehead, and their body seated on their heels; to the end that they may lean less on their elbows, and that it may be possible (without assisting themselves with their hands, but keeping them still joined to the top of their forehead) to raise themselves on their knees, and fall again upon their elbows, as they do thrice together, as often as they would speak to their king."

[309] In the French parliaments or courts, councillors were allowed to plead, and justice was administered in the king's name; but these parliaments had no legislative power, and had only to register the royal edicts before they became law.

they are elsewhere. Every passion seems in abeyance for a while, to give way to one passion only, during which the courtier neither pretends to be gentle, fawning, polite, nor pious.

(73.) Even the smallest trace of their former condition seems utterly obliterated in those who have made their fortune by gambling; they lose sight of their equals, and associate only with persons of the highest rank. It is true that the fortune of the die or *lansquenet*[310] often puts them in the same place whence it took them.[311]

(74.) I am not surprised that there are gambling houses, like so many snares laid for human avarice; like abysses where many a man's money is engulphed and swallowed up without any hope of return; like frightful rocks against which the gamblers are thrown and perish; that certain men are sent forth to find out the precise time some person has landed with newly got prize-money, or who has gained a lawsuit which has brought him in a goodly sum, or who has received some presents, or who has had a very lucky run at play; what young man of family has just come into a large inheritance, or what desperate clerk will venture the monies of his office on the turn of a card. Truly cheating is villainous and rascally, but it is an old and well-known trade, and practised at all times by the men we call professional gamblers. They have a sign outside their doors, and this may be the inscription: "Here cheating is done fairly;" for I suppose they do not pretend to be blameless. Every one knows that if a man gambles in one of these houses he is certain to lose. What to me is unaccountable, is that there should always be as many fools as gamblers want, to make a living by them.

(75.) Thousands have been ruined by gambling, and yet they tell you very coolly they cannot do without it. What an idle excuse is this! Is there any violent and shameful passion in existence to which we cannot apply the same language? Would any one be allowed to say, he cannot live without stealing, murdering, or rushing into all kinds of excesses? It is allowable to gamble in a frightful manner, without intermission, shame, or limit; to have no other aim but the total ruin of your adversary; to be carried away by a desire for gain, thrown into despair by losing or consumed by avarice; to risk on the turn of a card or die your own future and that of your wife and children; or should we do without it yet? And are there not sometimes worse consequences than these at the gambling-table, when men are entirely stripped, obliged to do without clothes and food, and cannot provide these for their families?

I allow no one to be a knave, but I will allow a knave to play high, but not an honest man, for it is too silly to expose oneself to a heavy loss.[312]

---

[310] A game of chance played with cards.

[311] Those who made their fortune by gambling were, according to the "Keys," Courcillon, Marquis de Dangeau, who left behind him a very valuable Journal of the sayings and doings of the court of Louis XIV., which has often been printed; but he did not owe his success in life to gambling alone; and Morin, already mentioned, page 155, note 1.

[312] All the "Keys" give as the model of a perfect gambler a certain Louis Robert, Seigneur de Fortille, who made his fortune as intendant of different army-corps, and lost almost everything he possessed; but as the passion for gambling was very common, and as the king was the first to give the example of it, ruined gamblers were to be found in plenty.

(76.) There is but one sorrow which is lasting, and that is one produced by the loss of property; time, which alleviates all others, sharpens this; we feel it every moment during the course of our lives when we miss the fortune we have lost.

(77.) The man who spends his fortune without marrying his daughters, paying his debts, or lending it out on good security, may be well enough liked by every one except by his wife and children.

(78.) Neither the troubles, Zenobia,[313] which disturb your empire, nor the war which since the death of the king, your husband, you have so heroically maintained against a powerful nation, diminish your magnificence in the least. You have preferred the banks of the Euphrates to any other country for erecting a splendid building; the air is healthy and temperate, the situation delightful; a sacred wood shades it on the west; the Syrian gods, who sometimes visit the earth, could not choose a finer abode; the adjacent country is peopled with men who are constantly busy shaping and cutting, coming and going, rolling or carting away the timber of Mount Lebanon, brass and porphyry; the air rings with the noise of cranes and machinery; and that noise instils a hope in the breasts of those who pass that way to go to Arabia, that, on their return home, they may see that palace finished, with all the splendour you design to bestow on it before you, or the princes, your children, make it your dwelling. Spare nothing, great queen; make use of your gold and of the best workmanship of first-class artists;[314] let the Phidiasses and Zeuxisses[315] of your century display the utmost of their skill on your walls and ceilings; lay out expensive and delightful gardens, so enchanting that they do not seem created by the hand of man; exhaust your treasures and your energy in this incomparable edifice; and, after you have brought it to perfection, one of those herdsmen who dwell in the neighbouring sandy deserts of Palmyra, and who has enriched himself by farming the tolls of your rivers, will purchase one day, with ready money, this royal demesne, and add fresh embellishments to it, so as to render it more worthy of him and his fortune.[316]

(79.) This palace, this furniture, these gardens, those handsome waterworks charm you, and on first beholding such a delightful mansion, you cannot forbear expressing your opinion that its owner ought to be superlatively happy. He is no more, and he never enjoyed it so pleasantly and so quietly as you did; he never Cheating at play was also not rare.

[313] Zenobia, queen of Palmyra, after the death of her husband Odenathus, waged war for five years against the Romans, and was vanquished by Aurelian in the year 273.

[314] Ouvrier, in the original, is sometimes used by our author for "artist."

[315] Phidias (490-432 B.C.) was a Greek sculptor of renown; Zeuxis (424-400 B.C.), a Greek painter, who is said to have painted grapes so well that some birds came and pecked at them.

[316] The "herdsman" alluded to in the above paragraph seems to have been the financier La Touanne, trésorier de l'extraordinaire des guerres. He had a mansion near the park of Saint Maur, part of an estate formerly belonging to Catherine de Medici (Zenobia), on which he spent enormous sums, whilst the other part belonged to the Prince de Condé, who in vain tried to induce the parvenu to sell him his property. Hence the attack of our author on the man who dared to oppose the wishes of his noble patron. However, when this paragraph appeared, La Touanne did not yet live at Saint Maur.

knew a cheerful day or a quiet night; he sunk beneath the debts he contracted in adorning it with those beauties which so delight you. His creditors drove him from it, and then he turned round his head and looked upon it for the last time; this affected him so much that it caused his death.[317]

(80.) We cannot avoid observing the strokes of fate or the freaks of fortune which happen in certain families, and which a hundred years ago were never heard of because they did not exist. Providence, on a sudden, bestows its favours on them; and more than once showers on them wealth, honours, and dignities, so that they bask in prosperity. Eumolpus,[318] one of those men who never had any ancestors, was raised so high that he obtained everything he desired during the course of a long life. Was this owing to the superior intelligence and to the profound capacity of either father or son, or to favourable circumstances? Fortune, at last, smiles on them no longer; it leaves them to sport elsewhere, and treats their descendants as it did their ancestors.

(81.) The immediate cause of the ruin and overthrow of gentlemen of the long robe and the sword is that they have to spend their money, not according to their income, but according to their rank in society.

(82.) If you have omitted nothing towards making your fortune, how great has been your labour! If you have neglected the most trifling thing, how lasting will be your repentance!

(83.) Giton has a fresh complexion, a full face, pendulous cheeks, a steady and resolute look, broad shoulders, a huge chest, a firm and deliberate gait; he speaks with assurance, must have every word repeated that is said to him, and is not greatly pleased with what is told him. He takes a large handkerchief out of his pocket, and blows his nose with a tremendous noise: he expectorates about the room, and sneezes very loud; he sleeps by day, by night, and that soundly, for he snores in company. He takes up more room than any one else at table or whilst walking, and walks in the middle of the road when with his equals; he stops and they stop; he goes forward and they go forward; all are governed by what he does. He interrupts and corrects those who are talking, but is never interrupted, and people listen to him as long as he likes to speak, for their ideas are like his, and they take it for granted that the news he tells them is perfectly true. If he sits down he throws himself into an easy-chair, crosses his legs, frowns, pulls his hat over his eyes so as to see no one, or suddenly draws it back to show a supercilious and bold countenance; he is merry, ever laughing, impatient, impudent, a freethinker,[319] and a politician full of secrets about the affairs of the day; he thinks he has talents and intelligence; he is wealthy.

---

[317] According to the commentators, this refers to Jacques Bordier, intendant des finances, who, after having spent more than a million on his estate at Raincy, was obliged to leave it; but his creditors did not expel him, for it was sold by his heirs after his death.

[318] The Marquis de Seignelay is supposed by some to have been the original of Eumolpus; he did not, however, enjoy a long life. (See page 149, note 255.

[319] Libertin, in the original, which first meant a man of free-and-easy manners, came to be chiefly used in the second half of the seventeenth century for a "freethinker."

Phædo has sunken eyes, a reddish complexion, a lean body and an emaciated countenance; he sleeps very little, and his slumbers are light; he is absent-minded, pensive, and, with some intelligence, looks like a dolt; he forgets to say what he knows or to speak about those incidents with which he is acquainted; if he says something now and then, he does it badly; he thinks he bores those persons to whom he addresses himself, and therefore tells his story briefly but coldly, so that he is never listened to nor taken notice of, for he makes nobody laugh. He praises and laughs at other persons' jests, is of their opinions, and runs and flies to render them some small services; he is over polite, and flatters and waits on them; he is close about his own affairs, and does not always tell the truth about them; he is very peculiar,[320] scrupulous, and timorous. He steps lightly and softly, and seems afraid to tread the ground; he walks with his eyes downward, and dares not raise them to face the passers-by; he never joins in any conversation, but places himself behind the person who speaks; picks up by stealth all that has been said, and withdraws if any one looks at him. He does not take up any room nor fill a place anywhere; he walks about with his arms close to his body, his hat over his eyes that he may not be seen, and wraps and folds himself up in his cloak. There is no street nor gallery so crowded and filled with people, but he finds a way to get through without jostling, and to steal along unperceived. If they beg him to sit down, he seats himself on the edge of a chair, and talks in a low voice and not very distinctly; he freely expresses, however, his opinion on public affairs, is angry with the age, and but indifferently pleased with the cabinet and the ministers; he seldom opens his mouth but to reply; he coughs and blows his nose with his hat before his face, he almost expectorates on himself, and does not sneeze till he is alone, or if it does happen, no one hears it, so that no one has to say "God bless you." He is poor.[321]

---

[320] Superstitieux sometimes had the above meaning; Littré gives two examples of it in his dictionary.

[321] Giton and Phædo do not apply to any one in particular, though some commentators maintain that by the first the Marquis de Barbézieux, the son of Louvois, was meant.

THE TUILERIES

VII.

OF THE TOWN.[322]

(1.) PEOPLE in Paris, without giving any notice beforehand, and as if it were some public assignation, meet every evening on the Cours[323] or in the Tuileries, to stare around and criticise one another.

They cannot dispense with those very persons whom they do not like and whom they deride.

---

[322] Now we speak of town and country, but in La Bruyère's time people mentioned the town or city and the court, wholly different in customs and manners. Boileau begins his Satires with the two following lines—

"Damon, ce grand auteur dont la muse fertile,
Amusa si long-temps et la cour et la ville."

Our author places his chapter "Of the Town" before that "Of the Court" and "Of the Great," and leads up to that "Of the Sovereign."

[323] Le Cours la Reine, familiarly called Le Cours, was a part of the Champs-Elysées, planted with trees by order of Maria de Medici, the wife of Henri IV.; hence the name. The theatre finished then at seven o'clock, when it was not too late to take a walk in summer-time. See also Molière's Les Fâcheux, act i. scene 1.

They wait for one another in these public walks,[324] and they examine one another; carriages, horses, liveries, coats of arms, nothing escapes their gaze; everything is looked at keenly or maliciously, and they respect or contemn the persons they meet according to the greater or lesser splendour of their equipages.

(2.) Everybody knows that long bank[325] which borders and confines the Seine where it joins the Marne on entering Paris; close by men come to bathe during the heat of the dog-days, and people at a little distance see them amuse themselves by jumping in and out of the water. Now, as long as there is no bathing, the city ladies never walk that way, and when the season is over they walk there no longer.[326]

(3.) In those places of general resort, where the ladies assemble only to show their fine dresses, and to reap the reward for the trouble they have taken with their apparel, people do not walk with a companion for the pleasure of conversation, but they herd together to get a little more confidence, to accustom themselves to the public, and to keep one another in countenance against criticisms. They talk but say nothing, or rather they talk to be taken notice of by those for whose sake they raise their voices, gesticulate, joke, bow carelessly, and walk up and down.

(4.) The town is split up into several sets, which, like so many little republics, have their peculiar laws, customs, dialects, and jests. As long as such a set remains in force, and as long as the conceit lasts, nothing is allowed to be well said or well done which it had no hand in, and it cannot enjoy anything from strangers; it even contemns those who have not been initiated in its mysteries. An intelligent man, whom chance has thrown amongst the members of such a set, is a stranger to them: he is, as it were, in a distant country, where he is ignorant of the roads, the language, the manners and the laws; he sees a sort of people who talk, rattle, whisper, burst out laughing, and presently relapse into a gloomy silence; he does not know what to do, and can hardly tell where to put in a word, or even when to listen. Some sorry buffoon is ever at hand who is the head and, as it were, the hero of such a set, and has always to keep them merry and to make them laugh before he has uttered a single word. If at any time a woman comes amongst them, who is not one of them, these jolly fellows are amazed she does not laugh at things she cannot understand, and appears not to be amused with some nonsense they would not understand themselves, if it were not their own; they will not overlook her tone of voice, her silence, her figure, her dress, her coming or going out of the room. This same set, however, does not last two years; in the first year are already sown those seeds of division which break it up the following year; quarrels about some woman, disputes at play, extravagant entertainments, which, though moderate at first, soon degenerate into pyramids of viands and sumptuous banquets, overthrow the commonwealth, and finally give it a mortal blow, and in a little while there is no more talk about them than about last year's flies.

(5.) There are in town lawyers belonging to the *grande robe*, and others to the

[324] The favourite and fashionable walk, during the latter part of the seventeenth century, was from Paris to Vincennes.

[325] That bank is now the quays Saint-Bernard and Austerlitz.

[326] Bourdaloue (1632-1704), a celebrated preacher, censures a similar behaviour in his sermon on Les Divertissements du Monde.

petite robe;[327] and the first take on the second their revenge for the contempt and the supercilious way in which they are treated by a court of justice. It is not easy to know where the *grande robe*[328] begins and the *petite* ends; there is even a large number of lawyers who refuse to belong to the second class and who are yet not considered to be of the first; they will, however, not abandon their pretensions, but, on the contrary, endeavour, by their sedate carriage and by the money they spend, to show themselves the equals of the magistrates; they have often been heard to say that their sublime duties, the independence of their profession, their eloquence, and their personal merits, balance at least the bags of money which the sons of financiers and bankers have paid for their offices.

(6.) You are very inconsiderate to sit musing, or perhaps dozing, in your carriage. Rouse yourself, and take a book or your papers, and begin to read; and hardly return the bows of those people who pass you in their carriages, for they will believe you to be very busy, and say everywhere that you are hard-working and indefatigable, and that you read and work even in the streets or on the highroad.[329] You may learn from a pettifogger that you should ever seem to be immersed in business, knit your brows and muse most profoundly about nothing at all; that you should not always have the time for eating or drinking, and that as soon as you are in the house you should vanish like a ghost, and betake yourself to your dark private room, hide yourself from the public, avoid the theatre, and leave that to those who run no risk in appearing there, though they have hardly the leisure for it, to the Gomons and the Duhamels.[330]

(7.) There are a certain number of young magistrates with large estates and fond of pleasure, who have become acquainted with some of those men who are called at court "dandies;" they imitate them, behave in a manner unbecoming the gravity of a judge, and believe that on account of their youth and fortune they have no need to be discreet or passionless. They borrow from the court the very worst qualities, appropriate to themselves vanity, effeminacy, intemperance, and indecency, as if all those vices were their privilege, thus affecting a character quite the opposite to what they ought to maintain, and, in the end, according to their wishes, become exact copies of very wicked originals.[331]

(8.) A gentleman of the legal profession is not like the same man in the city

---

[327] To the grande robe belonged all magistrates; to the petite robe all avoués and procureurs, somewhat like attorneys and solicitors; the avocats or barristers were between the two, and the court of justice or parlement above them all.

[328] The avocats were generally not considered to belong to the grande robe, and La Bruyère was one of them; the latter part of the paragraph is a direct attack on the sale of legal offices.

[329] This applies, according to the "Keys," to a certain M. de la Briffe, a maître des requêtes, or to M. de Saint-Pouange. (See page 134, note 259.)

[330] Two celebrated barristers of La Bruyère's time.

[331] J. H. de Mesmes, who became président à mortier in 1688, when he was only twenty-seven years old, is said to have been a constant companion of profligate young noblemen. A mortier was a round velvet cap, worn by the Chancellor and Presidents of parliaments.

and at court; when he has returned home he resumes his natural manners, look, and gestures, which he left behind, and is no longer so embarrassed nor so polite.

(9.) The Crispins join and club together to drive out with six horses to their carriage, and with a swarm of men in livery, to which each has furnished his share; they figure at the Cours or at Vincennes[332] as brilliantly as a newly-married couple, or as Jason who is ruining himself, or as Thraso who wishes to get married, and who has deposited the money to buy an important place.[333]

(10.) I hear a good deal of talk about the Sannions; about "the same name, the same arms, the elder branch, the younger branch, the younger sons of the second branch; about the first bearing their arms plain, the second with a label, and the third with a *bordure* indented." Their colour and metal are the same as those of the Bourbons, and, like them, they bear two and one;[334] it is true these are not "fleurs de lis," but they are satisfied; perhaps, in their inmost hearts, they believe their bearings as noble; at least, they are the same as those of lords of the highest rank who are quite content with them. We see them on their mourning hangings,[335] and on the windows of their chapels, on the gates of their castle, on their justiciary pillar, where many a man is condemned to be hanged who only deserved banishment; they are visible anywhere, on their furniture and their locks, while their carriages are covered with them, and the liveries of their servants do not disgrace their escutcheon. I should like to tell the Sannions that their ostentation is too precipitate; that they should have waited at least until their race had existed a century; that those persons who knew and conversed with their grandfather are old and cannot live long, and that, after their death, no one will be able to say where he kept his shop, and what a very dear one it was.

The Sannions and the Crispins[336] had rather be thought extravagant than covetous; they tell you a long story of a feast or a collation they gave, of their losses at play, and express aloud their regrets they have not lost more. They mention in their peculiar language certain ladies of their acquaintance; they have ever many pleasant things to tell each other, are always making new discoveries, and confide to one another their successes with the fair. One of them, coming lately to his country-house, hastens to bed, and rises with the dawn, then puts on his gaiters and a linen suit, and fastens on his belt and his powder-horn, ties back his hair, takes

---

[332] See page 165, note 324.

[333] The original has *et qui a consigné*, a meaning which we have still in the English word "consignment." The explanation of this word is given by the author himself.

[334] An allusion to the three fleurs de lis of the Bourbons.

[335] Litre, in the original, is a kind of mourning hangings, or, rather, a broad velvet band on which the coats of arms of certain nobles were painted, and which was placed around the church, inside as well as outside. The right of using the litre belonged only to noblemen who had founded a church, or to those who had exercised a certain jurisdiction in their domains.

[336] The commentators hint at several magistrates as the originals of the Crispins, and imagine that the Sannions were the family of Leclerc de Lesseville, the descendants of rich tanners, who became ennobled for having lent 20,000 crowns to Henry IV. after the battle of Ivry.

his gun, and is a sportsman, if he did but shoot well. He returns at night, wet and weary, without any game, but goes shooting again on the morrow, and spends the whole day in missing thrushes and partridges.

Another man[337] speaks of some wretched dogs he has as "his pack of hounds;" he knows where the meet is held, and goes there; he is at the starting,[338] and enters the thicket with the huntsmen, with his horn by his side; he does not ask, like Menalippus, "Do I enjoy myself?"[339] but he thinks he does; he forgets the law and all lawsuits, and would be thought an Hippolytus.[340] Menander, who yesterday was engaged in a lawsuit, paid him a visit, but to-day would not know again his judge. To-morrow you may see him at court, where a weighty and capital case is going to be tried; he gets his learned brethren about him, and informs them that he did not lose the stag, but that he is quite hoarse with hallooing after the hounds which lost the scent, or after those sportsmen who were at fault, and that, with half a dozen hounds, he was in at the death; but the clock strikes, and he has no more time to talk of the stag being at bay, or of the quarry: he must take his seat with the other magistrates and administer justice.

(11.) How great is the infatuation of certain men, who, being possessed of the wealth their fathers acquired by trade, which they have just inherited, imitate princes in their dress and retinue, and by excessive expenditure and ridiculous pomp provoke the remarks and sneers of the whole town they think to dazzle, and thus ruin themselves to be laughed at!

Some have not even the sorry advantage of having their follies talked about beyond their immediate neighbourhood, and the only spot where their vanity is displayed. They do not know in the Ile that André makes a figure and squanders his patrimony in the Marais.[341] If he were only better known in town and in the suburbs, perhaps, amongst so large a number of citizens, who are not all able to judge sensibly of everything, possibly one of them might declare André has a magnificent spirit, and give him credit for his banquets to Xanthe and Ariston, and for his entertainments to Elamire; but he ruins himself obscurely, and hastens to become poor only for the sake of two or three persons, who do not esteem him in the least, and though at present he rides in his coach, in six months he will hardly be able to go on foot.[342]

[337] This "other man" was a certain President de Coigneux, who neglected his legal duties to spend all his time in sport.

[338] Laisse-courre in French; formerly courre was used instead of courir, as a sporting term.

[339] A. M. Jérôme de Nouveau, the head of the post-office, is said to have asked his head huntsman a similar question.

[340] Hippolytus, son of Theseus, king of Athens, "a youth who never knew a woman," thrown from his chariot and killed, is the hero of Racine's tragedy Phèdre.

[341] The Ile meant nearly always the Ile Saint-Louis; the Quartier du Temple, formerly the Marais, is even sometimes now called by that name.

[342] The commentators have given the names of several obscure people for those "infatuated men," and for André as well; but it is surely not a rare thing for men to ruin themselves through vanity.

(12.) Narcissus[343] rises in the morning to lie down at night; he spends as many hours in dressing as a woman; he goes every day to mass at the Feuillants or the Minims;[344] is very agreeable in company, and in his parish they reckon on him to make a third man at ombre or reversis.[345] He sits for hours together at

Aricia's, where every night he ventures his five or six golden pistoles;[346] he never misses reading the *Gazette de Hollande* or the *Mercure Galant*;[347] he has read Bergerac,[348] Desmarets,[349] Lesclache,[350] Barbin's[351] stories, and some collections of poetry; he walks with the ladies on the Plaine or the Cours,[352] and is scrupulously punctual in his visits; he will do to-morrow precisely what he has done to-day and did yesterday; thus he lives, and thus he will die.

(13.) "I have seen this man somewhere," you'll say,[353] "and, though his face is familiar to me, I have forgotten where it was." It is familiar to many other people, and, if possible, I will assist your memory. Was it on the Boulevard,[354] in a carriage, or in the large alley of the Tuileries, or else in the dress-circle at the theatre? Was it at church, at a ball, or at Rambouillet;[355] or, rather, can you tell me where you have not seen him, and where he is not to be met with? If some well-known criminal is going to be executed, or if there are any fireworks, he makes

---

[343] The Abbé de Villars, who died in 1691, was a son of the Marquis de Villars, French ambassador to the Court of Spain, and is said to have been the original of Narcissus.

[344] The Convent of the Feuillants, a branch of the Cistercian monks, was in the Rue Saint-Honoré; that of the Minims, an order founded by St. Francis of Paula in 1453, was near the Place Royale.

[345] Ombre, a Spanish game of cards, often mentioned by English authors of the eighteenth century; Pope has a poetical description of it in his "Rape of the Lock." Reversis is another game of cards, played by four persons, and in which those who make the fewest tricks win the game.

[346] A golden pistole was usually worth eleven livres.

[347] The Gazette de Hollande was a newspaper published in Holland, and in which everything was put that could not be printed or said in France. For the Mercure Galant, see page 24, note 86.

[348] Cyrano de Bergerac (1620-1655) was the author of the Histoires Comiques des Etats et Empires de la Lune, etc., of a tragedy, Agrippine, and of a comedy, Le Pédant Joué, from which Molière borrowed two scenes.

[349] Desmarets de Saint-Sorlin (1596-1676), an author of various plays, novels, and poems, and one of the first in France to attack the authority of the ancients.

[350] Louis de Lesclache (1620-1661), a grammarian and a writer on philosophy.

[351] Barbin, a well-known publisher at the time our author wrote.

[352] The Plaine was probably the Plaine des Sablons; for the Cours, see page 164, note 2.

[353] The "Keys" are unanimous in saying that the Prince of Mecklenburg-Schwerin, who had married a sister of the Maréchal de Luxembourg, and who died at the Hague in 1692, is meant by "this man."

[354] This was the boulevard of the Porte Saint-Antoine, sometimes called the Nouveau Cours, on the road to Vincennes.

[355] A large garden in the Faubourg Saint-Antoine was called thus, after a financier of the same name who had laid it out.

his appearance at a window at the town-hall; if some one enters the town in state, you see him in the reserved seats; if a *carousel*[356] is ridden, he enters and takes his place on some bench; if the king gives an audience to an ambassador, he sees the whole procession, is present at the reception, and thrusts himself in the ranks when it returns. His presence is as essential at the solemn renewal of the alliance between the Swiss Cantons as that of the Lord Chancellor or the Helvetian pleni- potentiaries.[357] You see his face on the almanacks amongst the people or the by- standers;[358] if there is a public hunt going on or a *Saint Hubert*,[359] he will be present on horseback; they say to him that a camp is going to be pitched or that a review is going to be held, and off he will start for Houilles or Achères;[360] he is very fond of the army, the militia, and war, of which he has seen a good deal, even the taking of Fort Bernardi.[361] Chamlay knows something of marches, Jacquier of the commissariate, du Metz of the artillery,[362] but our gentleman is a looker-on, has grown old in the service of looking-on, and is a spectator by profession; he does not do anything that a man ought to do, and he does not know anything that a man ought to know; but he boasts that he has seen everything that was to be seen, and now does not regret to die. But what a loss will his death be for the whole town! Who will inform us, as he did, that the Cours is closed, and nobody is walking there, that the pond of Vincennes has been filled up and is now a raised moat, and that no carriage will any more be upset on that spot? Who will acquaint us when there is a concert, a choral service in church, or something wonderful to be seen at the fair? Who will let us know that Beaumavielle[363] died yesterday, and that Rochois[364] has got a cold and will not be able to sing for a week? Who will inform us that Scapin bears the "fleur de lis" on his arms, and who is very glad he does so? Who will pronounce, with the most boastful emphasis, the name of a mere citizen's wife, or who will be better provided with topical songs? Who will lend to the ladies the *Annales Galantes* and the *Journal Amoureux*?[365] Who will sing

[356] A sort of mock tilting-match on horseback.

[357] The alliance between France and Switzerland was always solemnly sworn, and this was done for the last time in 1663 in Notre-Dame.

[358] Every year under Louis XIV.'s reign there were published large engravings, in which the king, the princes, and the principal persons of the court were represented, whilst lower down the citizens, the people, etc., were looking on, and the real almanack was past- ed quite at the bottom.

[359] Saint Hubert was the patron saint of the chase, and on the 5th of November, when his festival was held, the king and the greatest personages of the court hunted at Versailles.

[360] Two small places near Versailles where often soldiers encamped and reviews were held.

[361] Bernardi was the director of a celebrated gymnasium at that time, and every year his pupils attacked and defended an artificial fort, erected by his orders.

[362] The Marquis de Chamlay was a noted tactician; Jacquier had been the head of the commissariate, and died in 1684; and Berbier du Metz, lieutenant-general of the artillery, was killed at the battle of Fleuras in 1690.

[363] Beaumavielle, a celebrated basso-singer at the opera, died about 1688.

[364] Marthe de Rochois sang at the opera from 1678 till 1697.

[365] The Annales Galantes were published in 1670, and written by Madame de Ville-

at table a whole dialogue of an opera, or the madness of "Roland"[366] in a *ruelle*, as well as he does?[367] To conclude, since there are in the city and elsewhere some very foolish people as well as some dull and idle people, who have nothing to do, who will so exactly suit every one of them as he did?

(14.) Theramenes[368] was rich and had some merit; some property was left him, and therefore he is now much wealthier and has a great deal more merit; all the women set to work to make him their gallant, and all the young girls to get him for a husband; he goes from house to house, to make the mothers believe that he is inclined to marry. As soon as he has taken his seat they withdraw, to leave full liberty to their daughters to be amiable and to Theramenes to declare his intentions. Here he is the rival of a magistrate;[369] there he throws into the shade a military man or a nobleman. The ladies could not covet more passionately any rosy-cheeked, gay, brisk, witty young fellow, nor could he be better received; they snatch him out of one another's hands, and can hardly find leisure to vouchsafe a smile to any other person who visits them at the same time. How many gallants is he going to defeat! how many good matches will be broken off on his account! Will he bestow his hand on the large number of heiresses who court him? He is not only the terror of husbands, but the dread of all these who wish to be so, and to whom marriage is the only resource for obtaining a sufficient sum to replace the money they paid for their official situations.[370] A man so happy and so wealthy[371] ought to be banished from a well-governed city, and the fair sex should be forbidden, under pain of being considered insane or degraded, to treat him better than if he were merely a person of merit.

(15.) The people in Paris commonly ape the court, but they do not always know how to imitate it; they by no means resemble it in those agreeable and flattering outward civilities with which some courtiers, and particularly the ladies, affably treat a man of merit, who possesses nothing but merit. Such ladies never inquire after that man's means or his ancestors; they find him at court, and that is sufficient for them; they give themselves no airs, they esteem him, and do not ask whether he came in a carriage or on foot, or whether he has a post, an estate, or followers; as they are satiated with pomp, splendour, and honour, they like to recreate themselves with philosophy or virtue. If a city lady hears the rattling of a carriage stopping at her door, she is anxious to be acquainted with any person who is in it, and to be polite to him, without at all knowing him; but from her window she has caught a glance of a set of fine horses, a good many liveries, is dazzled

---

dieu; no Journal Amoureux ever saw the light.

[366] Roland, an opera by Quinault (see page 28, note 99) and Lulli (see page 25, note 88, and page 46, note), was represented for the first time at Versailles in the beginning of 1685, and Mademoiselle de Rochois played the part of Angelica in it.

[367] See page 65, note 161.

[368] M. de Terrat, the chancelier of Monsieur, the brother of Louis XIV., is hinted at here, probably merely on account of his name.

[369] Le mortier, in the original. See page 168, note 331.

[370] La Bruyère employs le vide de la consignation. See page 169, note 333.

[371] Pécunieux our author uses in its Latin meaning.

by the numerous rows of finely gilt nails,[372] and is very impatient to behold such a military man or a magistrate in her apartments. How well will he be received! She'll never take her eyes off him. Nothing is lost upon her, and she has already given him credit for the double braces and springs of his carriage, which make it go easier, and she esteems him the more and loves him the better for them.

(16.) The infatuation of some city women in their wretched imitation of those at court is more offensive than the coarseness of the women of the people and the rusticity of country-women, since it is a mixture of both, and of affectation as well.

(17.) What a cunning contrivance to give during courtship valuable presents which cost nothing, and which after marriage have to be returned in kind![373]

(18.) It is sensible and praiseworthy in a man to spend on his nuptials one-third of his wife's dowry; to begin with deliberately impoverishing himself by buying and collecting superfluous things; and already to take from his capital in order to pay Gaultier,[374] the cabinet-maker, and the milliner!

(19.) Truly it is a charming and judicious custom which, in defiance of modesty and decency, and through some kind of shamelessness, compels a newly-married bride to lie on her bed for show, and to render herself ridiculous for some days, by exposing her to the curiosity of a few men and women whom she may know, or who may be strangers to her, and who hasten from all quarters of the town to look on such a sight as long as it lasts.[375] There is nothing wanting to make this custom seem very absurd and incomprehensible, except to see it mentioned in print in some book of travels in Mingrelia.

(20.) What a painful habit and what a troublesome kind of obligation it must be for certain persons to be continually anxious of meeting one another, yet when they meet to have nothing but trifles to say to one another, and to communicate reciprocally things which were previously known to both and of no matter of importance to either; to enter a room merely to leave it again; to go out after dinner,[376] only to come home in the evening, highly satisfied with seeing in five hours three Swiss,[377] a woman they hardly knew, and another they scarcely liked. Whoever

[372] Gilt nails were the principal ornaments of the heavy and unwieldy coaches of the age of Louis XIV.

[373] Some unprincipled suitors borrowed costly jewels which they put in the trousseau of their brides, but which had to be returned after the marriage.

[374] Gaultier was the proprietor of a well-known warehouse for the sale of silks and gold and silver-embroidered stuffs in the Rue des Bourdonnais, in Paris, during the latter part of the seventeenth century.

[375] According to an immemorial custom in Paris, a young wife showily dressed had to sit up on her bed during the first three days after marriage to receive visits. Several memoirs and letters of the time refer to it. Addison in "The Spectator," No. 45, speaks also of the "English ladies ... brought up the fashion of receiving visits in their beds."

[376] People were then (1688-1694) in the habit of dining at twelve o'clock, and of taking supper at seven or eight; hence the reference to the "five hours."

[377] We do not know if this refers to Swiss porters or Swiss guards; I should think it meant the former, and intends to point out that the lady made three calls. (See also page 134, note 260.)

will rightly consider the value of time, and how irreparable its loss is, must lament bitterly such wretched trifling.[378]

(21.) In town, people are brought up in complete ignorance of rural and country affairs; they can scarcely distinguish flax from hemp, wheat from rye, and neither of them from meslin; they are satisfied with eating, drinking, and dressing. Do not mention to a large number of townsfolk such words as fallowland, staddles, layers, or after-grass, if you wish to be understood, for they will not think it is their mother-tongue. Speak to some of them of measures, tariffs, taxes,[379] and to others of appeals, petitions, decrees, and injunctions; for they know the world, and above all, what is ugly and vulgar in it; but they do not know Nature, its beginning, growth, gifts, and bounteousness. Their ignorance often is voluntary, and based on the conceit they have of their own callings and talents. There is not a low pettifogger in his dark and grimy room, his brain teeming with the most wicked legal quibbles, who does not prefer himself to a husbandman, who, blest of Heaven, cultivates the land, sows when it is needed, and gathers a rich harvest; and if at any time the former hears mention made of the first men or the patriarchs, their rural lives and their husbandry, he wonders how people could have been living in those days without lawyers, commissioners, presidents, or solicitors, and cannot understand how they could ever have done without rolls-offices, courts of judicature, and refreshment-rooms.

(22.) When the Roman emperors were making their triumphal entries, they never protected themselves in a more effeminate, easy, and efficacious manner against the wind, the rain, the dust, and the sun, than the citizens of Paris do when they are driven from one end of the town to another. What a difference between their habits and the mules on which their forefathers rode! The latter did not know how to deprive themselves of the necessaries of life to get superfluities, nor to prefer show to substance; their houses were never illuminated with wax-candles, and they never warmed themselves by a little fire, for in their time such candles were only used at the altar and in the Louvre;[380] they never ate a bad dinner in order to keep a carriage; they were convinced that men had legs given them to walk, and they did walk. In dry weather they kept themselves clean; in wet they did not mind to dirty their shoes and stockings, and to cross a street or passage with the same alacrity as a sportsman rides over ploughed fields, or a soldier gets wet in the trenches. They had not then invented the harnessing of two men to carry them in a Sedan chair; then several magistrates walked to the two courts,[381] and with as good a grace as Augustus formerly went on foot to the Capitol. Pewter in those days shone on the tables and the sideboards, brass and iron in the chimneys,

---

[378] This paragraph alludes, of course, to the visits ladies pay one another.

[379] Sou pour livre, or a penny in the pound, in the original, was a tax on merchandise of a twentieth part of their value.

[380] Wax-candles were a luxury at the time La Bruyère wrote, and chiefly manufactured at Bougiah, on the coast of Africa; hence their name, bougie.

[381] In every parliament there were originally two courts, and two kinds of barristers or conseillers; one court was called the grand'chambre, where the cases were heard; in the other court, the chambre des enquêtes, reports in writing were made of all cases.

whilst silver and gold lay safe in coffers. Women were then waited on by women, and there were even women in the kitchen. Such fine names as "governor" and "governess" were not unknown to our forefathers, for they knew to whom the children of kings and of great princes were intrusted;[382] but their children had the same servants they had, and they themselves were satisfied to superintend their education. Everything they did was calculated; their expenses were in proportion to their means; their liveries, their carriages, their furniture, their household expenses, their town and country houses were all in accordance with their incomes and their station in life. Outward distinctions existed, however, amongst them, so that it was impossible to mistake the wife of an attorney for the wife of a judge, and a commoner or a mere servant for a nobleman. Less desirous to spend or enlarge their patrimony than to keep it, they left it entire to their heirs, led a tranquil life, and died a peaceful death; then, there was no complaint of hard times, of excessive misery, of scarcity of money; they had less than we have, and yet they had enough, richer through their economy and their moderation than through their incomes or estates. To conclude, in former days people observed this maxim, that what is splendour, pomp, and magnificence in nobles of high rank, is extravagance, folly, and stupidity in private gentlemen.[383]

[382] The nobleman or lady of high rank to whom the education of the children of royalty was intrusted in France bore the title of gouverneur, or gouvernante des enfants de France.

[383] Voltaire attacked this paragraph, and maintained it was ridiculous to praise our forefathers for being calculating, slow, coarse, and not very cleanly. Moreover, money should not be stowed away in coffers, but circulate. One of the latest commentators of La Bruyère, M. Destailleur, observes rightly that our author only praises economy, simplicity, and moderation, and not avarice and uncleanliness, and that he merely attacks the pretended showiness of men wishing to imitate people of high rank; hence the last sentence.

VIII.

OF THE COURT.

(1.) THE most honourable thing we can say of a man is, that he does not understand the court; there is scarcely a virtue which we do not imply when saying this.[384]

(2.) A perfect courtier can command his gestures, his eyes, and his countenance; he is profound and impenetrable; he seems to overlook every injury; he smiles on his enemies, controls his temper, disguises his passions, belies his inclinations, and both speaks and acts against his opinions. Such a quintessence of refinement is usually called "falsehood," and is, after all, sometimes of no more use to a courtier's success than frankness, sincerity, and virtue.

(3.) A court is like certain changeable colours; which vary according to the different lights they are exposed in. He who can define these colours can define the court.

(4.) A man who leaves the court for a single moment renounces it for ever; the

---

[384] Not alone La Bruyère, but many of the most eminent persons of his time, such as Saint-Simon, Bourdaloue, Fénelon, Massillon, Madame de Maintenon, the Duke of Orléans and his mother, had the same opinion of the court and courtiers.

courtier who was there in the morning must be there at night, and know it again next day, in order that he himself may be known there.

(5.) A man must appear small at court, and let him be never so vain, it is impossible to prevent it; but it is the common lot, and the highest nobles themselves are there of no consequence.

(6.) People who live in the provinces consider the court admirable; but if they visit it, its beauties diminish, like those of a fine drawing of perspective viewed too closely.

(7.) It is difficult to get accustomed to the spending of our lives in ante-chambers, courtyards, or on staircases.

(8.) The court does not satisfy a man, but it prevents him from being satisfied with anything else.

(9.) A cultured gentleman should have some experience of the court; as soon as he enters it he will discover a new world, as it were, wholly unknown to him, where vice and politeness have equal sway, and where good and evil alike may be of use to him.

(10.) The court is like a marble structure, for the courtiers are very polished and very hard.

(11.) Sometimes people go to court only to come back again, so that, on their return, they may be taken notice of by the nobility of their county or by the bishops of their diocese.

(12.) There would be no use for embroiderers and confectioners, and they would open their shops in vain, if all the people were modest and temperate; courts would be deserts and kings almost left alone, if every one was void of vanity and self-interest. Men are willing to be slaves in one place if they can only lord it in another. It seems that at court a proud, imperious, and commanding mien is delivered wholesale to the great for them to retail in the country; they do exactly what is done unto them, and are the true apes of royalty.

(13.) Nothing disparages some courtiers so much as the presence of a prince; their faces are scarcely to be recognised; their features are altered and their looks debased; the more proud and haughty they are, the greater is the change in them, because they have suffered a greater loss; whilst a gentlemanly and modest man bears it much better, as there is nothing in him to alter.

(14.) Courtly manners are contagious; they are caught at Versailles,[385] as the Norman accent is at Rouen and Falaise; we partly find them amongst quartermasters, superintendents, and confectioners;[386] a man with no very great intellect

[385] It was only in the sixth edition of the "Characters" that our author printed Versailles in full; until then it was only "V ..."

[386] The French has fourriers, petits contrôleurs, and chefs de fruiterie. The first looked after the lodgings of the persons following the court when the king was travelling; the second superintended the expenses of the king's table and household; and the third set out the dessert and provided the wax-candles for the king's dining-room. A fourrier is still a non-commissioned officer in the French army who has charge of the quarters and provi-

may become proficient in them; one with a lofty genius and of solid worth does not sufficiently value such accomplishments to make it his principal business[387] to study and acquire them; he contracts them imperceptibly, and does not trouble himself to get rid of them.

(15.) N ...,[388] in a great flutter, comes up to the king's chamber, turns everybody aside, and clears the way; he scratches at the door, nay, almost raps; he gives his name, and the people around him recover now their breath; after some time he is admitted, but it is with the crowd.[389]

(16.) Courts are haunted by certain bold adventurers, of free-and-easy manners, who introduce themselves, pretend to possess greater abilities than others in their profession, and are believed on their sole assertion.[390] In the meanwhile they take advantage of this general belief, or of the fondness of some men for novelty; they make their way through the crowd, and reach the ear of the prince, with whom the courtier sees them talking, whilst he thinks himself happy if he only obtains a glance. It is not difficult for great people to get rid of them, for as they are only admitted on sufferance, and are of no consequence, their dismissal is of no importance: then they disappear, at once rich and out of favour; and the very men who so lately were deceived by them are ready to be deceived by others.

(17.) Some men, on entering a room, make but a slight bow, stretch their shoulders and thrust out their chests like women; they ask you a question, look another way, and speak in a loud tone, to show that they think themselves above every one present; they stop, and everybody gathers around them; they do all the talking, and seem to take the lead. This ridiculous and simulated haughtiness continues until some really great person makes his appearance, when they shrink away at once, and are reduced to their natural level, for which they are all the better.

(18.) Courts cannot exist without a class of courtiers who can flatter, are complaisant, insinuating, devoted to the ladies, whose pleasures they direct, whose weaknesses they study, and whose passions they flatter; they whisper some naughty words to them, speak of their husbands and lovers in a proper manner,

---

sions of the men.

[387] Faire son capital, in the original, a phrase much in vogue during the sixteenth and seventeenth centuries.

[388] This paragraph is said to apply to a certain M. de Barète, unknown to fame, or to the brother of Madame de Maintenon. (See page 65, note 164.)

[389] It was not considered etiquette to knock or to rap at the door of the king's chamber, or at the door of any nobleman's room; but a person asking to be admitted simply scratched the door with his nails, whilst the fashionables used their combs, which they always carried about with them to comb their long wigs. Only the princes, the grand officers of the crown, and some favourite nobles were admitted to the grand levée of Louis XIV., then officers of an inferior rank and a certain number of courtiers were allowed to enter the room; the crowd were not admitted, but had to wait till the king left the room, and then stood aside.

[390] This is said to be an allusion to a certain Italian quack, Caretto or Caretti, then the fashion, who is mentioned by Saint-Simon in his Mémoires and by Madame de Sévigné in her Letters.

conjecture when they are sad, ill, or expect a baby; they head the fashions, refine on luxury and extravagance, and teach the fair to spend in a short time large sums on clothes, furniture, and carriages; they wear nothing themselves but what shows good taste and riches, and will not live in an old palace till it be repaired and embellished; they eat delicately and thoughtfully; there is no pleasure they have not tried and of which they cannot tell you something; they owe their position to themselves, and they keep it with the same ability they made it. Disdainful and proud, they no longer accost their former equals, and scarcely bow to them; they speak when every one else is silent; enter, and at inconvenient hours thrust themselves into places where men of the highest rank dare not intrude; and when such men, after long services, their bodies covered with wounds, filling great posts or occupying high official positions, do not look so confident, and seem embarrassed. Princes listen to what these courtiers have to say, who share all their pleasures and entertainments, and never stir out of the Louvre or the Castle,[391] where they behave themselves as if quite at home and in their own house; they seem to be in a thousand different places at one and the same time; their countenances are sure always to attract the notice of any novice at court; they embrace and are embraced, they laugh, talk loud, are funny, tell stories, and are of an easy disposition; they are agreeable, rich, lend money, but, after all, are of no importance.[392]

(19.) Would any person not think that to Cimon and Clitandre alone are intrusted all the details of the State, and that they alone are answerable for them? The one manages at least everything concerning agriculture and land, and the other is at the head of the navy. Whoever will give a sketch of them must express bustle, restlessness, curiosity, activity, and paint Hurry itself. We never see them sitting, standing, or stopping; no one has ever seen them walk; for they are always running, and they speak whilst running, and do not wait for an answer; they never come from any place, or go anywhere, but are always passing to and fro. Stop them not in their hurried course, for you would break their machinery; do not ask them any questions, or, if you do, give them at least time to breathe and to remember that they have nothing to do, can stay with you long, and follow you wherever you are pleased to lead them. They do not, like Jupiter's satellites,[393] crowd round and encompass their prince, but precede him and give notice of his coming: they rush with impetuosity through the crowd of courtiers, and all who stand in their way are in danger. Their profession is to be seen again and again, and they never go to bed without having acquitted themselves of such an important duty, so beneficial to the commonwealth. They know, besides, all the circumstances of every

[391] By the Castle is meant Versailles.

[392] This seems a more correct portrait of M. de Langlée than the one to be found in the chapter "Of the Gifts of Fortune," § 21 (see also page 139, note 279). Saint-Simon, in his Mémoires, often mentions him and his mother, who was the queen's chamber-maid, and through her influence at court got him introduced amongst the highest of the land. He also speaks of de Langlée's successes at play, his intimacy with the king, and the king's mistresses, favourites, and family, his want of intelligence, and his great tact, except in continually using obscene words, and finally his being an arbiter elegantiarum. Madame de Sévigné also refers to him and his familiarity.

[393] See p. 135, note 264.

petty accident, and are acquainted with anything at court people wish to ignore; they possess all the qualifications necessary for a small post. Nevertheless they are eager and watchful about anything they think will suit them as well as slightly enterprising, thoughtless, and precipitate. In a word, they both carry their heads very high, and are harnessed to the chariot of Fortune, but are never likely to sit in it.

(20.) A courtier who has not a pretty name ought to hide it under a better;[394] but if it is one that he dares own,[395] he should then insinuate that his name is the most illustrious of all names, and his house the most ancient of all others; he ought to be descended from the princes of Lorraine, the Rohans, the Châtillons, the Montmorencys,[396] and, if possible, from princes of the blood; he ought to talk of nothing but dukes, cardinals, and ministers; to introduce his paternal and maternal ancestors in all conversations, as well as the *Oriflamme*[397] and the Crusades; to have his apartments adorned with genealogical trees, escutcheons with sixteen quarters, and portraits of his ancestors and of the relatives of his ancestors; to value himself on his having an old castle with turrets, battlements, and portcullises; to be always speaking of his race, his branch, his name, and his arms; to say of a man that he is not a man of rank, of a woman that she is not of noble extraction;[398] or to ask whether Hyacinthus is a nobleman when they tell him he has drawn a great prize in the lottery.[399] If some persons laugh at such absurd remarks, he lets them laugh on; if others make erroneous comments, they are welcome; he will always assert that he takes his place after the royal family, and, by constantly repeating it, he will finally be believed.

(21.) It shows a simple mind to acknowledge at court the smallest alloy of

---

[394] Some commentators think this refers to the Duke de Bouillon, because his name means also "beef-tea," and because he wished to add to his family name, La Tour, that of d'Auvergne, but the name was illustrious. A modern commentator, M. Hémardinquer, rightly thinks it might apply to the ministers of Louis XIV., who all were descended from citizens, and took for their titles Marquis de Louvois, de Seignelay, de Barbézieux, Count de Maurepas, de Maillebois, etc., all of which titles might be considered "not pretty" as names.

[395] This points to M. de Clermont-Tonnerre, bishop of Noyon, who always boasted of his lineage, and thought himself a wit because he had been elected a member of the French Academy by the desire of the king.

[396] By the princes of Lorraine are probably meant the Guises, whose family name was de Lorraine; they were, however, princes de Joinville. The Rohans were one of the oldest families in Brittany; the Châtillons, of whom the Admiral de Coligny was one, were related to the Montmorencys, who date from the tenth century, and had been chiefly rendered famous in history by the connétable de Montmorency (1492-1567), the rival of the Duke de Guise.

[397] The Oriflamme was the banner of the Abbey of Saint-Denis, and only brought out by order of the king the moment the battle began.

[398] Demoiselle was originally the appellation given to any married or unmarried lady of noble birth, but in La Bruyère's time it was generally applied to ladies of plebeian origin. In several legal contracts our author's mother is called demoiselle veuve.

[399] There was no public lottery in France before the year 1700, but the king often had one drawn, and not seldom gave permission to hospitals and other public institutions also to have them drawn.

common blood, and not to set up for a nobleman.

(22.) At court people go to bed and rise only with a view to self; it is what they revolve in their own minds morning and evening, night and day; it is for this they think, speak, are silent or act; it is with this disposition that they converse with some and neglect others, that they ascend or descend; by this rule they measure all their assiduity, complaisance, esteem, indifference, or contempt. Whatever progress any of them seems to make towards moderation and wisdom, they are carried away by the first motive of ambition along with the most covetous, the most violent in their desires, and the most ambitious. Can they stand still when everything is in motion, when everything is stirring, and forbear running whither every one runs? Such people even think they only owe their success in life to themselves; and a man who has not made it at court is supposed not to have deserved it; and this judgment is without appeal. However, is it advisable for a man to leave the court without having obtained any advantage by his stay, or should he remain there without favour or reward? This question is so intricate, so delicate, and so difficult to decide, that a very large number of courtiers have grown old without coming to any affirmative or negative conclusion, and died, at last, without having arrived at any final resolution.

(23.) There is nothing at court so worthless and so contemptible as a man who cannot assist us in the least to better our position; I am amazed such a person dares appear there.

(24.) A man who sees himself raised far above his contemporaries, whose rank was formerly the same as his own, and who made their first appearance at court at the same time as he did, fancies it is a sure proof of his superior merit, and thinks himself better than those other people who could not keep up with him; but he forgets what he thought of himself before he became a favourite, and what he thought of those who had outstripped him.

(25.) It proves a good deal for a friend, after he has become a great favourite at court, still to keep up an acquaintance with us.

(26.) If a man who is in favour dares to take advantage of it before it is all over; if he makes use of a propitious gale to get on; if he keeps his eye on any vacancies, posts, or abbeys, asks for them, obtains them, and is stocked with pensions, grants, and reversions,[400] people will blame him for being covetous and ambitious, and will say that everything tempts him and is secured by him, his friends and his creatures; and that through the numberless and various favours bestowed on him, he, in his own person, has monopolised several fortunes. But what should he have done? I judge not so much by what people say, as by what they would have done themselves under similar circumstances, and that is precisely what he has done.

We blame those persons who make use of their opportunities for bettering their positions, because we are in a very inferior situation, and, therefore, despair

---

[400] The king usually allowed the holders of certain offices to appoint their successors, or to hold such posts conjointly. But they had to pay heavily for such survivances, as they were called, to the royal tax-gatherers and to the original holders. (See also page 130, note 254.)

of being ever in such circumstances that will expose us to a similar reproach. But if we were likely to succeed them, we should begin to think they were not so much in the wrong as we imagined, and would be more cautious in censuring them, for fear of condemning ourselves beforehand.

(27.) We should not exaggerate things, nor blame the court for evils which do not exist there. Courtiers never endeavour to harm real merit, but they leave it sometimes without reward; they do not always despise it when they have once discerned it, but they forget all about it; for a court is a place where people most perfectly understand doing nothing, or very little, for those whom they greatly esteem.

(28.) It would be very wonderful indeed, if among all the instruments I employ for building up my fortune, some of them were not to miscarry. A friend of mine who promised to speak for me does not say a single word; another speaks without any spirit; a third speaks by accident against my interests, though it was not his intention to do so. One lacks the will, another sagacity and prudence; and none of them would be sufficiently delighted in seeing me happy, and do everything in their power for making me so. Every one remembers well enough what pains he took in establishing his own position, and what assistance he got in clearing his way to obtain it. We should not be averse to acknowledge the services which certain people have rendered us, by rendering to others some service on similar occasions, if our chief and only care were not to think of ourselves when we have made our fortune.

(29.) Courtiers never employ whatever intelligence, skill, or perspicacity they may possess to find out means of obliging those of their friends who implore their assistance, but they only invent evasive answers, plausible excuses, or what they call impossibilities for moving in the matter; and then they think they have satisfied all the duties which friendship and gratitude require.

No courtier cares to take the initiative in anything, but he will offer to second him who does, because, judging of others by himself, he thinks that no one will make a beginning, and that therefore he shall not be obliged to second any one. This is a gentle and polite way of refusing to employ his influence, good offices, and mediation in favour of those who stand in need of them.

(30.) How many men almost stifle you with their demonstrations of friendship, and pretend to love and esteem you in private, who are embarrassed when they meet you in public, and at the king's levée, or at mass at Versailles, look another way, and do all they can to avoid you. There are few courtiers who have sufficient greatness of soul or confidence in themselves to dare to honour in public a man of merit but who does not occupy a grand post.

(31.) I see a man surrounded and followed by a crowd, but he is in office. I see another to whom every one says a few words, but he is a court favourite; a third is embraced and caressed even by persons of high rank, but he is wealthy; a fourth is stared at by all, and pointed at, but he is learned and eloquent. I perceive one whom nobody omits bowing to, but he is a bad man. I should like to see a man courted who is merely good and nothing else.

(32.) When a man is appointed to a new post he is inundated with praises, which flood the courtyards, the chapel, overflow the grand staircase, the vestibules, the galleries, and all the rooms of the palace;[401] he has quite enough of them, and can no longer bear it. There are not two different opinions about him; those of envy and jealousy are the same as those of adulation; every one is carried away by the raging torrent which forces a person to say what he thinks of such a man, or what he does not think of him, and often to commend a man of whom he has no knowledge. If such a man has any intelligence, merit, or valour, he becomes in one moment a genius of the first order, a hero, a demi-god; he is so extravagantly flattered in all the portraits painted of him that he appears disagreeably ugly when compared with any of them; it is impossible for him ever to reach the point to which servility and adulation would have him rise; he blushes at his own reputation. But let him not be so firmly established in the post in which he has been placed as people thought he was, and the world will without difficulty entertain another opinion. If his downfall be complete, then the very men who were instrumental in raising him so high by their applause and praise are quite ready to overwhelm him with the greatest contempt; I mean, there are none who will despise him more, blame him with greater acrimony, or deny him with more contumely than those very men who were most impassioned in speaking well of him.[402]

(33.) It may be justly said that it is easier to get appointed to an eminent and difficult post than to keep it.

(34.) We see men fallen from a high estate for those very faults for which they were appointed to it.

(35.) At court there are two ways of dismissing or discharging servants and dependants; to be angry with them, or to make them so angry with us that they leave us of their own accord.

(36.) Courtiers speak well of a man for two reasons: firstly, that he may know they have commended him; and secondly, that he may say the same of them.

(37.) It is as dangerous at court to make any advances as it is embarrassing not to make them.

(38.) There are some people who, if they do not know the name or the face of a man, make this a pretence for laughing at him. They ask who that man is; it is not Rousseau, Fabry, or La Couture,[403] for then they would know him.

[401] The original has tout l'appartement. The rooms where the courtiers danced attendance at Versailles were called thus.

[402] Some commentators imagine this refers to the Marshal de Luxembourg, who in 1675 was appointed to succeed the Prince de Condé as commander-in-chief of the army—an appointment which gave general satisfaction—and four years later fell into disgrace and was exiled. The hero who "appears deformed when compared to his portraits," seems also to refer to the Marshal, who was humpbacked. However, many other and earlier authors have made similar remarks about favourites of fortune fallen from their high estate.

[403] There were three persons named Rousseau, well known to the courtiers: an innkeeper near the Porte Saint-Denis, the doorkeeper of the King's chamber, and the fencing-master of the young royal princes. Fabry was a man who was "burned at the stake for his infamous vices about twenty years ago," says La Bruyère; and La Couture, the tailor of

(39.) I am told so many bad things of this man, and see so few in him, that I begin to suspect he has some merit which is so vexatious that it eclipses the merit of others.

(40.) You are an honest man,[404] and do not make it your business either to please or displease the favourites. You are merely attached to your master and to your duty; you are a lost man.

(41.) None are impudent by choice; but they are so constitutionally, and though it is quite wrong, yet it is natural; a man who is not born so is modest and cannot easily pass from one extreme to another. It would be useless to advise such a man to be impudent in order to be successful; a bad imitation will not do him any good, and would ensure his failure. Without real and ingenious effrontery there is not doing anything at court.

(42.) We seek, we hurry, we intrigue, we worry ourselves, we ask and are refused; we ask again and get what we ask for; but we pretend we obtained it without ever having asked for it, or so much as thought about it, and even when we had quite another thing in view. This is an obsolete style, a silly falsehood, which deceives nobody.

(43.) A man intrigues to obtain an eminent post, lays all his plans beforehand, takes all the right measures, and is on the point of being as successful as he wishes; some people are to initiate the business in hand, others are to second it; the bait is already laid, and the mine ready to be sprung; and then the candidate absents himself from the court. Who would dare suspect that Artemon ever aimed at so fine a post when he is ordered to leave his seat or his government to fill it?[405] Such an artifice and such a policy has become so stale, and the courtiers have so often employed it, that if I would impose upon the world and mask my ambition, I should always be about the prince to receive from his own hand that favour which I had solicited so passionately.

(44.) Men do not like us to pry into their prospects of bettering their position, or to find out what post they are anxious to occupy, because, if they are not successful, they fancy their failure brings some discredit upon them; and if they succeed, they persuade themselves it redounds more to their credit that the giver thought them worthy of it than that they thought themselves worthy of it, and, therefore, intrigued and plotted; they appear decked in their stateliness as well as in their modesty.[406]

Which is the greater shame, to be refused the post which we deserve, or to be put into one we do not deserve?

Difficult as it is to obtain a place at court, it is yet harder and more difficult to

the Dauphine, had become insane, and was always about the court.

[404] See page 43, note 121.

[405] The "Keys" pretend that Artemon is the Marquis de Vardes, who, after having been in exile for twenty years, intrigued to be appointed governor of the youthful Duke of Burgundy, and died in 1688, before he was successful; about a year afterwards the Duke de Beauvilliers was appointed to the vacant post.

[406] An allusion to the Duke de Beauvilliers, mentioned in the preceding note.

be worthy of filling one.

A man had better be asked by what means he obtained a certain post than why he did not obtain it.

People become candidates for any municipal office, or try to get a seat in the French Academy,[407] but formerly they endeavoured to obtain a consulship. Why should a man not labour hard during the early years of his life to render himself fit for eminent posts, and then ask openly and fearlessly, without mystery and without any intriguing, to serve his fatherland, his prince, and the commonwealth?

(45.) I never yet have seen a courtier whom a prince has appointed governor of a wealthy province, given a first-rate place, or a large pension, who does not protest, either through vanity, or to show himself disinterested, that he is less pleased with the gift than with the manner in which it was given. What is certain and cannot be doubted is that he says so.

To give awkwardly denotes the churl; the most difficult and unpleasant part is to give; then, why not add a smile?

There are, however, some men who refuse with more politeness to grant you what you ask than others know how to give;[408] and some of whom it has been said that you have to ask them so long, and they give so coldly and impose such disagreeable conditions on whatever favour you have to tear from them, that their greatest favour would be to excuse us from receiving any.[409]

(46.) There are some men at court so covetous that they catch hold of any rank or condition to reap its benefits; governments of provinces, offices, benefices, nothing comes amiss to them; they are so situated that, by virtue of their official position, they can accept any kind of favour; they are amphibious, live by the church and the sword, and one day or other will discover the secret of including the law also.[410] If you ask what those men do at court, you will be told that they receive and envy every one to whom anything is given.

(47.) A thousand people at court wear out their very existence by embracing, caressing, and congratulating all persons who have received favours, and die without having any bestowed on themselves.

---

[407] The French Academy, composed of forty members, was established on the 2d of January 1635, and still exists.

[408] It is said that the Minister of State Abel Servien (1598-1639) refused politely, and that Cardinal Mazarin (1602-1661) did not know how to give.

[409] P. Corneille, in his comedy Le Menteur (act i. scene 1), says also—

> "Tel donne à pleines mains qui n'oblige personne:
> La façon de donner vaut mieux que ce qu'on donne."

[410] Saint-Simon adopts the word amphibie from our author, and names, among others, a certain M. Saint-Romain, who was ambassador at the court of Portugal, and enjoyed the income of two abbeys. Some commentators think this paragraph refers to M. de Villeroy, who was archbishop as well as governor of Lyons, and died in 1693; whilst others suppose it alludes to the Chevalier de Hautefeuille, grand prieur d'Aquitaine, and lieutenant-general to boot.

(48.) Menophilus[411] borrows his manners from one profession and his dress from another; he goes masked all the year, though he does not conceal his countenance; he appears at court, in town, and elsewhere, always under a certain name and in the same disguise. He is found out and known by his face.

(49.) There is a highroad or a beaten road, as it is called, which leads to grand offices, and there is a cross or bye-way which is much the shortest.

(50.) We run to get a look at some wretched criminals, we line one side of the street, and we stand at the windows to observe the features and the bearing of a man who is doomed and knows he is going to die, impelled by a senseless, malignant, inhuman curiosity. If men were wise, they would avoid public executions, and then it would even be considered infamous to be present at such spectacles.[412] If you are of such an inquisitorial turn of mind, exercise your curiosity on a noble subject, and look on a happy man on the very day he has been appointed to a new post, and when he is congratulated on his nomination; read in his eyes, through his affected composure and feigned modesty, his delight and latent exultation; observe how quiet his heart beats and how serene his countenance looks now that he has obtained all he wished; how he thinks of nothing but his long life and health; how, at last, his joy bursts forth and can no longer be concealed; how he bends beneath the weight of his happiness, and how coolly and stiffly he behaves towards those who are no longer his equals; he vouchsafes them no answer, and seems not to see them; the embraces and demonstrations of friendship of men of high rank, whom he views now no more from a distance, finish his ruin; he becomes bewildered, dazed, and for a short time his brain is turned. You who would be happy and in your prince's favour, consider how many things you will have to avoid.[413]

(51.) When a man has once got into office, he neither makes use of his reason nor of his intelligence to regulate his behaviour and manners towards others, but shapes them according to his office and his position; this is the cause of his forgetfulness, pride, arrogance, harshness, and ingratitude.[414]

(52.) Theonas having been an *abbé*[415] for thirty years, grows weary of being so

---

[411] Menophilus is said to be either Father la Chaise (1624-1709), the Jesuit confessor of Louis XIV., or the celebrated Capuchin monk Joseph (1577-1638), the confidant of Cardinal Richelieu. Most likely the portrait was intended for neither.

[412] When our author wrote, it was the fashion for gentlemen and ladies of the best society to be present at public executions. Even Madame de Sévigné went with some ladies of the court to see the poisoners the Marchioness de Brinvilliers and la Voisin executed (1670 and 1680).

[413] This "happy" individual seems to have been a certain M. Boucherat, who after his nomination as chancelier de France became very arrogant.

[414] Some commentators appear to think this refers to M. de Pontchartrain (see page 143, note 288), who had been Secretary of State for more than a year when this paragraph first appeared in 1691; but this Minister was a friend and patron of our author.

[415] There were two kinds of abbés. The abbé régulier, who was always a priest, wore the habit of his order, not seldom was a high dignitary of the Church, and the abbé commendataire, who was a layman, and only enjoyed the revenues of the abbey; in time many a layman, who had no revenues whatever, either from an abbey or from any other source,

any longer. Others show less anxiety and impatience in being clad in purple than he displays in wearing a golden cross on his breast;[416] and because no great festival at court has ever made any alteration in his position,[417] he rails at the times, declares the state badly governed, and forebodes naught but ill for the future. Convinced in his heart that in courts merit is prejudicial to a man who wishes to better his position, he at last makes up his mind to renounce the prelacy; but some one hastens to inform him that he has been appointed to a bishopric, and full of joy and conceit at news so unexpected he says to a friend, "You'll see I shall not remain a bishop for ever; I shall be an archbishop yet."

(53.) There must be knaves at court[418] about the great and the Ministers of State, even if those are animated with the best intentions; but to know when to employ them is a very difficult question, and requires a certain amount of shrewdness. There are times and seasons when others cannot fill their places; for honour, virtue, and conscience, though always worthy of our respect, are frequently useless, and therefore in certain emergencies an honest man[419] cannot be employed.

(54.) An ancient author, whose very words I shall take the liberty to quote,[420] for fear I should weaken the sense of them by my translation, says: "To forsake the common herd, nay, one's very equals, to despise and vilify them; to get acquainted with rich men of rank; to join them in their private amusements, deceits, tricks, and bad business; to be brazen-faced, shameless, bankrupt in reputation; to endure the gibes and jokes of all men, and, in spite of all this, not to fear to go on, and that skilfully, has been the cause of many a man's fortune."

(55.) The youth of a prince is the making of many courtiers.

(56.) Timantes,[421] still the same, and possessed of that very merit which at first got him reputation and rewards, has deteriorated in the opinion of the courtiers, who are weary of respecting him; they bow to him coldly, forbear smiling on him, no longer accost nor embrace him, nor take him into a corner to talk mysteriously about some trivial affair; they have nothing more to say to him. He receives a pension, or is honoured by being appointed to a new post; and his virtues, almost dead in their memories, revive whilst their thoughts are refreshed; now they treat him as they did at the beginning, and even better.

(57.) How many friends, how many relatives of a new Minister, spring up in a single night! Some men pride themselves on their former acquaintance, on their

---

adopted the semi-clerical dress of an abbé and called himself so.

[416] A bishop wore a golden cross on his breast; cardinals wear purple dresses.

[417] Louis XIV. used on festive occasions to bestow various gifts on his courtiers, as well as abbeys and ecclesiastical appointments on clerical dignitaries.

[418] The "Keys" give the names of several well-known financiers as those "knaves."

[419] In the original homme de bien. (See page 43, note 121.)

[420] Our author imitates some old French writer, or at least employs antiquated words, of which the only one worthy of notice is saffranier, stained with saffron, because the houses of bankrupt traders were formerly stained yellow; hence saffranier meant "a bankrupt."

[421] Another allusion to the disgrace of the Duke de Luxembourg. (See page 195, note 402), which happened from 1679 to 1681.

having been his fellow-students or neighbours; others ransack their genealogy, go back to their great-grandfather, and recall their father and mother's side, for in some way or other every one wishes to be related to him; several times a day people affirm they are his relatives, and they would even gladly print it. They say presently: "The Minister is my friend; I am very glad of his promotion, and I ought to share in it, for he is a near relative of mine." Would those silly men, those servile votaries of fortune, those effete courtiers, have said this a week ago? Has the Minister become a more virtuous man, or more worthy of his sovereign's choice, or were they waiting for this appointment to know him better?[422]

(58.) What supports me and comforts me when sometimes men of high rank or my equals slight me, is the feeling that perhaps those very men only despise my position; and they are quite right, for it is a very humble one; but they would doubtless worship me if I were a Minister.

Am I suddenly to obtain some post, and do people know it, or foresee it, because they forestall me and bow to me first?

(59.) A man who tells us he has dined the day before at Tibur, or is going to have supper there tonight, and repeats it often, who brings in the name of Plancus'[423] about a dozen times during a few minutes conversation, such as, "Plancus asked me...." or "I said to Plancus...." is told that very moment that his hero has been snatched away by sudden death. He starts off at a tangent, gathers around him the people in the market-place or underneath the porticoes; accuses the deceased, rails at his conduct, and blackens his administration; he even denies him a knowledge of those details which the public own he had mastered, will not allow him to have had a good memory, refuses to praise him for his steadiness of character and power of work, and will not do him the honour to believe that among all the enemies of the State there was one who was Plancus' enemy.

(60.) I think it must be a pretty sight for a man of merit to observe at a meeting, or at a public entertainment, that the very seat which has been refused him is given up before his face to a man who has neither eyes to see nor ears to hear,[424] nor sense to know and to judge, and who has nothing to recommend him but his court-dress as a favourite,[425] which now he himself is above wearing.

(61.) Theodotus[426] is staid in dress, whilst his countenance, as theatrical as

[422] This new Minister was, according to some, M. Claude le Peletier (see page 54, note 1), appointed contrôleur-général des finances in 1683, and with whom the Duke de Villeroy, afterwards defeated by Marlborough at Ramillies, 1706, claimed relationship, though without any foundation. It seems more likely to have referred to M. de Pontchartrain. (See page 201, note 414.)

[423] Plancus is the Minister for War, Louvois, who died suddenly in 1691, about a year before this paragraph appeared: Tibur stands for Meudon, near Paris. In the ancient Tibur, a town of Latium to the east of Rome, and now called Tivoli, the Latin poet Horace had his country-seat; Plancus, the Consul, was one of his friends.

[424] This is a reference to Psalm cxxxv. 16, 17.

[425] In French certaines livrées, certain liveries. Can this be an allusion to the justaucorps à brevet, or coats only worn by the King's permission?

[426] The commentators suppose that a certain Abbé de Choisy (1644-1724) is meant,

an actor's who has to appear on the stage, harmonises with his voice, his carriage, gestures, and attitude. He is cunning, cautious, insinuating, mysterious; he draws near you and whispers, "It is fine weather; it is thawing." If he has no grand qualifications, he has all the little ones, even those which would scarcely become a youthful *précieuse*.[427] Imagine the application of a child building a house of cards or catching a butterfly; such is Theodotus, engaged on an affair of no consequence, and which is not worth any one's attention; he, however, treats it seriously, and as if it were of the greatest importance; he moves about, bestirs himself, and is successful; then he takes breath and rests awhile, as indeed he should, for he has given himself a good deal of trouble. Some people are intoxicated, and bewitched with the favour of the great; they think of them all day, and dream of them all night; they are always trotting up and down the stairs of a Minister's apartment, go in and come out of his ante-chamber, but they have nothing to say to him, though they speak to him; they speak to him a second time, and they are highly pleased, for they have spoken. Press them, squeeze them, and nothing will be got from them but pride, arrogance, and presumption; address them, and they do not answer; they know you not, they look bewildered, and their brain is turned; their relatives should take care of them and lock them up, lest in time their folly should drive them frantic, and make them harm some one. Theodotus has a gentler hobby; he immoderately loves favour, but his passion is less impetuous, and he worships it secretly, and fosters and serves it mysteriously; he is ever on the watch to discover who are the new favourites of the king;[428] if these wish for anything, he offers to serve them, and to intrigue for them; and stealthily sacrifices to them merit, connections, friendship, engagements, and gratitude. If the place of Cassini[429] were vacant, and a Swiss porter or postillion of a favourite were applying for it, he would support his pretensions, judge him worthy of the place, and think him capable of making observations and calculations, and of discussing about parhelions and parallaxes.[430] Should you like to know whether Theodotus be an author or a plagiary, original or a copyist, I will give you one of his works, and bid you read and judge. Who can decide, from the picture I have drawn, whether he is really pious, or merely a courtier?[431] I can with more assurance proclaim whether the stars will be propitious to him. Yes, Theodotus, I have calculated your nativity; you will obtain an appointment, and that very soon; so abandon your lucubra-

---

who passed a great part of his life dressed as a woman.

[427] See page 121, note 227.

[428] The original has tout ce qui paraît de nouveau avec les livrées de la faveur. See also page 205, note 425.

[429] The Italian astronomer T. D. Cassini (1625-1712) was the head of the Parisian Observatoire for astronomical studies.

[430] A parhelion is a mock sun or meteor near the sun, sometimes tinged with colours; a parallax is the difference between its position as seen from some point on the earth's surface and its position as seen from some other conventional point.

[431] This is a hit at the courtiers, who all simulated piety after the king had married Madame de Maintenon and revoked the edict of Nantes in 1685, and when he was wholly governed by the Jesuits. This paragraph first appeared in the seventh edition of the "Characters" in 1692.

tions, and print no more any of your writings; the public begs for quarter.

(62.) Never more expect candour, frankness, justice, good offices, services, kindness, generosity, steadiness from a man who for some time has spent all his days at court, and secretly wishes to better his fortunes. Do you know him by his face or conversation? He no longer calls things by their proper names; for him there exist no longer any knaves, rogues, fools, or impertinent people; if by chance he should say of any man what he thinks of him, that very man might come to know it, and prevent him from getting on.[432] Though he thinks ill of everybody, he speaks ill of none, for he only wishes success to himself, but would make believe that he wishes it to everybody, so that all may assist him, or at least that nobody may oppose him. Not satisfied with being insincere himself, he cannot endure that any one should be otherwise; truth offends his ear; he is indifferent, and does not care what remarks are made about the court and courtiers, but because he knows what they mean, he fancies himself an accomplice, and answerable for them. A tyrant in society and a martyr to his ambition, he is mournfully circumspect in his conduct and in his language; his raillery is innocent, but cold and constrained; his laughter is forced, his demonstrations of friendship deceptive, his conversation desultory, and his absence of mind frequent: he is profuse in his praises, and, if I may say so, pours out torrents of them whenever any man in office and a favourite does or says the smallest thing; but for any other person he is as sparing with his words as if he were consumptive. He has different formulas for complimenting people on entering or leaving a room, as well when he visits as when he is visited, and none of those who are satisfied with mere appearances and forms of speech ever leaves him discontented. He aims at getting patrons as well as partisans, and is a mediator, a confidant, and a go-between; he wishes to rule; he is as anxious as a novice to do every trifling thing that has to be observed at court; he knows where a man must stand to be seen; he can embrace you, share in your joy, ask you one question after another about your health and your affairs; and while you are answering him, he loses the thread of his curiosity, interrupts you, and begins another subject; or if he happens to see some one whom it is necessary to address in a different way, he finishes his congratulations to you whilst condoling with the other person; he weeps with one eye and laughs with the other. Sometimes, in imitation of the Ministers or the favourite, he speaks in public of trivial things, such as the wind or the frost, but, on the contrary, is silent and very mysterious about some important things he does know, and still more so about some he does not know.

(63.) There is a country[433] where all joy is conspicuous but false, and all grief hidden but real. Who would imagine that the anxiety to be present at entertainments, the raptures and applause at Molière's or Harlequin's comedies,[434] the banquets, the chase, the ballets, and *carrousels*,[435] conceal so much uneasiness, so many cares and such various interests, so many fears and expectations, so many

[432] Cheminer, in the original; a word much employed by the courtiers of Louis XIV.
[433] This country is, of course, the court.
[434] By Harlequin's comedies the Italian stage is meant.
[435] See page 174, note 356.

ardent passions, and such serious matters of business.

(64.) Court life is a serious, sad game, requiring application; a man must arrange his pieces and his plans, have a design, pursue it, thwart his adversaries, now and then venture something, and play capriciously; yet after all those fancies and contrivances he may be kept in check, and not seldom be checkmated; whilst often with well-handled men he may queen it and win the game; the most skilful or the most fortunate player obtains the victory.

(65.) The wheels, the springs, the movements of a watch are hidden, and only the hands can be seen gradually going round and finishing their course. This is a true image of a courtier, who goes over a great deal of ground, but often returns to the very same point whence he started.

(66.) "Two-thirds of my life are already gone; why, then, should I perplex myself so much about the remainder? The most brilliant career neither deserves the anxiety I suffer, nor the meannesses I accidentally commit, nor the humiliations and mortifications I have to bear. In thirty years those giants of power whom we can hardly perceive without raising our heads will be destroyed; I, who am so small, and those to whom I looked up with so much anxiety and from whom I expected all my greatness, will have disappeared. The best of all good things, if such there be in this world, is repose, retirement, and a place you can call your own." N ... was of this opinion when he was in disgrace, but he forgot it in his prosperity.[436]

(67.) A nobleman who resides in his own province, lives free, but without patronage; if he lives at court he will be patronised, but is a slave; so one thing compensates for another.

(68.) Xantippus,[437] at the uttermost end of his province, under an old roof and in a wretched bed, dreamt one night that he saw his prince, spoke to him, and felt great joy at this; when he awoke he was melancholy, told his dream, and exclaimed, "What strange fancies a man may have in his sleep!" Xantippus some time afterwards went to court, saw the prince, and spoke to him; and then his dream was more than realised, for he became a favourite.

(69.) Nobody is a greater slave than an assiduous courtier, unless it be a courtier who is more assiduous.

(70.) A slave has but one master; an ambitious man has as many masters as there are people who may be useful in bettering his position.

(71.) A thousand men scarcely known appear every day in crowds at the levée,[438] to be seen by their prince, who cannot see a thousand at a time; if to-day

---

[436] All the "Keys" say this is an allusion to the Cardinal de Bouillon; but the "Keys" are wrong, for his disgrace did not end until 1690, when this paragraph had already been two years published.

[437] Xantippus is supposed to be M. de Bontemps, the son of one of the premiers valets de chambre of the king; but this supposition seems not correct, for he was brought up at court, and was never what can be called "a favourite."

[438] See page 186, note 389.

he only sees those whom he saw yesterday and will see tomorrow, how many must be unhappy![439]

(72.) Of all those persons who dangle after men of rank, and pay their respects to them, a few honour them in their hearts, a great number follow them out of ambition or interest, but the motive of the largest number is a ridiculous vanity or a silly impatience to be noticed.

(73.) There are certain families who, according to the ways of the world, and what we call decency, ought never to be reconciled to one another; however, now they are good friends, for those whom religion could not induce to lay aside their feuds, interest, without much trouble, has linked together.

(74.) People say there exists a certain country where old men are gallant, well-mannered, and polite, young men, on the contrary, unfeeling, rude, ill-mannered, and impolite; they no longer entertain a passion for the fair sex at an age when, in other countries, young men begin to entertain it; and prefer to that sex feasts, revelry, and ridiculous amours. Amongst those people a man is considered sober and moderate who is never intoxicated with anything but wine, the excessive use of which makes it appear insipid; they endeavour by brandy, and by the strongest liquors, to revive their taste, which is already gone, and want nothing to complete their excesses but to drink *aquafortis*. The women of that country hasten the decay of their beauty by their artifices to preserve it; they paint their cheeks, eyebrows, and shoulders, which they bare, together with their breasts, arms, and ears, as if they were afraid of concealing those parts which they think will please, or of not showing enough of themselves. The countenance of the inhabitants of this country is not clear, but blurred and shrouded with a mass of hair that does not belong to them, but which they prefer to their own, and which is woven into a something to cover their heads, hanging down half way their bodies, altering all their features, and preventing people from being known by their natural faces. This nation has, besides, its God and its king: the high and mighty among them go at a fixed time every day to a temple they call a church; at the upper end of that temple stands an altar consecrated to their God, where a certain priest celebrates some mysteries, called by them holy, sacred, and formidable. The high and mighty men stand in a large circle at the foot of the altar, with their back to the priest and the holy mysteries, and their faces towards their king, who is seen kneeling in a raised and open pew, and towards whom all minds and all hearts seem directed. However, a certain kind of subordination is to be observed whilst this is going on; for this people seem to adore their prince, and their prince appears to worship God. The natives of this country call it.... It is situated about forty-eight degrees northern latitude, and more than eleven hundred leagues by sea from the Iroquois and the Hurons.[440]

(75.) Whoever will consider that a king's presence constitutes the entire hap-

[439] See also page 213, § 75.

[440] The court, Versailles, and the mass which Louis XIV. attended daily in the royal chapel are alluded to in the above paragraph. The Iroquois and the Hurons, both tribes of North American Indians, were, at the time La Bruyère wrote, considered as typical savages, and are often mentioned in the literature of the period.

piness of courtiers, that their sole occupation and satisfaction during the whole course of their lives is to see and be seen by him,[441] will in some measure understand how to behold God may constitute the glory and felicity of the saints.[442]

(76.) Great noblemen show their respect for their prince; this concerns them, as they have also their dependants. Courtiers of inferior rank are more relaxed in those duties, assume a kind of familiarity, and live like men whose examples none will follow.

(77.) What is there wanting in the youth of the present time? They can do and they know everything; or at least if they do not know as much as it is possible to know, they are as positive as if they did.

(78.) How weak are men! A great lord says of your friend Timagenes that he is a blockhead, but he makes a mistake. I do not require you to reply that Timagenes is a clever man, but only dare think he is not a blockhead.

He says also that Iphicrates is a coward; and you have seen him perform an act of bravery. But do not be uneasy. I do not insist you should relate it, but, after what you have heard this lord say, still remember that you saw him perform it.

(79.) To know how to speak to a king is perhaps the sole art of a prudent and pliant courtier. One word escapes him, which the prince hears, recollects, and sometimes lodges in his heart; there is no recalling it; all the care and skill that can be used to explain or soften it, serves only to impress it the more and to bite it in deeper. If the courtier has only spoken against himself, though this misfortune is very unusual, the remedy is at hand; he must take warning by his fault, and bear the punishment of his levity; but if another be the victim, he ought to feel dejected and contrite. Is there a better rule in such a dangerous conjuncture than to talk to our sovereign of others, of their persons, works, actions, manners, or conduct, at least with the same reserve, precaution, and care with which we talk of ourselves?

(80.) I would say that a man who tries to be witty must have a most wretched character, if it had not been said before.[443] Those persons who injure the reputation or position of others for the sake of a witticism deserve to be punished with ignominy; this has not been said before, and I dare say it.

(81.) There are a certain number of ready-made phrases which we store and use when we wish to congratulate one another. Though we often utter them without really feeling what we say, and are received without gratitude, yet we must not omit them, because, at least, they represent the very best thing in this world, namely, friendship; and since men cannot depend on one another in reality, they seem to have agreed to be satisfied with appearances.

[441] De Bussy-Rabutin, Madame de Sévigné, the Marshal de Villeroy, and the Duke de Richelieu, all describe in their writings the misery they felt on not seeing the king.

[442] This seems to be an ironical allusion to the idolatrous worship the courtiers felt, or at least pretended to feel, for Louis XIV., whom they considered "the image of the Divinity on earth."

[443] Pascal expresses a similar thought in his Pensées, vi. 19, and so do other authors. The commentators mention as known court-wits the Count de Grammont, the Duke de Roquelaure, the Duke de Lauzun, the Count de Bussy-Rabutin, and others.

(82.) With five or six terms of art, and nothing else, we set up for connoisseurs in music, painting, architecture, and gastronomy; we fancy we have more pleasure than others in hearing, seeing, or eating; we impose on our fellow-creatures and deceive ourselves.

(83.) At court there are always a certain number of people to whom a knowledge of the world, politeness, or fortune supply the want of merit;[444] they know how to enter and to leave a room; they are never embarrassed in their conversation, because they never engage in one; they please by their very taciturnity, and make themselves appear of importance by their prolonged silence, or by uttering, at most, a few monosyllables; they answer you by a glance, an intonation, a gesture, and a smile; their understanding, if I may venture on the expression, is only two inches deep, and if you fathom it, you will soon come to the bottom.

(84.) There are some men on whom favour lights as it were accidentally; they are the first it surprises and even alarms; they recollect themselves at last, and think they are worthy of their good fortune; and, as if stupidity and fortune were two things incompatible, or as if it were impossible to be lucky and foolish at one and the same time, they fancy they are intelligent, and venture, or I should rather say, are conceited enough, to speak on all occasions, on every possible subject, and without any regard for their audience. I might add that at last they become terrible, and disgust every one by their fatuity and nonsense. This is at least certain; they infallibly discredit those who assisted them in their promotion.[445]

(85.) What shall we call those who are only shrewd in the opinion of fools? I know this, that able men rank them with the people they impose upon.

A man must be very shrewd to make other people believe that he is not so sharp after all.

Shrewdness is neither too good nor too bad a quality, but is something between a virtue and a vice; there is scarcely any circumstance in which prudence cannot supply its place, and, perhaps, in which it ought not to do so.

Shrewdness is a near neighbour of rascality; there is but a step from the one to the other, and that a slippery one; falsehood only makes the difference, for add shrewdness to it, and the result is rascality.

Amongst those people who, out of shrewdness, hear everything and talk little, be sure to talk less; or, if you must talk much, say little.

(86.) You have a just and important business depending on the consent of two persons; and one of them says to you that he will favour it provided the other will agree to it, which the latter does, though he wishes to know what the first intends doing. Meanwhile nothing comes of it; and months and years roll on to no purpose. You say you are bewildered, that it is a complete mystery to you, and that

---

[444] M. de Bontemps and the Marquis de Dangeau, both of whom we have already mentioned (see page 210, note 437, and page 156, note 311), seem to be meant.

[445] The commentators give the names of several personages, all already mentioned before, such as the Count d'Aubigné, the Chancellor Boucherat, the Archbishop of Rheims, Le Tellier, and others.

all that was necessary for your success was for these two persons to meet together and to converse about it. I tell you I see through it all, and it is no mystery to me; they have met and conversed about your business.

(87.) Methinks a man who solicits for others shows the confidence of a person asking for justice, whilst he who speaks or acts for himself is as embarrassed and bashful as if he were asking a favour.

(88.) If a courtier be not continually upon his guard against the snares laid for him to make him ridiculous, he will, with all his sagacity, be amazed to find himself duped by people far less intelligent than he is.

(89.) In life some circumstances may happen when truth and simplicity prove the best policy.

(90.) If you are in favour, whatever you do is well done; you commit no faults, and every step you take leads you to the goal; but if you are not in favour, everything you do is faulty and useless, and whatever path you take leads you out of the way.

(91.) A man who has schemed for some time can no longer do without it; all other ways of living are to him dull and insipid.

(92.) Intelligence is requisite to be a schemer; yet a man may have a sufficient amount of it to be above scheming and plotting, and above subjecting himself to such things; in such a case he takes other means for bettering his fortune, or for acquiring a brilliant reputation.

(93.) Fear not, O Aristides, with your sublime intellect, your universal learning, your well-tried honesty, and your highly accomplished merits, to fall into disgrace at court, or to lose the favour of men of high rank so long as they need you.[446]

(94.) Let a favourite watch his actions very narrowly; for if I have to wait in his anteroom not so long as usual; if his countenance be more open, his forehead less clouded; if he listens to me more patiently, and sees me to the door a little farther than he used to do, I shall think he is tottering, and shall not be mistaken.

Man has but very little strength of mind, for disgrace or mortifications are needed to make him more humane, pliable, less rude, and more of a gentleman.

(95.) If we observe certain people at court, their discourses and their whole conduct show that they think neither of their grandfathers nor grandchildren; they only care for the present, and that they do not enjoy, but abuse.

(96.) Straton[447] is born under two planets, equally fortunate and unfortunate;

[446] All the "Keys" say that M. de Pomponne (1618-1699) is meant by Aristides; but he was still in disgrace when this paragraph was published (1689), and remained so for two years longer.

[447] Straton is undoubtedly the Duke de Lauzun, and his brother-in-law, the Duke de Saint-Simon, admits it. Lauzun had been a great favourite of the king, and had nearly married Louis XIV.'s cousin, Mademoiselle de Montpensier, but he was disgraced, imprisoned for ten years, partly reinstated in the king's favour, banished again from the court, and finally sent with an army of French auxiliaries to assist James II. in Ireland, where he was

his life is a romance, but with even less probability. Adventures he had none, but good and bad dreams in abundance, or, if I may say so, no dreams come up to his life. Fate has been to none more kind than to him; he is acquainted with the mean and the extremes of life; he has made a figure, been in distress, led an ordinary life, and gone through all vicissitudes. He has made himself valued for those virtues which he seriously asserted he possessed; he has said of himself, "I have intelligence and courage," and every one said after him, "He has intelligence and courage." In his good and bad fortune he has experienced the disposition of courtiers, who said of him perhaps more good and more ill than ever he deserved. When people praised him they called him pretty, amiable, rare, wonderful, and heroic; and words quite the contrary have also been employed to vilify him. His character is heterogeneous, mixed and confused; his life has been an enigma, which is not yet wholly solved.

(97.) Favour raises a man above his equals, and disgrace throws him below them.

(98.) He who one day or other deliberately abandons a great name, a great authority, or a large fortune, frees himself at once from many troubles, many restless nights, and sometimes from many crimes.

(99.) The world will be the same a hundred years hence as it is now; there will be the same stage and the same decorations, though not the same actors. All who were glad to receive favours, as well as those who were grieved and in despair for boons that were refused, shall have disappeared from the boards; others have already made their entrances who will act the same parts in the same plays, and in their turn make their exits, whilst those who have not yet appeared one day will also be gone, and fresh actors will take their places. What reliance is there to be placed on any actor?

(100.) Whoever has seen the court has seen the most handsome, the best-looking, and the most decked-out part of the world. He who despises the court after having seen it, despises the world.

(101.) The city makes a man take a dislike to the country; the country undeceives him as to the city and cares of the court.

A healthy mind acquires at court a liking for solitude and retirement.[448]

---

present at the battle of the Boyne. The Duke died in 1723, at the age of ninety.

[448] The first and last paragraphs of this chapter are an epitome of the whole.

THE GREAT

IX.

OF THE GREAT.

(1.) THE common people are so blindly prepossessed in favour of the great, and so enthusiastic about their bearing, looks, tone of voice, and manners, that if the latter would take it into their heads to be good, this prepossession would become idolatry.

(2.) If you are intrinsically vicious, O Theagenes[449] I pity you; if you have become so out of weakness for those men who have an interest in your being debauched, who have conspired to corrupt you, and boast already of their success, you will excuse me if I despise you. But if you are wise, temperate, modest, polite, generous, grateful, industrious, and besides of a birth and rank which ought to set examples rather than copy those others give, and to make rules rather than to receive them, agree with such a class of men, and be complaisant enough to imitate

---

[449] Nearly all commentators suppose that Theagenes is Phillippe de Vendôme (1655-1727), grand prieur de Malte, a grandson of Henry IV. and Gabrielle d'Estrées, and one of the most profligate men of his age; but it is more likely that La Bruyère wished to reprove his former pupil, the Duke de Bourbon, who at the time this paragraph appeared (1691) was but twenty-three years old, and addicted to very bad company.

their disorders, vices, and follies, after the respect they owe you has obliged them to imitate your virtues. This is a bitter but useful ironical remark, very suitable for securing your morals, for ruining all their projects, and for compelling them to remain as they are, and leave you as you are.

(3.) In one thing great men have an immense advantage over others; they may enjoy their sumptuous banquets, their costly furniture, their dogs, horses, monkeys, dwarfs, fools, and flatterers; but I envy them the happiness of having in their service their equals, and sometimes even their superiors, in feelings and intelligence.

(4.) Great lords delight in opening glades in forests, in raising terraces on long and solid foundations, in gilding their ceilings, in bringing a good deal of water where there was none before, in growing oranges in hothouses; but they are not anxious to restore peace to the distracted, to make joyful the afflicted, and to forestall urgent necessities, or to relieve them.

(5.) The question arises, whether, in comparing the different conditions of men, their troubles and advantages, we cannot observe such a mixture or balance of good and evil as seems to place them on an equality, or at least as makes one scarcely more desirable than another. Those men who are powerful, rich, and who want nothing may put the question, but the decision must be left to the indigent.

There is, however, a kind of charm belonging to each of those different conditions, and which lasts till misery removes it. The great please themselves in excess, their inferiors in moderation: these delight in lording and commanding; those are pleased, and even proud, to serve and to obey: the great are surrounded, complimented, and respected; the little surround, compliment, and cringe; and both are satisfied.

(6.) Good words cost the great so little, and their rank gives them such a dispensation for not keeping what they have most solemnly promised, that they really are moderate in being so sparing of those promises.

(7.) "Such a person," says some great man, "has grown old and feeble, and has worn himself out in my service. What can I do for him?" A younger competitor steps in, and obtains the post which had been refused to this unfortunate man for no other reason but that he too well deserved it.

(8.) "I do not know how it happens," you exclaim with a cold and disdainful air, "that Philanthes, though he possesses merit, intelligence, is agreeable, exact in fulfilling his duties, faithful and fond of his master, is not greatly valued by him, cannot please, and is not at all liked." — "Explain yourself; do you blame Philanthes or the great man whom he serves?"

(9.) It is often more advantageous to quit the service of great men than to complain of them.

(10.) Who can explain to me why some men get a prize in a lottery and others find favour with the great?

(11.) The great are so happily situated that in the whole course of their lives they never feel the loss of their best servants, or of persons eminent in their various capacities, and from whom they have obtained all the pleasure and profit they could. As soon as those unique persons, so difficult to replace, are dead, a host of flatterers are ready to expose their supposed weaknesses, from which, according to them, their successors are entirely free; they are convinced that these successors, whilst possessing all the skill and knowledge of their predecessors, will have none of their faults; and this is the language which consoles princes for the loss of worthy and excellent servants, and makes them satisfied with indifferent ones.[450]

(12.) The great feel a contempt for intelligent men, who have nothing but intelligence; men of intelligence despise the great, who possess nothing but greatness; a good man pities them both, if their greatness or intelligence is not allied with virtue.

(13.) When, on the one hand, I see some brisk, busy, intriguing, bold, dangerous, and obnoxious persons at the table of the great, and sometimes intimate with them, and, on the other hand, consider what difficulty a man of merit has to obtain an interview with them, I am not always inclined to believe that the wicked are tolerated out of interest, or that good men and true are looked upon as useless; but I am rather confirmed in my opinion that rank and sound judgment do not always go together, and that a liking for virtue and virtuous people is a distinct quality.

(14.) Lucilius chooses to spend his life rather in being admitted on sufferance by a few of the great than in being reduced to his living familiarly with his equals.

The custom of associating with people who are our superiors in rank ought to have some restrictions; it often requires extraordinary talents to put it into practice.[451]

(15.) Theophilus' disease seems to be incurable; he has suffered from it these thirty years, and now he is past recovery. He was, is, and will always be desirous of governing the great; death alone can extinguish with his life this craving for swaying and ruling other minds. Is it in him zeal for his neighbour's weal, or is he accustomed to it, or is it an excessive good opinion he has of himself? He insinuates himself into every palace, and does not stop in the middle of an apartment, but goes on to a window-niche or a closet; other people wait to be seen or to have an audience till he has finished his speech, which lasts generally a goodly time, during which he gesticulates much. He penetrates the secrets of many families, has a share in their good or bad fortunes; forestalls many an occasion, offers his services, and forces himself upon people so discreetly[452] that he must be admitted. The care of ten thousand souls, for which he is accountable to Providence as <u>much as for his </u>own, is not sufficient to employ his time or satisfy his ambition;

[450] This seems to be an allusion to Louis XIV., who never felt the loss of any of his ministers or officers. The latter part of the above paragraph probably refers to the successors of Turenne, Condé, and Colbert, who had all been dead some time before the year 1689, when it first appeared.

[451] If the Abbé de Choisy (see page 205, note 426) ever told La Bruyère how he was brought up, as he mentions in his Mémoires, there can be no doubt he was the original of Lucilius.

[452] In the original, il se fait de fête; an expression also used by other authors in La Bruyère's time.

there are others of a higher rank, and of more consideration, for whom he is not responsible, but of whom he officiously takes charge. He listens and watches for anything that may gratify his spirit of intrigue, meddling and muddling. A great man has scarcely set foot on shore, but he gets hold of him, and pounces upon him; and we hear that Theophilus is his guide and director before we could even suspect he had so much as thought of it.[453]

(16.) A coldness or incivility from our superiors in rank makes us hate them; but a bow or a smile soon reconciles us.

(17.) There are some proud men whom the success of their rivals humbles and mortifies; it is a disgrace which even sometimes makes them return your bow; but time, which alleviates all things, restores them at last to their natural disposition.

(18.) The contempt the great feel for the common people renders them so indifferent to their flattery or praises, that it does not feed their vanity. In like manner, princes praised continually and unreservedly by the great and the courtiers, would be more elated if they had a better opinion of those who praise them.

(19.) The great believe themselves the only persons who are the pink of perfection, and will hardly allow any sound judgment, ability, or refined feelings in any of a meaner rank; but they arrogate to themselves those qualities by virtue of their birth. However, they are greatly in error in entertaining such absurd prejudices, for the best thoughts, the best discourses, the best writings, and perhaps the most refined behaviour, have not always been found among them. They have large estates and a long train of ancestors, and there is no arguing about those facts.[454]

(20.) Have you any intelligence, grandeur of mind, capacity, taste, sound judgment? Can I believe prejudice and flattery which so boldly proclaim your merit? No! I suspect and reject them. I will not be dazzled by that look of capacity and grandeur which makes it appear as if you could act, speak, and write better than any one else; which makes you so niggardly of bestowing praise, and renders it impossible to obtain the smallest approbation from you. Hence I naturally infer that you are a favourite, have influence, and are very wealthy. How shall we describe you, Telephon?[455] We can only approach you as we do fire, namely, from a certain distance; and to form an opinion of you in a sensible and rational manner, we ought to strip you, handle you, and confront you with your equals. Your confidant, your most intimate friend, who gives you advice, for whom you give up the

---

[453] Theophilus is generally believed to have been the Abbé Roquette (1623-1707), Bishop of Autun, the supposed prototype of Molière's Tartuffe, and, according to Saint-Simon, "a man all sugar and honey, and mixed up in every intrigue." The "great man ... scarcely set foot on shore" was James II. of England, who came to France in 1689, two years before the above paragraph was published. The Abbé Roquette's character seems not so black as it has been painted, at least according to M. J. Henri Pignot's Life of him, published in 1876.

[454] Compare in the chapter "Of Personal Merit," § 33.

[455] Telephon, an odd name now, is said to be a portrait of François d'Aubusson (1625-1691), Count de la Feuillade, Duke de Rouanez, and Marshal of France, who at his cost erected a bronze monument to the glory of Louis XIV. on the Place des Victoires in Paris, where it still stands.

society of Socrates and Aristides, with whom you laugh, and who laughs louder than yourself, Davus,[456] in short, I know thoroughly; and this is enough for me to make you out.

(21.) There are some persons who, if they did know their inferiors and themselves, would be ashamed to be above them.

(22.) If there are but few excellent orators, are there many who can understand them? If good writers are scarce, are there many who can read? Thus we are always complaining of the paucity of persons qualified to counsel kings, and assist them in the administration of affairs; but if such able and intelligent personages make their appearance, and act according to their ideas and knowledge, are they beloved and esteemed as much as they deserve? Are they commended for what they plan and do for their country? They exist, that is all; they are censured if they fail, and envied if they succeed. Let us then blame the people for whom it would be ridiculous to find an excuse. The great and those in power look on their dissatisfaction and jealousy as inevitable; and, for this reason, they have been gradually induced not to take into account and to neglect their opinions in whatever they undertake, and even to consider this a rule in politics.

The common people hate one another for the injuries they reciprocally do each other; the great are execrated by them for all the harm they do, and for all the good they do not, whilst they are also blamed for their obscurity, poverty, and misfortunes.

(23.) The great think it too much condescension to have the same religion and the same God as the common people, for how can they be called Peter, John, or James, as any tradesman or labourer? Let us avoid, they say, to have anything in common with the multitude; let us affect, on the contrary, a distinction which may separate us from them; the people are welcome to the twelve apostles, their disciples, and the first martyrs, fit patrons for such folks; let them every year rejoice on some saint's day, which each celebrates as if it were his birthday;[457] but for us great people, let us have recourse to profane names, and be baptized by such patronymics as Hannibal, Cæsar, and Pompey, for they were indeed great men; by that of Lucretia, for she was an illustrious Roman lady; or by those of Rinaldo, Rogero, Oliviero, and Tancredo,[458] who were paladins and among the most marvellous heroes of romance; by those of Hector, Achilles, or Hercules, all demigods: even by those of Phœbus and Diana; and who shall prevent us from calling

---

[456] Davus is a certain Prudhomme, a proprietor of bath-and wash-houses, with whom M. de la Feuillade lodged before he became a favourite, in whom he had always the greatest confidence, and whose daughter he is supposed to have married after the death of his first wife.

[457] It is even now usual for strict Roman Catholics abroad to celebrate the day of the saint after which they are named, instead of the day on which they are born.

[458] Rinaldo is the Achilles of the Christian army in Tasso's "Jerusalem Delivered," and the rival of Orlando in Ariosto's "Orlando Furioso;" the second is the true hero of the latter poem, the third the friend and companion of Orlando, and the fourth the greatest of the Christian warriors except Rinaldo, in Tasso's poem, already mentioned.

ourselves Jupiter, Mercury, Venus, or Adonis?[459]

(24.) While the great neglect to become acquainted not only with the interests of their princes and with public affairs, but with their own, while they ignore how to govern a household or a family, boast of this very ignorance, and are impoverished and ruled by their agents, while they are satisfied with being dainty in eating and drinking,[460] with visiting Thais and Phryne,[461] talking of various packs of hounds, telling how many stages there are between Paris and Besançon or Philipsburg,[462] some citizens instruct themselves in what is going on within and without the kingdom, study the art of government, become shrewd politicians, are acquainted with the strength and weakness of an entire state, think of bettering their position, obtain a place, rise, become powerful, and relieve their prince of a portion of the cares of state. The great, who disdained them, now respect them, and think themselves fortunate in being accepted as their sons-in-law.[463]

(25.) If I compare the two most opposite conditions of men, I mean the great and the common people, the latter appear satisfied if they only have the necessities of life, and the former fretful and poor amidst superfluities. A man of the people can do no harm; a great man will do no good, and is capable of doing great mischief; the first only plans and practises useful things, the second adds to them what is hurtful. Here rusticity and frankness show themselves ingenuously; there a malignant and corrupt disposition lies hidden under a veneer of politeness. If the common people have scarcely any culture, the great have no soul; the first have a good foundation and no outward appearances; the latter are all outward appearance and but a mere superstratum. Were I to choose between the two, I should select, without hesitation, being a plebeian.

(26.) However able the great at court may be, and whatever skill they may possess in appearing what they are not, and in not appearing what they are, they cannot conceal their malice and their inclination to make fun of other people, and often to render a person ridiculous who is not really so. These fine talents are discovered in them at the first glance, and are admirable without doubt to ensnare a dupe or make a fool of a man who already was one, but are still better suited to deprive them of the pleasure they might receive from a person of intelligence, who knows how to vary and adapt his conversation in a thousand agreeable and pleasant ways, and would do so, if the dangerous inclination of a courtier to ridicule any one did not induce him to be very reserved; he, therefore, assumes a grave air,

[459] Among the great there were such names as Tancrède de Rohan, Hercule de Fleury, Achille de Harlay, Phébus de Foix, Cyrus de Brion, etc.; even citizens took grand classical or romantic names.

[460] The original has côteaux, most probably because some noblemen only drank certain wines which grew on some hill-slopes, called côteaux in French.

[461] Thais, an Athenian courtesan, mentioned in Dryden's "Alexander's Feast;" Phryne was another Athenian courtesan, said to have been Apelles' model.

[462] Philipsburg, an ancient fortified town of the Grand Duchy of Baden, had been taken by the Dauphin in 1688, after a month's siege.

[463] Among the citizens who had "become powerful" may be reckoned J. B. Colbert (see page 132, note 255), whose three daughters married dukes, and whose son married a relative of the Bourbon family.

and so effectively entrenches himself behind it, that the jokers, ill disposed as they are, cannot find an opportunity of making fun of him.

(27.) Ease, affluence, and a smooth and prosperous career are the cause why princes can take some delight in laughing at a dwarf, a monkey, an imbecile, or a wretched story; men less fortunate never laugh but when they ought to.

(28.) A great man loves champagne and hates wine from La Brie; he gets intoxicated with better wine than a man of the people; and this is the only difference between orgies in the two most opposite conditions of life, that of a lord and of a footman.

(29.) It would seem, at the first glance, that the pleasures of princes always are a little seasoned with the pleasure of inconveniencing other people. But this is not so; princes are like other men; they only think of themselves, and follow their own inclinations, passions, and convenience, which is quite natural.

(30.) One would think that the first rule of companies, of people in office and in power, is to provide those who depend on them in their business with as many obstructions as they dread those dependants might place in their way.

(31.) I cannot imagine in what a great man is happier than others, except perhaps in having more often the power as well as the opportunity of rendering a service; and if such an opportunity occurs, it seems to me that by all means he ought to embrace it. If it is for an honest man, he should be afraid of letting it slip; but as it is right to act thus, he should forestall any solicitation, and not be seen until thanks are due to him for his success: if it is an easy thing to render such a service, he should not set any value on it; if he refuses to assist this honest man, I pity them both.

(32.) Some men are born inaccessible, and yet these are the very men of whom others stand in need, and on whom they depend; they move about continually, are as restless as quicksilver, turn on their heels, gesticulate, shout, and are always in motion. Like those cardboard temples erected for fireworks during public festivals, they scatter fire and flames, thunder and lightning; and there is no approaching them until they are extinguished and have fallen down, and then only they can be handled, but are of no more use, and good for nothing.

(33.) A Swiss hall-porter, a *valet-de-chambre*, a footman, if they have no more sense than belongs to their station in life, do no longer estimate themselves by the meanness of their condition, but by the rank and fortune of those whom they serve, and without discrimination think that all people who enter by the door or ascend the staircase where they are in waiting are inferior to them and their masters; so true is it that we are doomed to suffer from the great and from all who belong to them.[464]

(34.) A man in office ought to love his prince, his wife, his children, and, next to them, men of intelligence; he ought to befriend them, surround himself with them, and never be without them; he cannot repay, I will not say with too many pensions or kindnesses, but with too great an intimacy and too many demonstrations of

---

[464] La Bruyère had, no doubt, experienced this when at the Duke de Condé's.

friendship, the assistance and the services they render him even when he does not suspect it. What rumours do they not scatter to the winds? How many stories do they not prove to be but fable and fiction? How well do they understand to justify want of success by good intentions, and demonstrate the soundness of a project and the correctness of certain measures by a prosperous issue; raise their voices against malice and envy, and prove that good enterprises proceed from the best of motives; put a favourable construction on wretched appearances, palliate slight faults, exhibit only virtues and place them in the best light; spread on innumerable occasions a report of facts and details which redound to their patron's honour, and make a jest of those who dare doubt it or advance anything to the contrary. I know it is a maxim with great men to let people speak, while they themselves continue to act as they think fit; but I also know that it not seldom happens that their carelessness in paying attention to what people say of them prevents them from performing the actions they intended.

(35.) To be sensible of merit, and, when known, to treat it well, are two great steps quickly to be taken one after another, but of which few great men are capable.

(36.) You are great, you are powerful, but this is not enough; act in such a manner that I can esteem you, so that I should be sorry to lose your favour, or sorry I was never able to obtain it.

(37.) You say of a great man or of a person in office, that he is very obliging, kind, and delights in being serviceable; and you confirm this by giving details of everything he has done in a certain business, in which he knew you took some interest. I understand what you mean; you succeed without any solicitation, you have influence, you are known to the ministers of state, you stand well with the great. What else would you have me understand?

A man tells you, "I think I am not very well treated by a certain personage; he has become proud since he has bettered his position; he treats me with contempt and no longer knows me." You answer, "I have no reason to complain of him; on the contrary, I must commend him; he even seems to be to be very civil." I believe I understand you too. You would let us know that some person in office has a regard for you, that in the anteroom he selects you from a large number of cultured gentlemen from whom he turns aside, to avoid the inconvenience of bowing to them or smiling on them.

"To commend some one, to commend some great man," is a nice phrase to start with, and which doubtless means to commend ourselves, when we relate all the good some great man has done to us, or never thought of doing to us.

We praise the great to show we are intimate with them, rarely out of esteem or gratitude; we often do not know the persons we praise; vanity and levity not seldom prevail over resentment; we are very dissatisfied[465] with them, and yet we praise them.

---

[465] The original has mal content, for, during the seventeenth century, mal was more generally placed before an adjective than now; at present mécontent would be used, which, when La Bruyère wrote, had often the meaning of "a rebel."

(38.) If it is dangerous to be concerned in a suspicious affair, it is much more so when you are an accomplice of the great; they will get clear and leave you to pay double, and for them and for yourself.[466]

(39.) A prince's fortune is not large enough to pay a man for a base complacency, if he considers what it costs the man whom he would reward; and all his power is not sufficient to punish him, if he measures the punishment by the injury done to him.

(40.) The nobility expose their lives for the safety of the state and the glory of their sovereign, and the magistrates relieve the prince of part of the burden of administering justice to his people. Both these functions are sublime and of great use, and men are scarcely capable of performing higher duties; but why men of the robe and the sword reciprocally despise each other is beyond my comprehension.

(41.) If it be true that the great venture more in risking their lives, destined to be spent in gaiety, pleasure, and plenty, than a private person who ventures only a life that is wretched, it must also be confessed that they receive a wholly different compensation, namely, glory and a grand reputation. The common soldier entertains no thoughts of becoming known, and dies unnoticed, among many others; he lived indeed very much in the same way, but still he was alive; this is one of the chief causes of the want of courage in people of low and servile condition. On the contrary, those personages whose birth distinguishes them from the common people, and who are exposed to the gaze of all men, to their censures and praises, exert themselves more than they were predisposed to do, even if they are not naturally courageous;[467] and this elevation of heart and mind, which they derive from their ancestors, is the cause of courage being usually found among persons of noble birth, and is perhaps nobility itself.

Press me into the service as a common soldier, I am Thersites; put me at the head of an army for which I am responsible to the whole of Europe, and I am Achilles.[468]

(42.) Princes, without any science or rules, can form a judgment by comparison; they are born and brought up amidst the best things, with which they compare what they read, see, and hear. Whoever does not approach Lulli, Racine, and Le Brun[469] they condemn.

(43.) To talk to young princes of nothing but their rank is an excess of precaution, while all courtiers consider it their duty and part and parcel of their politeness to respect them; so that they are less apt to ignore the regard due to their

---

[466] Gaston d'Orléans (1608-1660), the brother of Louis XIII., and even the Prince de Condé were examples of such "great."

[467] The original has vertu, in the sense of the Latin virtus, courage.

[468] Thersites, according to the Iliad, was squinting, humpbacked, loquacious, loud, coarse, and scurrilous, but he was not a "common soldier," but a chief. Achilles was the hero of the allied Greek army besieging Troy.

[469] Le Brun (1616-1690), a celebrated painter, was still alive when this paragraph appeared. For Lulli and Racine, see page 46, note 124, and page 11, note 33. Compare also page 226, § 19.

birth than to confound persons, and treat all sorts of ranks and conditions of men indifferently, or without distinction. They have an innate pride which they show when needed; they only have to be taught how to regulate it, and how to acquire kindness of heart, culture, gentlemanly manners, and sound discrimination.

L.F. BRUN

(44.) It is downright hypocrisy in a man of a certain position not at once to take the rank due to him, and which every one is willing to yield; he need not trouble himself to be modest, to mingle with the crowd that opens and makes way for him, to take the lowest seat at a public meeting, so that every one may see him there and run to lead him to a higher place. Modesty in men of ordinary condition is more trying; if they push themselves into a crowd, they are almost crushed to death, and if they choose an uncomfortable seat, they may remain there.[470]

(45.) Aristarchus hies to the market-place with a herald and a trumpeter, who blows on his instrument, so that a crowd comes running and gathers round him: "Oyez! Oyez! people!"[471] exclaims the herald, "be attentive; silence! silence! This very Aristarchus, whom you see before you, is to do a good action to-morrow." I would have said, in more simple and less ornate style: "Aristarchus has done well; is he now going to do better? If so, let me not know that he does well, or at least let me not suspect that I should be told it."[472]

(46.) The best actions of men are spoiled and weakened by their manner of doing them, which sometimes leaves even a suspicion of the purity of their intentions. Whoever protects or commends virtue for virtue's sake, or condemns and blames vice for the sake of vice, acts without design, naturally, without any artifice or peculiarity, pomp or affectation; he neither replies demurely and sententiously, and still less makes sharp and satirical remarks;[473] he never acts a part for the benefit of the public, but he shows a good example and acquits himself of his duty; he is not a subject to be talked about when ladies visit one another, nor for the *cabinet*,[474] nor amongst the newsmongers;[475] he does not provide an amusing gentleman with a subject for a funny story. The good he does is, indeed, a little less known, but good he does, and what more could he desire?

(47.) The great ought not to like the early ages of the world, for they are not favourable to them, and they must feel mortified to see that we are all descended from one brother and sister. All mankind form but one family, and the whole difference is merely in the nearer or remote degree of relationship.

(48.) Theognis[476] is very dandified in his dress, and goes abroad decked out like a lady; he is scarcely out of the house, and already his looks and countenance are arranged in a studied manner, so that he is fit to appear in public, and that the

---

[470] Achille de Harlay (1639-1712), President of the Parliament of Paris, and descended from an illustrious line of magistrates, is said to have feigned an excess of modesty which was not natural to him. See also page 45, note 122.

[471] This beginning of every English town-crier's oration, pronounced "Oh yes! Oh yes!" is merely the imperative of the defective French verb, ouir, "to hear," now seldom used, except in the present infinitive and in proverbial phrases.

[472] Aristarchus also refers to the above President, whose liberality, according to public rumour, was somewhat ostentatious.

[473] Another allusion to M. de Harley, whose "wise saws and modern sayings" were proverbial.

[474] A cabinet was a sort of social circle in Paris, where people generally met to exchange small talk and to hear the news or lectures on all subjects.

[475] See page 19, note 68.

[476] M. de Harlay (1625-1695), Archbishop of Paris, is said to have been the original of Theognis. (See page 46, § 26.) He was the nephew of the President mentioned on the previous page, note 122.

passers-by may behold him gracefully bestowing his smiles on them. If he enters any apartments at court, he turns to the right, where there is a large number of people, and to the left, where there are none; he bows to those who are there and to those who are not; he embraces the first man he meets, presses his head against his bosom, and then asks his name. Some one wants his assistance in a very easy matter of business; he waits on Theognis, and presents his request, to which the latter kindly listens, is delighted in being of use to him, and entreats him to procure him opportunities of serving him; but when the other comes to the point, Theognis tells him it lies not in his power to help him, begs him to fancy himself in his position, and to judge for himself. The postulant leaves, is seen to the door and caressed by Theognis, and becomes so embarrassed that he is almost satisfied with his request being refused.

(49.) A man must have a very bad opinion of mankind and yet know them well to believe he can impose on them with studied demonstrations of friendship and long and useless embraces.

(50.) Pamphilus[477] does not converse with the people he meets in the apartments at court or in the public walks; but some persons would think by his serious mien and his loud voice that he admits them into his presence, gives them audience, and then dismisses them. He has a stock of phrases, at once civil and haughty; an imperious, gentlemanly kind of civility, which he makes use of without any discrimination; a false dignity which debases him, and is very troublesome to his friends who are loth to despise him.

A true Pamphilus is full of his own merit, keeps himself always in view, and never forgets his ideas about his grandeur, alliances, office, and dignity; he takes everything belonging to his escutcheon, and produces it when he wants to show off; he speaks of his order and his blue ribbon,[478] which he displays or hides with equal ostentation. A Pamphilus, in a word, would be a great man, and believes he is one; but he really is not, and is only an imitation one. If at any time he smiles on a person of the lower orders, or a man of intelligence, he chooses his time so well that he is never caught in the fact; and were he unfortunately caught in the least familiarity with a person neither rich, powerful, nor the friend of a minister of state, his relative, nor one of his household,[479] he would blush up to his ears; he is very severe, and shows no mercy to a man who has not yet made his fortune. One day he sees you in a public walk and avoids you; the next day he meets you in a less public place, or, if it be public, in the company of some great man, and he takes courage, comes up to you, and says, "Yesterday you pretended not to see

---

[477] Pamphilus is the Marquis de Dangeau, of whom we have already spoken (see page 156, note 311), and who made himself ridiculous by his excessive vanity. Saint-Simon, in his Mémoires, calls the Marquis un Pamphile, but our author speaks of les Pamphiles, and describes them at three different times, namely, in 1681, 1691, and 1692.

[478] See page 47, note 127. When this paragraph appeared, the Marquis de Dangeau had been already three years a Knight of the Order of the Holy Ghost. The knights of this order wore a cross hanging from a broad blue ribbon, which were both depicted around their escutcheon.

[479] See page 70, note 171.

me." Sometimes he will leave you abruptly to go and speak to some lord and to the secretary of some minister,[480] and sometimes, finding that you are in conversation with them, he will pass between you and them[481] and take them away. Meet him at any other time and he will not stop; you must run and then he'll speak so loud as to expose you and him to all within hearing. Thus the Pamphiluses live, as it were, always on a stage; they are a class nurtured in dissimulation, who hate nothing more than to be natural, and who are real actors as much as ever Floridor and Mondori[482] were.

We can never say enough of the Pamphiluses; they are servile and timorous before princes and ministers; proud and overbearing to people who are merely virtuous; dumbfounded and embarrassed before the learned; brisk, forward, and positive before the ignorant. They talk of war to a lawyer and of politics to a financier; they pretend to know history among women, are poets among doctors, and mathematicians among poets. They do not trouble themselves about maxims, and less about principles; they live at random, are wafted onward and carried away by a blast of favour and the attractions of wealth; they have no feelings of their own, but they borrow them as they want them, and the person to whom they apply is neither a wise, able, nor virtuous man, but a man of fashion.

(51.) We nourish a fruitless jealousy and an impotent hatred against the great and men in power, which, instead of avenging us for their splendour and position, only adds to our own misery the galling load of another's happiness. What is to be done against such an inveterate and contagious disease of the mind? Let us be satisfied with little, and, if possible, with less; let us learn to bear those losses which may occur; the prescription is infallible, and I will try it. Then I shall refrain from bribing a doorkeeper or from mollifying a secretary;[483] from being driven from the door by a large crowd of candidates and courtiers which a minister's house[484] disgorges several times a day; from repining in an ante-chamber, from presenting to him, whilst trembling and stammering, a well-founded request; from bearing with his stateliness, his bitter laugh and his laconism. Now I neither hate nor envy him any more; he begs nothing of me, nor I of him; we stand on the same footing, unless perhaps that he is never at rest, and that I am.

(52.) If the great have frequent opportunities of doing us good, they seldom wish to do so; and if they wanted to injure us it lies not always in their power; therefore the sort of worship we pay them may frustrate our expectations, if rendered from other motives but hope or fear. A man may sometimes live a long

---

[480] Such an official was in our author's time called le premier commis.

[481] The original has il vous coupe, "he will cut you," an expression also used by Saint-Simon and Madame de Sévigné; the English phrase "to cut a person," in the sense of passing by him without pretending to see him, seems almost to have the same primary meaning.

[482] Two celebrated actors of the seventeenth century; Floridor, whose real name was Josias Soulas de Frinefosse, died in 1672, and Mondori in 1651.

[483] See page 240, note 480.

[484] This minister is said to have been Louvois (see page 204, note 423), who liked to have many postulants about him.

while without depending on them in the least, or being indebted to them for his good or bad fortune. We ought to honour them, as they are great and we little, and because there are others less than ourselves who honour us.

(53.) The same passions, the same weaknesses, the same meannesses, the same eccentricities, the same quarrels in families and among relatives, the same jealousies and antipathies prevail at court and in town.[485] You find everywhere daughters-in-law, mothers-in-law, husbands and wives; divorces, separations, and patched-up reconciliations; everywhere fancies, fits of passion, partialities, tittle-tattle, and what is called evil-talking. An observer would easily imagine that the inhabitants of a small town or of the Rue Saint-Denis were transported to V ... or to F....[486] In these two last places people display, perhaps, more pride, haughtiness, and perhaps more decorum in hating one another; they injure one another with more skill and refinement; their outbursts of rage are more eloquent, and they insult one another with more politeness and in a more select phraseology; they do not defile the purity of the language, they only offend men or blast their reputations; the outside of vice is handsome, but in reality, I say it again, it is the same as in the most abject conditions, for whatever is base, weak, and worthless is found there. These men so eminent by their birth, by favour, or by their position, these minds so powerful and so sagacious, these women so polished and so witty, are themselves but common people, though they despise common people.

The words "common people" include several things; they are a comprehensive expression, and we may be surprised to see what they contain and how far they extend. The common people, in opposition to the great, signify the mob and the multitude; but, as opposed to wise, able, and virtuous men, they include the great as well as the little.

(54.) The great are governed by sensations; their minds are unoccupied, and everything makes immediately a strong impression on them. If anything happens, they talk about it too much; soon after they talk about it but little, and then not at all, nor ever will; actions, conduct, execution, incidents are all forgotten; expect from them neither amendment, foresight, reflection, gratitude, nor reward.

(55.) We are led to two opposite extremes with regard to certain persons. After their death satires about them are current among the people, while the churches re-echo with their praises. Sometimes they deserve neither those libels nor these funeral orations, and sometimes both.

(56.) The less we talk of the great and powerful the better; if we say any good of them, it is often almost flattery; it is dangerous to speak ill of them whilst they are alive, and cowardly when they are dead.

---

[485] See page 164, note 322.

[486] The Rue Saint-Denis was a street in Paris crowded with small tradesmen, and still exists. Our author was nearly always afraid of clearly mentioning Versailles or Fontainebleau, and very often employed only the initial letters and asterisks or dots.

THE PRICE OF GLORY

X.

OF THE SOVEREIGN AND THE STATE.[487]

(1.) WHEN we have cursorily examined all forms of government without partiality to the one of our fatherland, we cannot decide which to choose; they are all a mixture of good and evil; it is, therefore, most reasonable to value that of our native land above all others, and to submit to it.

(2.) Tyranny has no need of arts or sciences, for its policy, which is very shallow and without any refinement, only consists in shedding blood; it prompts us to murder every one whose life is an obstacle to our ambition; and a man naturally cruel has no difficulty in doing this. It is the most detestable and barbarous way of maintaining power and of aggrandisement.

(3.) It is a sure and ancient maxim in politics that to allow the people to be lulled by festivals, spectacles, luxury, pomp, pleasures, vanity, and effeminacy, to occupy their minds with worthless things, and to let them relish trifling frivolities, is efficiently preparing the way for a despotism.

----

[487] The original république, which was inserted for the first time in the fourth edition of the "Characters," is used in the sense of the Latin respublica.

(4.) Under a despotic government the love for one's native land does not exist; self-interest, glory, and serving the prince supply its place.

(5.) To innovate or introduce any alterations in a state is more a question of time than of action; on some occasions it would be injudicious to attempt anything against the liberties of the people, and on others it is evident that everything may be ventured on. Today you may subvert the freedom, rights, and privileges of a certain town, and to-morrow you must not so much as think of altering the sign-boards of their shops.[488]

(6.) In public commotions we cannot understand how the people can ever be appeased, nor in quiet times imagine as little what can disturb them.

(7.) A government connives at certain evils in order to repress or prevent greater ones. There are others which are only evils because they originally sprang from abuses or bad customs, but these are less pernicious in their consequences and practice than would be a juster law or a more reasonable custom. Some kind of evils, which indeed are very dangerous, are curable by novelty and change: other evils are hidden and under ground, as filth in a common sewer; these are buried in shame, secrecy, and obscurity, and cannot be stirred up or raked about, without exhaling poison and infamy; so that the ablest men sometimes doubt whether it be more judicious to take notice of them or to ignore them. The State not seldom tolerates a comparatively great evil to keep out millions of lesser ills and inconveniences which otherwise would be inevitable and without remedy. Some there are,[489] which are greatly complained of by private persons, but which tend to benefit the public, though the public be only an aggregate of those self-same private persons; other ills a person suffers which turn to the good and advantage of every household; others, again, afflict, ruin, and dishonour certain families, but tend to benefit and preserve the working of the machinery of the State and of the government. Finally, there are some which subvert governments and cause fresh ones to arise on their ruins; and instances can be quoted of others which have undermined the foundations of great empires, and utterly destroyed them, merely to diversify and renew the surface of the globe.

(8.) What does the State care whether Ergastes be rich, has a good pack of hounds, invents new fashions in carriages and dress, and wantons in superfluities? Is the interest of a private person to be considered when the interest and convenience of the public are in question? When the burdens of the people weigh a little heavy, it is some comfort for them to know that they relieve their prince and enrich him alone; but they do not think they are obliged to contribute to the fortune of Ergastes.

----

[488] During the reign of Louis XIV., the signboards, which were often very large, swung above the heads of the passers-by, and the police tried in vain to reduce their dimensions or to have them fixed against the walls. Sometimes the government interfered in the municipal or provincial elections without any opposition, and sometimes a diminution of town councillors, or a promulgation of a stamp act for legal documents, was violently resisted, and the rebellion had to be quenched by an armed force, as, for example, in Guienne and Brittany from 1673 till 1675.

[489] Taxes are meant here.

(9.) Even in the most remote antiquity, and in all ages, war has existed, and has always filled the world with widows and orphans, drained families of heirs, and destroyed several brothers in one and the same battle. Young Soyecourt![490] I mourn your loss, your modesty, your intelligence, already so developed, so clear, lofty, and communicative; I bewail that untimely death which carried you off, as well as your intrepid brother, and removed you from a court where you had barely time to show yourself; such a misfortune is not uncommon, but nevertheless should be deplored! In every age men have agreed to destroy, burn, kill, and slaughter one another, for some piece of land more or less; and to accomplish this with the greater certainty and ingenuity, they have invented beautiful rules, which they call "strategy." When any one brings these rules into practice, glory and the highest honours are his reward, whilst every age improves on the method of destroying one another reciprocally. An injustice committed by the first men was the primary occasion for wars, and made the people feel the necessity of giving themselves masters to settle their rights and pretensions. If each man could have been satisfied with his own property and had not infringed on that of his neighbours, the world would have enjoyed uninterrupted peace and liberty.

(10.) They who sit peaceably by their own firesides among their friends, and in the midst of a large town, where there is nothing to fear either for their wealth or their lives, breathe fire and sword, busy themselves with wars, destructions, conflagrations, and massacres, cannot bear patiently that armies are in the field and do not meet; or, if in sight, that they do not engage; or, if they engage, that the fight was not more sanguinary, and that there were scarcely ten thousand men killed on the spot. They are sometimes so infatuated as to forget their dearest interests, their repose and security, for the sake of change, and from a liking for novelty and extraordinary events; some of them would even be satisfied with seeing the enemy at the very gates of Dijon or Corbie,[491] with beholding chains stretched across the streets and barricades thrown up, for the satisfaction of hearing and of communicating the news.

(11.) Demophilus, on my right, is full of lamentations, and exclaims, "Everything is lost; we are on the brink of ruin; how can we resist such a powerful and general league?[492] What can we do, I dare not say to vanquish, but to make head

---

[490] Adolphe de Belleforière, Chevalier de Soyecourt, a captain of the gendarmes of the Dauphin, died two days after the battle of Fleurus (July 1, 1690), of wounds received in this battle, in which his elder brother, the Marquis de Soyecourt, was also killed. Both those young men were the sons of Maximilien Antoine, Marquis de Soyecourt, grand veneur, who died in 1679, and was the original of Dorante in Molière's comedy Les Fâcheux. The name of the Marquis is often mentioned in the lampoons of the times for his reputation of valour in other fields than those of Mars. La Bruyère was a friend of the family, whose name was always pronounced Saucourt, and even sometimes written so.

[491] Dijon, the former capital of Burgundy, had been besieged in 1515 by thirty thousand men, who retired after the conclusion of a treaty of peace which the king, Francis I., did not ratify. Corbie, a town in Picardy, was taken when Burgundy and Picardy were invaded by the Imperials in 1636.

[492] This refers to the League of Augsburg, a coalition of England, Germany, Spain, Holland, Sweden, and Savoy against Louis XIV., with whom they were at war when this

by ourselves against so many and such powerful enemies? There never was anything like it as long as the monarchy has existed! A hero, an Achilles, would have to succumb! Besides," adds he, "we have committed some very serious blunders; I know what I am talking about, for I have been a soldier myself; I have seen some battles, and have learned a good deal from studying history." Then he falls to admiring Olivier le Daim and Jacques Cœur,[493] who, according to him, were men after his own heart, and ministers indeed. He retails his news, which is sure to be the most melancholy and disadvantageous that could be invented. Now a party of our soldiers has fallen into an ambush, and are cut to pieces; presently some of our troops, shut up in a castle, surrender at discretion, and are all put to the sword. Should you tell him that such a report is incorrect, and wants confirmation, he will not listen to you, but affirms that a general has been killed, and though it is certain that he has only been slightly wounded, and you tell him so, he deplores his death, is sorry for the widow, the children, and the State, and is even sorry for himself, for he has lost a good friend and an influential person. He tells you the German horse are invincible, and turns pale if you but name the Imperial cuirassiers.[494] "If we attack such a place," continues he, "we shall be obliged to raise the siege; we shall have to remain on the defensive without engaging in action, or if we do fight, we shall certainly be beaten, and then the enemy will be upon the frontiers." Demophilus gives them wings, and brings them presently into the heart of the kingdom; he fancies he already hears the alarm-bells ring in the towns, and thinks of his property and his estate; he does not know where to take his money, his movables, and his family, and whether to escape to the Swiss Cantons or to Venice.

But Basilides, on my left, raises suddenly an army of three hundred thousand men, and will not abate a single troop; he has a list of all the squadrons, battalions, generals, and officers, not omitting the artillery and baggage. All these troops are at his entire disposal; some he sends into Germany, others into Flanders, reserves a certain number for the Alps, a smaller quantity for the Pyrenees, and conveys the rest beyond seas; he knows their marches, he can tell what they will do, and what they will not do; you would think he had the King's ear, or was the minister's confidant. If the enemies are beaten,[495] and lose about nine or ten thousand men, he positively avers it was thirty, neither more nor less; for his numbers are always as settled and certain as if he had the best intelligence. Tell him in the morning we have lost a paltry village, he not only puts off a dinner to which the day before he had invited his friends, but does not take any dinner himself on that day; and if he eats a supper it is without appetite. If we besiege a town strong through its natural

paragraph was published in 1691.

[493] Olivier le Daim, first the barber of Louis XI. (1423-1483), became his favourite, but was hanged in 1484, after that king's death. Jacques Cœur, a rich merchant, rendered great services to Charles VII. (1403-1461), became his treasurer, and was accused of peculation; thrown into prison, he escaped, and died in exile in 1461. The characters of both these men were not very well known when La Bruyère wrote.

[494] The Imperial cavalry had a well-deserved reputation for cruelty and rapaciousness.

[495] Another allusion to the battle of Fleurus, won by the Marshal de Luxembourg about a year before this paragraph was published (1691).

position, and regularly fortified,[496] well stored with provisions and ammunition, defended by a good garrison, commanded by a brave general, he tells you the town has its weak spots, which are badly fortified, is in want of powder, has a governor who lacks experience, and will capitulate eight days after the trenches are opened. Another time he runs himself quite out of breath, and after he has recovered himself a little he exclaims, "I have some important news for you; our enemies are beaten and totally routed; the general and principal officers, or at least the greater part of them, are all killed, or have perished. What a tremendous slaughter! We certainly have been very lucky!" Then he sits down and takes a rest, after having told us the news, which only wants a trifle more confirmation; for it is certain there has been no battle at all. He assures us further that some prince, dreading our arms, has abandoned the League and left his confederates in the lurch, and that a second is inclined to follow his example; he believes firmly, with the populace, that a third is dead,[497] and names you the place where he is buried; and even when the common people[498] are undeceived, he offers to lay a wager it is true. He knows for a fact that T. K. L. is very successful against the Emperor,[499] that the Grand Turk[500] is making formidable preparations, and will not hear of peace; and that the Vizier will once more show himself before Vienna.[501] He claps his hands and is as delighted as if there were not the smallest doubt about it. The triple alliance[502] is a Cerberus[503] with him, and the enemy only so many monsters to be knocked on the head. He talks of nothing but laurels, palm-branches, triumphs, and trophies; in conversation he speaks of "our august hero, our mighty potentate, our invincible monarch," and whatever you do, you will not get him to say simply, "The King has a great many enemies; they are powerful, united, and exasperated; he has conquered them, and I hope he will always do so." This style, too bold and decisive for Demophilus, is not sufficiently pompous or grandiloquent for Basilides; his head is full of other expressions; he is planning inscriptions for triumphal arches and pyramids to adorn the capital when the conqueror will enter it; and as soon as he hears that the armies are in sight of each other, or that a town is invested, he has his clothes hung out and aired, so that they should be

---

[496] This refers to Mons, besieged by Vauban, and taken on the 9th of April 1691.

[497] In the month of July 1690, a rumour spread in Paris that William III. was dead, upon which many people publicly rejoiced, until the news came that the report was false. The "Keys" of the old English versions name for the first and second prince "the Duke of Savoy and the king of Spain."

[498] The original has halles et fauxbourgs, "markets and suburbs."

[499] The letters T. K. L. stand for Tækely, a Hungarian nobleman who broke out in open rebellion against the Emperor of Austria, Leopold I. (1640-1705), and gained a victory over the Imperial troops on the 21st of August 1690.

[500] At that time the Sultan was Soliman II., who only reigned from 1687 until 1691.

[501] The Grand Vizier Kara-Mustapha laid siege to Vienna in 1683.

[502] A league formed in the Hague against France was called "The Triple Alliance," and was entered upon in 1668 between England, Holland, and Sweden. Sometimes the treaty formed in 1717 between George I., the Regent of France, and the United Provinces is also called "Triple Alliance."

[503] Cerberus, a dog with three heads, which keeps guard in the infernal regions.

ready when a *Te Deum* is sung in the cathedral.[504]

(12.) A business which has to be discussed by the plenipotentiaries or by the diplomatic agents of crowned heads and republics must needs be unusually intricate and difficult if its conclusion requires a longer time than the settling of the preliminaries, nay, even than the mere regulating of ranks, precedences, and other ceremonies.

A minister or a plenipotentiary is a chameleon or a Proteus;[505] sometimes, like a practised gambler, he hides his temper and character, either to avoid any conjectures or guesses, or to prevent any part of his secret escaping through passion or weakness; and at other times he knows how to assume any character most suited to his designs, or which is required, as it may be his interest artfully to appear to other people as they think he really is. Thus when he intends to conceal that his master is very formidable or very weak, he is resolute and inflexible to prevent any large demands; or he is easygoing, so as to give others an opportunity of making some demands, and so secure the same liberty. At other times he is either diplomatic and disingenuous, so as to veil a truth whilst telling it, because it is of some importance to him to have it divulged but not believed; or else he is free and open, so that when he wishes to conceal what should not be known, people should nevertheless believe that he is acquainted with everything they wish to know, and be convinced that they have been told everything. In like manner he is fluent and verbose to excite others to talk, or prevent their saying what he does not wish or ought not to hear; to speak of many and various things which modify and destroy each other, and leave the mind hovering between confidence and distrust; to make amends for an expedient thoughtlessly proposed by suggesting another; or he is sedate and taciturn to induce others to talk, to listen for a long time, so that he may afterwards obtain the same favour himself, speak with authority and weight, and utter promises or threats which will influence people and produce a strong impression. He begins and speaks first, the better to discover the opposition and contradictions, the intrigues and cabals, of foreign ministers about some proposals he has made, to take his measures and reply to them; and at another meeting he speaks last, that he may be sure not to speak in vain, and to be exact, so as perfectly to be aware on what support he can reckon for his master and his allies, as well as to know what he ought to ask and what he can get. He knows how to be clear and explicit, or still better, how to be ambiguous and obscure, and to use words and phrases with a double meaning, which he can render more or less forcible as the occasion or his interest may require. He asks for a little because he will not grant much; he asks for much to make sure of a little. At first he insists upon getting a few trifling things, which he afterwards pretends to be of small value, so as not to prevent him for asking for one of greater value; he avoids, on the contrary, to gain at first an important point, if it is likely to prevent him from obtaining several

[504] According to the commentators, two insignificant newsmongers are supposed to be portrayed in Demophilus and Basilides, an Abbé de Sainte-Hélène and a certain du Moulinet, whom some think might have been an abbé or a magistrate, because instead of clothes he speaks of his robe or gown.

[505] Proteus, in the mythology, is a sea-god residing in the Carpathian Sea, who could change his form at will.

others of less importance, but which, when united, exceed the other in value. His demands are extravagant, but he knows beforehand they will be denied, so he is provided with a convenient excuse for refusing those he knows will be made, and which he does not wish to grant; as industrious to aggravate the enormity of these demands, and to let his adversaries admit, if possible, that there may be reasons why they cannot agree, as to weaken those which they pretend to have for not granting him what he solicits so urgently; and as diligent in vaunting and in enlarging upon the little he has to offer as he is in despising openly the little they are willing to grant. He pretends to make some extraordinary proposals which beget distrust, and cause to be rejected what indeed, if accepted, could not be performed; this also serves to colour his exorbitant demands, and throws on his antagonists the responsibility of a refusal. He grants more than is asked, so as to get still more than he gives. You have to pray, entreat, and beseech him for a long time to obtain some trifling favour, so as to destroy all expectations and uproot all thoughts of asking anything more important of him; or, if he is persuaded to grant it, it is always on such conditions that he may share in its profits and advantages. He directly or indirectly espouses the interest of an ally, if he finds it at the same time conducive to the advancing of his own pretensions; he talks of nothing but peace and alliances, the public tranquillity and the public interests, and thinks, indeed, only of his own, or rather of his master's and the State's he represents. Sometimes he reconciles some people who were opposed to one another, and sometimes he divides those who were united; he intimidates the powerful and encourages the weak; he draws several weak States into a league against a more powerful one, under the pretence of a balance of power, and then joins the former to turn the scale; but his protection and his alliance are always expensive. He knows how to interest those with whom he treats, and by a dexterous management and by shrewd and subtle subterfuges he makes them perceive what private advantage, profits, and honours they may derive through a certain pliability, which does not in the least clash with their instructions nor with the intentions of their masters. And in order not to be thought impregnable on his side, he betrays some anxiety to better his fortunes, and then receives some proposals which unveil to him the most secret intentions, the most profound designs, and the last resource of his opponents, and which he turns to his own advantage. If sometimes he is a loser by certain stipulations, which have at last been settled, he clamours loudly; and if he is not, he is still louder, and puts the losers on their justification and defence. His court has laid down rules of conduct for his guidance, all his measures are preconcerted, and his smallest advances arranged beforehand; and yet, whilst subjects of the greatest difficulty are treated and certain points are most strenuously contested, he behaves as if his yielding was voluntary, unexpected, and purely a condescension on his part; he dares even pledge his word that a certain proposal will be approved of, and that his master will not disavow his proceedings; he allows false reports to be spread concerning his instructions, which are represented as very limited, but he knows he has some private instructions which he never discloses until obliged to do so, and when it would damage him not to bring them forward. All his intrigues aim at something solid and substantial, for which he always is ready to sacrifice punctilios and imaginary points of honour. He possesses a great deal of coolness, is armed with courage and patience, and wearies and discourages others, but is never weary himself! He takes precautions and is hardened against all delays and procrastination, against all reproaches, suspicions, mistrust, difficulties, and obstacles, convinced that time and circumstances will influence the minds of his opponents, and accomplish the desired end. He goes so far as to pretend he has a secret purpose in breaking off the negotiations, while he passionately desires their continuance; but, on the contrary, when he has strict orders to do his utmost to break them off, he thinks the best way to effect it is to urge they should be continued and speedily despatched. If some important event happens, he affects either haughtiness or affability, as it may be to his advantage or prejudice; and if he is so perspicacious as to foresee it, he hurries it on or temporises according as the state for whom he labours dreads or desires it, and acts according to these emergencies. He shapes his actions to suit time, place, and opportunities, his own strength or weakness, the genius of the nation he has to deal with, and the mood and character of the personages with whom he is negotiating. All his designs and maxims, all the devices of his policy, tend only to prevent his being deceived, and to deceive others.[506]

(13.) The French nation require their sovereign to be grave in his deportment.[507]

(14.) One of the misfortunes of a prince is to be often overburdened with a secret of which the communication would be dangerous; he is fortunate if he can meet with a faithful confidant to whom he can unbosom himself.[508]

(15). A prince can get everything he wants except the pleasures of a private life: only the charms of friendship and the fidelity of his friends can console him for such a great loss.

(16.) A monarch who deservedly fills a throne finds it pleasant sometimes to be less grand, to quit the stage, to leave off the theatrical cloak and buskins,[509] and act a more familiar part with a confidant.

(17.) Nothing is more creditable to a prince than the modesty of his favourite.

(18.) No ties of friendship or consanguinity affect a favourite; he may be surrounded on all sides by relatives and friends, but he does not mind them; he is detached from everything, and, as it were, isolated.

(19.) The best thing a man can do who has fallen into disgrace is to retire from the court, for it would be better for him to disappear than to wander about in society as a former favourite, and to act a wholly different part from his first one. If

[506] This paragraph is the longest La Bruyère has written; it covers between eight and nine pages in the original edition.

[507] An indirect homage to the assumed gravity of Louis XIV.

[508] Most probably this is a discreet allusion to Madame de Maintenon, whom the king had married in 1684, and in whose room generally a Council of State was held.

[509] Bas de saye, in the original, is a plaited petticoat worn in Louis XIV.'s time by actors in classical tragedies; it owes its name to the Latin sagum, a military cloak of the ancient Gauls. Brodequins was the name given to the buskins of comic actors; the tragic actors strutted in their cothurnes.

he does this and remains in solitude, his career will be looked upon as marvellous; and though he dies, as it were, before his time, people will only remember his splendour and his kindness.

A favourite who has fallen into disgrace can behave still better than by becoming a hermit and trying to be forgotten, namely, by attempting some lofty and noble deed, if he can do so, for which he will be greatly praised, his reputation exalted, or, at least, confirmed; and by which also it will be clearly proved that he deserved his former favour, so that people will pity his downfall, and partly blame his ill-luck.[510]

(20.) I do not doubt that a favourite who has a sufficiently powerful and lofty mind must often feel embarrassed and abashed at the meanness, littleness, and flattery, at the superfluous cares and frivolous attentions of those who run after him, follow him, and cling to him, like the vile creatures they are; no doubt he laughs and sneers at them in private to make amends for the restraint he has to impose on himself in public.

(21.) Ye who are in office, ministers of state or favourites, give me leave to offer you some advice. Do not trust to your progeny to look after your reputation when you are gone, or expect that they will preserve the lustre of your name; titles pass away, a prince's favour is evanescent, honours are lost, wealth is spent, and merit degenerates. It is true you have children worthy of you, and I shall even add, capable of maintaining the position you leave them; but can you say the same thing of your grandchildren? Do not believe me, but cast your eyes for once on some men whom you despise, and who are descended from the very persons to whom you succeed, though you are now in such a high position. Be virtuous and humane; and, if you ask what more is necessary, I will tell you: "Humanity and virtue." Then you can command the future and be independent of posterity; then you can be certain to last as long as the monarchy. And when in ages to come some people will point out the ruins of your castles, and perhaps only the spot where they once existed, the thought of your praiseworthy deeds will still remain fresh in their minds; they will look eagerly at portraits and medallions of you, and will say, "The man[511] whose effigies you behold was one who dared to address his prince forcibly and freely, and was more afraid of injuring than of displeasing him; he did not oppose his being good and generous, nor his speaking of his good cities and of his good people. In this other personage whose portrait you see[512] you will observe strongly marked lineaments and an austere and majestic air; his

---

[510] This paragraph only appeared for the first time in the fourth edition of the "Characters," published in 1689, and disappeared, never to be printed again, two years afterwards. It was probably suppressed for fear of offending either Louis XIV., who had allowed his former favourites, Bussy-Rabutin and Lauzun, to reappear at court (see page 18, note 65, and page 218, note 447), or of hurting the feelings of these two noblemen, above all of Bussy-Rabutin, who, after being admitted to the presence of the King, twice left a court where he felt he was not wanted, and could not obtain any command in the army.

[511] This refers to Cardinal Georges d'Amboise (1460-1510), Prime Minister of Louis XII.

[512] Cardinal Richelieu (1585-1642) is meant.

reputation increases every year, and the greatest politicians cannot compete with him. His chief design was to establish the authority of the prince, and to ensure the lives and property of the people by destroying the power of the great; from this, neither the opposition of various parties, conspiracies, treacheries, the risk of being assassinated, nor his own infirmities, were able to divert him; he accomplished it, and yet he had leisure to commence another enterprise, since continued and completed by the best and greatest of our princes, the extirpation of heresy."[513]

(22.) The most artful and plausible snare that ever was set for great men by their men of business, or for kings by their ministers, has been the advice of liquidating their debts whilst enriching themselves.[514] Such advice is admirable, such a maxim is useful and productive, and proves a gold mine and a Peru, at least to those who have hitherto had the address to instil it into their masters' minds.[515]

(23.) Happy indeed is that nation whose prince appoints the very same persons for his confidants and ministers whom the people would have chosen themselves if they could have done so.

(24.) The mastering of the details of business and a diligent application to the smallest necessities of the state are essential to a good administration, though, in truth, too much neglected in these latter times by kings and their ministers; it is a knowledge greatly to be desired in a prince who is ignorant of it, and highly to be valued in him who has acquired it.[516] Indeed, what benefits and what increase

---

[513] In politics, La Bruyère was in advance of his age, but not in religious questions. He shared the idea of "the extirpation of heresy," not alone with almost all the prelates of his time, but with some of the most eminent men in science, art, and literature, who all applauded the revocation of the Edict of Nantes (1685), and advocated the notion of one religion for the whole State.

[514] This is an allusion to the reduction of the interest on the French debt, and the calling in and recoining of certain monies, a measure which was often taken by the French kings, and even by Louis XIV., who, however, made no profit by it. See also page 152, note 300.

[515] Colbert has been wrongly accused of having made money by those means; an accusation which was also brought against Mazarin, Fouquet, and the fermiers généraux, on far better grounds.

[516] Our author had to conciliate Louis XIV. at a time when it was supposed the publication of the "Characters" might make him many enemies. Hence the direct and indirect flatteries he bestows on the king, who prided himself on his complete mastery of details, for which he was praised by some and blamed by others; and amongst these latter must be reckoned Fénelon, who in his Telemachus (Book xvi.) criticises Louis XIV. in the character of Idomeneus. That the king had a talent for mastering details cannot be doubted, and this is even admitted by the late John Richard Green, in his "Short History of the English People," chap. ix. sect. vii., whose opinion of Louis XIV. I transcribe here, as a corrective of the flatteries scattered on this royal despot by La Bruyère: "Louis the Fourteenth, bigoted, narrow-minded, commonplace as he was, without personal honour or personal courage, without gratitude and without pity, insane in his pride, insatiable in his selfishness, had still many of the qualities of a great ruler; industry, patience, quickness of resolve, firmness of purpose, a capacity for discerning greatness and using it, an immense self-belief and self-confidence, and a temper utterly destitute indeed of real greatness, but with a dramatic turn for seeming to be great."

of pleasure would accrue to a people by their prince extending the bounds of his empire into the territories of his enemies, by their sovereignties becoming provinces of his kingdom, by his overcoming them in sieges and battles, by neither the plains nor the strongest fortifications affording any security against him, by the neighbouring nations asking aid of one another, and entering into leagues to defend themselves and put a stop to his conquests, by their leagues being in vain, by his continual advances and triumphs, by their last hopes being frustrated by the monarch recovering his health,[517] and thus affording him the pleasure of seeing the young princes, his grandchildren, maintain and enhance his glory, beholding them lead an army into the field, take the strongest fortresses, conquer new states, command old and experienced officers rather by their genius and merit than by the privilege of their noble birth, observing them tread in the footsteps of their victorious father and imitate his goodness, his willingness to learn, his justice, vigilance, and magnanimity. What signifies it to me, in a word, or to any of my fellow-subjects, that my sovereign be successful and overwhelmed with glory, through his own actions as well as through those of his family and servants; that my country is powerful and dreaded, if, sad and uneasy, I have to live oppressed and poor; if, while I am secured against any inroads of the enemy, I am exposed in the public squares or the streets of our cities to the dagger of the assassin; or if rapine and violence are less to be feared in the darkest nights amidst the densest forests than in our streets; if security, order, and cleanliness have not rendered the residing in our cities so delightful, and have not introduced there plenty as well as the pleasures of social intercourse; or if, being weak and defenceless, my property is to be encroached upon by some great man in the neighbourhood; if there is not a provision made to protect me against his injustice; if I have not within reach so many masters, and excellent masters too, to instruct my children in sciences and arts, which will one day raise their fortunes; if the improvement of trade will not facilitate my providing myself with more decent clothing[518] and wholesome food for my sustenance, at a reasonable rate; if, to conclude, through the care my sovereign takes of me, I am not as satisfied with my lot as his virtues must needs make him with his own?

(25.) Eight or ten thousand men are to a prince like money; with their lives he buys a town or a victory; but, if he can obtain either at a cheaper rate, and is sparing of them, he is like a man who is bargaining and knows better than any other the value of money.

(26.) All things succeed in a monarchy where the interests of the state are identical with those of the prince.

(27.) To call a king the father of his people[519] is not so much to eulogise him

[517] An allusion to an operation for fistula performed on Louis XIV. in 1686.

[518] Voltaire, in his Siècle de Louis XIV., says: "From 1663 until 1672 every year some new manufactory was established. The fine cloths formerly imported from England and Holland were manufactured at Abbeville.... The cloth manufactories of Sedan, which had almost gone to wreck and ruin, were re-established." See also page 48, note 133.

[519] Louis XII. was called by the States-General assembled at Tours (1506) the "father of his people."

as to call him by his name and to define what he is.

(28.) There exists a sort of interchange or permutation of duties between a sovereign and his subjects, and between them and him; and I shall not decide which are most obligatory and most difficult. On the one hand, we have to determine what are the bounden duties of reverence, assistance, service, obedience, and dependence, and on the other what are the indispensable obligations of goodness, justice, and protection. To say the prince can dispose of the lives of the people, is to tell us only that through their crimes men have become subjected to the laws and justice which the king administers; to add that he is absolute master of all his subjects' goods without any considerations, without rendering any accounts, or without discussion, is the language of flattery, the opinion of a favourite who will recant on his deathbed.[520]

(29.) When on a fine evening a numerous flock of sheep is seen on a hill quietly browsing thyme and wild thyme, or nibbling in a meadow the short and tender grass which has escaped the scythe of the reaper, the careful and diligent shepherd is amongst them; he does not lose sight of them, but follows them, leads them, changes their pasture; if they wander, he calls them together; if a hungry wolf approaches, he sets his dog on to beat him off; he keeps them and defends them; and when the sun rises he is already in the fields, which he leaves at its setting. What an amount of care, watchfulness, and assiduity is needed! Which condition seems to you the most delicious and the most unfettered, that of the sheep or of the shepherd? Was the flock made for the shepherd or the shepherd for the flock? This is an artless representation of a nation and its prince, but then the prince must be good.

A gorgeous and sumptuous monarch is like a shepherd adorned with gold and jewels, with a golden crook in his hands, with a collar of gold about his dog's neck, and a silken and golden string to lead him. What is his flock the better for all this gold, or what avails it against the wolves?

(30.) How happy is that station which every instant furnishes opportunities of doing good to thousands of men! how dangerous is that post which every moment exposes its occupant to injure millions!

(31.) If men in this world cannot feel a more natural, praiseworthy, and sensible pleasure than to know that they are beloved, and if kings are men, can they purchase the hearts of their people at too high a rate?

(32.) There are very few general rules and unvariable regulations for governing well; they depend on times and circumstances, as well as on the prudence and designs of the rulers. A perfect government is, therefore, a masterpiece of the intellect; and perhaps it would be impossible to attain it, if the subjects did not contribute their moiety towards it by their habits of dependence and submission.

(33.) Those persons who, under a very great monarch, fill the highest offices, have no very intricate duties to perform, and they do this without any trouble; everything goes on easily; the authority and the genius of the prince smoothes

[520] Such was, however, the opinion of Louis XIV. himself, who states in his Mémoires: "Kings are absolute masters, and naturally dispose fully and entirely of all the property possessed by the clergy and laity."

their way, rids them of all difficulties, and makes everything prosper beyond their expectations; their merit consists in being subordinates.[521]

(34.) If the care of a single family be so burdensome, if a man has enough to do to answer for himself, what a weight, what a heavy load must be the charge of a whole realm! Is a sovereign rewarded for all his anxieties by the pleasures which absolute power seems to afford and by the prostrations of his courtiers? When I think of the difficult, hazardous, and dangerous paths he sometimes is forced to tread to attain public tranquillity; when I think of the extreme but necessary means he often is obliged to employ to compass a good end; when I am aware he is accountable to God for the welfare of his people, that good and evil are in his hands, and that he cannot plead ignorance as an excuse, I cannot forbear asking myself the question if I should like to reign? A man who is tolerably happy as a private individual should not abandon it for a throne, for, even to one who occupies it by hereditary right, it is almost unbearable to be born a monarch.

(35.) How many gifts Heaven must bestow on a prince for him to become a good ruler! He must be of royal blood, have an august and commanding air, a presence to satisfy the curiosity of a crowd anxious to see the prince, as well as to command respect from his courtiers.[522] His temper must be always the same; he must be averse to ill-natured raillery, or, at least, be so sensible as to refrain from it; he must never threaten, reproach, nor give way to passion, yet he must be always obeyed; he should be complacent and engaging, so frank and sincere that all may think they plainly see the bottom of his heart, which will tend to gain him friends, partisans, and allies; yet he must be secret, close, and impenetrable in his motives and plans; he must be very grave and serious in public; be brief, precise, and dignified in his answers to ambassadors, as well as in his expressions in council; be careful in choosing fit objects for his favours, and bestow them with that peculiar charm which enhances them; great must be his sagacity to penetrate into the minds, qualifications, and tempers of men, to nominate them to various posts and places, as well as to select his generals and ministers of state. His opinions should be so settled, sound, and decisive in matters of state, as immediately to point out what is the best and most honest thing to do; his mind ought to be so upright and just as sometimes to decide against himself and in favour of his subjects, allies, or enemies; so comprehensive and ready should be his memory as to remember the necessities of his subjects, their faces, names, and petitions.[523] His capacious intelligence should not only exercise itself on foreign affairs, commerce, maxims of state, political designs, extension of the frontiers by conquering new provinces, and ensuring their safety by numerous and inaccessible forts; but also look after the affairs of his own kingdom, and study them in detail; banish from it a false,

[521] This is another flattery intended for Louis XIV., who thought that his ministers got their talents "by virtue of their office." The word subalternes, "subordinates," seems also out of place applied to such men as Colbert and Louvois.

[522] Louis XIV. was certainly not displeased when his presence awed those who were presented to him.

[523] All those excellent qualities, which La Bruyère thinks are necessary to a sovereign, were those generally attributed to Louis XIV., and which Saint-Simon also ascribes to him in his Mémoires.

insidious, and anti monarchical sect,[524] if such a one exists; abolish all barbarous and impious customs, if they are to be found there;[525] reform the abuses of laws and usages, for such may have crept in;[526] render his cities more safe and comfortable by establishing new police regulations, more splendid and magnificent by sumptuous edifices; punish severely scandalous vices; increase the influence of religion and virtue by his authority and example;[527] protect the Church and clergy, their rights and liberties;[528] and govern the nation like a father, always intent on relieving it and making the subsidies as light as those levied in the provinces[529] without impoverishing them. He must have great talents for war, be vigilant, diligent, and unwearied, able to command numerous armies, and be composed in the midst of danger; he ought to be sparing of his own life for the good of the state, and prefer its welfare and glory to that very life; his power must be absolute, to leave no room for indirect influence, intrigues and factions, and sometimes to lessen that vast distance which exists between the great and the common people, so that they may be drawn closer together, and obey that power equally; the knowledge of the prince should be extensive, that he may see everything with his own eyes, act immediately and by himself, so that his generals, though at a distance, are but his lieutenants, and his ministers but his ministers;[530] he should be sagacious enough to know when to declare war, when to conquer and make the best use of a victory, when to make peace, and when to break it; when, sometimes, to compel his enemies to accept it, according to the various interests at stake; to set bounds to his vast ambition, and how far to extend his conquests; he should find leisure for games, festivals, and spectacles; cultivate arts and sciences, and erect magnificent structures, even when surrounded by secret and declared enemies. To conclude, he should possess a superior and commanding genius, which renders him beloved by his subjects and feared by strangers, and makes of his court, and even of his entire realm, as it were, one family, governed by one head, living in perfect unison and harmony with one another, and thus formidable to the rest of the world. All these admirable virtues seem to me comprised in the notion of what a sovereign ought to be. It is true we rarely see them all combined in one man, for too many

---

[524] Another hit at the revocation of the Edict of Nantes.

[525] A reference to the royal edicts against duelling.

[526] Louis XIV., from 1667 to 1685, promulgated several laws reforming abuses in civil and criminal jurisprudence, and abolishing certain restrictions on trade, commerce, etc.

[527] To say that Louis XIV. increased by his example the influence of religion and virtue, can only apply to him after his marriage with Madame de Maintenon. See page 258, note 508.

[528] An allusion to the declaration of the liberties of the Gallican Church, published in 1682, and said to be written by Bossuet.

[529] The commentators of La Bruyère do not explain why the subsidies to be granted to the king were lighter in the provinces. Can it be that in certain provinces, called pays d'état, the subsidies voted by the provincial states were smaller than those voted by the authorities appointed by the king in those provinces not belonging to the pays d'état, and called pays d'élections?

[530] This allusion must greatly have pleased Louis XIV., who thought himself great as a strategist and as a politician.

adventitious qualities, such as intelligence, feelings, outward appearances, and natural disposition, must be found at the same time in him; it therefore appears to me that a prince who unites all these in his single person well deserves the name of Great.[531]

LOUIS XIV

---

[531] Although this paragraph is only half the size of paragraph 12, page 253, there is only one full stop in it in the original, and that is at the end.

THE CONSULTATION

XI.

OF MANKIND.

(1.) LET us not be angry with men when we see them cruel, ungrateful, unjust, proud, egotists, and forgetful of others; they are made so; it is their nature; we might just as well quarrel with a stone for falling to the ground, or with a fire when the flames ascend.

(2.) In one sense men are not fickle, or only in trifles; they change their habits, language, outward appearance, their rules of propriety, and sometimes their taste; but they always preserve their bad morals, and adhere tenaciously to what is ill and to their indifference for virtue.

(3.) Stoicism is a mere fancy, a fiction, like Plato's Republic. The Stoics pretend a man may laugh at poverty; not feel insults, ingratitude, loss of property, relatives, and friends; look unconcernedly on death, and regard it as a matter of indifference which ought neither to make him merry nor melancholy; not let pleasure or pain conquer him; be wounded or burned without breathing the slightest sigh or shedding a single tear; and this phantasm of courage and imaginary firmness they are pleased to call a philosopher. They have left man with the same faults they found in him, and did not blame his smallest foible. Instead of depicting vice as something terrible or ridiculous, which might have corrected him, they have limned an idea of perfection and heroism of which man is not capable, and they exhorted him to aim at what is impossible. Thus, the philosopher that is to be, but will never exist except in imagination, finds himself naturally, and without any exertions of his own, above all events and all ills; the most excruciating fit of the gout, the most severe attack of colic, cannot draw from him the least complaint; Heaven and earth may be overturned, without dragging him along in their downfall; and he remains calm and collected amidst the ruins of the universe, whilst a man really beside himself utters loud exclamations, despairs, looks fierce, and is in an agony for the loss of a dog or for a China dish broken into pieces.

(4.) Restlessness of mind, inequality of temper, fickleness of affections, and instability of conduct, are all vices of the mind, but they are all different; and, in spite[532] of their appearing analogous, are not always found in one and the same subject.

(5.) It is difficult to decide whether irresolution makes a man more unfortunate than contemptible, or even whether it is always a greater disadvantage to take a wrong step than to take none at all.

(6.) A man of variable mind is not one man, but several men in one; he multiplies himself as often as he changes his taste and manners; he is not this minute what he was the last, and will not be the next what he is now; he is his own successor. Do not ask what is his nature, but what are his proclivities; nor what mood he is in, but how many sorts of moods he has. Are you not mistaken, and is it Eutichrates whom you accost? To-day he is cool to you, but yesterday he was anxious to see you, and was so demonstrative that his friends were jealous of you. Surely he does not remember you; tell him your name.

(7.) Menalcas[533] goes down-stairs, opens the door to go out, and shuts it again; he perceives that he has his nightcap on, and on looking at himself with a little more attention, he finds that he is but half shaved, that he has fastened his sword on the wrong side, that his stockings are hanging on his heels, and that his shirt is bulging out above his breeches. If he walks about, he feels something strike <u>him all at once in</u> the stomach or in the face, and he cannot imagine what it is, un-

[532] The original has avec, which, in the seventeenth century, often was used for "in spite of."

[533] The author adds in a note: "This is not so much a portrait of one individual, as a collection of anecdotes of absent-minded persons. If they please, there cannot be too large a number of them, for as tastes differ, my readers can pick and choose." The chief traits of Menalcas are based on stories related by the Count de Brancas, who died eleven years before the above paragraph first saw the light (1691); others are said to have happened to the Prince de la Roche-sur-Yon, afterwards Prince de Conti (1664-1709), and to a certain Abbé de Mauroy, chaplain to Mademoiselle de Montpensier. Eustace Budgell (1685-1736) depicts in No. 77 of the "Spectator" "an absent man," and also speaks of Monsieur Bruyère, who "has given us the character of an absent man with a great deal of humour;" and then prints "the heads" of Menalcas' portrait. According to Watt's Bibliotheca Britannica, Budgell was the author of a translation of La Bruyère's "Characters," published 1699 and 1702; but in the edition of 1702 there is on the title-page, "made English by several hands."

til he opens his eyes and wakes up, when he finds himself before the shaft of a cart, or behind a long plank a workman is carrying. He has been seen to run his head against a blind man, and to get entangled between his legs, so that both fell backwards. Often he meets a prince face to face, who wishes to pass; he recollects himself with some difficulty, and scarcely has time to squeeze himself up against the wall to make room for him.[534] He searches about, rummages, shouts, gets excited, calls his servants one after another, and complains that everything is lost or mislaid; he asks for his gloves which he holds in his hands, like the woman who asked for the mask she had on her face. He enters the rooms at Versailles,[535] and passing under a chandelier, his wig gets hooked on to one of the brackets and is left hanging, whilst all the courtiers stare and laugh. Menalcas looks also, and laughs louder than any of them, staring in the meanwhile at all the company to see what man shows his ears and has lost his wig.[536] If he goes into town,[537] before he has gone far he thinks he has lost his way, gets uneasy, and asks some of the passers-by where he is, who name to him the very street he lives in; he enters his own house, runs out in haste, and fancies he is mistaken. He comes out of the *Palais de Justice*, and finding a carriage waiting at the bottom of the great staircase, he thinks it is his own and enters it; the coachman just touches the horses with his whip, and supposes all the while he is driving his master home; Menalcas jumps out, crosses the courtyard, mounts the stairs, and passes through the ante-chamber and ordinary rooms into the study; but nothing is strange or new to him; he sits down, takes a rest, and feels himself at home. When the real master of the house arrives, he rises to receive him, treats him very politely, begs him to be seated, and believes he is doing the honours of his own room; he talks, muses, and talks again; the master of the house is tired and amazed, and Menalcas as much as he, though he does not say what he thinks, but supposes the other is some bore who has nothing to do, and will leave soon—at least he hopes so, and remains patient; yet it is almost night before he is undeceived, and that with some difficulty. Another time he pays a visit to a lady, and imagines that she is visiting him; he sits down in her arm-chair[538] without any thought of giving it up; it then seems to him that the lady is somewhat long in her visit, and he expects every moment that she will rise and leave him at liberty; but as she delays, he is growing hungry, and night coming on, he invites her to have some supper with him, at which she bursts out in such loud laughter that he comes to himself. He marries in the morning, but has forgotten it at night, and does not sleep at home on his wedding-night; some time afterwards his wife dies in his arms, and he is present at her funeral; the next day one of the servants informs him that dinner is on the table, when he asks if his wife is already dressed and if they have told her it is served up. He enters a church, and takes a

---

[534] Many of the streets in Paris were so narrow when our author wrote, that two people could hardly pass abreast; it was, therefore, the fashion to "give the wall," as it was called, to persons of a superior rank.

[535] See page 243, note 486.

[536] The wigs were already worn very long, and completely concealed the ears.

[537] See page 164, note 322.

[538] There was usually only one or two arm-chairs in a reception-room, reserved for the master or mistress of the house, or for both.

blind man, always stationed at the door, for a pillar, and the plate he holds in his hands for a holy-water basin, into which he dips his hands; and when he makes the sign of the cross on his forehead, he, on a sudden, hears the pillar speak and beg for alms; he walks through the aisle, and fancying he sees a praying-chair, throws himself heavily on it; the chair bends, gives way, and strives to cry out;[539] Menalcas is surprised to find himself kneeling on the legs of a very little man, and leaning on his back, with both his arms on his shoulders, his folded hands extended, taking him by the nose and stopping his mouth; he is quite confused, withdraws, and goes and kneels elsewhere. He takes out his prayer-book as he thinks, but he pulls out a slipper instead, which he had inadvertently put into his pocket before he went out; he has hardly left the church when a footman runs after him, comes up to him, and asks him, with a laugh, if he has not got the bishop's slipper; Menalcas produces his, and assures him that he has no other slippers about him; but, however, after searching he finds the slipper of his lordship, whom he has just been visiting, had found indisposed at his fireside, and whose slipper he had pocketed before he took his leave, instead of one of his gloves he had dropt; so that Menalcas returns home with one slipper less. One day whilst gambling he lost all the money he had about him, and, as he wished to continue, he went into his private room, unlocked a cupboard, took out his cash-box, helped himself to whatever he pleased, and then thought he put it back again in its former place; but he heard some barking going on in the cupboard he just locked, and, quite astonished at this marvellous occurrence, he opened it again, and burst out laughing on beholding his dog he had locked up instead of his cash-box. Whilst he is playing backgammon he asks for something to drink, which is brought him; it is his turn to play, and, holding the box in one hand and the glass in the other, and being very thirsty, he gulps down the dice and almost the box, whilst the water is thrown on the board, and quite wets the person he is playing with. One day being in a room with a family with whom he was very intimate, he spits on the bed, and throws his hat on the ground, thinking he is spitting on the floor and shying his hat on the bed. Once on the river he asked what o'clock it was; they hand him a watch, but it is scarcely in his hands when he forgets both the time and the watch, and throws the latter into the river as a thing which bothers him. He writes a long letter, throws some sand on his paper,[540] and then pours the sand into the inkstand; but that is not all. He writes a second letter, and after having sealed both, he makes a mistake in addressing them; one of them is sent to a duke and peer of the realm, who, on opening it, reads: "Mr. Oliver,—Pray don't fail to send me my provision of hay as soon as you receive this letter." His farmer receives the other letter, opens it, has it read to him, and finds in it: "My lord,—I receive with the utmost submission the orders which it has pleased your highness," and so on. He writes another letter at night, and after sealing it, puts out the light; yet is surprised to be on a sudden in the dark, and is at a loss to conceive how it has happened. Coming down the Louvre staircase, Menalcas meets another person coming up, and exclaims that the

[539] It was reported that Brancas, chevalier d'honneur of the queen-mother, Anne of Austria (1602-1666), behaved in almost a similar manner to his royal mistress.

[540] Blotting-paper was not invented when our author wrote; even now it is not unusual abroad to find the ink of letters dried with sand, either plain or coloured.

latter is the very man he is looking for; he takes him by the hand, and they go down-stairs together, cross several courtyards, enter some apartments, and come out again; he moves about, and returns whence he started; then, looking more narrowly at the man he has thus been dragging after him for a quarter of an hour, he wonders who it is, has nothing to say to him, lets go his hand, and turns another way. He often asks a question, and is almost out of sight before it is possible to answer him; or else he will ask you, whilst he is running about, how your father is, and when you answer him that he is seriously unwell, he will shout to you that he is very glad to hear it. Another time, if you fall in his way, he is delighted to meet you, and says he has just come from your house to talk to you on a certain matter of business; then, looking at your hand, he exclaims, "That's a fine ruby you wear; is it a balass ruby?"[541] and then he leaves you, and goes on his way; this is the important matter of business he was so anxious to talk to you about. If he is in the country, he tells some person he must feel happy he has been able to leave the court in the autumn and to have spent on his estate all the time the court was at Fontainebleau;[542] whilst to other people he talks about something else; then, going back to the first, he says to him, "You have had some very fine weather at Fontainebleau, and you must have followed the royal hunt pretty often." He begins a story which he forgets to finish; he laughs to himself, and that aloud, at something he is thinking of, and replies to his own thoughts; he hums a tune, whistles, throws himself into a chair, sends forth a pitiful whine, yawns, and thinks himself alone. When he is at a dinner-party he gradually gathers all the bread on his own plate, and his neighbours have none; and he does the same with the knives and forks, which do not remain long in their hands. Lately some large spoons, convenient for helping every one, have been introduced at certain tables; he takes one of these spoons, plunges it into the dish, fills it, puts it into his mouth, and is highly astonished to see the soup he has just taken all over his clothes and linen. He forgets to drink at dinner, or, if he remembers it, thinks there is too much wine poured out for him; he flings more than half of it in the face of a gentleman seated at his right hand, drinks the rest with a great deal of composure, and cannot understand why everybody should burst out laughing for throwing on the floor the wine he did not wish to drink.[543] He keeps his bed a day or two for a slight indisposition, and a goodly number of ladies and gentlemen visit him, and converse

[541] Balais in French, a kind of pale-coloured ruby, so called, according to Littré's Dictionnaire, from Balakschan or Balaschan, not far from Samarcand.

[542] The king used to hunt at Fontainebleau almost every day in October. See also page 174, note 359.

[543] There existed a great deal of coarseness at the court of Louis XIV. underneath a semblance of extreme polish and refinement, and some of the stories told by Saint-Simon of the habits and customs of the king himself would not bear repeating at the present time, and even be considered disgraceful by the lowest classes of society. As an example of this general coarseness, it will, no doubt, have been observed that it was the usual habit of decent people to expectorate on the floor (see page 277, line 12), as well as to throw there the wine they did not wish to drink; for Menalcas is only laughed at for his absence of mind, and not for his bad habits. See also in the chapter "Of the Gifts of Fortune," § 83, the character of Phædo, page 161, and in the chapter "Of Society, etc.," the character of Troïlus, page 106, § 13.

with him in the *ruelle;*[544] in their presence he lifts up the blankets and spits in the sheets. He is taken to the Convent of the Carthusians, where they show him a gallery adorned with paintings, all executed by the hand of a master;[545] the monk who explains the subjects persistently expatiates on the life of Saint Bruno, and points out the adventure with the canon in one of the pictures.[546] Menalcas, whose thoughts are all the while wandering away from the gallery, and far beyond it, returns to it at last, and asks the monk whether it is the canon or Saint Bruno who is damned. Being once, as it happened, with a young widow, he talks to her of her deceased husband, and asks of what he died; this conversation renews all the sorrows of the lady, who, amidst tears and sobs, tells him all the particulars of her late husband's illness, from the night he first was attacked by fever to his final agony; whereupon Menalcas, who apparently listens to her narrative with great attention, asks her if the deceased was her only husband. One morning he gets it into his head to hurry on everything for dinner; but he rises before the dessert is brought on, and leaves his guests by themselves. That day he is sure to be seen everywhere in town except on the spot where he has made an appointment about the very business which prevented him finishing his dinner, and made him walk, for fear it would take too long a time to get the horses and carriage ready. You may frequently hear him shout, scold, and get in a rage about one of his servants being out of the way. "Where can that man be?" says he;

"what can he be doing? what has become of him? Let him never more present himself before me; I discharge him this very minute!" The servant makes his appearance, and he asks him, in a contemptuous tone, where he comes from; the man replies he has been where he was sent to, and gives a faithful account of his errand. You would often take Menalcas for what he is not, for an idiot; for he does not listen, and speaks still less; for a madman, because he talks to himself, and indulges in certain grimaces and involuntary motions of the head; for proud and discourteous, because when you bow to him, he may pass without looking at you, or look at you and not return your bow; for a man without any feeling, for he talks of bankruptcy in a family where there is such a blot; of executions and the scaffold before a person whose father has been beheaded; of plebeians before plebeians who have become rich and pretend to be of noble birth. He even intends to bring up his illegitimate son in his house, and pretends he is a servant; and though he would have his wife and children know nothing about the matter, he cannot forbear calling him his son every hour of the day. He resolves to let his son marry the daughter of some man of business, yet he now and then boasts of his birth and ancestors, and that no Menalcas has ever made a misalliance. In short, he seems to be absent minded, and to pay no attention to the conversation going

[544] See page 65, note 161.

[545] In the Convent of the Carthusians, then near the Luxembourg, were to be found the twenty-two celebrated pictures of Eustache Lesueur (1616-1655), representing the history of Saint Bruno, founder of that order, who died in 1101. The greater part of these pictures is now in the Louvre.

[546] This picture represents the burial of an eloquent and learned canon, who, whilst being carried to the tomb, rose in his coffin, exclaimed that he was damned, and fell back again.

on; he thinks and speaks at the same time, but what he says is seldom about what he thinks; so that there is hardly any coherence and sequence in his talk; he often says "yes" when he should say "no," and when he says "no," you must suppose he would say "yes." When he answers you so pertinently, his eyes are fixed on your countenance, but it does not follow that he sees you; he looks neither at you nor at any one, nor at anything in the world. All that you can draw from him, even when he is most sociable and most attentive, are some such words as these: "Yes, indeed; it is true; very well; really; indeed; I believe so; certainly; O Heaven!" and some other monosyllables, even not always used on the right occasions. He never is with those with whom he appears to be; he calls his footman very seriously "Sir," and his friend "La Verdure;"[547] says "Your Reverence" to a prince of the royal blood, and "Your Highness" to a Jesuit. When he is at mass, and the priest sneezes, he cries out aloud, "God bless you!" He is in the company of a magistrate of serious disposition, and venerable by his age and dignity, who asks him whether a certain event happened in such and such a way, and Menalcas replies, "Yes, miss." As he came one day from the country, his footmen plotted to rob him and succeeded; they jumped down from behind his coach, presented the end of a torch to his breast, and demanded his purse, which he gave up.[548] When he came home he told his friends what had happened, and when they asked for details he said they had better inquire of his servants, who also were present.

(8.) Impoliteness is not a vice of the mind, but the consequence of several vices; of foolish vanity, of ignorance of one's duties, of idleness, of stupidity, of absence of mind, of contempt for others, and of jealousy. Though it only shows itself outwardly, it is not the less odious, because it is a fault which is always visible and manifest; however, it gives more or less offence, according as the motives for displaying it are more or less offensive.

(9.) If we say of an angry, captious, quarrelsome, melancholy, formal, capricious person, that it is all owing to his temper, it is not to find an excuse for him, whatever people may think, but an involuntary acknowledgment that such great faults admit of no remedy.

What we call good temper is a thing too much neglected among men; they ought to understand that they should not alone be good, but also appear to be so, at least if they are inclined to be sociable and disposed to friendly intercourse; in other words, if they would be men. We do not require wicked men to be gentle and urbane; in these qualities they are never wanting, for they employ them to ensnare the simple, and to find a larger field for their operations; but we wish kind-hearted men always to be tractable, accessible, and courteous; so that there should no longer be any reason for saying that wicked men do harm and that good men make others uncomfortable.

(10.) The generality of men proceed from anger to insults; others act different-

[547] See page 138, note 272.

[548] Tallemant des Réaux, in his Historiettes, tells a more probable story of de Brancas, how one day, being on horseback and stopped by footpads, he mistook them for footmen, and ordered them to let go his horse, and how he did not find out his mistake till they clapt a pistol to his breast.

ly, for they first give offence and then grow angry; our surprise at such behaviour always supersedes resentment.

(11.) Men do not sufficiently take advantage of every opportunity for pleasing other people. When a person accepts a certain post, it seems that he intends to acquire the power of obliging others without using it; nothing is quicker and more readily given than a refusal, whilst nothing is ever granted until after mature reflection.

(12.) Know exactly what you are to expect from men in general, and from each of them in particular, and then mix with the people around you.

(13.) If poverty is the mother of all crimes, lack of intelligence is their father.

(14.) A knave can hardly be a very intelligent man; a clear and far-seeing mind leads to regularity, honesty, and virtue; it is want of sense and penetration which begets obstinacy in wickedness as well as in duplicity; in vain we endeavour to correct such a man by satire; it may describe him to others, but he himself will not know his own picture; it is like scolding a deaf man. It would be well, please gentlemen of sense and culture, and avenge everybody, if a rogue were not so constituted as to be without any feeling whatever.

(15.) There are some vices for which we are indebted to none but ourselves, which are innate in us, and are strengthened by habit; there are others we contract which are foreign to us. Sometimes men are naturally inclined to yield without much difficulty, to be urbane, and to desire to please; but by the treatment they meet from those whom they frequent and on whom they depend, they soon lose all moderation, and even change their disposition; they grow melancholy and peevish to a degree ere this unknown to them; their temper is completely changed, and they are themselves astonished at their being rude and tetchy.

(16.) Some people ask why the whole bulk of mankind does not constitute one nation, and does not like to speak the same language, obey the same laws, and agree among themselves to adopt the same customs and the same worship? For my part, observing how greatly minds, tastes, and sentiments differ, I am astonished to see seven or eight persons, living under the same roof and within the same walls, constitute one family.[549]

(17.) There are some extraordinary fathers, who seem, during the whole course of their lives, to be preparing reasons for their children for being consoled at their deaths.[550]

(18.) Everything is strange in the dispositions, morals, and manners of men: one person who during his whole lifetime has been melancholy, passionate, avaricious, fawning, submissive, laborious, and egotistical, was born lively, peaceable, indolent, ostentatious, and with lofty feelings, abhorring anything base; want, circumstances, and dire necessity have compelled him and caused such a great

---

[549] Compare what our author says in the above paragraph with the remarks he makes in § 21, page 260, and § 34, page 266.

[550] One of these fathers appears to have been the Duke de Gesvres (1620-1704), who spent all his money on purpose not to leave any to his children.

change. Such a man's inmost feelings can really not be described, for too many external things have altered, changed, and upset him, so that he is not exactly what he thinks he is himself or what he appears to be.

(19.) Life is short and tedious, and is wholly spent in wishing; we trust to find rest and enjoyment at some future time, often at an age when our best blessings, youth and health, have already left us. When at last that time has arrived, it surprises us in the midst of fresh desires; we have got no farther when we are attacked by a fever which kills us; if we had been cured, it would only have been to give us more time for other desires.

(20.) A man requesting a favour from another, surrenders himself at discretion to the personage from whom he expects it, but when he is quite sure it will be granted, he temporises, parleys, and capitulates.

(21.) It is so usual for men not to be happy, and so essential for every blessing to be acquired with infinite trouble, that what is obtained easily is looked upon with suspicion. We can hardly understand how anything which costs us so little can be greatly to our advantage, or how by strictly honest means we can so easily obtain what we want; we may think we deserve our success, but we ought very seldom to depend on it.

(22.) A man who says he is not born happy may at least become so by the happiness his friends and relatives enjoy, but envy deprives him even of this last resource.

(23.) Whatever I may somewhere have said,[551] it is, perhaps, wrong to be dejected. Men seem born to misfortune, pain, and poverty, and as few escape this, and as every kind of calamity seems to befall them, they ought to be prepared for every misfortune.

(24.) Men find it so very difficult to make business arrangements, they are so very touchy where their smallest interests are concerned, they are so bristling over with difficulties, so willing to deceive and so unwilling to be deceived, they place so high a value on what belongs to themselves, and are so apt to undervalue what belongs to others, that I admit I cannot understand how and in what way marriages, contracts, acquisitions, conventions, truces, treaties, and alliances are brought about.

(25.) Among some people arrogance supplies the place of grandeur, inhumanity of decision, and roguery of intelligence.

Knaves easily believe others as bad as themselves; there is no deceiving them, neither do they long deceive.

I would rather at any time be considered a fool than a rogue.

We never deceive people to benefit them, for knavery is a compound of wickedness and falsehood.

(26.) If there were not so many dupes in this world there would be fewer of those men called shrewd or sharp, who are honoured for having been artful

---

[551] See the chapter "Of Society," § 63.

enough in deceiving others during the whole course of their lives, and are proud of having done so. Why should you expect Erophilus not to presume on himself and his shrewdness, whose breach of faith, bad actions, and roguery, instead of doing him any harm, have procured him favours and rewards, even from those whom he has either never served or to whom he has done an ill turn?

(27.) We hear nothing in the squares and in the streets of great cities, and out of the mouths of the passers-by, but such words as "writs, executions, interrogatories, bonds, and pleadings." Is there not the smallest equity more left in this world? Or is it, on the contrary, full of people who coolly ask for what is not due to them, or who distinctly refuse to pay what they owe?

The invention of legal documents to remind men of what they promised, and to convince them that they did so, is a shame to humanity.

If you suppress passion, interest, and injustice, how quiet would the greatest cities be! The necessities of life, and the means of satisfying them, are the cause of nearly half the difficulties.

(28.) Nothing is of greater assistance to a man for bearing quietly the wrongs done to him by relatives and friends than his reflections on the vices of humanity; on the difficulty men have in being constant, generous, and faithful, or on their loving anything better than their own interests. He knows the extent of their power, and does not require them to penetrate solid bodies, to fly in the air, or to give every one his due; he may dislike mankind in general for having no greater respect for virtue; but he finds excuses for individuals, and even loves them from higher motives, whilst he does his best to require himself as little indulgence as possible.

(29.) There are certain things which we most passionately desire, and of which the mere thought carries us away and throws us into an ecstasy: if we happen to obtain them, we are less sensible of them than we thought we should be, and we enjoy them the less because we aspire to get some of greater importance.

(30.) There exist some evils so terrible and some misfortunes so horrible that we dare not think of them, whilst their very aspect makes us shudder; but if they happen to fall on us, we find ourselves stronger than we imagined; we grapple with our ill luck, and behave better than we expected we should.

(31.) Sometimes a pretty house which we inherit, or a fine horse, or a handsome dog which is given to us, or some hangings, or a clock presented to us, will alleviate a great grief, and make us feel less acutely a great loss.

(32.) Suppose men were to live for ever in this world, I do not think I could discover what more they could do than they do at present.

(33.) If life be wretched, it is hard to bear it; if it be happy, it is horrible to lose it; both come to the same thing.

(34.) There is nothing men are so anxious to keep, and yet are so careless about, as life.

(35.) Irene is at great cost conveyed to Epidaurus;[552] she visits Æsculapius in

---

[552] Epidaurus, a city of Peloponnesus, where Æsculapius, the god of medicine and a

his temple, and consults him about all her ailings. She complains first that she is weary and excessively fatigued, and the god replies that the long journey she just made is the cause of this; she says that she is not inclined to eat any supper, and the oracle orders her to eat less dinner; she adds she cannot sleep at night, and he prescribes her to lie a-bed by day; she complains of her corpulency, and asks how it can be prevented; the oracle replies she should get up before noon and now and then use her legs to walk; she declares that wine disagrees with her, the oracle bids her drink water; she suffers from indigestion, and he tells her she must diet herself. "My sight begins to fail me," says Irene. "Use spectacles," says Æsculapius. "I grow weak," continues she; "I am not half so strong nor so healthy as I was." "You grow old," says the god. "But how," asks she, "can I get rid of this disease?" "The shortest way to cure it, Irene, is to die, as your mother and grandmother have done." "Son of Apollo!" exclaimed Irene, "is this all the advice you give me? Is this the skill praised by all, and for which every one reveres you? What rare and secret things did you tell me, and what remedies have you prescribed for me, which I did not know before?" "Why did you not take these, then," the god replied, "without coming such a long distance to consult me, and shortening your days by such a tedious journey?"[553]

(36.) Death happens but once, yet we feel it every moment of our lives; it is worse to dread it than to suffer it.

(37.) Restlessness, fear, and dejection cannot delay death, but, on the contrary, hasten it; I only question whether man, who is mortal, should indulge in much laughing.

(38.) Whatever is certain in death is slightly alleviated by what is not so infallible; the time when it shall happen is undefined, but it is more or less connected with the infinite, and what we call eternity.

(39.) When we are sighing for the loss of our past blooming youth, which will return no more, let us think that decrepitude will come, when we shall regret the mature age we have reached and do not sufficiently value.

(40.) The fear of old age disturbs us, yet we are not certain of becoming old.

(41.) We hope to grow old, and yet we dread old age; or, in other words, we are willing to live, and afraid to die.

(42.) A man had better yield to nature and fear death, than be engaged in continual conflicts, provide himself with arguments and reflections, and be always son of Apollo, was worshipped.

[553] This paragraph appeared for the first time in the eighth edition of the "Characters," published in 1694, three years after the former favourite of Louis XIV., Madame de Montespan, had left the court, and about ten years after he had married Madame de Maintenon. Madame de Montespan had then become an imaginary invalid, and made frequent journeys to take the waters at different places, and chiefly to Bourbon-l'Archambaud, where, it is said, a doctor made her a similar answer as recorded above. It is doubtful whether La Bruyère would have spoken of her corpulency, failing sight, and her growing old if Madame de Montespan had still remained a favourite; his former pupil, the Duke de Bourbon, had married, in 1685, Mademoiselle de Nantes, one of her daughters by Louis XIV.

combating his own feelings in order not to fear it.

(43.) If some persons died, and others did not die, death would indeed be a terrible affliction.

(44.) A long disease seems to be a halting-place between life and death, that death itself may be a comfort to those who die and to those who are left behind.

(45.) Humanly speaking, there is something good in death, namely, that it puts an end to old age. That death which prevents decrepitude comes more seasonably than that which ends it.

(46.) Men regret their life has been ill-spent, but this does not always induce them to make a better use of the time they have yet to live.

(47.) Life is a kind of sleep; old men have slept longer than others, and only begin to wake again when they are to die. If, then, they take a retrospect of the whole course of their lives, they frequently discover neither virtues nor commendable actions to distinguish one year from another; they confound one time of their life with another time, and see nothing of sufficient note by which to measure how long they have lived. They have dreamt in a confused, indistinct, and incoherent way; but, nevertheless, they are aware, as all people who wake up, that they have slept for a long while.

(48.) There are but three events which concern man: birth, life, and death. They are unconscious of their birth, they suffer when they die, and they neglect to live.

(49.) There is a time preceding the power of reasoning, when, like animals, we live by instinct alone, and of which memory retains no vestiges. There is a second period, when reason is developed, formed, and might act, if it were not obscured and partly extinguished by vices of the constitution, and a sequence of passions following one another till the third and last age; reason then, being in its full strength, should produce something; but it is chilled and impaired by years, disease, and sorrow, and rendered useless by the machinery getting old and out of gear; yet these three periods constitute the whole life of man.

(50.) Children are overbearing, supercilious, passionate, envious, inquisitive, egotistical, idle, fickle, timid, intemperate, liars, and dissemblers; they laugh and weep easily, are excessive in their joys and sorrows, and that about the most trifling objects; they bear no pain, but like to inflict it on others; already they are men.

(51.) Children are neither for the past nor the future, but enjoy the present, which we rarely do.

(52.) There seems to be but one character in childhood; at that age morals and manners are nearly all the same, and it is only by paying great attention that we can perceive any difference, which, however, increases in the same proportion as reason does, whilst the passions and vices gather strength as well; these alone make men so unlike each other and so at variance with themselves.

(53.) Children already possess those faculties which are extinct in old men, namely, imagination and memory, and which are very useful to them in their little sports and amusements; by the help of these they repeat what they have heard, imitate what they see done, exercise all trades, either in busying themselves with many small labours or in copying the movements and gestures of various workmen; are guests at a sumptuous feast and entertained most luxuriously; are transported to enchanted palaces and places; have splendid carriages and a large retinue, though they are by themselves; are at the head of armies, give battle, and enjoy the delights of obtaining a victory; converse with kings and with the greatest princes; are themselves monarchs, have subjects, possess treasures which they make of leaves or sand; and know then, what they will ignore in after-life, to be satisfied with their fortune and to be masters of their own happiness.

(54.) There are no outward vices, nor bodily defects, which children do not perceive; they observe them at once, and know how to describe them in suitable terms, for more exact definitions could not be invented; but when they become men, they, in their turn, contract the same imperfections which they ridiculed.

The only anxiety children have is to find out the weaknesses of their masters, and of the persons they have to obey; as soon as they have taken once advantage of these, they get the upper hand, and obtain an influence over these people which they never part with: for what once deprived these persons of their superiority will always prevent them recovering it.

(55.) Idleness, indolence, and laziness, vices so natural to children, disappear as soon as they begin to play; they are then lively, attentive, exact observers of rule and order, never pardon the least slip, and several times begin again one and the same thing, in which they failed; these are sure forebodings that they may, hereafter, neglect their duties, but will forget nothing that can promote their pleasures.

(56.) To children everything seems great; courtyards, gardens, houses, furniture, men, and animals; to men the things of the world appear so, and, I dare say, for the same reason, because they are little.

(57.) Children begin among themselves with a democracy, where every one is master; and what is very natural, it does not suit them for any length of time, and then they adopt a monarchy. One of them distinguishes himself from among the rest, either by greater vivacity, strength, and comeliness, or by a more exact knowledge of their various sports and of the little laws which regulate them; all the others submit to him, and then an absolute government is established, but only in matters of pleasure.

(58.) Who can doubt but that children conceive, judge, and reason consistently? If only in small things consider they are children, and without much experience; if they make use of an indifferent phraseology it is less their fault than their parents' and masters'.

(59.) It destroys all confidence in the minds of children, and alienates them as well, to punish them for faults they have not committed, or even to be severe with them for trifling offences; they know exactly, and better than any one, what they deserve, and seldom deserve more than they dread; when they are chastised, they know if it is justly or unjustly, whilst unjust punishments do them more harm than not to be punished at all.

(60.) Man does not live long enough to be benefited by his faults; he is committing them during the whole course of his life, and it is as much as he can do, if, after many errors, he dies at last improved.

Nothing revives more a man than the knowledge that he has avoided doing some foolish action.

(61.) Men are loath to particularise their faults; they conceal them or blame some other person for them, and this gives the "spiritual director"[554] an advantage over the father-confessor.

(62.) The faults of blockheads are sometimes so great and so difficult to foresee, that wise men are puzzled by them; they are only of use to those who commit them.

(63.) A party spirit betrays the greatest men to act as meanly as the vulgar herd.

(64.) Vanity and propriety lead us to act in the same way and in the same manner as we should do through inclination or a feeling of duty; a man died lately in Paris of a fever which he got by sitting up at night with his wife, for whom he did not care.[555]

(65.) All men in their hearts covet esteem, but are loath any one should discover their anxiety to be esteemed; for men wish to be considered virtuous; and men would no longer be thought virtuous, but fond of esteem and praises, and vain, were they to derive any other advantages from virtue than virtue itself. Men are very vain, and of all things hate to be thought so.

(66.) A vain man finds it to his advantage to speak well or ill of himself; a modest man never talks of himself.

We cannot better understand how ridiculous vanity is, and what a disgraceful vice it is, than by observing how careful it is not to be seen, and how often it hides itself underneath a semblance of modesty.

False modesty is the highest affectation of vanity; it never shows a vain man in his true colours, but, on the contrary, enhances his reputation, through the very virtue which is the opposite of the vice constituting his real character; it is a falsehood. False glory is the rock on which vanity splits; it induces a desire in men to be esteemed for things they indeed possess, but which are frivolous and unworthy of being noticed; it is an error.

(67.) Men speak of themselves in such a manner, that though they admit they are guilty of some trifling faults, these very faults imply noble talents or great qualities. Thus they complain of a bad memory, though quite satisfied with the large amount of common sense and sound judgment they possess; submit to being reproached for absence of mind and musing, imagining them the concomitants

[554] See page 68, note 170.

[555] This refers to the Prince de Conti (1661-1685), a cousin of the Duke de Bourbon, the pupil of our author. When the Prince's wife, formerly Mademoiselle de Blois, a daughter of Louis XIV. and Mademoiselle de la Vallière, was attacked by the small-pox, he nursed her so well that she recovered, but he died.

of intelligence; acknowledge being awkward and not able to do anything with their hands, and comfort themselves for being without these small qualities by the knowledge of possessing those of the understanding or those innate feelings which every one allows them. In owning their indolence they always intimate they are disinterested and entirely cured of ambition; they are not ashamed of being slovenly, which shows they merely are careless of little things, and seems to imply that they solely occupy themselves with solid and important matters. A military man affects to say that it was rashness or curiosity which carried him into the trenches on a certain day, or in a dangerous spot, without being on duty or ordered to do so; and he adds that the general reprimanded him for it. Thus a man possessing brains or a solid genius and an innate circumspection which other men endeavour in vain to acquire; a man who has strengthened his mind by a long experience; to whom the number, weight, variety, difficulty, and importance of affairs merely procure some occupation without embarrassing him; who, by his extensive knowledge and penetration masters all events; who does not consult all the remarks ever written on the art of governments and politics, but is, perhaps, one of those sublime minds created to sway others, and from whose example those rules were first made; who is diverted, by the great things he does, from those pleasant and agreeable things he might read, and who, on the contrary, loses nothing by recapitulating and turning over, as it were, his own life and actions: a man, so constituted, may easily, and without compromising himself, admit that he knows nothing of books and never reads.[556]

(68.) Men intend sometimes to conceal their imperfections, or attenuate the opinion of others about them, by frankly acknowledging them. "I am very ignorant," says some man who knows nothing; "I am getting old," says a second above threescore; "I am far from rich," says a third who is wretchedly poor.

(69.) There is either no such thing as modesty, or it is mistaken for something quite different, if we think it to be an inward sentiment, debasing man in his own eyes, and which is a supernatural virtue we call humility. Man naturally thinks of himself with pride and conceit, and thinks thus of no one but himself; modesty only aims at modifying this disposition so that no one shall suffer by it; it is an external virtue, which commands our looks, gait, words, tone of voice, and obliges a man ostensibly to act with others as if in reality he did not despise them.

(70.) There are many people in this world who inwardly and habitually draw a comparison between themselves and others, always give a decision in favour of their own merits, and behave accordingly.

(71.) You say, "Men must be modest;" that is what all intelligent men desire; but then people tyrannise over those who yield through modesty, and should not crush them when they give way.

Again some say, "People should be quiet in their dress;" intelligent men do not wish for anything else; but the world requires ornaments, and we comply with its demands; it runs eagerly after superfluities, and we display them. Some

---

[556] According to the "Keys," this paragraph alludes to Louvois. See page 132, note 255, and page 242, note 484.

people value others only for the fine linen or the rich silks they wear, and we do not always refuse to purchase esteem, even on those terms. There are some places where every person shows himself, and where you will be admitted or refused admittance according as your gold lace is broader or narrower.

(72.) Vanity, and the high value we set upon ourselves, makes us imagine that others treat us very haughtily, which is sometimes true and often false; a modest man is not so susceptible.

(73.) We ought not to be so vain and imagine that others are anxious to have a look at us, and to esteem us, and that our talents and merits are the topics of their conversations, but we should have so much confidence in ourselves as not to fancy when people whisper that they speak ill of us, or laugh only to make fun of us.

(74.) What is the reason that to-day Alcippus bows to me, smiles and almost throws himself out of his coach to take notice of me. I am not rich, and on foot; therefore, according to the present fashion, he ought not to have seen me. Is it not because a person of the highest rank is with him in his carriage?

(75.) Men are so full of themselves, that everything they do is connected with self; they like to be seen, to be shown about, even by those who do not know them, and who, if they omit this, are said to be proud, for they should guess who and what those men are.

(76.) We never look for happiness within ourselves, but in the opinions of men we know to be flatterers, insincere, unjust, envious, whimsical and prejudiced. How eccentric!

(77.) We might think that people laugh only at something really ridiculous; yet there are certain people who laugh just as much at what is not so as at what is. If you are foolish and thoughtless, and some unbecoming expression escapes you, they laugh at you; if you are wise, and say nothing but what is sensible, and as it should be said, they laugh at you all the same.

(78.) Those who, by violence or injustice, steal our property, or rob us of our honour by slander, show effectually that they hate us; but this is not an undoubted proof that they no longer esteem us; therefore, it is not impossible that we may forgive them, and, one day or other, again become their friends. Ridicule, on the contrary, is of all wrongs the least to be excused, for it is the language of contempt, and one of the ways in which it is most plainly expressed; it attacks a man in his last intrenchment, namely, the good opinion he has of himself; it aims at making him ridiculous in his own eyes; and thus convinces him that the person who ridicules him is very badly disposed towards him, so that he resolves never to be reconciled to him.

It is monstrous to consider how easy it is for us to ridicule, censure, and despise others, and how we enjoy it; and yet how enraged we are when others ridicule, censure, and despise us.

(79.) Health and wealth prevent men from experiencing misfortunes, and thus make them callous to their suffering fellow-creatures; whilst they who already are burdened by their own miseries feel most tenderly those of others.

(80.) In well-constituted minds,[557] festivals, spectacles, and music bring more vividly before us, and make us feel the more the misfortunes of our relatives or friends.

(81.) A great mind is above insults, injustice, grief, and raillery, and would be invulnerable were it not open to compassion.

(82.) We feel somewhat ashamed of being happy at the sight of certain miseries.

(83.) Men have a very quick perception of their smallest advantages and are as backward in discovering their faults. They never ignore they have fine eyebrows and well-shaped nails, but scarcely know they have lost an eye, and not at all when they are wanting in understanding.

Argyra pulls off her glove to show her fine hand, and does not forget to let us have a peep of her little shoe, which makes us think she has a small foot; she laughs at serious as well as at funny observations to show her fine teeth; if she does not hide her ears it is because they are well shaped; and if she does not dance, it is because she is not too well satisfied with her waist, which is not very slender. She knows perfectly well what she is about, with the exception of one thing: she is always talking, and has not one grain of sense.

(84.) Men do not value very highly the affections of the heart, but idolise the gifts of body and mind. A person who, in speaking of himself, would coolly say that he is good, constant, faithful, sincere, just, and grateful, does not imagine he offends against modesty; but he would not venture to say that he is sprightly, or that he has fine teeth or a soft skin; that would be rather too much of a good thing.

It cannot be denied that men admire two virtues, courage and liberality, because they highly value two things which these virtues cause us to neglect, namely, life and money; yet no one boasts that he is courageous or liberal.

No one in speaking of himself will say, especially without any foundation, that he is handsome, generous, eminent, for men value those qualities too highly, and so they are satisfied with thinking they possess them.

(85.) Whatever similarity is apparent between jealousy and emulation, they differ as much as vice and virtue.

Jealousy and emulation have the same object, which is the prosperity or merit of another, but with this difference, that the latter is a voluntary sentiment, as courageous as sincere, which fertilises the mind and induces it to take advantage of great examples, so that it not seldom excels what it admires; whilst the first, on the contrary, is violent in its action, and, as it were, a forced acknowledgment of a merit it does not possess; it goes so far as even to deny merit whenever it exists; or, if it is compelled to admit its existence, refuses to commend it, and envies the reward it receives. Jealousy is a barren passion, which leaves a man in the same state

---

[557] The original has "aux âmes bien nées," a very favourite expression of the French authors of the seventeenth century; thus P. Corneille, amongst others, says in the Cid:

"Pour des âmes bien nées,
La valeur n'attend point le nombre des années."

it finds him, fills him with high ideas of himself and of his reputation; causes him to become callous and insensible to the actions and labours of others; and inspires him with astonishment on perceiving in this world other talents than his own, or other men with the same talents on which he prides himself; this disgraceful vice, which by its very excess always turns to vanity and presumption, does not so much persuade the person infected with it that he has more intelligence and merit than others, as that he alone is intelligent and praiseworthy.

Emulation and jealousy are always found in persons practising the same art, possessing the same talents, and filling the same positions. The meanest artisans are most subject to jealousy; those persons who follow the liberal arts or literature, as artists, musicians, orators, poets, and all who pretend to write, ought not to be capable of anything but emulation.

Jealousy is never free from some sort of envy; and these two passions are often taken for one another. But this is wrong: envy may sometimes exist without jealousy, as, for example, when a position very superior to our own, a large fortune, royal favour, or a secretaryship of state have caused it.

Envy and hatred are always united, and fortify each other in one and the same person; they can only be distinguished from one another in this, that the latter aims at the individual, the former at his position and condition in life.

An intelligent man is not jealous of a cutler who has made a first-rate sword, nor of a sculptor who has just finished a fine piece of statuary; he knows there are rules and methods in those arts beyond his ken; that tools have to be handled with which he is unacquainted, and of whose very names and shapes he is ignorant; it is sufficient for him to be aware that he has never served an apprenticeship to such a trade, and he consoles himself, therefore, that he has not mastered them. But he may, on the contrary, envy, and even be jealous of a minister of state, and of those who govern; as if reason and common sense, of which he has a share as well as they have, are the only things required for ruling a nation and for the administration of public affairs, and as if they could take the place of regulations, directions, and experience.

(86.) We meet with few utterly dull and stupid men, but with fewer sublime and transcendental ones. The generality of mankind hovers between these two extremes; the gap is filled by a great number of men of ordinary talents, but who are very useful and serviceable to the State, and efficient as well as agreeable; as, for example, in commerce, finances, during war, in navigation, arts, trades, in the possession of a good memory, in gambling,[558] in society, and in conversation.

(87.) All the intelligence of the world is useless to a man who has none, for having no ideas himself, he cannot be improved by those of others.

(88.) To feel the want of reasoning faculties is the next thing to possessing them;

---

[558] Gambling was highly valued at court (see page 154, § 71); the Marquis de Dangeau (see page 156, note 311) owed partly his position to his successes at the gambling-table; and the mathematician Sauveur, a member of the Academy of Sciences, used to give scientific demonstrations before the king and the court of the various combinations of the fashionable games.

a madman cannot have this sensation. Thus the next best thing to intelligence is the consciousness that we have none, for then we might do what is considered impossible, and, without intelligence, neither be a fool nor a fop nor impertinent.

(89.) A man who has not a large amount of intelligence is grave and all of a piece; he does not laugh, he never jokes nor trifles; and is as incapable of rising to great things as of suiting himself, by way of change, to small ones; he hardly knows how to play with his children.

(90.) Everybody says of a coxcomb that he is a coxcomb, but no one dares to tell him so; he dies without knowing it and without anybody being avenged on him.

(91.) What a dissonance is there between the mind and the heart! Some philosophers lead bad lives though they have large stores of "wise saws;" and some politicians, full of schemes and ideas, cannot govern themselves.

(92.) The mind wears out like other things; sciences are its aliment; they nourish it and wear it out.

(93.) Men of inferior rank are sometimes burdened with a thousand useless virtues, but they have no opportunities of making use of them.

(94.) We meet with some men who bear with ease the weight of the royal favour and of power, who get accustomed to their grandeur, and remain steady though they occupy the highest posts. On the contrary, those men whom fortune, without any choice or discrimination, has almost blindly overwhelmed with its blessings, behave insolently and extravagantly; their looks, their carriage, their tone of voice, and their manner of receiving people, show for some time the admiration they have for themselves, as well as for beholding themselves on such an eminence; they become at last so restless that their downfall alone can tame them.

(95.) A stout and robust fellow, who has a wide chest and a broad pair of shoulders, carries heavy burdens quickly and gracefully, and has still one hand at liberty, while a dwarf would be crushed by half his load. Thus eminent stations make great men yet more great, and little ones less.

(96.) Some men gain by being eccentric; they scud along in full sail in a sea where others are lost and dashed to pieces; they are successful by the very means which would seem to prevent all success; they reap from their irregularity and folly all the advantages of consummate wisdom; they are men who devote themselves to other men, to high-born nobles, for whom they have sacrificed everything, and in whom they have placed their last hope; they do not serve, but amuse them. Obsequious men of merit are useful to the great; they are necessary to them, and grow old whilst retailing their witticisms, for which they expect to be rewarded as if they had done some noble deeds; by dint of being funny they obtain posts of great importance, and rise to the highest dignities by continually buffooning, until finally and unexpectedly they find themselves in a position they neither dreaded nor anticipated. Nothing remains of them in this world but an example of their success, which it would be dangerous to imitate.[559]

---

[559] The Marshal de la Feuillade is supposed to be meant. Besides the monument he

(97.) People might expect that certain persons who once performed some noble and heroic actions known to the entire world, would not be exhausted by so arduous an effort, and should at least be as rational and judicious in their behaviour as men commonly are; that they should be above any meanness unworthy of the great reputation they have acquired; and that by mixing less with the people they should not give them an opportunity of viewing them too closely, so that curiosity and admiration might not change to indifference, and perhaps to contempt.[560]

(98.) It is easier for some men to enrich themselves with a thousand virtues than to correct a single vice; it is unfortunate for them that this vice is often the least suitable to their condition in life, and renders them highly ridiculous; it weakens their splendid and grand qualities, and prevents them from becoming perfect and keeping their reputation stainless. We do not require these men to be more enlightened and incorruptible, more fond of order and discipline, more assiduous in doing their duties, more zealous for the public good, or more solemn in their deportment; we could only desire them to be less amorous.[561]

(99.) Some men in the course of their lives alter so much in feeling and intelligence, that we are sure to make a mistake if we judge merely of them by what they appeared in their early youth. Some were pious, wise, and learned, who have been spoiled by the favours fortune bestowed on them, and are so no longer;[562] others began their lives amidst pleasures, and devoted all their intelligence in their pursuit, but, being no longer in favour, they now are religious, wise, and temperate.[563] These latter commonly become great men, who may be relied upon; their honesty has been tried by patience and adversity; they, moreover, show great politeness, which they owe to the society of ladies, and display in every circumstance, as well as a spirit of order, thoughtfulness, and sometimes lofty capacities, acquired by study and the leisure of a shattered fortune.

All men's misfortunes proceed from their aversion to being alone; hence gambling, extravagance, dissipation, wine, women, ignorance, slander, envy, and forgetfulness of what we owe to God and ourselves.

erected to Louis XIV. (see page 227, note 455), there are many other proofs of his eccentricity, as, for example, his going with two hundred volunteers to wrest Candia from the Turks, and his voyage to Spain to challenge a certain M. de Saint-Aunay, who was accused of having calumniated Louis XIV.

[560] The commentators speak of a certain captain of the guard, Boisselot, and of an Irish officer, Macarthy, one of the generals of James II.; but there would have been nothing astonishing in their "mixing with the people." It may be that this paragraph points at the Duke of Orléans, a brother-of Louis XIV., who had shown some valour at the battle of Cassel in 1677, but who was never more employed, and was not very "judicious."

[561] All the "Keys" say the Archbishop of Paris, M. de Harlay, was meant. See also page 238, note 476.

[562] The Cardinal de Bouillon (1644-1715) is supposed to be meant by this remark; he was, however, according to Saint-Simon, always very dissolute in his manners. See page 210, note 436.

[563] Some "Keys" name here wrongly Boutillier de Rancé, the founder of the Trappists, whilst others speak of Le Camus, bishop of Grenoble (see page 47, note 4). La Bruyère's allusion is far more general.

(100.) Men are sometimes unbearable to themselves; darkness and solitude unsettle them, and throw them into a state of imaginary dread and groundless terror; at such a time the least harm that can befall them is a lassitude of everything.

(101.) Idleness is the mother of listlessness, and chiefly induces men to hunt after diversions, gambling, and company. He who loves work requires nothing else.

(102.) Most men employ the first years of their life in making the last miserable.

(103.) There are some works which begin with the first letter of the alphabet and end with the last; good, bad, and indifferent things are all inserted; nothing of a certain nature is forgotten; and these, though made up of far-fetched jokes and affectations, are called "sports of wit."[564] The same kind of sport also rules our conduct; a certain matter once commenced must be finished, and we have to go on till the end. It would have been much better to alter our plan or entirely to drop it; but it is far more odd and difficult to proceed with it, and therefore we go on, and are stimulated by contradiction; vanity encourages us, and takes the place of reason, which abandons and leaves us. Such eccentricity is even carried on in the most virtuous actions, and often in some of a religious nature.

(104.) To do our duty is an effort to us, because when we do it we only perform our obligations, and seldom receive those eulogies which are the greatest incentive to commendable actions, and support us in our enterprises. N ... loves to make a display of his charity, so he is appointed a superintendent of a charity-board, and a steward to its revenues, whilst his house becomes a public office for the distribution of them;[565] his doors are open to all clergymen or to Sisters of Charity;[566] and every one sees and talks about his liberality in relieving the poor. Who would dare to imagine N ... was not an honest man, unless it were his creditors?

(105.) Géronte dies of mere decrepitude, and without having made the will he intended to make for those last thirty years; as he died intestate, about half a score of relatives share his estate among them. For a long time he was only kept alive through the care taken of him by his wife, Asteria, who, though young, always attended on him, never let him go out of her sight, nursed him in his old age, and at last closed his eyes. He has not left her money enough to rid her of the necessity

----

[564] All the "Keys" say this refers to the Dictionnaire de l'Académie, but its first edition only appeared in 1694, and this paragraph was published four years before. See page 9, note 46. It alludes probably to those encyclopedias called Traités sur toutes les sciences, très abrégés à l'usage de la noblesse, or to some collection of anecdotes, a kind of omnium gatherum, entitled Bibliothèque des gens de cour; perhaps it might also apply to some verses then in vogue, and called vers abécédaires, of which the first line began with an "a," the second with a "b," and so on. Those "sports of wit," which our author calls by the name of jeux d'esprit, witticisms, also existed later in England, e.g., "The Foundling Hospital for Wit."

[565] Several persons have been named whose duty it was to distribute charity to the poor, but it has been rightly observed that the person alluded to in this paragraph "makes a display of it," and therefore it cannot have been his duty.

[566] In French, sœurs grises, grey sisters, because the Sisters of Charity wore grey dresses. Bands were then worn by every one, but clergymen's bands were plain and called petits collets, the name our author gives them.

of taking another old man for a husband.

(106.) When people are loth to sell or give up their posts and offices, even when in extreme old age, it is a token they are possessed of the notion that they are immortal; or if they think they may die, it is a sign they love nobody but themselves.[567]

(107.) Faustus is a rake, a prodigal, a free-thinker, as well as ungrateful and passionate; yet his uncle Aurelius neither hates him nor disinherits him.

Frontin, his other nephew, after twenty years of acknowledged honesty and of blind complacency for the old man, never gained his favour; and the only legacy left to him is a small pension, which Faustus, the sole heir, has to pay him.

(108.) Hatred is so lasting and stubborn, that reconciliation on a sick-bed certainly forebodes death.

(109.) We insinuate ourselves into the favour of others, either by flattering those passions which animate them, or by pitying the infirmities which afflict their bodies; and this is the only way by which we can show our regard for them; hence the healthy and those who do not desire anything, are less easy to be swayed.

(110.) Want of vigour and voluptuousness are innate in man and cease with him, and fortunate or unfortunate circumstances never make him abandon them; they are the fruits of prosperity or become a solace in adversity.

(111.) The most unnatural sight in the world is an old man in love.

(112.) Few men remember that they have been young, and how hard it was then to live chaste and temperate.

The first thing men do when they have renounced pleasure, through decency, lassitude, or for the sake of health, is to condemn it in others. Such conduct denotes a kind of latent affection for the very things they left off; they would like no one to enjoy a pleasure they can no longer indulge in; and thus they show their feelings of jealousy.

(113.) It is not the dread of one day wanting money which renders old men avaricious, for some of them have such a large quantity of it that this cannot make them uneasy; besides, how can the fear disturb them of being in want of the common necessities of life when they are old, since by their own free will they deprive themselves of these to satisfy their avarice. Neither do they wish to leave great riches to their children, for they naturally love nobody better than themselves; moreover, there are many misers who have no heirs. Avarice seems rather an effect of age and of the disposition of old men, who as naturally give themselves up to it as they did to pleasure in their youth, or to ambition in their manhood. Neither vigour, youth, nor health are needed to become a miser; nor is there any necessity

[567] Holders of certain legal or financial offices had the right of reversion or next nomination whilst they were alive, and not seldom delayed exercising it until they were very old; but unless they did so within forty days of their death, and had paid an annual tax called le droit de paulette, so called after Charles Paulet, a minister of Henri IV. who established it in 1604, and which tax varied from a sixtieth to a fourth of the value of the office, the king had a right to make fresh appointments. See also page 192, note 400.

for people hurrying themselves, nor for those who hoard being in the slightest degree active; a man has nothing to do but let the money lie in his coffers, and deny himself everything; this is not very difficult for old people, who must have some passion or other because they are men.[568]

(114.) There are some people who dwell in wretched houses, have hardly any beds, are badly clad and worse fed; who are exposed to all the severity of the seasons, deprive themselves of the society of their fellow-creatures, and live in continual solitude; who grieve for the present, the past, and the future; whose lives are a perpetual penance, and who have thus discovered the secret of going to perdition by the most troublesome way: I mean misers.

(115.) The remembrance of their youth remains green in the heart of old men; they love the places where they lived; and the persons with whom they then began an acquaintance are dear to them; they still affect certain words in use when they first began to speak; they prefer the ancient style of singing and dancing; and boast of the old fashions in dress, furnishing, and carriages; they cannot bring themselves to disapprove of those things which served their passions, and are always recalling them. Can any one imagine these old men would prefer new customs and the latest fashions, which they do not adopt, and from which they have nothing to expect, which young men have invented, and which give them, in their turn, such a great advantage over their elders?

(116.) An old man who is careless in his dress, or else overdressed, increases his wrinkles, and looks as senile as he really is.

(117.) An old man is proud, disdainful, and unsociable if he is not very intelligent.

(118.) A courtier of a ripe old age, who is a sensible man and has a good memory, is an inestimable treasure; he is full of anecdotes and maxims; he knows a good many curious circumstances of the history of the age, which are never met with in books; and from him we may learn such rules for our conduct and manners which can be depended upon, because they are based on experience.[569]

(119.) Young men can bear solitude better than old people, because their passions occupy their thoughts.

(120.) Though Philip[570] is rather old, he is over-natty and effeminate, and only cares for little dainties; he has studied the art of eating, drinking, sleeping, and taking exercise, and scrupulously observes the smallest rules he has prescribed for himself, which all tend to his comfort; even a mistress, if his system allowed

[568] Jean François, Marquis d'Hautefort, who was, it is said, the original of Harpagon in Molière's Avare, seems to be partly portrayed in this paragraph.

[569] Some of the commentators pretend that the "courtier of a ripe old age" was the Marshal Nicolas de Villeroy, the former governor of Louis XIV., who died in 1685, and whose son, the Duke, is mentioned on page 54, note 3, and on page 204, note 1.

[570] It is said that by Philip our author intended to portray the Marquis de Sablé, a son of the finance minister Servien, who was the proprietor of Meudon, sold it to Louvois (see the chapter "Of the Court," page 204, note 423), and seems to have been chiefly known by his love for eating and drinking, his eccentricities and his debauchery.

him to keep one, could not tempt him to break them; he is overburdened with superfluities, to which he is so accustomed that he cannot do without them. He thus increases and strengthens the ties which bind him to life, and employs the remainder of it in making its loss more grievous. Was he not already sufficiently afraid of dying?

(121.) Gnathon[571] lives for no one but himself, and the rest of the world are to him as if they did not exist. He is not satisfied with occupying the best seat at table, but he must take the seats of two other guests, and forgets that the dinner was not provided for him alone, but for the company as well; he lays hold of every dish, and looks on each course as his own; he never sticks to one single dish until he has tried them all, and would like to enjoy them all at one and the same time. At table his hands serve for a knife and fork; he paws the meat over and over again, and tears it to pieces, so that if the other guests wish to dine, it must be on his leavings. He does not spare them any of those filthy and disgusting habits which are enough to spoil the appetite of the most hungry; the gravy and sauce run over his chin and beard; if he takes part of a stew out of a dish, he spills it by the way over another dish and on the cloth, so you may distinguish him by his track. He eats with a great deal of smacking and noise, rolls his eyes, and uses the table as a manger, picks his teeth and continues eating; he makes every place his home, and will have as much elbow-room in church and in a theatre as if he were in his own room. When he rides in a coach, it must always be forward, for he says that any other seat will make him fall in a swoon, if we can believe him. When he travels he is always in advance of his companions, so as to get first to the inn, and choose the best room and the best bed for himself; he makes use of everybody, and his own and other people's servants run about and do his errands; everything is his he lays his hands on, even clothes and luggage; he disturbs every one, but does not inconvenience himself for anybody; he pities no one, and knows no other indispositions but his own, his over-feeding and biliousness; he laments no person's death, fears no one's but his own, and to redeem his own life, would willingly consent to see the entire human race become extinct.

(122.) Clito[572] never had but two things to do in his life, to dine at noon and to eat supper in the evening;[573] he seems only born for digestion, and has only one subject of conversation, namely, the *entrées* of the last dinner he was present at, and how many different kinds of *potages*[574] there were; he then talks of the roasts and *entremets*; remembers precisely what dishes were brought up after the first course, does not forget the side-dishes, the fruit and the *assiettes*;[575] names all the

____

[571] Louis Roger Danse, a canon of the Sainte-Chapelle, and a noted gourmand, is supposed to have sat for Gnathon, as well as for the stout Canon Evrard in Boileau's Lutrin.

[572] The Count d'Olonne, a well-known lover of good cheer, who died in 1690, is said to have been limned as Clito; others think it was another gourmet, M. de Bruslard, Count de Broussain, who lived until 1693.

[573] See page 179, note 376.

[574] The potages, in La Bruyère's time, different from what is now understood by them, seem to have been a sort of stew.

[575] These were either entremets or side-dishes not larger than could be contained in

wines and every kind of liquor he has drunk; shows himself as well acquainted as a man can possibly be with culinary language, and makes his hearer long to be at a good dinner, provided he were not there. He prides himself on his palate which cannot be imposed upon, and has never been exposed to the terrible inconvenience of being compelled to eat a wretched stew or to drink an indifferent wine. He is a remarkable person in his way, who has brought the art of good living to the highest perfection; there never will be another man who ate so much and so nicely; he is, therefore, the supreme arbiter of dainty bits, and it would hardly be allowable to like anything he did not approve of. But he is no more! When he was almost dying he still would be carried to the table, and had guests to dinner on the day of his death. Wherever he may be he is sure to eat; and should he rise from the grave it will be to eat.

(123.) Ruffinus' hair begins to turn grey, but he is healthy; his ruddy cheeks and sparkling eyes promise him at least twenty years more; he is lively, jovial, familiar, and does not care for anything; he laughs heartily, even when he is alone, and without any cause; he is satisfied with himself, with his family, his little fortune, and calls himself fortunate. Some time since he lost his only son, a young man of great promise, who might have become an honour to his family; other people shed tears, but he did not, and merely said, "My son is dead, and his mother will soon follow him," and then he was comforted. He has no passions, no friends nor enemies; no one troubles him; everybody and everything suits him; he speaks to those he never saw before with the same freedom and confidence as to those he calls his old friends, and very soon tells them his bad jokes and stories. Some people address him and then leave him, but he does not mind it, and the tale he began to one person he finishes to another who has just come.

(124.) N ... is less worn with age than disease, for he is not more than threescore and eight, but he has the gout and suffers from nephritic colic; he looks quite emaciated and has a greenish complexion, which forebodes no good; yet he has his lands marled, and reckons he has no need to manure them these fifteen years; he has some young wood planted, and hopes that in less than twenty years it will afford him a delicious shade. He has a house built of free-stone, and at the corners are iron clasps to make it stronger; he assures you, coughing, and in a weak and feeble tone of voice, that it will last for ever. He walks every day among the workmen, leaning on one of his servants' arms, shows his friends what he has done, and tells them what he purposes to do. He does not build for his children, for he has none, nor for his heirs, who are scoundrels and who have quarrelled with him; he only builds to enjoy it himself, and to-morrow he will be dead.

(125.) Antagoras has a familiar[576] and popular countenance; he is as well known to the mob as the parish beadle or as the saint carved in stone adorning the high altar. Every morning he runs up and down the courts and the offices of parliament,[577] and every evening up and down the streets and highways of the town. He has had a lawsuit these forty years, and has always been nearer his

---

a plate or assiette.

[576] Trivial in French. See page 136, note 265.

[577] See page 181, note 381.

death than the end of his legal troubles. There has not been any celebrated case or any long and difficult lawsuit tried that he has not had something to do with; his name is in the mouth of every barrister, and agrees as naturally with such words as "plaintiff" or "defendant" as an adjective does with a substantive. He is everybody's kinsman, and disliked by all; there is scarcely a family of whom he does not complain, or who does not complain of him; he is perpetually engaged in seizing some property, in asking for an injunction[578] to prevent the sale of an office[579] or some stocks, in using the privilege of pleading in certain cases[580] or of seeing some judgments put into execution; besides this, he is every day at some meeting of creditors, is appointed chairman of their committee,[581] and loses money by every bankruptcy; he finds some spare moments for a few private visits, and like an old gossip[582] talks about lawsuits, and tells you all the news about them. You leave him one hour at one end of the town and find him the next at another end,[583] where he arrived before you, and has been giving again all the details of his lawsuit. If you yourself are engaged in a lawsuit and wait early the next morning on your judge,[584] you are sure to meet Antagoras, who must first leave before you can be admitted.[585]

(126.) Some men pass their long lives in defending themselves and in injuring other people, and die at last, worn out with age, after having caused as many evils as they suffered.

(127.) There must, I confess, be seizures of land, distraint on furniture, prisons, and punishments; but without taking into consideration justice, law, and stern necessity, it has always astonished me to observe with what violence some men treat other men.

(128.) Certain wild animals, male and female, are scattered over the country, dark, livid, and quite tanned by the sun, who are chained, as it were, to the land they are always digging and turning up and down with an unwearied stubbornness; their voice is somewhat articulate, and when they stand erect they discover a human face, and, indeed, are men. At night they retire to their burrows, where they live on black bread, water, and roots; they spare other men the trouble of sowing, tilling the ground, and reaping for their sustenance, and, therefore, deserve not to be in want of that bread they sow themselves.

---

[578] This asking for an injunction was called s'opposer au sceau, literally "to oppose one's self to the seal."

[579] See page 130, note 254, and page 192, note 400.

[580] Committimus, in the original.

[581] The chairman is the syndic de direction.

[582] Vieil meuble de ruelle. Vieil was, in La Bruyère's time, often used instead of vieux, even before a consonant. For ruelle, see page 65, note 161.

[583] The original speaks of the "Marais" (see page 172, note 341), and of the "Grand Faubourg," probably the "Faubourg Saint-Germain."

[584] See page 72, note 175.

[585] The "Keys" name for Antagoras two eccentric noblemen of the time now wholly unknown, a Count de Montluc and a Marquis de Fourille.

(129.) Don Fernando resides in his province, and is idle, ignorant, slanderous, quarrelsome, knavish, intemperate, and impertinent; but he draws his sword against his neighbours, and exposes his life for the smallest trifle; he has killed several men, and will be killed in his turn.[586]

(130.) A provincial nobleman, useless to his country, his family and himself, often without a roof to cover himself, without clothes or the least merit, tells you ten times a day that he is of noble lineage, despises all graduates, doctors, and presidents of parliaments[587] as upstarts, and spends all his time among parchments and old title-deeds, which he would not part with to be appointed chancellor.[588]

(131.) Power, favour, genius, riches, dignity, nobility, force, industry, capacity, virtue, vice, weakness, stupidity, poverty, impotence, plebeianism, and servility generally are combined in men in endless variety. These qualities mixed together in a thousand various manners, and compensating one another in many ways, form the different states and conditions of human life. Moreover, people who are acquainted with each other's strength and weakness act reciprocally, for they believe it their duty; they know their equals, are conscious that some men are their superiors, and that they are superior to some others; and hence familiarity, respect or deference, pride or contempt. This is the reason why, in places of public resort, we see each moment some persons we wish to accost or bow to, and others we pretend not to know, and still less desire to meet; and why we are proud of being with the first and ashamed of the others. Hence it even happens that the very person with whom you think it an honour to be seen, and with whom you are desirous to converse, deems you troublesome and leaves you; and that often the very person who blushes when he meets others, receives the same treatment when others meet him, and that a man who treated others with contempt is himself disdained, for it is common enough to despise those who despise us. How wretched is such a behaviour; and since it is certain that in this strange interchange we gain on one side what we lose on another, should we not do better to abandon all haughtiness and pride, qualities so unsuited to frail humanity, and make an arrangement to treat one another with mutual kindness, by which we should at once gain the advantage of never being mortified ourselves, and the happiness, which is just as great, of never mortifying others?

(132.) Instead of being frightened, or even ashamed, at being called a philosopher, everybody in this world ought to have a strong tincture of philosophy;[589] it suits every one: its practice is useful to people of all ages, sexes, and conditions; it

[586] In Louis XIV.'s time France was divided into thirty-three provinces, and as communications were difficult, the inferior noblemen were what our author describes them to be, and had no other amusements but duelling, dining, and drinking.

[587] The original has fourrures et mortiers; the gowns of bachelors, licentiates, and doctors of the various faculties were bordered and even sometimes lined with fur. For mortier see page 168, note 331.

[588] In French les masses d'un chancelier, for the mace was always carried before the Chancellor of France.

[589] La Bruyère adds in a note: "We can only mean that philosophy which is depending on the Christian religion."

consoles us for the happiness of others, for the promotion of those whom we think undeserving, for failures, and decay of strength and beauty; it steels us against poverty, age, sickness, and death, against fools and buffoons; it will help us to pass away our life without a wife, or to bear with the one with whom we have to live.

(133.) Men are one hour overjoyed at trifles, and the next overcome with grief for a mere disappointment; nothing is more unequal and incoherent than the emotions stirring their hearts and minds in so short a time. If they would set no higher value on the things of this world than they really deserve, this evil would be cured.

(134.) It is as difficult to find a vain man who believes himself as happy as he deserves, as a modest man who believes himself too unhappy.

(135.) When I contemplate the fortune of princes and of their Ministers, which is not mine, I am prevented from thinking myself unhappy by considering, at the same time, the fate of the vine-dresser, the soldier, and the stone-cutter.

(136.) There is but one real misfortune which can befall a man, and that is to find himself at fault, and to have something to reproach himself with.

(137.) The generality of men are more capable of great efforts to obtain their ends than of continuous perseverance; their occupation and inconstancy deprives them of the fruits of the most promising beginnings; they are often overtaken by those who started some time after them, and who walk slowly but without intermission.

(138.) I almost dare affirm that men know better how to plan certain measures than to pursue them, how to resolve what they must needs do and say than to do or to say what is necessary. A man is firmly determined not to mention a certain subject when negotiating some business; and afterwards, either through passion, garrulity, or in the heat of conversation, it is the first thing which escapes him.

(139.) Men are indolent in what is their particular duty, whilst they think it very deserving, or rather whilst it pleases their vanity, to busy themselves about those things which do not concern them, nor suit their condition of life or character.

(140.) There is as much difference between a heterogeneous character a man adopts and his real character as there is between a mask and a countenance of flesh and blood.

(141.) Telephus has some intelligence, but ten times less, if rightly computed, than he imagines he has; therefore, in everything he says, does, meditates, and projects, he goes ten times beyond his capacity, and thus always exceeds the true measure of his intellectual power and grasp. And this argument is well founded. He is limited by a barrier, as it were, and should be warned not to pass it; but he leaps over it, launches out of his sphere, and though he knows his own weakness, always displays it; he speaks about what he does not understand, or badly understands; attempts things above his power, and aims at what is too much for him; he thinks himself the equal of the very best men ever seen. Whatever is good and commendable in him is obscured by an affectation of doing something great and wonderful; people can easily see what he is not, but have to guess what he really is. He is a man who never measures his ability, and does not know himself; his true character is not to be satisfied with the one that suits him, and which is his own.

(142.) The intelligence of a highly cultivated man is not always the same, and has its ebbs and flows; sometimes he is full of animation, but cannot keep it up; then, if he be wise, he will say little, not write at all, and not endeavour either to draw upon his imagination, or try to please. Does a man sing who has a cold? and should he not rather wait till he recovers his voice?

A blockhead is an automaton,[590] a piece of machinery moved by springs and weights, always turning him about in one direction; he always displays the same equanimity, is uniform, and never alters; if you have seen him once you have seen him as he ever was, and will be; he is at best but like a lowing ox or a whistling blackbird; I may say, he acts according to the persistence and doggedness of his nature and species. What you see least is his torpid soul, which is never stirring, but always dormant.

(143.) A blockhead never dies; or if, according to our manner of speaking, he dies at one time or other, I may truly say he gains by it, and that, when others die, he begins to live. His mind then thinks, reasons, draws inferences and conclusions, judges, foresees, and does everything it never did before; it finds itself released from a lump of flesh, in which it seemed buried without having anything to do, and without any motion, or at least any worthy of that name; I should almost say, it blushes to have lodged in such a body, as well as for its own crude and imperfect organs, to which it has been shackled so long, and with which it could only produce a blockhead or a fool. Now it is equal to the greatest of those minds which animated the bodies of the cleverest or the most intellectual men, and the mind of the merest clodhopper[591] is no longer to be distinguished from those of Condé, Richelieu, Pascal, and Lingendes.[592]

(144.) A false delicacy in familiar actions, in manners or conduct, is not so called because it is simulated, but because it is really employed in things and on occasions where it is utterly out of place. On the other hand, a false delicacy in taste or temper is only so when it is feigned or affected. Emilia screams as loud as she can when a trifling accident happens, and when she is not a bit afraid; another lady affectedly turns pale at the sight of a mouse, or is fond of violets, and swoons at the scent of a tuberose.

(145.) Who would venture and flatter himself to satisfy mankind? Let no prince, however good and powerful, pretend to do so. Let him promote their pleasures,[593] let him open his palace to his courtiers, and even admit them amongst his

---

[590] An allusion to the theory of Descartes (see page 151, note 298), that beasts were only automatons without any consciousness of their acts.

[591] In French "Alain," the name of a rustic servant in Molière's École des Femmes.

[592] All the names given by our author have already been mentioned before, except that of Claude de Lingendes (1595-1660), one of the best preachers among the Jesuits, and whose reputation must have been great to quote him with such illustrious dead; and whilst Bossuet, Bourdaloue, and Fénelon were still alive.

[593] An allusion to the entertainments given by Louis XIV.

own followers; let him show them other spectacles in those very places of which the mere sight is a spectacle;[594] let him give them their choice of games, concerts, and refreshments, and add to this magnificent cheer, amidst the most complete liberty; join with them in their amusements; let the great man become affable, and the hero humane and familiar, and this would not be sufficient. Men finally tire of the very things which at first enraptured them; they would forsake the table of the gods; and nectar, in time, would become insipid. Through vanity and wretched over-refinement, they do not hesitate to criticise things which are perfect; in spite of every exertion, their taste, if we may believe them, can never be gratified, and even regal expenditure would be unsuccessful; malice prompts them to do what they can to lessen the joy others may feel in satisfying them. These same people, commonly so sycophantic and complaisant, are liable to forget themselves; sometimes they are scarcely to be recognised, and we see the man even in the courtier.

(146.) Affectation in gesture, speech, and manners is frequently the outcome of indolence or indifference; whereas a great passion or matters of importance seem to compel a man to become natural.

(147.) Men have no characters, or if they have, it is that of having no constant and invariable one, by which they may at all times be known; they cannot bear to be always the same, to persevere either in regularity or license; and if they sometimes forsake one virtue for another, they more often get disgusted with one vice through another vice. Their passions run counter to another, and their foibles contradict each other; extremes are easier to them than a regular and natural conduct would be; they dislike moderation, and are extravagant in good as well as evil things; and when they no longer are able to stand excesses they relieve themselves by change. Adrastes was such a profligate libertine that he found it comparatively easy to comply with the fashion and to become devout; he would have found it much more difficult to become an honest man.[595]

(148.) What is the reason that some people, who can meet the most trying disasters with coolness, lose all command over themselves and fly into a passion at the least inconvenience? Such conduct is not wise, for virtue is always the same and does not contradict itself; it is a vice, then, and nothing else but vanity, roused and stirred up by those events which make a noise in the world and when there is something to be gained, but which is negligent in all other things.

(149.) We seldom repent talking too little, but very often talking too much; this is a common and well-known maxim, which everybody knows and nobody practises.

(150.) To say things of our enemies which are not true, and to lie to defame them, is to avenge ourselves on ourselves, and give them too great an advantage over us.

(151.) If men knew how to blush at their own actions, how many crimes, and not only those that are hidden, but those that are public and well known, would

---

[594] Such places were, in our author's time, Versailles, Fontainebleau, Marly.

[595] This seems to hit at the courtiers of Louis XIV., who pretended to become devout in order to please the monarch and Madame de Maintenon.

never be committed!

(152.) If some men are not so honest as they might be, the fault lies in their bringing up.

(153.) There exists in some people a happy mediocrity of intelligence which contributes to keep them discreet.

(154.) Rods and ferulas are for children;[596] crowns, sceptres, caps, gowns, *fasces*, kettledrums, archers' dresses for men.[597] Reason and justice, without their gewgaws, would neither convince nor intimidate; man who has intelligence, is led by his eyes and his ears.

(155.) Timon, or the misanthrope, may have an austere and savage mind, but outwardly he is polite, and even ceremonious; he does not lose all command over himself, and does not become familiar with other men; on the contrary, he treats them politely and gravely, and in a manner that does not encourage any freedom to be taken; he does not desire to be better acquainted with them nor to make friends of them, and is somewhat like a lady visiting another lady.[598]

(156.) Reason is ever allied to truth, and is almost identical with it; only one way leads to it, but a thousand roads can lead us astray. The study of wisdom is not so extensive as that of fools and coxcombs; he who has seen none but polite and reasonable men, either does not know men, or knows them only by halves. Whatever difference may be noticed in disposition and manners, intercourse with the world and politeness produce the same appearance in all, and externally make men resemble one another in some way which mutually pleases, and being common to all, leads us to believe that everything else is in the same proportion. A man, on the contrary, who mixes with the common people, or retires into the country, will, if he has eyes, in a short time make some strange discoveries, and see things which are new to him, and which he never before imagined existed; gradually and by experience he increases his knowledge of humanity, and almost calculates in how many different ways man may become unbearable.

(157.) After having maturely considered mankind and found out the insincerity of their thoughts, opinions, inclinations, and affections, we are compelled to acknowledge that stubbornness does them more harm than inconstancy.

(158.) How many weak, effeminate, careless minds exist without any extraordinary faults, and who yet are proper subjects for satire! How many various kinds of ridicule are disseminated amongst the whole human race, which by their very eccentricity are of little consequence, and are not ameliorated by instruction or

[596] La Bruyère is not in advance of his times in what regards corporal punishment: Montaigne was.

[597] For "caps" and "gowns" the original has mortier and fourrures (see page 168, note 331, and page 318, note 587); for fasces see page 139, note 278.

[598] Some commentators think that the Marshal de Villeroy (see page 54, note 151) is meant by Timon, but this cannot be, as the Marshal was rather ostentatious, and not at all a misanthrope. Perhaps our author thought of giving another version of Molière's Alceste, as later on he gives another of Tartuffe, in his portrait of Onuphre, in the chapter "Of Fashion," page 395, § 24.

morality. Such vices are individual and not contagious, and are rather personal than belonging to humanity in general.

DIFFERENT OPINIONS

XII.

OF OPINIONS.

(1.) NOTHING is more like a deep-rooted conviction than obstinate conceit; whence proceed parties, intrigues, and heresies.

(2.) We do not always let our thoughts run on one and the same subject without varying them: infatuation[599] and disgust closely follow on one another.

(3.) Great things astonish and small dishearten us; custom familiarises us with both.

(4.) Two qualities quite opposed to one another equally bias our minds: custom and novelty.

(5.) There is nothing so mean and so truly vulgar as extravagantly to praise those very persons of whom we had but very indifferent opinions before their promotion.

---

[599] The original has entêtement, "infatuation," "obstinacy," which sometimes meant "enthusiasm," as in Molière's Femmes Savantes, act iii. scene 2, "J'aime la poésie avec entêtement."

(6.) A prince's favour does not exclude merit, nor does it even suppose its existence.

(7.) We are puffed up with pride and entertain a high opinion of ourselves and of the correctness of our judgment, and yet it is surprising we neglect to make use of it in speaking of other people's merit; fashion, the fancy of the people or of the prince, carry us away like a torrent; we extol rather what is praised than what is praiseworthy.

(8.) I doubt whether anything is approved and commended more reluctantly than what deserves most to be approved and praised; and whether virtue, merit, beauty, good actions, and the best writings produce a more natural and certain impression than envy, jealousy, and antipathy. A pious person[600] does not speak well of a saint, but of another pious person. If a handsome woman allows that another woman is beautiful, we may safely conclude she excels her; or if a poet praises a brother poet's verses, it is pretty sure they are wretched and spiritless.

(9.) Men do not easily like one another, and are not much inclined to commend each other. Neither actions, behaviour, thoughts, nor expression please them nor are satisfactory; they substitute for what is recited, told, or read to them what they themselves would have done in such a circumstance, or what they think and have written on such a subject; and are so full of their own ideas that they have no room for another's.

(10.) Men are generally inclined to become dissolute and frivolous, and such a large number of pernicious or ridiculous examples is to be found in this world, that I should feel inclined to believe that eccentricity, if kept within bounds and not gone too far, would almost be like correct reasoning and regular behaviour.

"We must do as others do" is a dangerous maxim, which nearly always means "we must do wrong" if it is applied to any but external things of no consequence, and depending on custom, fashion, or decency.

(11.) If men were not more like bears and panthers than men, if they were honest, just to themselves and to others, what would become of the law, the text and the prodigious amount of commentaries made on it; what of petitions and actions,[601] and everything people call jurisprudence? And to what would those persons be reduced who owe all their importance and pride to the authority with which they are invested for seeing those laws executed? If those very men were honest and sincere, and had no prejudices, the wrangles of the schoolmen, scholasticism, and all controversies would vanish. If all men were temperate, chaste, and moderate, what would be the use of that mysterious medical jargon, a gold-mine for those persons who know how to use it? What a downfall would it be for all lawyers, doctors, and physicians if we could all agree to become wise!

We would have been obliged to do without many men great in peace and war. Several arts and sciences have been brought to a high degree of exquisite perfection, which, so far from being necessary, were introduced into the world as

[600] Our author adds in a note, "a pretended pious person."
[601] The original has pétitoire et possessoire, printed in italics.

remedies for those evils only caused by our wickedness.

How many things have sprung up since Varro's[602] times, of which he was ignorant! Such a knowledge as Plato or Socrates possessed would now not satisfy us.

(12.) At a sermon, a concert, or in a picture gallery, we can hear in different parts of the room quite contrary opinions expressed upon the very same subject; and hence I draw the conclusion that in all kinds of works we may venture to insert bad things as well as good ones; for the good please some and the bad others; and we do not risk much more by putting in the very worst, for it will find admirers.

(13.) The phœnix of vocal poetry rose out of his own ashes, and in one and the same day saw his reputation lost and recovered. That same judge so infallible and yet so decided—I mean the public—changed his views regarding him, and either was, or is now, in error. He who should say to day that Q ... is a wretched poet would pronounce as bad an opinion as he who formerly said he was a good one.[603]

(14.) Chapelain was rich and Corneille was not; *La Pucelle* and *Rodogune* deserved a different fate;[604] therefore, it has always been a question why, in certain professions, one man makes his fortune and another fails? Men should look for the reason of this in their own whimsical behaviour, which, on most important occasions, when their business, their pleasures, their health, and their life are at stake, often makes them leave what is best and take what is worst.

(15.) The profession of an actor was considered infamous among the Romans, and honourable among the Greeks: how is it considered amongst us? We think of them like the Romans, and live with them like the Greeks.

(16.) It was sufficient for Bathyllus to be a pantomimist to be courted by the Roman ladies; for Rhoe to dance on the stage, or for Roscia and Nerina[605] to sing in the chorus to attract a crowd of lovers. Vanity and impudence, the consequences of being too powerful, made the Romans lose a taste for pleasures secretly and mysteriously enjoyed; they were fond of loving actresses, without any jealousy of the audience, and shared with the multitude the charms of their mistresses; they only cared to show they loved not a beauty nor an excellent actress, but an

---

[602] M. Terentius Varro (116-26 B.C.) was considered one of the most learned among the Romans. His principal works are De re rustica and De Lingua latina.

[603] This is an allusion to Quinault (see page 28, note 99), whose tragedies were all bad, but whose operas were considered well written. (See page 175, note 366.) He died in 1688, one year before the appearance of this paragraph.

[604] J. Chapelain (1595-1674), the author of La Pucelle d'Orléans, an epic poem of which only twelve cantos appeared, was the wealthiest of all the authors of his time. Rodogune, Princesse des Parthes, one of the most successful tragedies of Pierre Corneille, had been acted in 1644, and this great dramatist died in poverty and want twenty years later, at the age of seventy-eight, four years before the above paragraph was published.

[605] Bathyllus is Le Basque or Pécourt (see page 67, note 167); the names of several long-forgotten female dancers or singers are given for Rhoe, Roscia—the feminised name of the celebrated Roman actor Roscius—and Nerina.

actress.[606]

(17.) Nothing better demonstrates how men regard science and literature, and of what use they are considered in the State, than the recompense assigned to them, and the idea generally entertained of those persons who resolve to cultivate them. There is not a mere handicraft nor ever so vile a position, that is not a surer, quicker, and more certain way to wealth. An actor lolling in his coach[607] bespatters the face of Corneille walking on foot. With many people learning and pedantry are synonymous.

Often when a rich man speaks and speaks of science, the learned must be silent, listen, and applaud, at least if they would be considered something else besides learned.

(18.) A certain boldness is required to vindicate learning before some persons strongly prejudiced against learned men, whom they call ill-mannered, wanting in tact, unfit for society, and whom they send back, stripped in this way, to their study and their books. As ignorance is easy, and not difficult to acquire, many people embrace it; and these form a large majority at court and in the city, and overpower the learned. If the latter allege in their favour the names of d'Estrées, de Harlay, Bossuet, Séguier, Montausier, Wardes, Chevreuse, Novion, Lamoignon, Scudéry, Pellisson,[608] and of many other personages equally learned and polite; nay, if they dare mention the great names of Chartres, Condé, Conti, Bourbon, Maine, and Vendôme,[609] as princes who to the noblest and loftiest acquirements

[606] An allusion to the wife of Dancourt (1661-1725), an author and comic actor, who is, as an actress, said to have been neither beautiful nor excellent.

[607] According to the "Keys," the actor referred to was Baron (see page 67, note 167), or Champmeslé (1642-1701), an author and actor, and the husband of a lady known to posterity as a friend of the poet Racine.

[608] The Cardinal d'Estrées (1628-1714) was a member of the French Academy: his nephew, the Marshal, was considered a learned and polished gentleman. There were several magistrates of the name of Séguier, of whom the best known is the Chancellor Séguier (1588-1672). The Duke de Montausier, the former governor of the Dauphin, the husband of Mademoiselle de Rambouillet, and the supposed original of Molière's Misanthrope, was still alive when his name appeared, but died about a year later, in 1690. The Duke de Chevreuse, afterwards Duke de Luynes (1620-1690), an author of moral and religious works, was a friend of the Port-Royalists. The first President of the Parliament, Potier de Novion, was a member of the Academy, and died in 1693. There were two Lamoignons— the first, President of the Parliament, who died in 1677, and his son, Chrétien François, président à mortier, the friend of Boileau and Racine, who lived till 1709. Paul Pellisson (1624-1693), the friend and defender of Fouquet, became perpetual secretary to the French Academy, of which he wrote a history, and was considered the ugliest man of his time. M. de la Bruyère adds in a footnote, that in speaking of Scudéry, he meant Mademoiselle Scudéry, to distinguish her from her brother Georges, also an author; this lady wrote a good many novels then in vogue (see page 123, note 229), and died in 1701, more than ninety years old. For de Harlay see page 237, note 470; for Bossuet see page 47, note 128; and for Wardes or Vardes see page 197, note 405.

[609] The Duke de Chartres (1674-1723), only seventeen years old when this paragraph appeared, was reputed very clever for his age; he afterwards became the Regent d'Orléans. By Condé, either the great Condé, who died in 1686, or his son Henri-Jules, the father of La

add Greek atticism and Roman urbanity, those persons do not hesitate to reply that such examples are exceptional; and the sound arguments brought forward are powerless against public opinion. However, it seems that people should be more careful in giving their decisions, and at least not take the trouble of asserting that intellects producing such great progress in science, and making persons think well, judge well, speak well, and write well, could not acquire polite accomplishments.

No very great intelligence is necessary to have polished manners, but a great deal is needed to polish the mind.

(19.) A politician says: "Such a man is learned, and therefore not fit for business; I would not trust him to take an inventory of my wardrobe;" and he is quite right, Ossat, Ximenes, and Richelieu[610] were learned, but were they men of ability and considered able ministers? "He understands Greek," continues our statesman, "he is a pedant,[611] a philosopher." According to this argument an Athenian fruit-woman who probably spoke Greek was a philosopher, and the Bignons and Lamoignons[612] are mere pedants, and nobody can doubt it, for they know Greek. How whimsical and crack-brained was the great, the wise, and judicious Antoninus to say: "That a people would be happy whose ruler was philosophising, or who should be governed by a philosopher or a scribbler."[613]

Languages are but the keys or entrance-gates of sciences, and nothing more; he that despises the one slights the other. It matters little whether languages are ancient or modern, dead or living, but whether they are barbarous or polite and whether the books written in them are good or bad. Suppose the French language should one day meet with the fate of the Greek and Latin tongues; would it be considered pedantic to read Molière or La Fontaine some ages after French had ceased to be a living language?

Bruyère›s pupil, was meant. For François-Louis, Prince de Conti (1634-1709), see page 273, note 533; his father, Armand de Bourbon (1629-1666), had first been an admirer and then an antagonist of Molière. For Bourbon and Vendôme see page 221, note 449; there was also a celebrated general, the Duke de Vendôme (1654-1712). The Duke de Maine (1670-1736), the eldest of the children of Louis XIV. and Madame de Montespan, was twenty years old when his name appeared in the above paragraph, and was considered a prodigy of learning.

[610] The Cardinal d'Ossat (1536-1604) became an able diplomatist and statesman, after having been professor of rhetoric and philosophy at the University of Paris; Cardinal Ximenes (1437-1517) published several works of Aristotle, founded the University of Alcala, and promoted the publishing of a polyglot Bible before becoming prime minister of Charles V. of Spain. Richelieu (see page 261, note 512) wrote several theological works, some tragedies, and founded the French Academy.

[611] The original has grimaud, also used by Trissotin in addressing Vadius in Molière's Femmes Savantes, act iii, scene 5: "Allez, petit grimaud, barbouilleur de papier."

[612] Jérôme Bignon (1589-1656) was a celebrated magistrate; his son was also a scholar, and his grandson, the Abbé Jean-François (1662-1743), was a member of the French Academy. For the Lamoignons see page 333, note 608.

[613] Plato expresses this idea in the seventh book of his "Republic," but it was often in the mouth of the Roman Emperor Marcus Aurelius (121-180), called Antoninus, as being the adopted son of Antoninus Pius.

(20.) If I mention Eurypilus, you say he is a wit.

You also call a man who shapes a beam a carpenter, and him who builds a wall a bricklayer. Let me ask you where this wit has his workshop, and what is his sign? Can we recognise him by his dress? What are his tools? Is it a wedge, a hammer, an anvil? Where does he rough-hew or shape his work, and where is it for sale? A workman is proud of his trade; is Eurypilus proud of being a wit? If he is proud of it, he is a coxcomb, who debases the natural dignity of his intellect, and has a low and mechanical mind, which never seriously applies itself to what is either lofty or intellectual; and if he is not proud of anything, and this I understand to be his real character, then he is a sensible and intelligent man. Do you not bestow the title of "wit" on every pretender to learning and on every wretched poet? Do you not think you have some intelligence, and if so, no doubt a first-rate and practical one? But do you consider yourself, therefore, a wit, and would you not deem it an insult to be called so? However, I give you leave to call Eurypilus so, and this ironically, as fools do, and without the least discrimination, or as ignorant people do who console themselves by irony for the want of a certain culture which they perceive in others.

(21.) I do not wish to hear anything more about pen, ink, or paper, style, printer, or press! Venture no more to tell me: "Antisthenes, you are a first-rate author; continue to write. Shall we never see a folio volume of yours? Speak of all the virtues and vices in one connected and methodical treatise, without end," and they should also add, "without any sale." I renounce everything that either was, is, or will be a book! Beryllus swoons when he sees a cat,[614] and I on beholding a book. Am I better fed or warmer clothed; is my room sheltered against northern blasts; have I so much as a feather-bed,[615] after having had my works for sale for more than twenty years? You say I have a great name and a first-rate reputation: you may just as well tell me that I have a stock of air I cannot dispose of. Have I one grain of that metal which procures all things? The low pettifogger[616] swells his bill, get costs paid which never came out of his pocket, and a count or a magistrate becomes his son-in-law. A man in a red or filemot-coloured dress[617] is changed into a secretary, and in a little time is richer than his master, who remains a commoner whilst he buys a title for hard cash. B ...[618] enriches himself by some

---

[614] Henri III. of France is said to have fainted if he caught sight of a cat, and some commentators state a certain Abbé de Drubec (see page 112, note 217) had this weakness. Shakespeare, in the Merchant of Venice (act iv. scene 1) also says, "Some that are mad, if they behold a cat."

[615] In our author's time there were only feather beds or straw palliasses, but no flock beds.

[616] The original has praticien. See page 153, note 304.

[617] A footman. We have already seen in the chapter "Of the Town" (page 137, note 1) how many footmen became financiers of the highest order.

[618] This stands for Antoine Benoît, the royal waxwork maker, who had a gallery of waxworks called cercle royal.

waxwork show; B ... by selling some bottled river-water.[619] Another quack[620] arrives with one trunk from the other side of the Pyrenees; it is scarcely unpacked when pensions rain on him, and he is ready to return whence he came with plenty of mules and cartloads full of property. Mercury is Mercury,[621] and nothing else; and as gold alone cannot pay his go-betweens and his intrigues, he obtains, moreover, favour and distinctions. To confine myself to lawful gain, you pay a tiler for his tiles and a workman for his time and labour; but do you pay an author for his thoughts and writings? and if his thoughts are excellent, do you pay him liberally? Does he furnish his house or become ennobled by thinking or writing well? Men must be clothed and shaved,[622] have houses with doors that shut close; but where is the necessity of their being well informed? It were folly, simplicity, stupidity, continues Antisthenes, to set up for an author or a philosopher! Get me, if possible, some lucrative post which may make my life easy, enable me to lend some money to a friend, and give to those who cannot return it; and then I can write for recreation or indolently, just as Tityrus[623] whistles or plays on the flute; I'll have that or nothing, and will write on those conditions; I will yield to the violence of those who take me by the throat and exclaim, "You shall write!" I have the title of my new book ready for them: "Of beauty, goodness, truth, ideas, of first principles, by Antisthenes, a fishmonger."

(22.) If the ambassadors of some foreign princes[624] were apes who had learned to walk on their hind-legs, and to make themselves understood by interpreters, it could not surprise us more than the correctness of their answers, and the common sense which at times appears in their discourse. Our prepossession in favour of our native country and our national pride makes us forget that common sense is found in all climates, and correctness of thought wherever there are men. We should not like to be so treated by those we call barbarians; and if some barbarity still exists amongst us, it is in being amazed on hearing natives of other countries reason like ourselves.

All strangers are not barbarians, nor are all our countrymen civilised; in like manner every country is not savage,[625] nor every town polished. There exists

[619] B ... was a certain Barbereau who sold Seine water for mineral water, or perhaps Brimbeuf, another quack, who sold a specific for perpetual youth.

[620] This may be Caretti (see page 186, note 390), or Domenico Ammonio, another Italian quack.

[621] A good many panders at the court of Louis XIV. were politely called Mercuries, after the messenger of Jupiter; it is therefore difficult to say whom La Bruyère meant. Some say he spoke of Bontemps, first valet-de-chambre of the king; others imagine he wished to hit the Marquis de Lassay, who had the reputation of being pander to the Duke de Bourbon, the former pupil of our author.

[622] In La Bruyère's time people wore long wigs but were closely shaved.

[623] Tityrus is a shepherd, who, according to the first line uttered by Melibœus in Virgil's first "Eclogue," is one of those men who "lay at ease under their patrimonial beech trees."

[624] This is an allusion to the Siamese ambassadors, who came to Paris in 1686, and produced a great sensation.

[625] The original has agreste, taken with the meaning it sometimes has in Latin. La

in Europe, in a large kingdom, a certain place in a maritime province where the villagers are gentle and affable, and, on the contrary, the burgesses and the magistrates coarse, with a boorishness inherited from their ancestors.[626]

(23.) In spite of our pure language, our neatness in dress, our cultivated manners, our good laws and fair complexion, we are considered barbarians by some nations.

(24.) If we should hear it reported of an Eastern nation that they habitually drink a liquor which flies to their head, drives them mad, and makes them very sick, we should say they are barbarians.

(25.) This prelate seldom comes to court, lives retired, and is never seen in the company of ladies: he neither plays grand nor little *primero*,[627] is not present at feasts or spectacles, is not a party man, and does not intrigue; he is always in his diocese, where he resides, devotes himself to instructing his people by preaching and edifying them by his example; spends his wealth in charity, and wastes away through doing penance; he is strict in the observance of his duties, but his zeal and piety are like those of the apostles. Times are changed, and in the present reign he is threatened with a higher clerical dignity.[628]

(26.) Persons of a certain position, and members of a profession of great dignity, to say no more,[629] should understand that they are not to gamble, sing, and be as jocular as other men, so that the world may talk about them; if they see them so pleasant and agreeable, it will not be believed that they are elsewhere staid and severe. May we venture to hint that by acting in such an undignified manner they offend against those polished manners upon which they pride themselves, and which, on the contrary, modify outward behaviour and make it suit any condition of life, cause them to avoid strong contrasts, and never show the same man in these various shapes as a compound of eccentricity and extravagance.

(27.) At a first and single glance we ought not to judge of men as of a picture or statue; there is an inner man, and a heart to be searched; a veil of modesty covers merit, and a mask of hypocrisy covers wickedness. Few there are whose discernment authorises them to decide; it is but gradually, and even then, perhaps,

---

Bruyère says in a note: "This word is used here metaphorically."

[626] Our author was probably for a month either at Rouen or Caen as trésorier-général des finances, an office which he bought in 1673, and, whilst there, might have had a quarrel with some of his colleagues. This is the more likely as in the first three editions of the "Characters" the magistrates alone were named.

[627] A game played with four cards, formerly in use; it was primero when the hands were shown, and the four cards were of different colours; grand primero when more than thirty points were made. In Shakespeare's King Henry VIII. (act v. scene 1), Gardiner tells Sir Thomas Lovell that he left the king "at primero with the Duke of Suffolk."

[628] This is supposed to have been a portrait of M. de Noailles, who was Bishop of Châlons when La Bruyère wrote this paragraph, but who in 1695 became Archbishop of Paris and a Cardinal. The number of bishops residing in their dioceses was very small at the end of the seventeenth century.

[629] An allusion to some members of the clergy and legal profession who frequented fashionable society.

compelled by time and circumstances, that perfect virtue or absolute vice show themselves in their true colours.

(28.) A FRAGMENT.... "He said that the intelligence of this fair lady was like a diamond in a handsome setting," and, continuing to speak of her, he added: "Her common sense and agreeable manners charm the eyes and hearts of all who converse with her, so that they do not know whether to love or to admire her most; she can be a perfect friend, or produce such an impression that her admirers feel inclined to transgress the bounds of friendship. Too young and healthy-looking not to please, but too modest to affect it, she esteems men only for their merit, and believes she has only friends; her vivacity and sentiment surprise and interest us, and though she knows perfectly the delicacies and niceties of conversation, she sometimes suddenly makes some happy observations, which give a great deal of pleasure and need not be answered. She speaks to you like one who is not learned, who is not certain of anything, and wants to be informed; and she listens to you as a person who knows a great deal, highly values what you say, and on whom nothing of what you say is lost. Far from pretending to be witty by contradicting you, and by imitating Elvira, who had rather be thought sprightly than a woman of sense and sound judgment, she adopts your thoughts, thinks they are her own, enlarges on them, and embellishes them; and makes you pleased you have thought so correctly and expressed yourself better than you believed you did. She shows her contempt for vanity in her conversation and in her writings, and never employs witticisms instead of arguments, for she is aware that true eloquence is always unaffected. If it is to serve any one and to induce you to do the same, Arténice leaves to Elvira all pretty speeches and literary phraseology, and only tries to convince you by her sincerity, ardour, and earnestness. What she likes above everything is reading, as well as conversing with persons of merit and reputation, and this not so much to be known to them, as to know them. We may already commend her for all the wisdom she will have one day, and for all the merit she will have in time to come; her behaviour is without reproach; she has the best intentions, and principles which cannot be shaken, and are very useful to those who, like her, are exposed to be courted and flattered. She rather likes to be alone, without, however, altogether shunning society, and indeed without even being inclined to retirement, so that perhaps she wants nothing but opportunities, or, as some would call it, a large stage for the display of all her qualities.[630]

(29.) The more natural a handsome woman is, the more amiable she appears; she loses nothing by being not in full dress, and without any other ornaments than her beauty and her youth. An artless charm beams on her countenance and animates every little action, so that there would be less danger in seeing her adorned in splendid and fashionable apparel. Thus an honest man is respected for his own sake, independent of any outward deportment by which he endeavours to give

[630] According to the Abbé de Chaulieu, Arténice is Catherine Turgot, the wife of Gilles d'Aligres, Seigneur de Boislandry, who, after a scandalous lawsuit, separated from her one year before this "Fragment" appeared (1694). She was then only twenty-one, and became, it is said, the mistress of de Chaulieu; afterwards she married again a certain M. de Chevilly, a captain of the royal guards. Her friend, Mademoiselle de la Force, is supposed to have been Elvira.

himself a graver appearance and to make his virtue more apparent. An austere look, an exaggerated modesty, eccentricity in dress, and a large skull-cap, add nothing to his probity nor heighten his merit;[631] they conceal it, and perhaps make it appear less pure and ingenuous than it is.

Gravity too affected becomes comical; it is like extremities which join one another, and of which the centre is dignity; this cannot be called being grave, but acting the part of a grave man; a person who studies to assume a serious appearance will never succeed. Either gravity is natural, or there is no such thing, and it is easier to descend from it than to attain it.

(30.) A man of talent and of good repute, if he is peevish and austere, frightens young people and gives them a bad opinion of virtue, as they are afraid it requires too much austerity, and is too tiresome. If, on the contrary, he is cheerful and easily accessible, his example is instructive to them, for it teaches them that men may live happy, do a good deal of work, and yet be serious without giving up decent diversions; he thus is an exemplar they can follow.

(31.) We should not judge of men by their countenance; but it may serve to make a guess at their character.

(32.) A clever look in men is the same as regularity of features among women; it is a kind of beauty which the vainest endeavour to acquire.

(33.) When a man is known to have merit and intelligence, he is never ugly, however plain he may be; or if even he is ugly, it leaves no bad impression.[632]

(34.) A good deal of art is needed to return to nature; a good deal of time, practice, attention, and labour to dance with the same freedom and ease we walk with; to sing as we speak; to throw as much vivacity, passion, and persuasion in a studied speech to be publicly delivered as in one which we sometimes naturally use, without any preparation, and in familiar conversation.

(35.) They who without sufficient knowledge have a bad opinion of us, do not wrong us; they do not attack us, but a phantom of their own imagination.

(36.) Some trifling regulations have to be followed in certain places, some duties have to be fulfilled at certain times, and some decorum has to be observed by certain persons, which could not be divined by the most intelligent people, and which custom teaches without any trouble: we should, therefore, not condemn men who omit these things, as they have not been taught them, neither should we decide their characters by the shape of their nails or the curl of their hair; if we do form such a judgment we shall soon find out our error.

(37.) I doubt whether it be lawful to judge of some men by a single fault, or if extreme necessity, a violent passion, or a sudden impulse prove anything.

(38.) If we wish to know the truth about certain affairs or certain persons, we should believe the very opposite of the reports circulated about them.

---

[631] An allusion to the President de Harlay. See page 237, note 470.

[632] This paragraph and the preceding one seem to refer to Pellisson. See page 333, note 608.

(39.) Unless we are very firm and pay continual attention to what we utter, we are liable to say "yes" and "no" about the same thing or person in an hour's time, induced to do this merely by a sociable and friendly disposition, which naturally leads a person not to contradict men who hold different opinions.

(40.) A partial man is exposed to frequent mortifications; for it is as impossible for his favourites always to be happy or wise as for those who are out of his favour always to be at fault or unfortunate; and, therefore, he often is put out of countenance either through the failure of his friends, or some glorious deed done by those whom he dislikes.

(41.) A man liable to be prejudiced who ventures to accept an ecclesiastical or civil dignity is like a blind man wishing to be an artist, a dumb man who would be an orator, or a deaf man desiring to judge a symphony; these are but faint comparisons imperfectly expressing the wretchedness of prejudice. Besides, prejudice is a desperate and incurable disease, contaminating all who approach the patient, so that his equals, inferiors, relatives, friends, and even the doctors abandon him; it is past their skill to work any cure if they cannot make him confess what is his disease, and acknowledge that the remedies to heal it are to listen, to doubt, to inquire, and to examine. Flatterers, rogues, and slanderers, those who never open their mouths but to lie or to advance their own interests, are the quacks in whom he trusts, and who make him swallow all they please; they thus poison and kill him.

(42.) Descartes' rule never to decide on the slightest truth before it is clearly and distinctly understood is sufficiently grand and correct to extend to the judgment we form of persons.

(43.) Some men have a bad opinion of our intellect, morals, and manners; but we are well revenged when we see the worthless and base character of their favourites.

On this principle a man of merit is neglected and a blockhead admired.

(44.) A blockhead is a man without enough intelligence to be a coxcomb.

(45.) A blockhead thinks a coxcomb a man of merit.

(46.) An impertinent man is an egregious coxcomb; a coxcomb wearies, bores, disgusts, and repels you; an impertinent man repels, embitters, irritates, and offends; he begins where the other ends.

A coxcomb is somewhat of an impertinent man and of a blockhead, and is a medley of both.

(47.) Vices arise from a depraved heart; faults from some defect in our constitution; ridicule from want of sense.

A ridiculous man is one who, whilst he is so, has the appearance of a blockhead.

A blockhead is always ridiculous, for that is his character; an intelligent man may sometimes be ridiculous, but will not be so long.

An error in conduct makes a wise man ridiculous.

Foolishness is a criterion of a blockhead, vanity of a coxcomb, and impertinence of an impertinent man; ridicule seems sometimes to dwell in those who are really ridiculous, and sometimes in the imagination of those who believe they perceive ridicule where it neither is nor can be.

(48.) Coarseness, clownishness, and brutality may be the vices of an intelligent man.

(49.) A stupid man is a silent blockhead, and is more bearable than a talkative blockhead.

(50.) What is often a slip of the tongue or a jest from a man of sense is a blunder when said by a blockhead.

(51.) If a coxcomb would be afraid of saying something not exactly right he would no longer be a coxcomb.

(52.) One proof of a commonplace intellect is to be always relating stories.

(53.) A blockhead does not know what to do with himself; a coxcomb is free, easy, and confident in his manners; an impertinent man becomes impudent; and merit is always modest.

(54.) A conceited man is one in whom a knowledge of certain details, dignified by the name of business, is added to a very middling intellect.

One grain of sense and one ounce[633] of business more than there are in a conceited man, make the man of importance.

While people only laugh at a man of importance he has no other name; but when they begin to complain of him he may be called arrogant.

(55.) A gentleman is between a clever man and an honest man, though not as distant from the one as from the other.[634]

The difference between a gentleman and a clever man diminishes each day, and will soon disappear altogether.

A clever man does not blaze forth his passions, understands his own interests, sacrifices many things to them, has acquired some wealth, and knows how to keep it.

A gentleman is not a highwayman, commits no murders, and, in one word, has no flagrant vices.

It is very well known that an honest man is a gentleman; but it is comical to think that every gentleman is not an honest man.

An honest man is neither a saint nor a pretender in religion, but has only confined himself to being virtuous.

(56.) Genius, taste, intelligence, good sense, are all different, but not incom-

---

[633] A grain is the 576th part of an ounce, which is the 16th part of a pound.

[634] The original has honnête homme (see page 43, note 121) for "gentleman," homme de bien for "honest man" (see page 49, note 137), and habile homme for "clever man."

patible.

Between good sense and good taste there is as much difference as between cause and effect.

Intelligence is to genius as the whole is in proportion to its part.

(57.) Shall I call a man sensible who only practises one art, or even a certain science, in which I allow him to be perfect, but beyond that displays neither judgment, memory, animation, morals, nor manners; does not understand me; thinks not, and expresses himself badly; a musician, for example, who, after he has enraptured me with his harmony, seems to be shut up with his lute in the same case, and when he is without his instrument is like a machine taken to pieces, in which there is something wanting and from which nothing more is to be expected?

Again, what shall I say of a certain talent for playing various games, and who can define it to me? Is there no need of foresight, shrewdness, or skill in playing ombre[635] or chess? And if there is, how does it happen that we see men of hardly any intellect excel in these games, and others of great talent scarcely show moderate ability, and get confused and bewildered when they have to move a pawn or play a card?

There is something in this world, which, if possible, is still more difficult to understand. Some person seems dull, heavy, and stupefied; he knows neither how to speak, nor to relate what he has just seen; but, if he puts pen to paper, he can tell a tale better than any man; he makes animals, stones, and trees talk, and everything which does not speak; his works are light, elegant, natural, and full of delicacy.[636]

Another is simple, timorous, and tiresome in conversation; he mistakes one word for another, and judges of the excellence of his work merely by the money it brings him; he cannot read this work aloud, nor decipher his own handwriting. But let him compose, and he is not inferior to Augustus, Pompey, Nicomedes, and Heraclius; he is a king, and a great king, a politician and a philosopher; he undertakes to make heroes speak and act; he depicts the Romans, and in his verse they are greater, and more like Romans, than in their own history.[637]

Should you like to have an outline of another prodigy? Imagine a man, easy, gentle, affable, yielding, and then all of a sudden violent, enraged, furious, and capricious; represent to yourself a man simple, artless, credulous, sportive, and flighty, a grey-haired child; but let him recollect himself, or rather give himself up to the genius dwelling within him, and perhaps quite independent of him and without his knowledge, he will display rapture, lofty thoughts, splendid imagery, and pure latinity. You may well ask if I speak of one and the same man? Yes, of Theodas,[638] and of no one else. He shrieks, is quite agitated, rolls on the ground,

---

[635] For "ombre" see page 172, note 345.

[636] A portrait of La Fontaine (see page 335, § 19), who was still alive when this paragraph appeared (1691).

[637] This is a sketch of Pierre Corneille (see page 9, note 45, and page 18, note 61), and Augustus, Pompey, Nicomedes, and Heraclius are the names of some of his tragedies.

[638] Theodas is Santeul (1630-1697), one of the most elegant of the modern Latin poets,

rises, shouts, and roars; and yet amidst this whirlwind of words shines forth a brilliant effulgence which delights us. To speak plainly, he talks like a fool and thinks like a wise man; he utters truth in a ridiculous way, and sensible and reasonable sayings in a foolish manner; people are surprised to hear common sense arise and bud amidst so much buffoonery, so many grimaces and contortions. I may say also that he speaks and acts better than he understands; he has within him, as it were, two souls, which are unconnected and do not depend on one another, but act each in their turn and have quite distinct functions. This astonishing picture would want another touch should I omit to state that he is anxiously craving for praise, has never enough of it, and is ready to fly at any of his critics, but in reality is docile enough to profit by their censure. I begin to imagine I have drawn the portraits of two wholly different persons; and yet to find a third in Theodas is not quite impossible, for he is kind-hearted, agreeable, and has excellent qualities.

Next to sound judgment, diamonds and pearls are the rarest things to be met with.

(58.) One man is well known for his abilities, and is honoured and cherished wherever he goes, but he is slighted by his household and his own family, whom he cannot induce to esteem him; another man, on the contrary, is a prophet in his own country, has a great reputation among his friends, which does, however, not extend beyond his house, and prides himself on the rare and singular merit his family—whose idol he is—believe he is possessed of, but which he leaves at home every time he goes out, and takes nowhere with him.[639]

(59.) Every one attacks a man whose reputation is rising; the very persons he thinks his friends hardly pardon his growing merit, or that early popularity which seems to give him a share of the renown they already enjoy; they hold out as long as they can, until the king declares himself in his favour and rewards him; then they immediately gather in crowds round him, and only from that day he ranks as a man of merit.

(60.) We often pretend to praise immoderately some men who hardly deserve it, and to raise them, if it were possible, on a level with those who are really eminent, either because we are tired of admiring always the same persons, or because their fame, being divided, is less offensive to behold, and seems to us less brilliant and easier to be borne.

(61.) We see some men carried along by the propitious gale of favour, and, in one moment, they lose sight of land, and continue their course; everything smiles on them, and they are successful in whatever they undertake; their deeds and their works are extolled and well rewarded, and when they appear they are caressed and congratulated. A firm rock stands on the coast, and breakers dash against its base; all the blasts of power, riches, violence, flattery, authority, and favour cannot

whose character, immediately recognised by all his contemporaries, seems to have been the compound of folly and sense La Bruyère made it out to be; he is said to have died in consequence of having drunk a glass of wine and snuff given to him by the Duke de Bourbon, the father of our author's pupil.

[639] These two men are said to have been the brothers Le Peletier. See page 54, note 150.

shake it. The public is the rock against which these men are dashed to pieces.

(62.) It is usual, and, as it were, natural to judge of other men's labour only by the affinity it bears to our own. Thus a poet, filled with grand and sublime ideas, does not greatly prize an orator's speech, which is often merely about simple facts; and a man who writes the history of his native land cannot understand how any person of sense can spend his whole life in contriving fictions or hunting after a rhyme; and a divine, immersed in the study of the first four centuries,[640] thinks all other learning and science sad, idle, and useless, whilst he perhaps is as much despised by a mathematician.

(63.) A man may have intelligence enough to excel in a particular thing and lecture on it, and yet not have sense enough to know he ought to be silent on some other subject of which he has but a slight knowledge; if such an illustrious man ventures beyond the bounds of his capacity, he loses his way, and talks like a fool.

(64.) Whether Herillus talks, declaims, or writes, he is continually quoting; he brings in the prince of philosophers[641] to tell you that wine will make you intoxicated, and the Roman orator[642] to say that water qualifies it. When he discourses of morals, it is not he, but the divine Plato who assures us that virtue is amiable, vice odious, and that both will become habitual. The most common and well-known things, which he himself might have thought out, he attributes to the ancients, the Romans and Greeks; it is not to give more authority to what he says, nor perhaps to get more credit for learning, but merely for the sake of employing quotations.

(65.) We often pretend that a witticism is our own, and by doing this we run the risk of destroying its effect; it falls flat, and witty people, or those who think themselves so, receive it coldly, because they ought to have said it, and did not. On the contrary, if told as another's, it would meet with a better reception; it is but a jest which no one is obliged to know; it is related in a more insinuating manner, and causes less jealousy; it offends nobody; if it is amusing it is laughed at, and if excellent is admired.

(66.) Socrates was said to be insane, to be "an intelligent madman;" but those Greeks who gave such a name to so wise a man passed for madmen themselves. They exclaimed, "What odd portraits does this philosopher present us with! What strange and peculiar manners does he describe! In what dreams did he discover and collect such extraordinary ideas! What colours and what a brush has he! They are only idle fancies!" They were mistaken—all those monsters and vices were painted from life, so that people imagined they saw them, and were terrified. Socrates was far from a cynic; he did not indulge in personalities, but lashed the morals and manners which were bad.[643]

---

[640] Bachelors in theology and the canon law were the only graduates compelled to study the history of the first four centuries of the Christian era.

[641] Aristotle.

[642] Cicero.

[643] La Bruyère did not wish to give a sketch of Socrates, as he himself admitted in one of his letters to Ménage. It is supposed he meant to give a portrait of himself; at least he was

(67.) A man who has acquired wealth by his knowledge of the world is acquainted with a philosopher, and with his precepts, morals, and conduct; but not imagining that mankind can have any other goal in whatever they do than the one he marked out for himself during his whole lifetime, he says in his heart, "I pity this rigid critic; his life has been a failure; he is on a wrong track, and has lost his way; no wind will ever waft him to a prosperous harbour of preferment;" and, according to his own principles, he is right in his arguments.

Antisthius says: "I pardon those I have praised in my works, if they will forget me, for I did nothing for them, as they deserved to be commended. But I will not so easily pardon forgetfulness in those whose vices I have attacked, without touching their persons, if they owe me the invaluable boon of being amended; but as such an event never happens, it follows that neither the one nor the other are obliged to make me any return."

This philosopher continued saying: "People may envy my writings or refuse them their reward, but they are unable to diminish their reputation; and if they did, what should hinder me from scorning their opinions?"

(68.) It is a good thing to be a philosopher, but it does not much benefit a man to be thought one. It will be considered an insult to call any one a philosopher till the general voice of mankind has declared it otherwise, given its true meaning to this beautiful word, and granted it all the esteem it deserves.

(69.) There is a philosophy which raises us above ambition and fortune, and not only makes us the equals of the rich, the great, and the powerful, but places us above them; makes us contemn office and those who appoint to it; exempts us from wishing, asking, praying, soliciting, and begging for anything, and even restrains our emotion and our excessive exultation when successful. There is another philosophy which inclines and subjects us to all these things for the sake of our relatives and friends; and this is the better of the two.

(70.) It will shorten and rid us of a thousand tedious discussions to take it for granted that some persons are not capable of talking correctly, and to condemn all they have said, do say, or will say.

(71.) We only approve in others those qualities in which we imagine they resemble us; thus, to esteem any one seems to make him an equal of ourselves.

(72.) The same faults which are dull and unbearable in others are in their right place when we have them; they do not weigh us down, and are hardly felt. One man, speaking of another, draws a terrible likeness of him, and does not in the least imagine that at the same time he is painting himself.

If we could see the faults in other people, and could be brought to acknowledge that we possess the same faults, we would more readily amend them; it is when we are at a right distance from them, and when they appear what they really are, that we dislike them as much as they deserve.

(73.) A wise man's behaviour turns on two pivots, the past and the future. If he has a good memory and a keen foresight, he runs no danger of censuring in others

sometimes called "an intelligent madman."

what perhaps he has done himself, or of condemning an action which, in a parallel case, and in like circumstances, he sees it will be impossible for him to avoid.

(74.) Neither a soldier, a politician, nor a skilful gambler[644] create luck, but they prepare it, allure it, and seem almost to fix it. They not only know what a fool and a coward ignore, I mean, to make use of luck when it does come, but by their precautions and measures they know how to take advantage of a lucky chance, or of several chances together. If a certain deal or throw succeeds, they gain; if another happens, they also win; and often profit by one and the same in various ways. These sharp men may be commended both for their good fortune and prudent conduct, and they should be rewarded for their luck as other men are for their virtue.

(75.) I place nobody above a great politician but a man who does not care to become one, and who is more and more convinced that it is not worth troubling himself about what is going on in the world.

(76.) In the best of counsels there is something to displease us; they are not our own thoughts; and, therefore, presumption and caprice at first cause them to be rejected, whilst we only follow them through necessity or after having reflected.

(77.) This favourite has been wonderfully fortunate during his whole lifetime; he enjoyed an uninterrupted good fortune, was never in disgrace, occupied the highest posts, was in the king's confidence, had vast treasures, perfect health, and died quietly. But what an extraordinary account he will have to render of a life spent as a favourite, of advice given, of advice which was not tendered or not listened to, of good deeds omitted, and, on the contrary, of evil ones committed, either by himself or his instruments; in a word, of all his prosperity.[645]

(78.) When we are dead we are praised by those who survive us, though we frequently have no other merit than that of being no longer alive; the same commendations serve then for Cato and for Piso.[646]

"There is a report that Piso is dead; it is a great loss; he was an honest man, who deserved to live longer; he was intelligent and agreeable, resolute and courageous, to be depended upon, generous and faithful;" add: "provided he be really dead."

(79.) The way in which we exclaim about certain persons being distinguished for their good faith, disinterestedness, and honesty is not so much to their praise as to the disrepute of all mankind.

(80.) A certain person relieves the necessitous, but neglects his own family and

[644] A gambler was in La Bruyère's time a regular profession, perhaps not considered quite as respectable as any other of the learned professions, but still decent enough to entitle its professors to be received at court and in very good society. The gambler was almost as much admired for his pluck and dash as a gentleman-jockey is at present.

[645] It was generally believed that this paragraph refers to the minister Le Tellier (1603-1685) and to his son Louvois, for whom see pages 132 and 242, notes 255 and 484.

[646] Cato of Utica (95-46 B.C.). Lucius Calpurnius Piso, the father-in-law of Julius Cæsar, had been accused by Cicero in the year 59 B.C. of extortions, and of plundering Macedonia.

leaves his son a beggar; another builds a new house though he has not paid for the lead of the one finished ten years before; a third makes presents and is very liberal, but ruins his creditors. I would fain know whether pity, liberality, and magnificence can be the virtues of a man without sense, or whether eccentricity and vanity are not rather the causes of this want of sense.[647]

(81.) If we wish to be essentially just to others, we should be quick and not dilatory; to let people wait is to commit an injustice.

Those persons do well, or do their duty, who do what they ought. A man who allows the world to speak always of him in the future tense, and to say he will do well, behaves really very badly.

(82.) People say of a great man who has two meals a day, and spends the rest of his time in digesting what he has eaten, that he starves; all that they mean to express by this is that he is not rich, or that his affairs are not very prosperous; the remark about starving might be better applied to his creditors.

(83.) The culture, good manners, and politeness of persons of either sex, advanced in years, give me a good opinion of what we call "former times."[648]

(84.) Parents are over-confident in expecting too much from the good education of their children, and commit a grievous error if they expect nothing from it and neglect it.

(85.) Were it true, as several persons affirm, that education does not alter the heart and constitution of man, and that in reality the changes it produces transform nothing and are merely superficial, yet I would still maintain that it is beneficial to him.

(86.) He who speaks little has this advantage, that he is presumed to have some intelligence, and if he really is not deficient in it, it is presumed to be first-rate.

(87.) To think only of ourselves and of the present time is a source of error in politics.

(88.) Next to being convicted of a crime, it is often the greatest misfortune for a man his being accused of having committed one, and being obliged to clear himself from the charge. He may be acquitted in a court of justice and yet be found guilty by the voice of the people.[649]

(89.) One man faithfully observes certain religious duties and discharges them carefully, yet he is neither commended nor censured, he is not so much as thought of; another, after ten years' utter neglect of such duties, attends again to them and is commended and extolled. Every person has a right to his own opinion; I, for my part, blame the second man for having so long neglected those duties, and think his reformation fortunate for himself.

[647] See also the chapter "Of Mankind," pages 308 and 321, §§ 104 and 139.

[648] Our author had already praised people of a certain age in his chapter "Of the Court," page 211, § 74.

[649] An allusion to Pierre-Louis de Reich, Seigneur de Penautier, receiver-general of the clergy of France, who had been accused of having poisoned his father-in-law.

(90.) A flatterer has not a sufficiently good opinion of himself or others.

(91.) Some men are forgotten in the distribution of favours, and we ask what can be the reason of this; if they had not been forgotten we should have raised the question why they had received them. Whence proceeds this dissimilitude? Is it from the character of these persons, or the instability of our opinions, or rather from both?

(92.) We often hear the question asked, "Who shall be chancellor, primate,[650] pope?" People go even farther, and, according to their own wishes or caprice, often promote persons more aged and infirm than those who at present fill certain posts; and as there is no reason why any post should kill its occupant, but, on the contrary, often makes him young again, and reinvigorates his body and soul, it is not unusual for an official personage to outlive his appointed successor.[651]

(93.) Disgrace extinguishes hatred and jealousy. As soon as a person is no longer a favourite, and when we do not envy him any more, we admit that his actions are good, and we can pardon in him any merit and a good many virtues; he might even be a hero, and not vex us.

Nothing seems right that a man does who has fallen into disgrace; his virtues and merit are slighted, misinterpreted, or called vices. If he is courageous, dreads neither fire nor sword, and faces the enemy with as much bravery as Bayard and Montrevel,[652] he is called a "braggadocio," and they make fun of him, for there is nothing of the true hero about him.

I contradict myself; I own it; do not blame me, but blame those men whose judgments I merely give, and who are the very same persons, though they differ so much and are so variable in their opinions.

(94.) We need not wait twenty years to see a general alter his opinion on the most serious things as well as on those which appear most certain and true. I shall not venture to maintain that fire in its own nature, and independent of our sensations, is void of heat,[653] that is to say, nothing like what we feel in ourselves on approaching it, lest some time or other it may become as hot as ever it was thought; nor shall I advance that one straight line falling on another makes two right angles, or two angles equal to two right angles, for fear something more or less be discovered, and my proposition be laughed at; nor, to mention something else, shall I say, with the whole of France, that Vauban is infallible, and that this is

---

[650] The Archbishop of Lyons bore the title of primat des Gaules, which is in the original French.

[651] See page 192, note 400.

[652] Pierre du Terrail, Seigneur de Bayard (1475-1524), a great military commander, deservedly received the name of the "knight without fear and without reproach." Our author states in a footnote that the Marquis de Montrevel was commissioner-general of the cavalry, and lieutenant-general. Seven years after the death of La Bruyère, he became Marshal of France. Saint-Simon calls him "a very brave but a rather stupid, not over-honest and ignorant man," who died of fright by the upsetting of a salt-cellar.

[653] This theory was maintained by Descartes.

an undoubted fact,[654] for who will guarantee me but that in a short time it may be hinted that even in sieges, in which lies his peculiar pre-eminence, and of which he is considered the best judge, he does not make some blunders, and is as liable to mistakes as Antiphilus is?[655]

(95.) If you believe people who are exasperated against one another, and swayed by passion, a scholar is a mere sciolist,[656] a magistrate a boor or a pettifogger,[657] a financier an extortioner, and a nobleman an upstart; but it is strange these scurrilous names, invented by anger and hatred, should become so familiar to us, and that contempt, though cold and inert, should dare to employ them.

(96.) You agitate yourself, and give yourself a good deal of trouble, especially when the enemy begins to fly, and the victory is no longer doubtful, or when a town has capitulated; in a fight or during a siege you like to be seen everywhere in order to be nowhere; to forestall the orders of the general for fear of obeying them, and to seek opportunities rather than to wait for them or receive them. Is your courage a mere pretence?

(97.) Order your soldiers to keep some post where they may be killed, and where nevertheless they are not killed, and they prove they love both honour and life.

(98.) Can we imagine that men who are so fond of life should love anything better, and that glory, which they prefer to life, is often no more than an opinion of themselves, entertained by a thousand people whom either they do not know or do not esteem?[658]

(99.) Some persons who are neither soldiers nor courtiers make a campaign and follow the court; they do not assist in besieging a town, but are merely spectators,[659] and are soon cured of their curiosity about a fortified place, however wonderful; about trenches; the effects of shells and cannon, about surprises, and the order and success of an attack of which they catch a mere glimpse. The place holds out, bad weather comes on, fatigues increase, the mud has to be waded through, and the seasons have to be encountered as well as the enemy; the lines may be forced, and we may find ourselves between the town and an army, and reduced to dire extremities. The besiegers lose heart, begin to murmur, and ask if the raising of the siege will be of such great consequence, and if the safety of the

[654] Vauban (1633-1707), the great French military engineer, after the retaking of Namur by William III. in 1695, four years after this paragraph saw the light, was accused of having committed some errors in the erection of the fortifications of that town, but he proved those accusations to be unfounded.

[655] Antiphilus is Pope Innocent XI. (1676-1689), who held other opinions as a cardinal than he did as a pope; he opposed the liberties of the Gallican Church.

[656] The original has savantasse, a word always used with a bad meaning.

[657] In French praticien. See page 153, note 304.

[658] See the chapter "Of Mankind," page 299, § 76.

[659] An allusion to the siege of Namur, June 1692, which lasted one month, during which many courtiers and magistrates went there out of curiosity. Racine and Boileau were also present as the king's historians. The above paragraph appeared the same year the siege took place.

State depends on one citadel. They further add "that the heavens themselves declare against them; and that it is best to submit, and put off the siege until another season." They no longer understand the firmness, and, if they may say so, the obstinacy of the general, who is not to be overcome by obstacles, but is stimulated by the difficulty of his undertaking, and watches by night and exposes his life by day to accomplish his design. But as soon as the enemy has capitulated, the very men who lost heart boast of the importance of the conquest, foretell the consequences it will have, exaggerate the necessity there was in undertaking it, as well as the danger and shame there would have been in raising it, and prove that the army opposed to the enemy was invincible.[660]

They return with the court, and as they pass through the towns and villages, are proud to be looked upon by the inhabitants, who are all at their windows, as the very men who took the place; thus they triumph all along the road and fancy themselves very courageous. When they are home again they deafen you with flanks, redans, ravelins, counter breastworks,[661] curtains, and covert-ways; give you an account of the spots where curiosity led them, and where it was pretty dangerous, and of the risks they ran on returning of being killed or made prisoners; but they do not say one word about the mortal terror they were in.

(100.) It is no great disadvantage for a speaker to stop short in the middle of a sermon or a speech; it does not deprive him of his intelligence, good sense, imagination, morals, and learning; it robs him of nothing; but it is very surprising that, though it is considered more or less disgraceful and ridiculous, some men will expose themselves to so great a risk by tedious and often unprofitable discourses.

(101.) Those who make the worst use of their time are the first to complain of its brevity; as they waste it in dressing themselves, in eating and sleeping, in foolish conversations, in making up their minds what to do, and, generally, in doing nothing at all, they want some more for their business or for their pleasures, whilst those who make the best use of it have some to spare.

There is no minister of State so busy but he knows he loses two hours every day, which amounts to a great deal in a long life; and if this waste is still greater among other conditions of men, what a large loss is there of what is most precious in this world, and of which every one complains he has not enough.

(102.) There exist some of God's creatures called men, who have a spiritual soul, and who spend their whole lives in the sawing of marble, and devote all their attention to it; this is a very humble business and of not much consequence; there are other people who are astonished at this, yet who are of no use whatever, and spend their days in doing nothing, which is inferior to sawing marble.

(103.) Most men are so oblivious of their souls, and act and live in such a manner, that to them it seems to be of no use whatever; we therefore deem it no small

[660] A French army of eighty thousand men under the Marshal de Luxembourg (see page 195, note 402) prevented William III. from coming to the relief of Namur.

[661] According to M. G. Servois's preface to the Lexique of La Bruyère, ravelin, a synonym of demi-lune, and fausse-braie, a counter breastwork, are antiquated in French. However, "ravelin" and "demi-lune" are still found as English words in certain dictionaries.

commendation of any man to say he thinks; this has become a common eulogy, and yet it places a man only above a dog or a horse.

(104.) "How do you amuse yourself? How do you pass your time?" fools and clever people ask you. If I answer, in opening my eyes, in seeing, hearing, and understanding, in enjoying health, rest, and freedom, that is nothing; the solid, the great, and the only advantages of life are of no account. "I gamble, I intrigue," are the answers they expect.

Is it good for a man to have too great and extensive a freedom, which only induces him to wish for something else, which would be to have less liberty?

Liberty is not indolence; it is a free use of time; it is to choose our labour and our relaxation; in one word, to be free is not to do nothing, but to be the sole judge of what we wish to do and to leave undone; in this sense liberty is a great boon.

(105.) Cæsar was not too old to think of conquering the entire world; his sole happiness was to lead a noble life and to leave behind him a great name; being naturally proud and ambitious, and enjoying robust health, he could not better employ his time than in subjugating all nations. Alexander was very young for so serious a design; it is surprising that women or wine did not sooner ruin the undertaking of a man of such tender years.[662]

(106.) A young prince, of an august race,[663] the love and hope of his people, granted by Heaven to prolong the felicity of this earth, greater than his ancestors, the son of a hero who is his exemplar, has by his divine qualities and anticipated virtues already convinced the universe that the sons of heroes are nearer being so than other men.[664]

(107.) If the world is only to last a hundred million years, it is still in all its freshness, and has but just begun; we ourselves are so near the first men and the patriarchs, that remote ages will not fail to reckon us among them. But if we may judge of what is to come by what is past, what new things will spring up in arts, sciences, in nature, and, I venture to say, even in history, which are as yet unknown to us! What discoveries will be made! What various revolutions will happen in states and empires! What ignorance must be ours, and how slight is an experience of not above six or seven thousand years!

(108.) No way is too tedious for him who travels slowly and without being in a hurry; no advantages are too remote for those who have patience.

---

[662] Montaigne was of the opinion of La Bruyère and in favour of Cæsar; Pascal, in his Pensées, on the contrary, thought that Cæsar, assassinated at the age of fifty-six, was too old for the conquest of the world, and that it would have better suited the youthful Alexander. See also page 49, § 31.

[663] This paragraph in praise of the Dauphin (1661-1711), written in epigraphic style, was printed in capital letters, and published whilst he was in command of the army of the Rhine (1688).

[664] La Bruyère says in a note: "This is an opinion opposed to a well-known Latin maxim." Erasmus, in his Adagiorum Chiliades, gives the Latinised proverb, Filii heroum noxæ, "the sons of heroes degenerate," and our author alludes to this. As for the "divine qualities," see page 51, § 33.

(109.) To court nobody, and not to expect to be courted by any one, is a happy condition, a golden age, and the most natural state of man.[665]

(110.) Those who follow courts or live in towns only care for the world; but those who dwell in the country care for nature, for they alone live, or at least know that they live.

(111.) Why this coldness, and why do you complain of some expressions which escaped me about some of our young courtiers? You are not vicious, Thrasyllus? If you are, it is unknown to me; but you yourself tell me so; what I do know is that you are no longer young.

You are personally offended at what I said of some great men, but you should not cry out when other people are hurt. Are you haughty, wicked, a buffoon, a flatterer, or a hypocrite? I protest I was ignorant of it, and did not think of you; I was speaking of men of high rank.

(112.) Moderation and a certain prudent behaviour leave men unknown; in order to be known and admired they must have great virtues, or perhaps great vices.

(113.) Whether men are of a superior or of an inferior condition, as soon as they are successful, their fellow-men are prejudiced in their favour, delighted and in raptures; a crime which has not failed is almost as much commended as real virtue, and luck supplies the place of all qualities; it must be an atrocious action, a foul and nefarious attempt indeed, which success cannot justify.[666]

(114.) Men, led away by fair appearances and specious pretences, are easily induced to like and approve an ambitious scheme contrived by some great man; they speak feelingly of it; its boldness or novelty pleases them; it is already familiar to them, and they expect naught but its success. But should it happen to miscarry, they confidently, and without any regard for their former judgment, decide that the plan was rash and could never succeed.[667]

(115.) Certain designs are of such great splendour and of such enormous consequence, that people talk about them for a long time; that they lead nations to fear or to hope, according to their various interests, and that a man stakes his glory and his entire fortune on them. After appearing on the world's stage with such pomp he cannot slink away in silence; whatever terrible dangers he foresees will be the consequences of his undertaking; he must commence it; the smallest evil he has to expect will be a failure.

(116.) You cannot make a great man of a wicked man; you may commend his plans and contrivances, admire his conduct, extol his skill in employing the surest and shortest means to obtain his end; but if his purpose be bad, prudence has no share in it, and where prudence is wanting no greatness can ever exist.

---

[665] La Bruyère's feeling about the happiness of being his own master breaks out now and then. See also page 232, § 33.

[666] This paragraph, and almost all the following ones, refer to the revolution (1688) which placed William III. on the throne of Great Britain.

[667] An allusion to the abortive attempt of the French in Ireland to aid in the re-establishment of James II. See also page 218, note 447.

(117.) An enemy is dead who was at the head of a formidable army, and intended to cross the Rhine; he understood the art of war, and his experience might have been seconded by fortune. What bonfires were lit, and what rejoicings took place! But there are other men, naturally odious, who are disliked by every one; it is therefore not on account of their success, nor because people fear they might be successful, that the voice of the public is lifted up, and that the very children's hearts leap for joy as soon as it is rumoured abroad that the earth is at length rid of them.[668]

(118.) "O times! O morals!"[669] exclaims Heraclitus.[670] "O unfortunate age, rich in bad examples, when virtue is persecuted and crime is predominant and triumphant!" I will turn a Lycaon or an Ægistheus,[671] for I can never meet with a better opportunity nor a more favourable conjuncture; if, at least, I desire to be prosperous and to flourish. A certain personage[672] says, "I will cross the sea; I will dispossess my father of his patrimony; I will drive him, his wife, and his heir from their territory and kingdom;" and he not only says it but does it. What he had reason to dread was the resentment of many kings, insulted in the person of one monarch. But they side with him; they almost have said to him: "Cross the sea, rob your father; and let the entire world witness how a king can be driven from his kingdom, as if he were a petty lord turned out from his castle, or a farmer from his farm; show them that there is no longer any difference between private persons and ourselves. We are tired of these distinctions; teach the world that the nations whom God has placed underneath our feet may abandon us, betray us, and give us up, and themselves as well, into the hands of the stranger, and that they have less to fear from us than we have to dread them and their power."[673] What person can behold such a sad scene without shedding tears or being deeply moved! Every office has its privileges, and every official speaks, pleads, and agitates to defend them; the royal dignity alone enjoys no longer such privileges, and the kings themselves have renounced them. Only one among them, ever kind-hearted and magnanimous, opens his arms to receive an unhappy family;[674] all the others league themselves against him as if to avenge the assistance he lends to a cause which is theirs as well; spite and jealousy have more weight with them than considerations for their honour, religion, and rule, and even than domestic and

---

[668] The first-mentioned enemy was Charles V., Duke of Lorraine, who died in 1690; the second was William III., a rumour of whose death spread in Paris the same year, and caused great rejoicings.

[669] O Tempora! O Mores! is the opening of the first of Cicero's Catilinaria.

[670] Our author lets Heraclitus, the weeping philosopher, utter this paragraph, whilst he puts the following into the mouth of Democritus, the laughing, or better, the sneering philosopher of Abdera.

[671] According to the mythology, Lycaon, king of Arcadia, murdered his guests and served them up at his table, in order to test the divine knowledge of Jupiter, who changed him into a wolf. Ægistheus was the son of Thyestes, and the murderer of Agamemnon.

[672] William III.

[673] The "they have less to fear from us," &c., was also one of the arguments used by France during the first revolution.

[674] This, of course, refers to the hospitality Louis XIV. granted to James II.

personal interests; they do not perceive that, I will not say their election, but their very succession, and even their hereditary rights are at stake. Finally, in every one of them personal feelings prevail over those of a sovereign. One prince was going to set Europe free, and free himself as well from an ominous enemy; he was just on the point of reaping the glory of having destroyed a mighty empire when he abandoned his plan, and joined in a war in which success is far from certain.[675] Those rulers who by virtue of their position are arbitrators and mediators temporise; and when they could already have interfered and done some good, they only promise they will do so.[676] "O shepherds," continues Heraclitus, "O ye rustics who dwell in hovels and cottages; if the course of events does not affect you, if your hearts are not pierced by the malice of men, if man is no longer mentioned among you, but foxes and lynxes are the only subjects of your conversation, allow me to dwell with you, to appease my hunger with your black bread, and to quench my thirst with the water from your wells."

---

[675] Leopold I. (see page 252, note 499), Emperor of Germany, broke off a war in which he was engaged against the Ottomans, who had twice invaded Hungary, and entered the League of Augsburg (1686) against Louis XIV., because the latter had compelled him to accept the Treaty of Nimeguen, in 1679. See page 253, note 502.

[676] An allusion to Pope Innocent XI. (see page 361, note 655), who was too little of a friend of Louis XIV. to show much zeal on behalf of James II.

WILLIAM III

(119.) Ye little men, only six feet high, or at most seven, who, as soon as you have reached eight feet, are to be seen for money in booths at the fairs, as giants and wonders; who, without blushing, give yourselves the titles of "highnesses" and "eminences," which is the utmost that can be granted to those mountain-tops so near the sky that they see the clouds form underneath them; ye haughty, vain-glorious animals who despise all other creatures, and who cannot even be compared to an elephant or a whale, draw near, ye men, and answer Democritus. Do you not commonly speak of "hungry wolves, furious lions, and mischievous monkeys?" Pray, who are you? "Man is a rational creature" is continually dinned in my ears. Who gave you this appellation? Did the wolves, or the lions, or the monkeys do so, or did you take it yourselves? It is already very ridiculous that you should bestow on animals, your fellow-creatures, all the bad epithets, and take the best for yourselves; leave it to them to give names, and you will see that they will not forget themselves, and how you will be treated. I do not mention, O men, your frivolities, your follies and caprices, which place you lower than the mole or the tortoise, who wisely move along quietly and follow invariably their own natural instinct; but listen to me for a moment: You say of a goshawk if it be very swift-winged and swoops well down on a partridge, that it is a good bird; of a greyhound following a hare very close and catching it, that it is a first-rate dog; it is also quite right that you should say of a man who hunts the wild boar, brings it to bay, walks up to it and kills it with a spear, that he is a courageous man. But if you see two dogs barking at each other, provoke, bite, and tear one another to pieces, you say they are foolish creatures, and take a stick to part them. If any one should come and tell you that all the cats of a large country met in a plain in their thousands and tens of thousands, and that after they had squalled to their hearts' content they had fallen upon each other tooth and nail; that about ten thousand of them had been left dead on the spot and infected the air for ten leagues round with their evil-smelling carcasses; would you not say that it was the most disgraceful row you ever heard? And if the wolves acted in the same way, what a butchery would there be, and what howls would be heard! Now, if these two kind of animals were to tell you they love glory, would you come to the conclusion that this glory consists in their meeting together in such a way to destroy and annihilate their own species; and if you have come to such a conclusion, would you not laugh heartily at the folly of these poor animals? Like rational creatures, and to distinguish yourselves from those which only make use of their teeth and claws, you have invented spears, pikes, darts, sabres, and scimitars, and, in my opinion, very judiciously; for what could you have done to one another merely with your hands, except tearing your hair, scratching your faces, and, at best, gouging one another's eyes out; whilst now you are provided with convenient instruments for making large wounds and for letting out the utmost drop of your blood, without there being any fear of your remaining alive? But as you grow more rational from year to year, you have greatly improved the old fashion of destroying yourselves; you use certain little globes[677] which kill at once, if they but hit you on the head or chest; you have other globes, heavier and more massive,[678] which cleverly cut you in two or disembowel you, without counting those falling on your roof,[679] breaking through the floors from the garret to the cellar, which they destroy, and blowing up your wife who is lying-in, and the child, the nurse, and the house as well. And yet this is glory, which delights in all this hurly-burly and mighty hubbub! You have also defensive arms, and according to the rules and regulations, when waging war, you should put on a suit of iron, no doubt a pretty becoming dress, which always puts me in mind of those four famous fleas, formerly shown by a cunning artist, a quack, who knew how to keep them alive in a glass phial; each of those little animals wore a helmet, their bodies were covered by a breastplate; they had vambraces, knee-pieces, and a spear at their side; their accoutrements were quite perfect,

[677] Musket-balls.
[678] Cannon-balls.
[679] Shells.

and thus they skipped and jumped about in their bottle. Fancy a man of the size of Mount Athos,[680] and why not? Would a soul be puzzled to animate such a body, for it would have plenty of room to move about in? If such a man's sight were piercing enough to discover you somewhere upon earth, with your offensive and defensive arms, what do you think would be his opinion of a parcel of little marmosets thus equipped, and of what you call war, cavalry, infantry, a memorable siege, a famous battle? Shall I never hear any other sound buzz in my ears? Is the world only filled with regiments and companies? Has everything been changed to battalions and squadrons?—He takes a town, then a second, then a third; he wins a battle, two battles, he drives away the enemy, he conquers by sea, by land.—Do you say these things of one of you, or of a giant, a Mount Athos? There is a remarkable man amongst you, pale and livid,[681] with not ten ounces of flesh on his bones, and who would be blown down by the least gust of wind, one would think, and yet he makes more noise than half-a-dozen men, and sets everything in a blaze; he has just now been fishing in troubled waters, and caught a whole island at once; in another place, it is true, he is beaten and pursued, but escapes into the bogs,[682] and will hearken neither to peace nor to truce. He began betimes to show what he could do, and so severely bit his nurse's breast[683] that the poor woman died of it; I know what I mean, and that is sufficient. To conclude: he was born a subject and is no longer one; on the contrary, he is now the master, and those whom he has overcome and brought under his yoke are harnessed to the plough and till the ground with might and main; those good people seem even afraid of being un-yoked one day and of becoming free, for they have pulled out the thong and lengthened the handle of the whip of the man who drives them; they forget nothing that can increase their slavery; they let him cross the water so that he may get new vassals and acquire fresh territories; and to succeed in this he has, it is true, only to take his father and mother by the shoulders and throw them out of doors, and they aid him in this virtuous undertaking. The people on this side and that side of the water subscribe, and each pays his share, to render him every day more and more formidable to all; the Picts and the Saxons compel the Batavians to be silent, and the latter act in the same manner to the Picts and Saxons; they may all boast of being his humble slaves, as they wished to be. But what do I hear of certain personages who wear crowns? I do not mean counts or marquesses, who swarm on this earth, but princes and sovereigns. This man does but whistle, and they come at his call; they uncover as soon as they are in his anteroom, and never

[680] Athos was a mountain in Roumelia which the sculptor Dinocrates proposed to hew into a statue of Alexander. Our author refers to this; Byron has also an allusion to it in the twelfth canto of his "Don Juan."

[681] The enemies of William III. often alluded to the livid colour of his countenance, and Boileau in his wretched Ode sur la prise de Namur also speaks of "Nassau blème."

[682] The Prince of Orange ordered in 1672 the dykes in Holland to be opened to delay the advance of the French army; hence the allusion to "bogs."

[683] William III. became the adopted son of the Dutch republic on the death of his father in 1666, and on the proposal of John de Witt. Frenchmen pretend he was far more dictatorial in Holland than in England, and accuse him of having behaved ungratefully towards de Witt, his so-called "nurse."

speak but when he asks them a question.[684] Are these the same princes who cavil so much and are so precise about rank and precedence, and who spend whole months in regulating such questions whilst some Diet is assembled? What shall this new ruler[685] do to reward so blind a submission, and to satisfy the high opinion they have of him? If a battle is to be fought, he must win it, and in person; if the enemy besieges a town, he must go raise the siege and drive him away with ignominy, unless the ocean be between him and the enemy;[686] it is the least he can do to please his courtiers. Cæsar[687] himself comes and swells their number; at least he expects important services from him; for either the "archon" and his allies will fail, which is more difficult than impossible to conceive, or, if he succeeds, and nothing resists him, he is ready with his allies, who are jealous of Cæsar's religion and greatness, to rush upon him, snatch away his eagle, and reduce him and his heir to the "fasces argent"[688] and to his hereditary dominions. But there is no use saying anything more; they have all voluntarily given themselves up to the man whom they should perhaps have distrusted the most. Would Esop not have told them that "the feathered tribe of a certain country got alarmed and frightened at being near a lion, whose mere roar terrified them; they went to the animal, who persuaded them he would come to some arrangement, and take them under his protection. The end of it was that he gobbled them all up one after another."

---

[684] When William III. returned to the Hague (1690), several princes who had joined the League of Augsburg came to compliment him; it was even rumoured that the Elector of Bavaria had some time to wait before he could obtain an audience.

[685] In the original archonte, archon, the chief magistrate in ancient Athens.

[686] This seems to refer to the siege of Mons (1690), which William III. did not venture to raise.

[687] The Emperor of Germany.

[688] The arms of the house of Austria proper.

THE BIRD-FANCIER

XIII.

OF FASHION.

(1.) IT is very foolish, and betrays what a small mind we have, to allow fashion to sway us in everything that regards taste, in our way of living, our health, and our conscience. Game is out of fashion, and therefore insipid, and fashion forbids to cure a fever by bleeding. This long while it has also not been fashionable to depart this life shriven by Theotimus; now none but the common people are saved by his pious exhortations, and he has already beheld his successor.[689]

(2.) To have a hobby is not to have a taste for what is good and beautiful, but for what is rare and singular, and for what no one else can match; it is not to like things which are perfect, but those which are most sought after and fashionable. It is not an amusement but a passion, and often so violent that in the meanness of its object it only yields to love and ambition. Neither is it a passion for everything scarce and in vogue, but only for some particular object which is rare, and yet in

[689] Theotimus stands for M. Sachot, who was vicar of Saint-Gervais at the time La Bruyère wrote, and used to shrive all the fashionable people, but gradually was supplanted by Bourdaloue, who also succeeded him in his vicarage. The fashion of not bleeding during a fever still exists, and rightly so.

fashion.

The lover of flowers has a garden in the suburbs, where he spends all his time from sunrise till sunset. You see him standing there, and would think he had taken root in the midst of his tulips before his "Solitaire;" he opens his eyes wide, rubs his hands, stoops down and looks closer at it; it never before seemed to him so handsome; he is in an ecstasy of joy, and leaves it to go to the "Orient," then to the "Veuve," from thence to the "Cloth of Gold," on to the "Agatha," and at last returns to the "Solitaire," where he remains, is tired out, sits down, and forgets his dinner; he looks at the tulip and admires its shade, shape, colour, sheen, and edges, its beautiful form and calix; but God and nature are not in his thoughts, for they do not go beyond the bulb of his tulip, which he would not sell for a thousand crowns, though he will give it to you for nothing when tulips are no longer in fashion, and carnations are all the rage. This rational being, who has a soul and professes some religion, comes home tired and half-starved, but very pleased with his day's work; he has seen some tulips.[690]

Talk to another of the healthy look of the crops, of a plentiful harvest, of a good vintage, and you will find he only cares for fruit, and understands not a single word you say; then turn to figs and melons; tell him that this year the pear-trees are so heavily laden with fruit that the branches almost break, that there are abundance of peaches, and you address him in a language he completely ignores, and he will not answer you, for his sole hobby is plum-trees. Do not even speak to him of your plum-trees, for he only is fond of a certain kind, and laughs and sneers at the mention of any others; he takes you to his tree and cautiously gathers this exquisite plum, divides it, gives you one half, keeps the other himself, and exclaims: "How delicious! do you like it? is it not heavenly? You cannot find its equal anywhere;" and then his nostrils dilate, and he can hardly contain his joy and pride under an appearance of modesty. What a wonderful person, never enough praised and admired, whose name will be handed down to future ages! Let me look at his mien and shape whilst he is still in the land of the living, that I may study the features and the countenance of a man who, alone amongst mortals, is the happy possessor of such a plum.[691]

Visit a third, and he will talk to you about his brother collectors, but especially of Diognetes.[692] He admits that he admires him, but that he understands him less than ever. "Perhaps you imagine," he continues, "that he endeavours to learn something of his medals, and considers them speaking evidences of certain facts that have happened, fixed and unquestionable monuments of ancient history. If you do, you are wholly wrong. Perhaps you think that all the trouble he takes to

---

[690] The "Keys" speak of a certain lawyer, Cambout or Cabout, who belonged to the household of the Condés, and of a flute-player, Descosteaux, both passionately fond of flowers, as the supposed originals of the "lover of flowers."

[691] This lover of fruit was the financier Rambouillet de la Sablière, who had a large garden in the Faubourg Saint-Antoine. See also page 173, note 355.

[692] Four well-known antiquarians, the Duke d'Aumont, Vaillant, Le Nostre, and Father Menestrier, the latter author of an Histoire de Louis le grand par les médailles, have been supposed the originals of Diognetes.

become master of a medallion with a certain head on it is because he will be delighted to possess an uninterrupted series of emperors. If you do, you are more hopelessly wrong than ever. Diognetes knows when a coin is worn, when the edges are rougher than they ought to be, or when it looks as if it had been newly struck; all the drawers of his cabinet are full, and there only is room for one coin; this vacancy so shocks him that in reality he spends all his property and literally devotes his whole lifetime to fill it."

"Will you look at my prints?" asks Democedes,[693] and in a moment he brings them out and shows them to you. You see one among them neither well printed nor well engraved, and badly drawn, and, therefore, more fit on a public holiday to be stuck against the wall of some house on the "Petit-Pont" or in the "Rue Neuve"[694] than to be kept in a collection. He allows it to be badly engraved and worse drawn; but assures you it was done by an Italian who produced very little, and that hardly any of these prints have been struck off, so that he has the only one in France, for which he paid a very heavy price, and would not part with it for the very best print to be got. "I labour under a very serious affliction," he continues, "which will one day or other cause me to give up collecting engravings; I have all Callot's etchings,[695] except one, which, to tell the truth, so far from being the best, is the worst he ever did, but which would complete my collection; I have hunted after this print these twenty years, and now I despair of ever getting it; it is very trying!"

Another man criticises those people who make long voyages either through nervousness or to gratify their curiosity; who write no narrative or memoirs, and do not even keep a journal; who go to see and see nothing, or forget what they have seen; who only wish to get a look at towers or steeples they never saw before, and to cross other rivers than the Seine or the Loire; who leave their own country merely to return again, and like to be absent, so that one day it may be said they have come from afar; so far this critic is right and is worth listening to.

But when he adds that books are more instructive than travelling, and gives me to understand he has a library, I wish to see it. I call on this gentleman, and at the very foot of the stairs I almost faint with the smell of the Russia leather bindings of his books. In vain he shouts in my ears, to encourage me, that they are all with gilt edges and hand-tooled, that they are the best editions, and he names some of them one after another, and that his library is full of them, except a few places painted so carefully that everybody takes them for shelves and real books, and is deceived. He also informs me that he never reads nor sets foot in this library, and now only accompanies me to oblige me. I thank him for his politeness, but feel as he does on the subject, and would not like to visit the tan-pit which he calls a library.

------

[693] Several collectors of prints of the time have been named by the commentators as the original of Democedes.

[694] At the time La Bruyère wrote, the houses on the bridge called the "Petit-Pont" and those in the "Rue Neuve-Notre-Dame" were covered with hangings and adorned with common prints on the days when a procession was passing.

[695] Jacques Callot (1593-1655), a celebrated Lorraine artist and etcher.

Some people immoderately thirst after knowledge, and are unwilling to ignore any branch of it, so they study them all and master none; they are fonder of knowing much than of knowing some things well, and had rather be superficial smatterers in several sciences than be well and thoroughly acquainted with one. They everywhere meet with some person who enlightens and corrects them; they are deceived by their idle curiosity, and often, after very long and painful efforts, can but just extricate themselves from the grossest ignorance.

Other people have a master-key to all sciences, but never enter there; they spend their lives in trying to decipher the Eastern and Northern languages, those of both the Indies, of the two poles, nay, the language spoken in the moon itself. The most useless idioms, the oddest and most hieroglyphical-looking characters, are just those which awaken their passion and induce them to study; they pity those persons who ingenuously content themselves with knowing their own language, or, at most, the Greek and Latin tongues. Such men read all historians and know nothing of history; they run through all books, but are not the wiser for any; they are absolutely ignorant of all facts and principles, but they possess as abundant a store and garner-house of words and phrases as can well be imagined, which weighs them down, and with which they overload their memory, whilst their mind remains a blank.

A certain citizen loves building, and had a mansion erected so handsome, noble, and splendid that no one can live in it.[696] The proprietor is ashamed to occupy it, and as he cannot make up his mind to let it to a prince or a man of business, he retires to the garret, where he spends his life, whilst the suite of rooms and the inlaid floors are the prey of travelling Englishmen and Germans, who come to visit it after having seen the Palais-Royal, the palace L ... G ...[697] and the Luxembourg. There is a continual knocking going on at these handsome doors, and all visitors ask to see the house, but none the master.

There are other persons who have grown-up daughters, but they cannot afford to give them a dowry, nay, these girls are scarcely clothed and fed; they are so poor that they have not even a bed to lie upon nor a change of linen. The cause of their misery is not very far to seek; it is a collection crowded with rare busts, covered with dust and filth, of which the sale would bring in a goodly sum; but the owners cannot be prevailed upon to part with them.

Diphilus is a lover of birds, he begins with one and ends with a thousand; his house is not enlivened, but infested by them; the courtyard, the parlour, the staircase, the hall, all the rooms, and even the private study are so many aviaries; we no longer hear warbling, but a perfect discord; the autumnal winds and the most rapid cataracts do not produce so shrill and piercing a noise; there is no hearing one another speak but in those apartments set apart for visitors, where people will have to wait until some little curs have yelped, before there is a chance of seeing

[696] In the "Rue Vieille-du-Temple," in Paris, there was, at the time our author wrote, a mansion erected by M. Amelot de Bisseuil, which was considered one of the curiosities of Paris.

[697] According to some "Keys," this refers to the Hotel Lesdiguières; according to others, to the hotel of M. de Langlée. See page 188, note 392.

the master of the house. These birds are no longer an agreeable amusement for Diphilus, but a toilsome fatigue, for which he can scarcely find leisure; he spends his days—days which pass away and never come back—in feeding his birds and cleaning them; he pays a man a salary[698] for teaching his birds to sing with a bird-organ, and for attending to the hatching of his young canaries. It is true that what he spends on the one hand he spares on the other, for his children have neither teachers nor education. In the evening, worn out by his hobby, he shuts himself up, without being able to enjoy any rest until his birds have gone to roost, and these little creatures, on which he dotes only for their song, have ceased to warble. He dreams of them whilst asleep, and imagines he is himself a tufted bird, chirping on his perch; during the night he even fancies he is moulting and brooding.

Who can describe all the different kinds of hobbies? Can you imagine when you hear a certain person speak of his "Panther Cowry," his "Pen Shell," and his "Music Shell,"[699] and brag of them as something very rare and marvellous, that he intends to sell these shells? Why not? He has bought them for their weight in gold.

Another is an admirer of insects, and augments his collection every day; in Europe he is the best judge of butterflies, and has some of all sizes and colours.[700] What an unfortunate time you have chosen to pay him a visit! He is overwhelmed with grief, and in a fearful temper, which he vents on his family; he has suffered an irreparable loss; draw near him and observe what he shows you on his finger; it is a caterpillar, but such a caterpillar, lifeless, and but just expired.

(3.) Duelling is the triumph of fashion, which it sways tyrannically and most conspicuously. This custom does not allow a coward to live, but compels him to go and be killed by a man of more valour than himself, and to be mistaken for a man of courage. The maddest and most absurd action has been called honourable and glorious; it has been sanctioned by the presence of kings; in some cases it has even been considered a sort of duty to countenance it; it has decided the innocence of some persons,[701] and the truth or falsity of certain accusations of capital crimes; it was so deeply rooted in the opinion of all nations, and had obtained such a complete possession of the feelings and minds of men, that to cure them of this folly has been one of the most glorious actions of the greatest of monarchs.[702]

(4.) Some persons were formerly in high repute for commanding armies, for diplomacy, for pulpit eloquence, or for poetry, and now they are no longer fash-

[698] In the original, *il donne pension à un homme*, antiquated in this sense.

[699] The author states: "These are names of various shells." The original has "le Léopard, la Plume, la Musique," and the English names have been kindly suggested by M. Hugh Owen in "Notes and Queries" as equivalents for the French ones.

[700] A few years before La Bruyère wrote, there was quite a mania for butterflies at court, and in Paris.

[701] An allusion to the ordeal by duel, of which one of the last was fought between Jarnac and La Chateigneraye, in 1542, before Henri II. and his court. A treacherous thrust of the first-named nobleman has given rise to the proverbial saying *un coup de Jarnac*.

[702] Louis XIV. was strongly opposed to duelling, and several legal prohibitions of it were promulgated during his reign.

ionable. Do certain men degenerate from what they formerly were, and have their merits become antiquated, or is our liking for them worn out?

(5.) A fashionable man is not long the rage, for fashions are ephemeral; but if he happens to be a man of merit, he is not totally eclipsed, but something or other of him will still survive; he is as estimable as he formerly was, but only less esteemed.

Virtue is fortunate enough to be able to do without any help, and can exist without admirers, partisans, and protectors; lack of support and approbation does not harm it, but, on the contrary, strengthens, purifies, and perfects it; whether in or out of fashion, it is still virtue.

(6.) If you tell some men, and especially the great, that a certain person is virtuous, they will say to you, "they trust he may long remain so;" that he is very clever, and above all, agreeable and entertaining, they will answer you, "that it is so much the better for him;" that he is a man of culture and knows a great deal, they will ask you "what o'clock it is, or what sort of weather we have?" But if you inform them that a Tigellinus[703] has been gulping down a glass of brandy,[704] and, wonderful to relate, that he has repeated this several times during his repast, they will ask where he is, and tell you to bring him with you the next day, or that same evening, if possible. We bring him with us, and that very man, only fit for a fair or to be shown for money, is treated by them as a familiar acquaintance.

(7.) Nothing brings a man sooner into fashion and renders him of greater importance than gambling;[705] it is almost as good as getting fuddled.[706] I should like to see any polished, lively, witty gentleman, even if he were Catullus himself or his disciple,[707] dare to compare himself with a man who loses eight hundred *pistoles*[708] at a sitting.

(8.) A fashionable person is like a certain blue flower which grows wild in the fields, chokes the corn, spoils the crops, and takes up the room of something better; it has no beauty nor value but what is owing to a momentary caprice, which dies out almost as soon as sprung up. To-day it is all the rage, and the ladies are decked with it; to-morrow it is neglected and left to the common herd.[709]

[703] Sophonius Tigellinus, a favourite and accomplice of the Roman emperor Nero, was put to death about the year 70.

[704] In the original, souffler and jeter en sable, "to gulp down;" only the last word is found in the dictionary of the French Academy of 1694. The old English translators of La Bruyère have been greatly puzzled by the sentence beginning with the word "a Tigellinus," and give it: "a juggler, one who turns aqua-vita black, and performs other feats of legerdemain (other surprising things)," whilst the translation of 1767 speaks of "a fiddler, who, besides several odd performances on his instrument, gulps down," &c.

[705] See the chapter "Of the Gifts of Fortune," §§ 71,-75.

[706] In the original la crapule, now no longer used for "intoxication."

[707] C. Valerius Catullus (87-47 B.C.), the well-known Roman poet; is supposed to allude to the Abbé de Chaulieu (see page 342, note 630). The latter's disciple was the Chevalier de Bouillon.

[708] See page 173, note 346.

[709] During the summer of 1689 the fashionable ladies at court adorned themselves

A person of merit, on the contrary, is a flower we do not describe by its colour, but call by its name, which we cultivate for its beauty or fragrance, such as a lily or a rose; one of the charms of nature, one of those things which beautify the world, belonging to all times, admired and popular for centuries, valued by our fathers, and by us in imitation of them, and not at all harmed by the dislike or antipathy of a few.

(9.) Eustrates is seated in his small boat, delighted with the fresh air and a clear sky; he is seen sailing with a fair wind, likely to last for some time, but a lull comes on all of a sudden, the sky becomes overcast, a storm bursts forth, the boat is caught by a whirlwind, and is upset. Eustrates rises to the surface of the waters and exerts himself; it is to be hoped he will at least save himself and get hold of the boat; but another wave sinks him, and he is considered lost: a second time he appears above the water, and hope revives, when a billow all of a sudden swallows him up; he is never more seen again, he is drowned.

(10.) Voiture and Sarrazin[710] just suited the age they lived in, and appeared at the right time, when it seems they were expected; if they had not made such haste they would have come too late; and I question if, at present, they would have been what they were then. Light conversation, literary society, delicate raillery, lively and familiar epistolary interchange, and a select circle of friends, where intelligence was the only passport of admittance, have all disappeared. To say that these authors would have revived them is too much; all I can venture to admit in favour of their intellect is, that perhaps they might have excelled in another way. But the ladies of the present time are either devotees, coquettes, fond of gambling, or ambitious, and some of them all these together; court favour, gambling, gallants, and spiritual directors, have taken their places, and they defend them against men of culture.[711]

(11.) A coxcomb, who makes himself ridiculous as well, wears a tall hat, a doublet with puffs on the shoulders, breeches with ribbons or tags, and jackboots; at night he dreams what he shall do to be taken notice of the following day. A wise man leaves the fashion of his clothes to his tailor; it shows as much weakness to run counter to the fashion as to affect to follow it.

(12.) We blame a fashion that divides the shape of a man into two equal parts, and takes one of it for the waist, whilst leaving the other for the rest of the body; we condemn the fashion of making of a lady's head the basis of an edifice of several heights, the build and shape of which change according to fancy; which removes the hair from the face, though Nature designed it to adorn it; and ties it up and makes it bristle so that the ladies look like Bacchantes; this fashion seems to have been intended to make the fair sex change its mild and modest air for one much more haughty and bold. People exclaim against certain fashions as ridiculous; but they adopt them as long as they last, to adorn and embellish themselves, and they derive from them all the advantages they can expect, namely, to please. Methinks with bouquets of cornflowers.

[710] For Voiture see page 20, § 37, and note 72. Sarrazin (1603-1654) was a rival of Voiture in an affected and pretentious style.

[711] The original has gens d'esprit. See page 20, note 70.

the inconstancy and fickle-mindedness of men is to be admired; for they successively call agreeable and ornamental things directly opposed to one another; they use in plays and masquerades those same dresses and ornaments which, until then, were considered as denoting gravity and sedateness; a short time makes all the difference.[712]

(13.) N ... is wealthy; she eats and sleeps well; but the fashion of head-dresses alters, and whilst she does not think anything at all about it, and believes herself quite happy, her head-dress has quite grown out of fashion.

(14.) Iphis attends church, and sees there a new-fashioned shoe; he looks upon his own with a blush, and no longer believes he is well dressed. He only comes to hear mass to show himself, but now he refuses to go out, and keeps his room all day on account of his foot. He has a soft hand, which he preserves so by scented paste, laughs often to show his teeth, purses up his mouth, and is perpetually smiling; he looks at his legs and surveys himself in the glass, and no man can have a better opinion of his personal appearance than he has; he has adopted a clear and delicate voice, but fortunately lisps;[713] he moves his head about and has a sort of sweetness in his eyes which he does not forget to use to set himself off; his gait is indolent, and his attitudes are as pretty as he can contrive them; he sometimes rouges his face, but not very often, and does not do so habitually. In truth, he always wears breeches and a hat, but neither earrings nor a pearl necklace; therefore I have not given him a place in my chapter "Of Women."

(15.) Those very fashions which men so willingly adopt to adorn themselves are apt to be laid aside when their portraits are taken, as if they felt and foresaw how crude[714] and ridiculous these would look when they had lost the bloom and charm of novelty; they prefer to be depicted with some fancy ornaments, some imaginary drapery, just as it pleases the artist, and which often are as little suited to their air and face as they recall their character and personage. They affect strained or indecent attitudes, harsh, uncultivated, and foreign manners, which transform a young *abbé* into a swaggerer, and a magistrate into a swashbuckler, a Diana into a woman of the town, an amazon or a Pallas into a simple and timid woman, a Laïs into a respectable girl, and a Scythian, an Attila,[715] into a just and magnanimous prince.

Such is our giddiness, that one fashion has hardly destroyed another, when it is driven away by a newer one, again to make way for its successor, which will not be the last. Whilst these changes are going on, a century elapses, and all these gew-

[712] Those of my readers who wish to see the various fashions in dress of the end of the seventeenth century should look at the etchings at the head of each chapter, which faithfully represent them at the time La Bruyère wrote; the high head-dresses had been abandoned when he penned this paragraph (1691), but they became again the rage the following year (see Chapter iv., "Of Women," § 5), and continued so for a considerable period.

[713] In the original il parle gras; parler gras means usually "to speak thick," but is sometimes said, as it is here, of people who lisp, which generally in French is grasseyer.

[714] In the original indécence, "crudeness," "want of harmony," now antiquated with this meaning.

[715] Attila, king of the Huns, died 453.

gaws are ranked amongst things of the past, and exist no longer. Then the oldest fashion becomes again the most elegant, and charms the eye the most, it pleases as much in portraits as the *sagum* or the Roman dress on the stage, as a long black veil, an ordinary veil, and a tiara[716] do on our hangings and our pictures.

Our fathers have transmitted to us the history of their lives as well as a knowledge of their dresses, their arms,[717] and their favourite ornaments; a benefit for which we can make no other return than by doing our posterity the same service.

(16.) Formerly a courtier wore his own hair, breeches, and doublet, as well as large canions,[718] and was a freethinker;[719] but this is no longer becoming; now he wears a wig, a tight suit, plain stockings, and is devout. All this because it is the fashion.

(17.) Any man who, after having dwelt for a considerable time at court, remains devout, and contrary to all reason, narrowly escapes being thought ridiculous, can never flatter himself with becoming the fashion.

(18.) What will not a courtier do for the sake of advancing his interests? Rather than not advance them he will turn pious.[720]

(19.) The colours are all prepared, and the canvas is stretched, but how shall I fix this restless, giddy, and variable man, who adopts so many thousand different shapes? I depict him as devout, and I think I have caught his likeness; but I have missed it, and he is already a freethinker. Let him remain even in this bad position, and I shall succeed in portraying his irregularity of heart and mind so that he will be known; but another fashion is in vogue, and again he becomes devout.

(20.) A man who thoroughly knows the court is well aware what virtue and what piety is;[721] there is no imposing upon him.

(21.) To neglect going to vespers as obsolete and not fashionable; to keep one's place for morning service; to know all the ins and outs of the chapel at Versailles, and who sits in the seats next[722] to the royal tribune, and what is the best place where a man can be seen or remain unobserved; to be thinking at church of God and business; to receive visits there; to order people about and send them on mes-

---

[716] The "long black veil," coming down to the feet, worn by ladies in mourning, and during some grand ceremonies, was called a mante. Our author adds in a note: "Oriental habits." The tiara, or triple crown, was the head-dress of the ancient Persian potentates, of the Jewish high priest, and of the Pope. For the sagum, see page 259, note 509.

[717] The author says in a note: "Offensive and defensive."

[718] Canions, or canons in French, were large round pieces of linen, often adorned with lace or bunches of ribbons, which were fastened below the breeches, just under the knee.

[719] Libertin in the original. See page 161, note 319.

[720] It was two years after the revocation of the Edict of Nantes (1685) that La Bruyère made these remarks about "pretended piety," for since the influence of Madame de Maintenon over Louis XIV., all the courtiers were turning pious. See also page 207, note 431.

[721] Our author is careful to add in a note, "assumed piety."

[722] Connaître le flanc is used by La Bruyère. Some of the commentators think this is a military term used purposely by our author.

sages or wait for answers; to trust more to the advice of a spiritual director than to the teachings of the Gospel; to derive all sanctity and notoriety from the reputation of our director; to despise all people whose director is not fashionable, and scarcely allow them to be in a state of salvation; to like the word of God only when preached at home or from the mouth of our own director; to prefer hearing a mass said by him to any other mass, and the sacraments administered by him to any others, which are considered of less value; to satiate ourselves with mystical books, as if there were neither Gospels, Epistles of the Apostles, nor morals of the fathers; to read or speak a jargon unknown in the early centuries;[723] to be very circumstantial in amplifying the sins of others and in palliating our own; to enlarge on our own sufferings and patience; to lament our small progress in heroism as a sin; to be in a secret alliance with some persons against others; to value only ourselves and our own set; to suspect even virtue itself; to enjoy and relish prosperity and favour, and to wish to keep them only for ourselves; never to assist merit; to make piety subservient to ambition; to obtain our salvation through fortune and dignities; these are, at least in our days, the greatest efforts of the piety of this age.

A pious person[724] is one who, under an atheistical king, would be an atheist.

(22.) Devout people know no other crime but incontinence, or, to speak more exactly, the scandal and appearance of incontinence. If Pherecides passes for a man who is cured of his fondness for women, or Pherenicia for a wife who is faithful to her husband, they are quite satisfied; allow these devotees to continue a game that finally will be their undoing; it is their business to ruin their creditors, to rejoice at the misfortunes of other people and take advantage of it, to idolise the great, to despise their inferiors, to get intoxicated with their own merit, to pine away with vexation, to lie, slander, intrigue, and do as much harm as they can. Would you like them to usurp the functions of those honest men[725] who avoid pride and injustice as well as the more latent vices?

(23.) When a courtier shall be humble, divested of pride and ambition, cease to advance his own interests by ruining his rivals, be just and relieve the misery of his vassals, pay his creditors, be neither a knave nor a slanderer, shall abandon luxurious feasting and unlawful amours, pray not only with his lips, and even when the prince is not present, shall not be morose and inaccessible, not show an austere countenance and a sour mien, shall not be lazy and buried in thought, reconcile a multiplicity of employments by conscientious application, shall be able and willing to devote his whole mind and all his attention to those great and arduous affairs which especially concern the welfare of the people and of the entire state; when his character shall make me afraid of mentioning him in this paragraph, and

---

[723] None of La Bruyère's commentators have observed that the "unknown jargon" seems to refer to the mystic quietism taught by Jeanne-Marie Bouvier de la Motte-Guyon (1648-1717), who was at the height of her reputation when this paragraph was published for the first time in the eighth edition of the "Characters" in 1694. To our author has also been attributed "Dialogues sur le Quiétisme."

[724] La Bruyère is always very careful when he uses the word "devout" or "pious," in a bad sense, to add in a note, "assumed" or "false piety." See also § 22.

[725] See page 43, note 121.

his modesty prevent him from knowing himself, if I should not give his name; then I shall say of such a man that he is devout, or rather that he is a man given to this age as an example of sincere virtue as well as to detect hypocrites.[726]

(24.) Onuphrius' bed[727] has only grey serge valances, but he sleeps on flock and down; he also wears plain but comfortable clothes, I mean, made of a light material in summer, and of very soft cloth in winter; his body-linen is very fine, but he takes very good care not to show it; he does not call out for his "hair-shirt and scourge,"[728] for then he would show himself in his true colours, as a hypocrite, whilst he intends to pass for what he is not, for a religious man; however, he acts in such a way that people believe, without his telling it them, that he wears a hair-shirt and scourges himself. Several books lie about his apartments, such as the "Spiritual Fight," the "Inward Christian," the "Holy Year;"[729] his other books are under lock and key; if he goes along the streets and perceives from afar a man to whom he ought to seem devout, downcast looks, a slow and demure gait, and a contemplative air are at his command; he plays his part. If he enters a church, he observes whose eyes are upon him, and accordingly kneels down and prays, or else, never thinks of kneeling down and praying; if he sees an honest man and a man of authority approach him, by whom he is sure to be perceived, and who, perhaps, may hear him, he not only prays but meditates, has outbursts of devotion, and sighs aloud; but as soon as this honest man is gone, he becomes calm, and does not say a single word more. Another time he enters a chapel, rushes through the crowd, and chooses a spot to commune with himself, and where everybody may see how he humbles himself;[730] if he hears any courtiers speaking or laughing loud, and behave in chapel more boisterously than they would in an ante-chamber,[731] he makes a greater noise than they to silence them, and returns

---

[726] This "devout courtier" was Paul de Beauvillier, Dulce de Saint-Aignan, peer of France, gouverneur des enfants de France. See also page 197, note 405.

[727] Sainte-Beuve, in his Histoire de Port Royal, justly observes that La Bruyère showed more courage in writing the character of Onuphrius than Molière displayed in bringing out his Tartuffe, for the latter comedy made its appearance in 1667, and Onuphrius in 1691, five years after the revocation of the Edict of Nantes, when Louis XIV. was already under the influence of Madame de Maintenon, and had become devout.

[728] An allusion to the first words said by Tartuffe (act iii. scene 2) in Molière's play of that name: "Laurent, serrez ma haire avec ma discipline."

[729] The "Spiritual Fight," a religious work attributed to an Italian Theatine monk, Scupoli, had been already translated into French in 1608; the "Inward Christian," by Louvigny, was published in 1661, whilst there were two "Holy Years," one written by Bordier in 1668, and a second published ten years later by a certain clergyman, Loisel.

[730] In the original, il pousse des élans et des soupirs, a reminiscence of Molière's Tartuffe (act i. scene 5), where Orgon, in speaking of the hypocrite, says:

> "Il attirait les yeux de l'assemblée entière
> Par l'ardeur dont au ciel il poussait sa prière;
> Il faisait des soupirs, de grands élancements,
> Et baisait humblement la terre à tous moments."

[731] The "chapel" and the "anteroom" refer to the chapel and anteroom of the palace of Versailles.

to his meditations, in which he always disdainfully compares those persons to himself, to his own advantage. He avoids an empty church where he could hear two masses one after another, as well as a sermon, vespers, and compline, with no one between God and himself, without any other witnesses, and without any one thanking him for it; but he likes his own parish, and frequents those churches where the greatest number of people congregate, for there he does not labour in vain and is observed. He chooses two or three days of the year to fast in or to abstain from meat, without any occasion; but at the end of the winter he coughs; there is something wrong with his chest, he is more or less splenetic,[732] and feels very feverish; people entreat him, urge him, and even quarrel with him to compel him to break his fast as soon as it has begun, and he obeys them out of politeness. If Onuphrius is chosen as an umpire by relatives who have quarrelled, or in a lawsuit amongst members of one and the same family, he always takes the side of the strongest, I mean the wealthiest, and cannot be convinced that any person of property can ever be in the wrong. If he is comfortable at the house of a rich man whom he can deceive, whose parasite he is, and from whom he may derive great advantages, he never cajoles his patron's wife, nor makes the least advances to her, nor declares his love;[733] but rather avoids her, and will leave his cloak behind,[734] unless he is as sure of her as he is of himself; still less will he make use of devotional[735] cant to flatter and seduce her, for he does not employ it habitually, but intentionally, when it suits him, and never when it would only make him ridiculous. He knows where to find ladies more sociable and pliable than his friend's wife; and very seldom absents himself from these ladies for any length of time, if it were only to have it publicly stated that he has gone into religious retirement; for who can doubt the truth of this report, when people see him reappear quite emaciated, like one who has, not spared himself?

Moreover, those women who improve and thrive under the shelter of piety[736] suit him, but with this trifling difference, that he neglects those who are declining in years, and courts the young, and amongst these is only attracted by the best looking and the finest shape; he goes where they go, and returns when they return, and if they stay anywhere he stays there also; he has the consolation of seeing them at all times and places, and nobody needs be shocked about this, for they are devout, and so is he. Onuphrius is sure to make the best use he can of his friend's cecity and of his prepossession; sometimes he borrows money of him; at other times he acts so artfully that his friend offers to lend him some; people are very angry with him because he does not apply to his other friends when he needs money; now and then he refuses to receive a small sum unless he gives his note of hand for it, though he is quite certain never to take it up; at another time he says, with a <u>certain air, he is</u> not in want of anything, and that is, when he only needs a trifling

[732] Il a des vapeurs in the original, which, when our author wrote, was somewhat like the "out of sorts" of the present time.

[733] A reference to the declaration Tartuffe makes to Elmire, the wife of Orgon. See Molière's Tartuffe, act iii. scene 3.

[734] An allusion to Joseph's adventure with Potiphar's wife.

[735] La Bruyère is very careful to add again in a note: "False piety."

[736] Again our author adds "false piety," in a footnote.

amount; and on a certain occasion he publicly extols the generosity of his friend, on purpose to induce him to give him a considerable sum. He does not expect to succeed to the whole of the real estate of his friend, nor to get a deed of gift of all his property, especially if the son, the right and lawful heir, has to be set aside.[737] A pious man is neither a miser, nor prejudiced, unjust, nor selfish; and, though Onuphrius is not a pious man, he wishes to be thought one, and perfectly to imitate piety, though he does not feel it, in order secretly to forward his interests; he, therefore, would never aim at robbing the direct heirs of any family, nor insinuate himself where there is a daughter to portion, and a son to establish;[738] he knows their rights are too strong and inviolable to be upset without loud clamours, which he dreads, and without such an undertaking coming to the ears of the prince,[739] from whom he conceals his intrigues for fear of his true character being discovered. He selects collateral heirs, whom he can attack with greater impunity, and is the terror of male and female cousins, nephews and nieces, and of the flatterers and professed friends of all rich uncles; he gives himself out to be the legitimate heir of every wealthy old man who dies without issue, and who will have to disinherit him, if he wishes his relatives to get possession of his estate. If Onuphrius does not find means[740] to deprive them of the whole, he will, at least, rob them of a good share of it; a trifling calumny or even the slightest slander are sufficient for this pious purpose, and, indeed, Onuphrius is a perfect master of the art of slandering, and considers it sometimes his duty not to let it lie dormant, for there are men and women whom, according to him, he must decry for conscience' sake; and these are the people he does not like, whom he wishes to harm, and whose spoils he desires to get hold of. He compasses his ends without so much as opening his mouth; some persons talk to him of Eudoxus, he smiles or he weeps; they ask him why he does so, and they ask him again and again, but he does not reply; and he is right, for he has said quite enough.

(25.) "Laugh, Zelia,[741] be gay and frolicsome as you used to be. What has become of your mirth?" "I am wealthy," you reply, "I can do as I please, and I begin to breathe freely." "Laugh louder, Zelia, and louder still; what is the use of more riches if it makes you thoughtful and sad? Imitate the great, who are born in the lap of luxury; they laugh sometimes, and yield to their inclination; follow therefore yours, and do not let it be said that a new place, or a few thousand *livres* a year more or less, drive you from one extreme to another." "I only value favour because I can be thoughtful and sad," you answer. "I thought so, Zelia; but, believe

[737] Tartuffe, in the comedy of that name (act iii.), obtains from Orgon a deed of gift of all his property, to the detriment of his son and his second wife. This was against the French law, which obliged a man to leave a certain part of his goods, called la légitime (see page 95, § 71), to his wife and children; but this law did not apply to cousins, nephews, and nieces.

[738] Orgon, the patron of Tartuffe, has a son and a daughter.

[739] See Tartuffe, act v. scene 7.

[740] The original has ne trouve pas jour; the French noun has become antiquated in this sense.

[741] According to some commentators, Zelia was intended for the wife of de Pontchartrain, the contrôleur-général of the finances; but they seem to forget that La Bruyère was his friend and under some obligations to him.

me, do not leave off laughing, and smile on me, when I pass, as you did formerly: fear nothing; I shall not have a worse opinion of you and your post; I shall as firmly believe that you are wealthy and a favourite as well." "I have decided religious opinions," you answer. "That's quite enough, Zelia; and I ought to remember that persons whose conscience is at rest no longer care to show a calm and joyful countenance; gloomy and austere feelings are in the ascendancy and outwardly displayed; but such feelings proceed still further, and we are no longer surprised to observe that piety[742] makes a woman still more proud and disdainful than beauty and youth."

(26.) Arts and sciences have been greatly improved during this century, and have become highly refined; even salvation has now been reduced to rule and method, and to it have been added the most beautiful and sublime inventions of the human understanding. Devotion and geometry have each their own phraseology, or what are called "artistic expressions," and a person who ignores them is neither devout nor a mathematician. The first devout men, even those who were taught by the apostles, did not know them; those simple-minded people only had faith, practised good works, merely believed, and led righteous lives.

(27.) It is a delicate thing for a prince to reform his court and to introduce piety;[743] for knowing to what extent courtiers will carry their complaisance, and that they will make any sacrifices to advance their interests, he manages them with prudence, bears with them and dissembles, lest they should be driven to hypocrisy or sacrilege; he expects that Providence and time will be more successful than his zeal and his activity are.

(28.) Already in ancient times courts granted pensions and bestowed favours on musicians, dancing-masters, buffoons, flute-players, flatterers, and sycophants; they possess undoubted merits, and their talents are recognised and well known, for they amuse the great and give them a little breathing-time during the intervals of grandeur. It is well known that Fabien is a fine dancer, and that Lorenzani[744] composes beautiful anthems; but who can tell if a pious man be really virtuous? There is no pension to be got for him from the king's private purse, nor from the public treasury; and this is quite right, for piety is easy to counterfeit; and if it were rewarded, it would expose the prince to honour dissimulation and knavery, and to pension a hypocrite.

(29.) It is to be hoped the piety of the court, such as it is, will at least oblige prelates to reside in their dioceses.[745]

---

[742] In this and the following paragraph the author adds again in a note, "pretended piety."

[743] Already in the first edition of the "Characters" (1687), La Bruyère gave in the above paragraph his opinion about the danger of compelling the courtiers to become pious.

[744] Favier, a dancer at the opera, was also the dancing-master of the Duke de Bourbon, the pupil of La Bruyère. The anthems of Paolo Lorenzani, the music-master of Ann of Austria (1601-1666), were published in 1693.

[745] Many of the bishops in our author's time were continually dangling about the court, and not residing in their dioceses. See page 340, note 628.

(30.) I am convinced that true piety is the source from which repose flows; it renders life bearable and death without sting; hypocrisy does not possess such advantages.

(31.) Every hour in itself, and in respect to us, is unique; when once it is gone, it is entirely lost, and millions of ages will not bring it back again; days, months, and years, are swallowed up and irrevocably lost in the abyss of time; time itself shall be destroyed; it is but a point in the immense space of eternity, and will be erased. There are several slight and frivolous periods of time which are unstable, pass away, and may be called fashions, such as grandeur, favour, riches, power, authority, independence, pleasure, joy and superfluities. What will become of such fashions when time itself shall have disappeared? Virtue alone, now so little in fashion, will last longer than time.

NOBLE AND CITIZEN

XIV.

OF CERTAIN CUSTOMS.

(1.) Certain people want a fortune to become ennobled.[746]

Some of these would have been ennobled[747] if they could have put off their creditors half a year longer.

Others, again, are commoners when they lay down, and rise noblemen.[748]

How many noblemen are there whose relatives are commoners?

(2.) Some man disowns his father, who is known to keep an office or a shop,

[746] Our author added in a note of the first four editions, "secretaries of the king." Those offices were bought, and ennobled their holders, hence the nickname of savonnettes à vilain, literally, "soap balls for serfs." Other offices also gave a title to the persons who filled them, and this is probably the reason of the suppression of this note.

[747] La Bruyère's own note says "veterans," a name given to the conseillers (see page 181, note 381), who, after having practised for twenty years, sold their post, but retained all the privileges attached to it.

[748] Here our author gives the same note as above.

and only mentions his grandfather, who has been dead this long time, is unknown and cannot be found now; he enjoys a large income, has a grand post, great connections, and wants nothing but a title to become a nobleman.

(3.) Formerly the words "granting letters of nobility" were considered good French and habitually employed, but now they have become antiquated and out of date, and the courts of justice use the word "rehabilitation."[749] To rehabilitate supposes a wealthy man to be of noble descent, — for it is absolutely requisite he should be so, — and also his father to have forfeited the title by ploughing, digging, by becoming a pedlar, or by having been a lackey; it also supposes that the son only desires to be restored to the rights of his ancestors, and to wear the coat of arms his family always wore, though, perhaps, one of his own invention, and quite different from that on his old pewter ware; thus the granting of letters of nobility does not apply to his case, for they only confer an honour on a commoner, that is, on a man who has not yet discovered the secret of becoming rich.

(4.) A man of the people, by often affirming he was present when some prodigy happened, persuades himself that he has really seen it; another person, by concealing his age, comes to believe at last he is as young as he would be thought; and thus a commoner, who habitually asserts he is descended from some ancient baron, or from some noble lord, has the ideal pleasure of fancying himself of such illustrious descent.

(5.) What man is there, however meanly born, who having acquired some fortune, can be in want of a coat of arms, and with this coat, heraldic devices of the highest rank, a crest, supporters, a motto, and perhaps a war-cry? What is become of the distinction between head-pieces and helmets? They are no longer in use and not even mentioned; it does no more matter if they are worn in front or profile, open or closed, and with more or less bars; such niceties are out of date; coronets are worn, which is far simpler, for people think they deserve wearing them, and, therefore, bestow them on themselves. Some of the better sort of citizens have still a little shamefacedness left which prevents them using the coronet of a marquess, and they content themselves with an earl's, whilst a few do not even go a long way for their coat of arms, but take it from their sign-boards to put it on their carriages.[750]

---

[749] Commoners were ennobled by the grant of letters of nobility, whilst nobles whose ancestors had derogated were rehabilitated. However, commoners who had become wealthy often asked and obtained letters of rehabilitation, and, therefore, pretended to be of noble origin. "Rehabilitation," according to Thomas Blount's Law Dictionary, 1717, was in England: "one of those exactions ... claimed by the Pope ... and seems to signify a Bull or Breve for re-enabling a spiritual person to exercise his function, who was formerly disabled; or a restoring to former ability."

[750] The "war-cry" is a great proof of the nobility being ancient. The heaume, head-piece, is the same as the casque, helmet, which latter word was generally used in French heraldic language. According to certain rules which soon ceased to be practised, the vizard was open or shut, and showed more or less bars, whilst the helmet was in front or profile, according as the owner of the coat of arms was of ancient or modern nobility. The "Keys" refer to the Le Camus and Bezons families, as having taken the pictorial emblems of their father's signboards for their family arms. See also Molière's École des Femmes, Act i. Scene 1.

(6.) Provided a person is not born in a city, but in some lonely thatched house in the country, or in some ruins in the midst of marshes, dignified with the name of castle, he will be taken for a nobleman upon his own affirmation.

(7.) A man of noble descent wishes to pass for a small lord, and he compasses his end; a great lord pretends to be a prince, and employs so many precautions that, thanks to some fine appellations, quarrels about rank and precedence, and a genealogy not recognised by D'Hozier,[751] he at last is allowed to be a petty prince.

(8.) In everything great men mould themselves, and follow the example of people of higher rank, who, on their side, that they may have nothing in common with their inferiors, willingly abandon all honorific appellations and distinctions with which their rank is burdened, and instead of their slavery prefer a life of more freedom and ease.[752] Those who follow their steps vie already to observe the same simplicity and modesty. And thus, through a feeling of pride, all will condescend to live naturally and as the people do. How horribly inconvenient they must feel!

(9.) Some people are so fond of names that they have three for fear of wanting some; one for the country, another for the town, and a third which they use when on duty or in their office; others have a dissyllabic name which they ennoble by the particle "du" or "de" as soon as their circumstances improve; some, again, by suppressing a syllable make a name illustrious which was before obscure; by changing one letter of his name another person disguises himself, and he who formerly was Syrus becomes Cyrus.[753] Many suppress their whole names, though far from ignominious, to adopt others which sound better, and by which they get nothing but to be always compared to the great men from whom those names are borrowed. Finally, there are some, who, though born within the walls of Paris, pretend to be Flemish or Italian, as if every country had not its commoners, lengthen their French names, and give them a foreign termination, as if names were the better for being far-fetched.[754]

(10.) The want of money has reconciled the nobility to the commoners, and put an end to all disputes about the quartering of escutcheons.[755]

(11.) How many persons would be gainers by a law which should decree that

[751] The D'Hoziers were a family of genealogists, flourishing from 1592 till 1830. La Bruyère speaks most probably of Louis Roger and his brother Charles-René d'Hozier, who were of middle age when the "Characters" were published.

[752] It is said this is a hit at Monsieur, the brother of Louis XIV., who, in imitation of the king's son and grandsons, did no longer wish to be addressed as "Royal Highness," but simply as "you;" an example followed by all other French princes.

[753] A maître d'hôtel of Louis XIV., Delrieux, is said to have called himself De Rieux, and there had been a marshal of that name. Syris is the name of a slave in Plautus' and Terence's comedies; Cyrus, a celebrated king of Persia, was killed in battle against the Massagetæ, 529 B.C.

[754] Such men were a M. Sonnin, the son of a receveur-général, who called himself M. de Sonningen, and M. Nicolai, Marquis de Goussainville, descended from a M. Nicolas.

[755] The marriages of the Marquis de Tourville with a Mdlle. Langeois (see page 142, note 285), and of the Marshal de Lorges with Mdlle. Frémont, (see page 132, note 255), are examples of this, though many similar marriages took place almost daily.

nobility can be inherited from the mother's side, but how many more would be losers by it.[756]

(12.) There are few families but who are related to the greatest princes as well as to the common people.

(13.) There is nothing lost by being a nobleman; those who have a title neither want franchises, immunities, exemptions, privileges. Do you think it was purely for the pleasure of being ennobled that certain monks have obtained a title? They are not so foolish; it is only for the advantages they receive from it. It is, after all, much better than to get money by having an interest in farming the salt tax, and that not alone for every individual of the community, for it is against their vows, but even for the community itself.[757]

(14.) I here declare openly and desire all men to take notice of it, that none may hereafter be surprised: if ever any great man will think me worthy of his patronage, if ever I happen to make my fortune, I then shall claim descent from a certain Godfrey de la Bruyère, whom all chronicles of France mention as one of the many French noblemen of the highest rank who followed Godfrey of Bouillon to conquer the Holy Land.[758]

(15.) If nobility be virtue, a flagitious man loses his title; and if it be not virtue, is a very trifling thing.

(16.) Certain things are astonishing and incomprehensible if we consider their principles and why they were established. Who could imagine, for example, that these *abbés* who dress and are as effeminate and vain as any man or woman of rank can well be, and who vie for the ladies' favours with a marquess or a financier, and defeat them both, were originally and etymologically the fathers and heads of holy monks and humble anchorites to whom they should be exemplars. How powerful, how absolute, how tyrannical is custom! And, not to mention greater irregularities, is it not to be feared that one day or other some young *abbés* will fig-ure in grey-flowered velvet dresses like a certain cardinal, or will paint and wear patches like women?[759]

----

[756] An ironical remark referring to noblemen marrying the daughters of commoners, for nobility descended only from the father to the children, but not if the mother were a serf; in Champagne, however, nobility could be inherited from the mother's side.

[757] "Franchise" is a privilege or exemption from ordinary jurisdiction, and "immu-nity" the right of not paying taxes, or of paying less than the commonalty. La Bruyère, in speaking of "certain monks who obtained titles," adds in a note: "a certain convent was secretary to the king." The convent of the Celestines had already in the fourteenth cen-tury been appointed to a secretaryship, and received its emoluments, but never fulfilled its duties. The religious community said to have had an interest in the gabelle or salt tax, is supposed to have been that of the Jesuits, but this accusation seems to have been made without sufficient proof.

[758] A certain Geoffroy de La Bruyère had really taken part in the third crusade and died during the siege of St. Jean d'Acre in 1191, or almost a century after Godfrey of Bouil-lon (1061-1100). Our author only mentioned his ancestor's full name in the sixth edition of the "Characters," published in 1691.

[759] Abbé is derived from the Syrian aba, father; the "cardinal" may have been the

(17.) That the obscenities of the gods, the Venus, the Ganymede, and all the other nudities of Carracci are represented on pictures painted for certain princes of the Church who style themselves successors of the apostles, may be proved by visiting the palace of the Farnese.[760]

(18.) A thing, however handsome, loses somewhat of its beauty by being out of place; decorum adds a certain perfection and is based on reason; thus we never behold a jig danced in a chapel,[761] or hear stagey elocution in the pulpit; whilst no profane imagery is seen in churches, nor a crucifix and a picture of the Judgment of Paris[762] in these same holy places, nor the dress and retinue of a military man in a churchman.[763]

(19.) Shall I freely declare my thoughts about what the world calls a fine morning choral service, decorations often profane, places reserved and paid for, books distributed as in the theatre,[764] frequent assignations and interviews, deafening murmurings and talk, a certain person mounted in the pulpit, who holds forth in a familiar and jejune manner, without any other ambition than to get the people together and to amuse them until an orchestra begins to play, and, shall I say it, until singers are heard who have rehearsed for a considerable time? Does it become me to exclaim that I burn with zeal for the Lord's house? and must I draw aside the slender curtain which covers those mysteries, witnesses of such gross indecencies? What! must I call all this the church service because they do not yet dance at the TT....[765]

(20.) We hear of no vows nor pilgrimages made to any saint, in order to attain a higher degree of benignity, a more grateful heart, to be more just and less evil-doing, and to be cured of vanity, restless activity, and a propensity for buffoonery?

(21.) What can be more eccentric than for a number of Christians of both sexes

Cardinal de Bouillon, who always was gaily dressed. See page 306, note 560.

[760] In the palace Farnese at Rome, built by order of the Cardinal Alexander Farnese, who afterwards became Pope under the name of Paul III. (1534-1549), are to be found many works, such as Aurora and Cephalus, Diana and Endymion, Galathea, Polyphemus and Acis, and Ganymedes and Jupiter, painted by Annibale Carracci (1560-1609), and Domenichino (1581-1641), all representing nude figures, and not religious subjects.

[761] Richelet's Dictionary, published in 1680, mentions the gigue as "une danse anglaise, composée de toutes sortes de pas, qu'on danse sur la corde," and hence, he continues, "any dancing tune was thus called." But was a jig originally danced on the tight-rope? The "chapel" is of course the chapel-royal at Versailles.

[762] Paris, a son of Priam and Hecuba, had to decide whether Juno, Venus, or Minerva was the most beautiful, and should receive a "golden apple" as a prize. The three goddesses did not present themselves for this competition with too many clothes on.

[763] Hangings representing nude figures and profane subjects were seen until almost the last fifty years in some of the churches of the capital of France.

[764] Our author adds in a note, "an anthem translated into French by LL...." but no commentator has discovered who this unknown poet can have been.

[765] The TT ... were the Theatine monks, who settled in France about 1644, built a splendid church, and tried to raise money by charging for seats, during service, which was held with full orchestral and vocal music, about ten years before our author first published this paragraph, in 1694, in the eighth edition of his book.

to meet on certain days in a large room to applaud and reward a company of ex-communicated persons, who are only excommunicated for the very pleasure they give, and for which already they have been paid beforehand? Methinks either all theatres should be shut or a less severe anathema be fulminated against actors.[766]

(22.) On those days which are called holy a monk confesses, while the vicar thunders from the pulpit against the monk and his followers. A pious woman leaves the altar and then hears the preacher state in his sermon that she has committed sacrilege. Has the church no power either to make a clergyman hold his peace, or to suspend for a time the authority of a Barnabite?[767]

(23.) The fees in a parish church are higher for a marriage than for a christening, and amount to more for a christening than for confession; people would think them a tax laid upon the sacraments, which seem to be appreciated *ad valorem*; yet, after all, this is not the case; and those persons who receive money for these holy things do not think they sell them, whilst those who pay for them as little think they purchase them. Such an appearance of evil might indeed be avoided as well for the sake of the weak as for that of the scoffers.

(24.) A ruddy and quite healthy-looking parish priest,[768] wearing fine linen and Venice lace, has his seat in church near the cardinals and the doctors of divinity,[769] where he finishes to digest his dinner, whilst certain Bernardine or Franciscan monks come out of their cells or deserts to which decency and their own vows should confine them, to preach before him and his flock, and to be paid for their sermons as if they were vendible commodities. You will not let me continue, and you remark: "That such a censure is novel and unexpected, and that this shepherd and his flock ought not to be deprived from hearing the Word of God and receiving the bread of life." "By no means, I would have him himself preach that word as well as administer that bread morning and evening, in the churches, in the houses, on the market-places, from the housetops, and have none assume such a grand and laborious office but with intentions, capacities, and physical strength deserving of the handsome offerings and wealthy emoluments belonging to it. However, I am compelled to excuse the vicar's conduct, for it is customary, and he found it already established and will transmit it to his successors; but still I must blame this strange, unreasonable, and unwarrantable custom, whilst I approve still less the habit of his being paid four times for the same funeral, once for himself, a second time as his fees, a third for his being present, and a fourth for his officiating."

[766] Although this paragraph appeared when the "Characters" were first published in 1688, yet the great Bossuet went, five years later, out of his way to attack, in a sermon, Molière, the actor and playwright, although the latter had been dead more than twenty years.

[767] This paragraph reveals to us the quarrels raging between the secular and regular clergy, and seems to point out that, at the time our author wrote, the Barnabites were in vogue as confessors. The "monk" is supposed to have been a certain Father la Combe, the spiritual director of Madame Guyon. See page 393, note 723.

[768] Three parish priests have been named by the commentators as the originals of La Bruyère's portrait, but our author was far more general in his application.

[769] Les fourrures in the original. See page 318, note 587.

(25.) Titus served the church these twenty years in a small living, and is not yet held worthy of a better which becomes vacant; neither his talents, knowledge, his exemplary life, nor the wishes of his parishioners are sufficient to get him promoted; another clergyman starts up, as it were, from underground, and he obtains the preference; Titus is sent back and put off, but he does not complain, for custom will have it so.

(26.) "Who," asks the precentor, "will compel me to come to matins? Am I not master of the choir? My predecessor never went there, and I am as good a man as ever he was! Shall I allow my dignity to be debased while I hold office, or leave it to my successor as I found it?" The head of the school says: "I do not battle for my own interests, but for those of the prebend; it would be hard indeed for a superior canon to have to do duty with the choir, whilst the treasurer, the archdeacon, the penitentiary, and the grand vicar think themselves exempt from it." "It is my right," argues the head of the chapter, "to claim my dues, even if I should never come to prayers; for twenty years I slept every night without being disturbed; I will go on as I began, and never act derogatory to my dignity. Else, why should I be head of the chapter, if my example should be of no importance?" Thus each strives not to praise the Lord, and to show that, for a long time, it was neither customary nor compulsory to do so; whilst the emulation not to repair to divine service cannot be greater nor more fervent. The bells toll in the stillness of the night, and the same sounds which awaken the choristers and the singing-boys, lull the canons into a more sound and pleasant slumber, interspersed by delicious dreams; they rise late, and go to church to be paid for having slept.

(27.) Who would ever imagine, did not experience daily show it, how difficult it is for people to resign themselves to their being happy; and that there should be need of men dressed in a certain fashion, who by tender and pathetic speeches prepared beforehand, by certain inflexions of the voice, by tears and gestures, which make them perspire and exhaust them, finally induce a Christian and sensible man, who is desperately ill, not to be lost for ever but to ensure his own salvation.

(28.) Aristippus' daughter lies dangerously ill; she sends for her father, and is anxious to be reconciled to him and die happy. Shall so wise a man, the oracle of the whole town, take such a sensible step of his own accord, and persuade his wife to do the same? No! they will not stir without the interference of a spiritual director.

(29.) If a mother does not yield to the inclinations of her daughter, but induces her to become a nun, she takes upon herself the charge of another soul beside her own, and is responsible for such a soul to God. Such a mother will be lost for ever if the daughter be not saved.

(30.) A certain man gambles and is ruined, but nevertheless, when the eldest of his two daughters gets married, he gives her as a dowry all he has been able to rescue out of the clutches of some cheat;[770] the younger will shortly become a nun, without any vocation for it, but compelled by the losses of her father at play.

---

[770] The original has the proper name Ambreville, a noted rogue and head of a band of robbers, who was publicly burned at the stake in 1686.

(31.) Certain maidens, virtuous, healthy, enthusiasts in religion, and who feel they have a call, have not sufficient money to enter a wealthy nunnery and to take the vows of poverty.

(32.) A woman who hesitates whether she shall enter an abbey or a nunnery revives the old question about the advantages of a popular or a despotic rule.[771]

(33.) To play the fool and marry for love is to marry Melita, a handsome, sensible, thrifty, charming young woman who loves you, but is not so wealthy as Ægina, whose hand is proposed to you, with a large dowry, but who feels a strong inclination for spending it all, and your own fortune as well.

(34.) Formerly it was considered no trifling affair to get married; it was a settlement for life, a matter of importance which deserved a great deal of consideration; for a man had to take a wife for all his life, for better or worse; the same table and the same bed served them both; there was no getting rid of one another by separate maintenance, and a man with a household and children did not seem a rollicking bachelor.

(35.) I commend the bashfulness of a man who avoids being seen with a woman not his wife, and I can also understand his being loth to frequent persons of bad reputation. But what an impertinence for a man to blush being in the company of his own wife and being ashamed of appearing in public with a lady whom he has chosen as his companion for life, who should be his joy, his comfort, and his chief society; whom he loves and esteems, who adorns his home, and whose intelligence, merits, virtue, and connections reflect credit on him. Why did he not begin being ashamed of his marriage?

I am well aware of the tyranny, of custom, how it sways the mind and constrains the manners of men, even in things which are most senseless and needless; but I feel, nevertheless, I could be bold enough to walk on the Cours to be stared at in the company of the lady who is my wife.[772]

(36.) It is not a fault in a young man to marry a lady advanced in age, nor should he be ashamed of it, for he not seldom shows his prudence and foresight by acting thus. But it is infamous to treat his benefactress disgracefully, and to let her see she has been imposed upon by a hypocrite and an ungrateful fellow. If dissembling be ever excusable it is when it is done out of kindness; if deception is ever to be allowed, it is when sincerity would be cruelty. No man should behave cruelly even if his wife should live longer than he expected; for he did not stipulate, when he married her, that she should give up the ghost immediately after having made his fortune and paid his debts. Has she no longer to draw breath,

---

[771] The lady superior of an abbey was appointed by the king, but in a nunnery she was elected by the entire sisterhood; hence our author's remarks about "a popular or a despotic rule."

[772] When our author wrote, it was the fashion among the upper classes for a man never to be seen in public with his wife. Some years later people began even to be ashamed of being married, and if comedies hold the mirror up to nature, this may be observed in Le Philosophe marié (1727), by N. Destouches, and in Le Préjugé à la Mode (1735), by La Chaussée. For the Cours, see page 164, note 323.

and has she to take a dose of opium or hemlock after having performed such a fine stroke of business? Is it a crime in her to live? And is she to be blamed if the man should die before the woman, for whose funeral he had already made such nice arrangements, and for whom he intended to have the biggest bells tolled and the finest trappings brought out?

(37.) For some time a certain method has been in use for making the most of one's money,[773] which is still practised by some of our gentlemanly people, though it has been condemned by our most eminent divines.

(38.) In every commonwealth there are always some offices apparently created for no other purpose but to enrich one man at the expense of many; the property and the monies of private people flow continually and uninterruptedly in his coffers,[774] and they hardly ever come back, or if they do, it is after a long while. Each of these chests is like an abyss, a sea, which receives the waters of many rivers but disgorges none; or, if it does, it is imperceptibly, through secret and subterranean channels, without in the least abating its size and volume, and not till it has enjoyed these waters for a good while and can keep them no longer.

(39.) To sink money in an annuity was formerly considered quite safe; it was sure to be paid, and inalienable, but, now, through the fault of administrators, it may be considered irretrievably lost.[775] What other means are there for doubling an income or for hoarding? Shall I trust my money to the farmers of the *huitième denier*, or to those of the indirect taxes?[776] Shall I become a miser, a farmer of the revenue,[777] or an administrator of a hospital?

(40.) You have a silver coin, or even a gold coin in your possession, but that is not enough, for such coins only exercise their influence in large quantities; collect, if you can, a goodly number of them, make a heap of them, and then leave the rest to me. You are neither well-born, intelligent, talented, nor experienced, but what does it matter? only keep up your heap and I will take care to place you in such an eminent position that you shall stand covered before your master, if you have one; and he must be a very great man indeed, if, with the help of your daily increasing

---

[773] The author states in a note that by "making the most of one's money" he means "lending it out on bills and notes of hand," for which, according to the old French legislation and the old canonical law no interest could be charged, though some divines allowed trading companies to pay interest on borrowed monies.

[774] Several remarks had been made on this part of the above paragraph whilst La Bruyère was still alive, and a note of the ninth edition of the "Characters" (1696), published one month after the author's death, explained that it only referred to monies deposited in the greffe or clerk's office of certain tribunals whilst a lawsuit was going on.

[775] An allusion to the bankruptcy of some hospitals in Paris, which ruined many persons who had advanced money on annuities. This bankruptcy took place in the year 1689, and the fourth edition of the "Characters," in which the above paragraph first appeared, was published the same year. The original has also a play on words, on le fonds perdu, to sink money in an annuity, and un bien perdu, money irretrievably lost.

[776] For the huitième denier, see page 138, note 270. The aides were indirect taxes which the clergy and the nobility had to pay as well as the common people.

[777] The original has partisans. See page 136, note 266.

coin, I do not make him stand bareheaded in your presence.

(41.) Oranta has been at law these ten years to know in what court her cause is to be tried; her pretensions are well founded, of great importance, and her whole fortune is at stake. Perhaps about five years hence she may know who her judges are to be, and in what court she is to plead for the remaining years of her life.

(42.) The custom which has, of late, been adopted by our courts of judicature, of interrupting barristers whilst speaking, of preventing them from being eloquent and witty, of making them go back to the mere facts of a case, and to the bare proofs on which their clients base their rights, is very much approved of.[778] This harsh measure, which makes orators regret they have to leave out the finest parts of their speeches, banishes eloquence from the only spot where it is not out of place, and will make of our Parliaments[779] mute judicial tribunals, is founded on this sound and unanswerable argument, that it expedites the dispatch of business. I also wish the clerks would not forget to accelerate their business in the same way it is now done in court, and that not only barristers' speeches but the reports in writing might be curtailed.[780]

(43.) It is the duty of a judge to administer justice, but it is his profession to delay it; some judges know their duty and practise their profession.

(44.) Whenever a judge is solicited[781] it reflects no credit on him, for either his knowledge or his honesty is considered doubtful, and an attempt is made to prejudice him or to get him to commit an injustice.

(45.) With certain judges court favour, authority, friendship, and family connections, damage a good cause, and an affectation of wishing to appear incorruptible induces them to become unjust.

(46.) A magistrate who is either a dandy or a gallant has a far worse influence than if he were a dissolute man, for the latter conceals his behaviour and intrigues, so that often it is not known how to approach him, whilst the former with many professed foibles may be influenced by every woman he wishes to please.

(47.) Religion and justice are almost alike respected in a commonwealth, and the character of a magistrate is considered nearly as sacred as that of a priest. A legal dignitary can hardly dance at a ball, be seen in a theatre, or doff his plain and modest apparel, without bringing contempt upon himself; it is strange a law should be necessary to regulate his outward appearance, and compel him to assume a grave and highly respectable air.[782]

------

[778] The President Potier de Novion (see page 333, note 608) was the first, it is said, to adopt this custom, but a few months before this paragraph was published (1689), he had to resign his post on account of malversation and abuse of authority.

[779] See page 155, note 309.

[780] See page 181, note 381.

[781] See page 72, note 175.

[782] Counsellors of parliament (see page 181, note 381) were obliged to wear bands, by an order of Council obtained at the request of M. de Harlay (see page 45, note 122); before that time they wore cravats like other gentlemen. See also page 65, note 162.

(48.) There exists no profession in which an apprenticeship is not necessary; and in considering the various stations of men, it is manifest that, from the highest to the lowest, some time has been allowed to every person for qualifying himself by practice and experience for his profession, when his errors have been of no importance, but, on the contrary, led to perfection. War itself, which seems to owe its origin to confusion and disorder, and to be fostered by them, has its own rules; people do not destroy one another in the open field, in platoons, and in bands, without having been taught it, for killing is practised methodically. There is a school for military men; then why should magistrates not have one? There are established practices, laws, and customs, but no time is allowed, or at least not sufficient time, for digesting and studying them. The first attempt and apprenticeship of a youth who, fresh from school, dons red garments, and has been made a judge on account of his money,[783] is to decide arbitrarily of the lives and fortunes of men.[784]

(49.) The chief qualification of an orator is probity; without it he is no more than a declaimer, and disguises or exaggerates matters of fact, makes use of falsified quotations, slanders, adopts all the injustice and malice of his client, and may be ranked among those advocates of whom the proverb says, "that they are hired to insult people."[785]

(50.) I have heard it said: "It is true I owe a certain sum to such and such a person, and his claim is indisputable; but I wait to see if he will execute a small matter of form, and if he omits it, he can never retrieve his error; consequently he will then lose his debt, and his claim will be undoubtedly superseded. Now, he is pretty sure to forget it!" The man who utters such words has a real pettifogger's conscience.

An excellent, useful, sensible, wise, and just maxim for all courts of judicature would be the reverse of that which prefers form to equity.

(51.) Torture is an admirable invention, and infallibly destroys an innocent man who has a weak constitution, whilst it saves a guilty man who is hardy.[786]

(52.) The punishment of a villain is an example for his fellows; in the condemnation of an innocent man all honest men are concerned.[787]

[783] The counsellors of parliament wore red gowns, the magistrates red fur-lined cloaks. See page 318, note 587. The original of "on account of his money" is consignation. See page 169, note 333.

[784] In most of the courts of France the places of magistrates were bought and sold. See also the chapter "Of the Town," page 167, § 5.

[785] Marcus Valerius Martialis (43, was living 104) says: "Iras et verba locant."

[786] Montaigne, Montesquieu, and many other eminent Frenchmen attacked the legal employment of torture, but it was continued in France till 1788.

[787] Our author uses by exception honnêtes gens for honest men. A certain Marquis de Langlade was put on the rack (1688), and after having been innocently sentenced to the galleys on a false accusation of having robbed the Duke de Montmorency, died there in 1689; and a servant, Le Brun, accused of the murder of Madame Marel, died after having been cruelly tortured (1690). The real criminals were discovered some time afterwards, and this produced a great sensation at the time La Bruyère wrote (1691).

Speaking of myself, I would almost affirm never to become a thief or murderer, but I would not be so bold as to infer that I might never be punished as such.

Deplorable is the condition of an innocent person whose trial has been hurried, and who is found guilty. Can even that of his judge be more lamentable?

(53.) If I had been told that in former ages a *prévôt*, or one of those magistrates appointed for the apprehension and destruction of rogues and thieves, had been long acquainted with all such rascals, knew their names and faces as well as the number and quantity of their robberies, and all particulars about them; and had so far penetrated all their actions and was so completely initiated in all their horrible mysteries that, to prevent the clamour some great man was about to raise for the loss of a jewel, stolen from him in a crowd when coming from some party, he knew how to restore it to him, and that Parliament interfered and had this magistrate tried; I should class such an event with many others in history, which in the course of time have become incredible. How, then, can I believe, what may be inferred from recent, well-known, and clearly proved facts, that such a pernicious connivance exists even at the present time, is made a jest of, and is looked upon as a matter of course?[788]

(54.) There exists a large number of men, imperious towards the weak, firm and inflexible when solicited by commoners, without any regard for the inferior classes, rigid and severe in trifles, who will not accept the smallest present, nor be persuaded by their dearest friends and nearest relatives, and who only are to be bribed by women.[789]

(55.) It is not absolutely impossible for a man who is in high favour to lose his suit.

(56.) A person who is dying may expect his last will to be listened to as if it was an oracle; every man puts his own construction on it and explains it as he pleases, or rather, as it will suit his inclination or his interest.

(57.) There are some men of whom we may truly say that death does not so much determine their last will as that it deprives them of life as well as of their irresolution and restlessness: a fit of anger moves them to make a will, whilst they are living, but when the fit is over it is torn to pieces and burnt. They have as many wills in their strong box as there are almanacs on their table, for every year is sure to produce a new one; a second will is annulled by a third, which is rendered void by another better drawn up, again invalidated by a fifth and holographic will. Yet if a person who has an interest in suppressing this last will has neither an opportunity, nor a desire, nor the means of doing so, he must stand by its clauses and conditions; for what can more clearly prove the intentions of a man, however changeable, than a last deed, under his own hand, made so lately that he had no time to change his mind?

---

[788] It has been said that the wife of M. de Saint-Pouange (see page 134134, note 259) was robbed of a diamond buckle when leaving the opera, but that it was returned to her by M. de Grandmaison, grand prévôt de la connétablie.

[789] The "Keys" mention as one of these men the President de Mesmes. See page 168, note 331.

(58.) If there were no wills to regulate the rights of lawful heirs, I question whether men would need any tribunal to adjust their differences; the functions of a judge would almost be reduced to the sad necessity of sending thieves and incendiaries[790] to the gallows.

Whom do you see in the galleries[791] of the court, in the waiting-rooms, at the doors or in the rooms of the magistrates? Not heirs-at-law, for their rights are immutable; but legatees, going to law about the meaning of a clause or an article; disinherited persons who find fault with a will drawn up at leisure and with circumspection by a grave, able, and conscientious man, and not without the aid of a good lawyer; with a deed in which some cunning legal practitioner has not omitted an iota of his professional cant and his ordinary subtleties, signed by the testator and public witnesses, duly initialled, and which, notwithstanding all this, is set aside by the court and declared null and void.

(59.) Titius is present at the reading of a will; his eyes are red with weeping, and he is overcome with grief for the loss of a friend whose heir he expects to become. One clause of the will bequeaths him his friend's official position, another his municipal bonds, by a third he becomes master of an estate in the country, and a fourth gives him a furnished house in the middle of town, with all its appurtenances. His grief increases, his tears flow abundantly, and he cannot contain himself; he already beholds himself in an official position,[792] with a town and country house, both furnished in the same style; he intends to keep a good table and a carriage. "Was there ever a more gentlemanly or a better man than the deceased?" he asks. But a codicil is joined to the will which must also be read, by which Mævius is appointed sole heir, and Titius is sent back to the suburbs to trudge without money or titles. Titius wipes away his tears, and it is now Mævius' duty to grieve.[793]

(60.) Does not the law, in forbidding to kill, include also stabbing, poisoning, burning, drowning, lying in ambush, open violence, in a word, and all means tending to homicide? Does the law, which restrains husbands and wives from bequeathing property to one another, only refer to direct and immediate ways of giving?[794] Has it made no provision against those that are indirect? Was it the

[790] During the latter part of the reign of Louis XIV., fire-raising was very common in the rural districts of France, and it was one of the means the peasants chose for revenging themselves on their masters for their exactions and for fiscal cruelties.

[791] The original has lanternes, tribunes in Parliament whence people could see what was going on without being seen.

[792] Il se voit officier in the original. See page 153, note 304.

[793] Titius and Seius were often quoted in Roman law, as "A." and "B." are in English law, in stating a case to counsel. Mævius was a wretched poet of Virgil's time, and seems to be wrongly named by La Bruyère in apposition to Titius. According to some commentators, the mishap attributed to Titius really happened to a M. Hennequin, procureur général au grand conseil.

[794] The notary, M. de Bonnefoi, in Molière's Malade Imaginaire (act i. scene 9) explains to the hypochondriacal Argan: "You cannot give anything to your wife by your will ... Common law is opposed to it ... in Paris and in all countries where common law exists.... All the good which man and woman joined in wedlock can do to each other, is a mutual

cause of the introduction of trustees, and does it even tolerate them? When the dearest of wives outlives her husband, does a man bequeath his estate to a trusty friend as an acknowledgment of his friendship, or is it not rather a proof of his complete confidence and reliance on that friend who will make a right use of what has been intrusted to him? Will a man make over his estate to anyone whom he even suspects of not restoring it to the person for whom it is really intended? Is any speech or any letter needed, and is a contract or an oath necessary for such a collusion? Does not every man on such an occasion feel what he can expect from another man? If, on the contrary, the property of such an estate is vested in a trustee, why does he lose his reputation by retaining it? What, then, is the reason of all these satires and lampoons?[795] Why is he compared to a guardian who betrays his trust, to a servant robbing his master of a sum of money he has to take somewhere? Such a comparison is wrong. Is it considered infamous not to perform a piece of liberality, and for a man to keep for his own use what is his own? How strangely perplexed, how terribly burdened, must such a trustee feel! If a man, out of respect for the laws, appropriates to himself a trust, he can no longer be thought an honest man; if, out of love for a deceased friend, he fulfils his intentions, and restores to the widow what has been intrusted to him, he lends his name, and transgresses the law. The law, then, does not harmonise with the opinions of men. Perhaps so, but it does not suit me to say whether the law is wrong or whether the people are mistaken.

(61.) I have been told that certain individuals or certain bodies of men contest with one another for precedence, and that presidents of Parliaments[796] and peers dispute as to who shall go first. In my opinion either of the contending parties who avoids appearing when Parliament meets, yields, is conscious of its own weakness, and decides in favour of its competitors.

(62.) Typhon supplies a certain nobleman of high rank with horses, dogs, and everything. On the strength of that lord's protection he behaves most audaciously, and does what he likes in his own province, without fear of being punished; he becomes a murderer, perjures himself, sets fire to his neighbours' houses, and needs not look for a refuge. At last the prince is obliged to punish him himself.[797]

(63.) "Stews, liqueurs, entrées, side dishes," are words which should be for-

donation while living; and then there must be no children." And when Argan asks what he has to do to leave his wife his property, the honest notary replies: "You can quietly choose an intimate friend of your wife's, to whom you will give, in due form by your will, all that you can; and this friend shall afterwards give it all back to her."

[795] Vaudeville in the original, of which the primitive meaning was "a satirical song."

[796] Le mortier in French. See page 168, note 331. When the king was not present at a sitting of the Parliament, the president claimed the right to represent him, and therefore, to take precedence before any one.

[797] A certain de Charnacé, formerly lieutenant in the king's body-guard, committed several crimes in Anjou, even coined false money, and finally was obliged to flee for his life. In many of the provinces the conduct of the nobles was so inhuman and disgraceful, that the kings of France were often obliged to appoint special committees, called grands jours, to try and punish them, the latest and most celebrated of which had been held in Auvergne in 1665.

eign and unintelligible to us; such words should not be employed in times of peace, as they are only incentives to luxury and gluttony; but how come they to be continually mentioned in times of war, amidst public calamities, before an enemy, and on the very night before a battle, or during a siege? Where do we find any mention made of Scipio's or Marius's table? Do we read anywhere that Miltiades, Epaminondas, and Agesilaus were fond of good living? I should like no general to be commended for the goodness, elegance, and sumptuousness of his table, till everything that could be said about him had been told, and people had expatiated on all the details of some victory or the taking of some town. I should even be glad to see a general desirous of avoiding such commendations.[798]

(64.) Hermippus[799] makes himself a slave to what he calls "his little contrivances;" all habits, customs, fashions, decency itself, must be sacrificed to them; he looks for them everywhere, discards a lesser for a greater, and neglects none which is practicable; he studies them, and there is not a day but what he discovers a fresh one. Other men may take their dinners and suppers, but he objects to the very name of them, eats when he feels hungry, and then only of what he likes best. He must see his bed made, but no one is so skilful or fortunate to make it in such a way that he can sleep as he likes. He seldom leaves his house; he is partial to his own room, where he is neither idle nor busy, where he does no work, but muddles about in the garb of a man who has taken medicine. Other people are obliged to wait the leisure of a locksmith or a joiner, whenever they want them; but he has everything at hand: a file, if anything has to be filed: a saw, if anything has to be cut off, and a pair of pincers to pull out. You cannot mention any tools he has not got, and he fancies they are much better and more convenient than these workmen use; he has some new and unknown tools, without any name, of his own invention, and of which he has almost forgotten the use. There exists not a man who can be compared to him for performing in a short time and without much difficulty some labour which is perfectly useless. He was compelled to take ten steps to go from his bed to his lavatory; he has now so contrived his room as to reduce these ten to nine, so he saves a good many steps during the whole course of his life! Other people turn a key, and push and pull before a door opens, but this is very fatiguing and unnecessary, so he does without it. But he is not going to reveal by what means. In fact, he understands the use of springs and machinery, above all, of such machinery as the world can very well spare. Daylight is not admitted in Hermippus' apartment through the window, but in quite a different way; he has also discovered a secret for going up and down the house otherwise than by the stairs, and is now studying how to go in and out more conveniently than by the

---

[798] The "Keys" name Louis de Crevant, Duke d'Humières, who was made Marshal of France in 1668, and died in 1694; Jacques Henri de Durfort, Duke de Duras, brother to the Earl of Feversham, and also a Marshal of France, who died in 1704, at the age of seventy-four; and the Marshal de Créqui, as having displayed great luxury whilst in the field. The king, who had first given the example of such splendour, finally attempted to restrain it, and in vain promulgated edicts against it in 1672.

[799] Hermippus is supposed to be a certain Jean-Jacques Renouard, Count de Villayer, maître des requêtes, a member of the French Academy, who was very ingenious, and always invented new machinery—amongst others, a kind of lift—and who died in 1691.

door.

(65.) Physicians have been attacked[800] for a long time, and yet every one consults them; neither the sallies of the stage nor of satire diminish their fees;[801] they give dowries to their daughters, have sons magistrates and bishops;[802] and all this is paid for by the very persons who make fun of them. People who are in good health fall ill some day or other, and then they want a man whose trade it is to assure them they shall not die. As long as men are liable to die, and are desirous to live, a physician will be made fun of, but he will be well paid.

(66.) A good physician is a man who employs specifics, or, if he has not got any, allows those persons who have them to cure his patient

(67.) Quacks are rash, and therefore rarely successful; hence physic and physicians are in vogue; the latter let you die, the former kill you.

(68.) Carro Carri[803] lands in France with a recipe which he says cures in a short time, and which, sometimes, is a slow poison; it has been in the hands of his family for many years, but he has improved it. It is a specific against the colic, yet he cures quartan ague, pleurisy, dropsy, apoplexy, and epilepsy. Rack your memory a little, and mention the first disease you can think of, let us say hemorrhage; he can cure it. It is true he raises no one from the dead, and does not restore men to life, but he keeps them, of course, till they are decrepit, for it is by mere chance that his father and grandfather, who were acquainted with the secret, both died very young. Physicians receive for their visits the fees people give them, and some are even satisfied with thanks; but Carro Carri is so certain of his remedy, and of its effect, that he does not hesitate to take his fee beforehand, and expects to receive before he has given anything. If the disease be incurable, so much the better; it will be the more deserving of his attention and his remedy.[804] Begin with putting into his hands thousands of francs, make over to him some bonds,[805] and then you have no longer any need to be more uneasy about your cure than he himself is. The world is full of men with names ending in o and i, most respectable names, who are all rivals of this man, and impose on the patients and the disease. Fagon,[806] you will admit that neither your physicians nor those of all the faculties

[800] The original has improuver, now antiquated.

[801] Leurs pensions in French. See page 381, note 695.

[802] A d'Aquin (1629-1696), who was physician to Louis XIV., had one son a magistrate and another a bishop. See also page 273, note 533.

[803] See page 186, note 390. Some "Keys" also say that perhaps Adrien Helvétius, the grandfather of the philosopher, may be meant, but this seems hardly likely, for Helvétius was wealthy, gave his medicine gratis, was a very honest man, and the first to recommend the use of ipecacuanha in certain diseases.

[804] In Molière's Malade Imaginaire (act iii. scene 4), Toinette, the servant, dressed up as a physician, says almost the same thing.

[805] Constitution (de rentes) understood in the text.

[806] Guy Crescence Fagon (1638-1718) became in succession physician to the wife of the Dauphin, the queen, and the royal children, and in 1693, when d'Aquin fell into disgrace, first physician to Louis XIV. He was for his time an able and conscientious man. His eldest son became Bishop of Lombez, and his second intendant des finances.

in the world always cure or are certain of their cure; but those who have inherited their empirical medicine from their forefathers, and whose experience has come to them in the same way, always promise, and even pledge themselves by oath, to cure their patients. How sweet it is for men not to abandon hope even when attacked by a mortal disease, and still to think they are pretty well when expiring! Death is then an agreeable surprise, and comes without striking terror beforehand; so that a man feels it before he has thought of preparing for it and giving himself up to it. O Esculapius Fagon! Establish throughout the world the reign of Peruvian bark and of emetics;[807] carry to its perfection the science of those plants which are given to man for prolonging life;[808] observe in your practice, with more exactness and judgment than was ever done before, the influence of climate and weather, the various symptoms and the natural disposition of your patients; treat them in the only way which suits them and by which they can be cured; eradicate the most obscure and inveterate diseases from the human body, which has no secrets for you; but do not attempt the diseases of the mind, for they can never be cured, and leave, therefore, to Corinna, Lesbia, Canidia, Trimalcion, and Carpus, the passion, or rather the mania, they have for quacks.

(69.) Astrologers and fortune-tellers, who practise palmistry and calculate nativities, guess at things past by the motion of a sieve, and show undimmed truth in a looking-glass or in a cup of water, are publicly tolerated; such people are, indeed, not without their use; they predict to men they'll make their fortune, to girls they shall marry their sweethearts, console those children whose fathers are too long dying, and calm the restlessness of young women married to old men; in a word, they deceive, but not at a very high rate, those who wish to be deceived.

(70.) What is to be thought of magic and sorcery? Its theory is very obscure; its principles are vague, uncertain, and visionary, but some facts have been produced which are perplexing, and certified by serious-minded men who were present when they happened, or learned them from other men as reliable as they themselves are. To admit or to deny all these facts seems equally absurd, and I venture to say that in this and in other extraordinary things which deviate from nature's laws, a middle course has to be steered between mere credulity and obstinate rejection.[809]

(71.) Children can scarcely know too many languages, and methinks, all means should be taken to facilitate their acquiring them; there is no condition of life in which they are not useful, for they clear the way for the acquisition of solid

[807] Fagon was a strenuous defender of emetics and of Peruvian bark, which latter remedy was first imported into France in the seventeenth century, and had become so popular that Jean la Fontaine sang its praises in a pretty long poem, le Quinquina, the French name of the Peruvian bark, so called after the Countess del Cinchon, wife of the Viceroy of Peru, whence the bark was first sent to Europe.

[808] Fagon was also professor of botany and chemistry in the king's botanical garden, and one of the editors of its catalogue, called Hortus regius, published in 1665.

[809] The belief in sorcerers and witchcraft was very general when our author wrote, and there existed an almost universal idea that robbers and murderers might be discovered by means of the motion of a hazel rod. Even the magistrates in France tried sometimes such a rod to find out criminals.

learning, as well as for easy and pleasant acquirements. If this somewhat difficult study is put off to that more advanced age which is called youth, people have no longer the strength of mind and the will to follow it up, and if they do, they find it impossible to persevere; for in studying those languages they consume that very time which should be applied in speaking them, and confine themselves to mastering words when they wish to proceed beyond, and require facts; and thus they lose the first and most valuable years of their life. Such a grand foundation can never rightly be laid, unless it be when the soul naturally receives everything, is deeply impressed by it, and when the memory is fresh, quick, and steady; when the mind and the heart are yet void of passions, cares, and desires, and when those who have a right to dispose of us, induce us to labour for a considerable time. I am convinced the small number of true scholars and the great number of superficial ones is owing to the neglect of this rule.[810]

(72.) The study of the original texts can never be sufficiently recommended; it is the shortest, the safest, and the most pleasant way for all kinds of learning. Take things from the beginning, go to the main spring, read over the text repeatedly, learn it by heart, quote it upon occasions; above all, apply yourself to penetrate the sense of it to its fullest extent and in all its circumstances, reconcile an author's various sentiments, settle his principles, and draw your own conclusions. The early commentators were in the very position I should wish you to be; never borrow their explanations nor adopt their ideas unless your own fail you, for their interpretation is not yours and may easily slip out of your memory; on the contrary, your observations have sprung up in your own mind, will abide with you, and more readily recur in your conversations, consultations, and discussions. You will be delighted to observe that in your reading no insurmountable difficulties will present themselves except those that have nonplussed commentators and scholiasts themselves, who, moreover, have at their command such a rich and abundant store of vain and useless learning when passages are sufficiently clear and present no difficulties to themselves nor to others. This system of studying the original texts will convince you that men's laziness has encouraged pedants to increase the bulk of libraries rather than their worth, and to crush the text under a weight of commentaries; by doing this they have injured themselves and acted contrary to their own interests, as those same commentaries have caused an increase of reading, researches, and of that kind of labour which they intended to render useless.

(73.) What is it that governs men in their way of living and in their diet? Is it health and sobriety? That is the question. Whole nations first eat fruit and meat afterwards, whilst others do quite the contrary, and some begin their meal with one kind of fruit and finish it with another. Does this proceed from reason or custom? Is it for their health's sake that men wear their clothes buttoned up to their chin, and put on ruffs and bands after going for so many ages quite open-breasted?[811]

[810] Many eminent pedagogues have held a contrary opinion; for example, Malebranche in his Traité de Morale, and Jean Jacques Rousseau in his Emile, both maintain languages should be acquired when the child is not too young.

[811] The going "open-breasted" was the fashion of the time of Francis I.; ruffs and bands were worn in France during part of the reigns of Henri II. and Henri III., but were no longer in vogue when our author wrote; they were, however, still used in Spain.

Is it for the sake of decency, especially at a time when they have found the means of appearing undressed though they are dressed?[812] On the other hand, are women who expose their breasts and shoulders, less delicate in their constitution than men, or less inclined to decency? It is a strange kind of modesty which induces them to hide their legs and almost their feet, and at the same time allows them to bare their arms to the elbow.[813] How came men formerly to think they had to attack or defend themselves whilst waging war, and who taught them the use of offensive and defensive arms? What obliges them to-day to lay these aside, to put on boots to go to a ball, and to support the pioneers in the trenches, exposed to the whole fire of a counterscarp, without having any arms, and only dressed in a doublet.[814] Were our forefathers wise or senseless in not deeming such a practice useful to their king or their country? And who are our heroes renowned in history? A du Guesclin, a Clisson, a Foix, a Boucicault,[815] who all wore helmets and buckled on breastplates?

Who can account for the introduction of certain words and the proscription of others?[816]

Ains is lost; the vowel beginning it, and which could so easily be cut off, could not save it; it gave way to another monosyllable which at best is but its anagram.[817] *Certes* is beautiful in its old age, and has yet strength, though declining; it should be used in poetry, and our language is under some obligation to those authors who employ it in prose and defend it in their works. *Maint* is a word which should never have been forsaken, and on account of its adaptability for any style and for the sake of its French origin.[818] *Moult*, though descended from the Latin, possessed in its time the same merit, and I do not see why *beaucoup* should be

---

[812] This is an allusion to the wearing of very tight silk stockings and short breeches, showing the legs.

[813] It was never the custom in France for ladies to hide their feet, but in Spain it was considered highly improper and indecent even to show the smallest part of them (see the Countess d'Aulnoy, Relation du Voyage en Espagne, 1690); and as the wife of Louis XIV., Maria Theresa, was a daughter of Philip IV. of Spain, it is probable that the ladies at court followed the fashion set to them by the queen.

[814] According to Voltaire's Siècle de Louis XIV., chap, viii., the king and his officers went, however, to the trenches wearing head-pieces and breast-plates.

[815] Bertrand du Guesclin (1320-1380) was constable of France under Charles V., whilst Olivier de Clisson (1332-1407) filled the same high office under Charles VI.; Gaston de Foix (1331-1391), surnamed "Phœbus," was Viscount of Bearn, and Jean le Maingre de Boucicault (1364-1421) was Marshal of France. They all four distinguished themselves in the wars against the English during the fourteenth century.

[816] Our author now launches into a dissertation about the relative value of certain words which was far from unusual at the time he wrote, and is found in almost the same form in several contemporary writers. I also imagine the late Walter Savage Landor was influenced by La Bruyère's dissertation when he wrote in his "Imaginary Conversations" the two "Dialogues" between Dr. Johnson and Horne Tooke.

[817] Mais, says La Bruyère in a note, but this word is not an anagram of ains, which comes from the Latin ante, whilst mais is the Latin magis.

[818] It is not yet settled whether maint is of Latin, Celtic, or Teutonic origin.

preferred to it. *Car* has endured some persecution, and if it had not been protected by some men of culture, it would have been shamefully banished from a language which it had served so long; and this without knowing what word to put in its place.[819] When *cil* was in fashion it was one of the prettiest words of the French language; and it is a sad thing for the poets that it has become antiquated. *Doulou-reux* is, of course, derived from *douleur*, and so are *chaleureux* or *chaloureux* from *chaleur*: yet *chaloureux* is going out,[820] though it enriched our tongue, and was employed quite correctly when *chaud* was not the right expression. *Valeur* ought also to have given us *valeureux; haine, haineux; peine, peineux; fruit, fructueux; pitié, piteux; joie, jovial; foi, féal; cour, courtois; gîte, gisant; haleine, halené; vanterie, vantard; mensonge, mensonger; coutume, coutumier;* just as *part* should have produced *partial; point, pointu* and *pointilleux; ton, tonnant; son, sonore; frein, effréné; front, effronté; ris, ridicule; loi, légal; cœur, cordial; bien, benin;* and *mal, malicieux. Heur* was allowed when *bonheur* did not suit; from the first arose *heureux*, which is so French and yet exists no longer; if some poets have employed it, it is more for the sake of the measure than from choice. *Issue* prospers, and comes from *issir*, no longer in exis-tence. *Fin* is used, but not *finer*, which is derived from it, whilst *cesse* and *cesser* are still flourishing. *Verd* no longer gives *verdoyer*, nor *fête, fétoyer;* nor *larme, larmoyer;* nor *deuil, se douloir* and *se condouloir;* nor *joie, s'éjouir;* though it still makes *se réjouir* and *se conjouir*, whilst *orgueil* gives *s'enorgueillir.* Formerly *gent* was used, as in *le corps gent;* this easy word is not alone no longer in use, but it has involved *gentil* in its ruin. We employ *diffamé*, which proceeds from *fame*, which is out of date, and *curieux* is derived from *cure*, now obsolete. It was much better to say *si que* than *de sorte que* or *de manière que, de moi* instead of *pour moi* or *quant à moi; je sais que c'est qu'un mal*[821] than *je sais ce que c'est qu'un mal*, whether you consider the Latin anal-ogy, or the benefit we often derive from using a word less in a phrase.[822] Custom has preferred *par conséquent* to *par conséquence*, and *en conséquence* to *en conséquent; façons de faire* to *manières de faire*, and *manières d'agir* to *façons d'agir* ...; in the verbs *travailler* to *ouvrer; être accoutumé* to *souloir; convenir* to *duire; faire du bruit* to *bruire; injurier* to *vilainer; piquer* to *poindre;* and *faire ressouvenir* to *ramentevoir* ...; and in the nouns *pensées* to *pensers*, which is such a beautiful word and so suited for poetry; *grandes actions* to *prouesses; louanges* to *los; méchanceté* to *mauvaistié; porte* to *huis; navire* to *nef; armée* to *ost; monastère* to *monstier;* and *prairies* to *prées* ...; all words, equally fine, which might have been used together and rendered the language more copious. Through adding, suppressing, changing, or displacing some letters, custom has formed *frelater* from *fralater; prouver* from *preuver; profit* from *proufit; froment* from *froument; profil* from *pourfil; provision* from *pourveoir; promener* from *pourmener*, and *promenade* from *pourmenade.*[823] This same custom upon occasion

[819] Some purists wished to forbid the use of car, which was defended by Voiture. (See page 20, note 72.)

[820] A good many words which La Bruyère thought were going out of fashion are still in use at present.

[821] De moi and que c'est que have been employed several times by Malherbe (see page 21, note 76) and other good authors, but these expressions are now quite obsolete.

[822] Oraison, phrase in the original; antiquated in this sense.

[823] The people formally changed the Latin syllables pro and fro into prou or pour

makes the adjectives *habile, utile, facile, docile, mobile,* and *fertile* of different genders, without changing anything in their spelling; whilst, on the contrary, the masculine *vil* and *subtil* change in the feminine and become *vile* and *subtile*.[824] It has altered the old terminations, and of *scel* made *sceau*; of *mantel, manteau*; of *capel, chapeau*; of *coutel, couteau*; of *hamel, hameau*; of *damoisel, damoiseau*; of *jouvencel, jouvenceau*;[825] and yet all these differences and changes have been of no perceptible advantage to the French tongue. Is it, therefore, a progress for a language to be governed by custom, and would it not be better to shake off the yoke of such despotic sway? Or shall we in a living language only listen to reason, which prevents the use of words having a double meaning, traces these words to their roots, and discovers what relation they bear to those languages from which they sprang, if that very reason bids us follow custom?[826]

Whether our ancestors wrote better than we do, or whether we excel them in our selection of words, style, and expression, perspicuity and brevity, is a question often debated but never yet decided. But this question is not at an end, if people will compare, as they sometimes do, a dull writer of a past century to the most celebrated authors of the present age, or the verses of Laurent,[827] who is paid for not writing any more, to those of Marot and Desportes.[828] In order to judge sensibly in this case we should compare one age to another, and one first-rate piece of literary work to another, such as, for example, the best *rondeaux* of Benserade and Voiture[829] to the following two, which tradition has handed down to us, but without transmitting to us the name of the authors, or the time when they were written:[830] —

---

and into frou or four; hence proufit, fourment, or froument, from the Latin proficere and fromentum. The scholars of the sixteenth century brought back these words to their etymological form.

[824] In French adjectives in il derived from Latin words with a long i, on which the accent rests, form their feminine by adding an e, whilst adjectives with the termination ile for the masculine and feminine are formed from Latin words with a short i, not accentuated.

[825] In the French of the Middle Ages these substantives had the termination els, aus, or iaus in the nominative singular plural, and el in the accusative singular and the nominative plural; aus became generally adopted in all cases, but dropped the s.

[826] Vaugelas and his commentators insisted that all words not sanctioned by custom should not be admitted into the French language.

[827] Laurent was a wretched versifier at the time of La Bruyère, who published rhymed descriptions of all kinds of festivals.

[828] For Marot. See page 22, note 79. Philippe Desportes (1555-1606), an imitator of the Italian school of poetry, enjoyed a great reputation in his time.

[829] See page 122, note 228, and page 20, note 72.

[830] The original rondeaux which are given here are not so old as La Bruyère thought they were, and are merely very fair imitations, written probably about the end of the sixteenth century. The hero of the first rondeau is Ogier, generally called le Danois, which does not mean the Dane, but is a contraction of le D'Ardennois, from the Ardennes.

I owe the above translation to Mr. J. E. Barlas, of New College, Oxford, who has endeavoured to imitate the pseudo-antiquated style of the original, and to use several Chaucerian and Spenserian words.

In timely sort Ogier came into Fraunce,
Of Paynim misbegot to rid the lond;
Needs not that I should tell his puissaunce,
Sit never foeman durst his glaunce withstond.

Tho' when he hath set all in happy chaunce,
Forth on a perlous jorney bent, he fond
In Paradise the well of youth's joyaunce,
Wherewith he thought to stay time's threatening bond
In timely sort.

Tho' by this well his body, weak with years,
Upon a sodain changéd quight appears
To youthful wight, fresh, limber eke, and straight.
Great pitye 'tis such lesinges tell no truth!

Bien à propos s'en vint Ogier en France
Pour le païs de mescréans monder:
Jà n'est besoin de conter sa vaillance
Puisqu' ennemis n'osoient le regarder.

Or quand il eut tout mis en assurance,
De voyager il voulut s'enharder;
En Paradis trouva l'eau de jouvance,
Dont il se sceut de vieillesse engarder
Bien à propos.

Puis par cette eau son corps tout décrépite
Transmué fut par manière subite
En jeune gars, frais, gracieux et droit.

Grand dommage est que cecy soit sornettes:
Filles connois qui ne sont pas jeunettes,
A qui cette eau de jouvance viendroit
Bien à propos.

— —

De cettuy preux maints grands clercs ont écrit
Qu'oncques dangier n'étonna son courage:
Abusé fut par le malin esprit,
Qu'il épousa sous feminin visage.

Si piteux cas à la fin découvrit,
Sans un seul brin de peur ny de dommage,
Dont grand renom par tout le monde acquit,
Si qu'on tenoit très honeste langage
De cettuy preux.

Bien-tost après fille de Roy s'éprit
De son amour, qui voulentiers s'offrit
Au bon Richard en second mariage.

Donc sil vaut mieux ou diable ou femme avoir,
Et qui des deux bruit plus en ménage,
Ceulx qui voudront, si le pourront scavoir
De cettuy preux.

Virgins I wot of that bene past their youth,
To whom this bath had come, ere yet too late,
In timely sort.

— —

Of this prow knight full many clerks have penned
That never daunger could his corage scare:
Whom natheless the foul fiend, which unaware
He 'spoused in woman's shape, did foully shend.

So piteous case left his stout heart at end
Without one taint of fear or sordid care:
Whereof great praise throughout the world he bare—
If aught of credence we to tales may lend
Of this prow knight.

Eftsoones it chaunced the daughter of the king
Earned for his love, and made free offering
To Richard, of herself for second wife.

Then, if to keep a woman or a fiend
Be better, and which stirs more hellish strife,
He that would weet may question which was weened
Of this prow knight.

MONK PREACHING

XV.

OF THE PULPIT.[831]

(1.) A SERMON at present has become a mere show, in which there is not the least appearance of that evangelical gravity which is the very soul of it; a good appearance, a well-modulated voice, careful gestures, choice expressions, and prolonged enumerations supply its place. To listen attentively whilst Holy Writ is dispensed is no longer customary; going to church is an amusement, among numberless others, and is a diversion in which there exists rivalry and many persons bet on various competitors.

(2.) Profane eloquence is transferred from the bar, where Le Maître, Pucelle,

[831] The chapter "Of the Pulpit" was first published in 1688, and our author made additions to it until the eighth edition of the "Characters" saw the light, in 1694. He had heard all the best preachers of his time, such as the Jesuit Claude de Lingendes (see page 323, note 592), and the Oratorians Le Jeune and Senault, who both died in 1672, whilst Bossuet preached in Paris from 1659 to 1669. Bourdaloue began preaching there in 1663, Mascaron in 1666, Fléchier in 1670, and Fénelon in 1675. The only great pulpit-orator our author did not hear was Massillon, who did not preach in the capital until 1696. Several sermons on pulpit oratory were preached in France, and many books on the same subject had been published there before and after this chapter was printed.

and Fourcroy[832] formerly practised it, and where it has become obsolete,[833] to the Pulpit, where it is out of place.

Clergymen contest even the prize of eloquence at the altar and before the holy mysteries; every person in the congregation thinks himself a judge of the preacher, censures or applauds him, and is no more converted by the sermon he approves of than by the one he condemns. The orator pleases some and not others; but agrees with all in this: that as he does not endeavour to render them better, they never trouble their heads about becoming so.

An apprentice ought to be obedient and do what his master tells him; he profits by his instructions, and in time becomes himself a master; but man is more untoward, for he criticises the preacher's discourses as well as the philosopher's works, and thus becomes neither a Christian nor a philosopher.

(3.) Orators and declaimers will attract large congregations until that man returns who in a style, based on the Holy Scriptures, shall explain to the people the Word of God in a simple and familiar manner.[834]

(4.) Quotations from profane authors, dull allusions, bathos, antithesis, and hyperboles are no longer in vogue, and portraits[835] will also cease to be in fashion, and give way to a plain exposition of the gospel, accompanied by other means that produce conversion.

(5.) At length a man has made his appearance for whom I so impatiently longed, but whom I dared not expect to behold in this age. The courtiers, from delicacy of taste and a feeling of decorum, have applauded him; and what is almost incredible, have left the king's chapel to mingle among the crowd, and hear the Word of God preached by a truly apostolic man.[836] The town was not of the same opinion as the court, and in whatever city-church he spoke not one of the parishioners came, and the very churchwardens left their pew; the clergymen indeed stuck to him, but the flock was scattered and went to swell the congregations of neighbouring orators. This is what I should have foreseen; and therefore, I ought not

---

[832] Three barristers of repute in the seventeenth century, Antoine le Maître (1608-1658), whose Recueil de Plaidoyers has been printed; Claude Pucelle, and Bonaventure Fourcroy, a friend of Molière and Boileau, who died in 1691 and was a poet as well as a lawyer.

[833] See the Chapter "Of Certain Customs," § 42.

[834] A certain Abbé le Tourneur or le Tourneux, who died in 1680 at the age of forty-six, is said to have been such a man, but was, of course, not allowed to remain long at court.

[835] Bourdaloue (1632-1704) set the fashion of introducing in his sermons "portraits" or "Characters" of well-known individuals: a fashion which was much exaggerated by his imitators, and which also for some time prevailed in England. The Sermons of Dr. R. South (1633-1716), Prebendary of Westminster and Canon of Christ Church, Oxon, contain also many "portraits."

[836] Our author says in a note; "This was Father Seraphin, a Capuchin monk." Others have been less favourably inclined towards this preacher than La Bruyère was. This monk, who had been holding forth in Paris as early as 1671, preached in the parish church of Versailles, and four years later before the court and the king, in the palace.

to have advanced that such a man, whenever he appeared, would be universally followed, and would only have to open his mouth to be listened to, for I know how difficult it is to eradicate force of habit in mankind in all things. During the past thirty years, rhetoricians, declaimers, and enumerators have been listened to; and people run after preachers who depict in a grand style or in miniature. Not long since sermons were full of points and clever transitions, sometimes even so smart and pungent that they might have served for epigrams: now, I confess, these are somewhat softened, and may pass for madrigals. Three things, these preachers argue, are always absolutely indispensable, mathematically necessary, and worthy of your entire attention; one thing they prove in the first part of their discourse, another in the second, and another in the third; so that you are to be convinced of one truth, which is their first point of doctrine; of another truth, which is their second point; and of a third truth, which is their third point. In this manner the first reflection will instruct you in one of the fundamental principles of religion; the second in another principle which is not less fundamental; and the last reflection in a third and last principle, the most important of all, but which, for want of leisure, is reserved for another opportunity. In a word, to recapitulate and abridge this division, and to form a scheme of.... "Hold," you exclaim, "do these preachers require more preparation for a speech of not quite an hour's length which they have to deliver? The more these gentlemen strive to explain and make things clear to me, the more they bemuddle my brains."—I can well believe you, and it is the most natural result of such a mass and confusion of ideas which come all to one and the same thing, but with which they unmercifully burden the memory of their audience. To see them obstinately persist in this custom, people would almost think that the grace of being converted was inseparable of such long-winded divisions and sub-divisions. But how is it possible to be converted by apostles, whom we can hardly hear, follow, and keep in sight? I should like to ask them to condescend and rest several times, in the midst of their headlong career, and give their audience and themselves a short breathing time. But I may spare myself the trouble of addressing them and of wasting words on them. Homilies are out of date, and the Basils and Chrysostoms[837] could not restore them, for if they came back, people would take refuge in other dioceses, so as not to hear them nor their familiar and instructive discourses. Men in general like fine phrases and periods, admire what they do not understand,[838] fancy themselves well informed, and are satisfied with deciding between a first and second point of doctrine, or between the last sermon and the last but one.

(6.) Not a hundred years ago a French book consisted of a certain number of pages written in Latin, with here and there a line or two of French scattered on each page. But such passages, anecdotes, and quotations from Latin authors[839] did not only fill books; Ovid and Catullus, at the bar, decided finally in cases of

[837] Saint Basil (329-379) was bishop of Cesarea; Saint John Chrysostom was (347-407) bishop of Constantinople, called the "golden-mouthed" for his great eloquence.

[838] Our author makes the same observation about dramatic poets. See his Chapter "Of Works of the Mind," page 9, § 8.

[839] Compare in Racine's comedy of Les Plaideurs the speech of "L'Intimé" (act iii, scene 3), to ridicule similar quotations.

marriages and wills, and were of as much use to widows and orphans as the Pandects were.[840] Sacred and profane authors were inseparable, and seemed to have slipped together in the pulpit; Saint Cyril and Horace, Saint Cyprian and Lucretius, spoke by turns; the poets were of the same opinion as Saint Augustin[841] and the rest of the Fathers. Latin was the language spoken before women and churchwardens, for any length of time, and even sometimes Greek; there was no preaching so wretchedly without a prodigious amount of learning. But the times are changed, and customs alter; the text still continues in Latin, but the sermons are preached in French, and in the purest French, whilst the Gospel is not so much as quoted. Little learning is requisite now-a-days to preach very well.

(7.) Scholastic divinity is at last driven out of the pulpits of all the great towns in the kingdom, and confined only to hamlets and villages for the instruction and edification of ploughmen and vine-dressers.

(8.) A preacher must have some intelligence to charm the people by his florid style,[842] by his exhilarating system of morality, by the repetition of his figures of speech, his brilliant remarks and vivid descriptions; but, after all, he has not too much of it, for if he possessed some of the right quality he would neglect these extraneous ornaments, unworthy of the Gospel, and preach naturally, forcibly, and like a Christian.

(9.) An orator paints some sins in such alluring colours, and describes with such delicacy when they were committed, represents the sinner as having so much wit, elegance, and refinement that, for my part, if I feel no inclination to resemble his pictures, I have at least occasion to betake myself to some teacher who, in a more Christian style, may make me dislike those vices of which the other has given such a seductive description.

(10.) A fine sermon is an oratorical speech, which, in all its rules and freed from all its faults, is exactly governed by the same principles as any other piece of human eloquence, and decked out with all sorts of rhetorical ornaments. Not a passage nor a thought are lost to connoisseurs; they easily follow the orator in all the digressions in which he chooses to wander, as well as in his towering flights; he is a riddle to none but to the common people.

(11.) What a judicious and admirable sermon I have just heard! How beautifully brought forward were the most essential points of religion as well as the strongest motives for conversion! What a grand impression it must have produced on the minds and souls of the audience! They are convinced; they are moved and so deeply touched that they confess from their very souls the sermon they have

[840] The Pandects of the Roman emperor Justinian were a cyclopædia of legal decisions of Roman lawyers; and after they had been discovered at Amalfi in Italy about the year 1137, they changed the whole of the legal aspect of Europe.

[841] There were three saints of the name of Cyrillus, but the one mentioned above was probably bishop of Jerusalem (315-388); Saint Thascius Cæcilius Cyprianus (210-285) was bishop of Carthage: whilst Saint Aurelius Augustinus (354-430) was the celebrated author and bishop of Hippo.

[842] The preachers accused of a florid style were, according to the "Keys," the Oratorian Senault, and Fléchier, who in 1685 had been appointed bishop of Nîmes.

just heard Theodorus preach excels even the one they heard before.[843]

(11.) An indulgent and relax morality produces no more effect than the clergyman who preaches it;[844] for a man of the world is neither excited nor roused by it, and is not so averse to a rigid doctrine as some people think, but, on the contrary, likes to hear it from the person whose duty it is to preach it. There seems to be, therefore, in the church two classes of men wholly distinct from one another; the one declaring the truth in all its amplitude, without respect of persons, without disguise; the other listening to this truth with pleasure, satisfaction, admiration, and applause, but acting neither the better nor the worse for it.

(13.) It may be said, and justly so, that the heroic virtues of some great men have been the cause of the corruption of eloquence, or have, at least, enervated the style of most preachers. Instead of joining with the people in rendering thanks to Heaven for the extraordinary gifts it has bestowed on those great men, these very preachers have enrolled themselves among authors and poets, and become panegyrists; they have even uttered more extravagant praises than are found in dedications, verses, or prologues; they have turned the Word of God into a whole warp of praises, which, though well deserved, are out of place, bestowed from selfish motives, not required, and ill-suited to their calling. It is fortunate indeed, if, while they are celebrating their heroes in the sanctuary, they even mention the name of that God or of that religion they ought to preach. Some have wished to preach the Gospel, which is for all men, only to one person, and have been so disconcerted when by accident that person was kept away, that they were unable to pronounce a Christian discourse before an assembly of Christian men, because it was not prepared for them, so that other orators have been obliged to take their places, who had only sufficient leisure to praise God in an extemporary exhortation.[845]

(14.) Theodulus has been less successful than some of his hearers thought he would be; his discourse has gratified them, and so has he; but he would have pleased them much more, if instead of delighting their ears and their minds, he had flattered their feelings of jealousy.

(15.) Preachers and soldiers are alike in this; their vocation presents more risk than any other, but preferment is also more rapid.

(16.) If you are of a certain rank, and have no other talent but preaching dull sermons, preach away, however dull you may be, for you will obtain no preferment if you are utterly unknown. Theodotus has been well paid for his wretched phraseology and his tiresome monotony.

[843] Theodorus is supposed to be Bourdaloue (see page 165, note 326). Some other celebrated preachers have also been named.

[844] Charles Boileau, abbé de Beaulieu, and a member of the French Academy, who died in 1704 (see page 49, note 135), is said to have preached a morality such as is mentioned in the above paragraph.

[845] A certain Abbé de Roquette, a nephew of the Bishop of Autun (see page 226, note 453), had to preach one Holy Thursday before the king, but through some unfortunate accident Louis XIV. could not be present, and the preacher, disconcerted at the absence of the monarch, for whom probably he had prepared the most fulsome flatteries, did not dare to mount the pulpit and deliver his sermon.

(17.) Some men have been preferred to bishopricks for their preaching, whose talents now would not have procured them a mere prebend.

(18.) There is a certain panegyrist whose name seems always weighed down by a heap of titles and qualities, of which a large number is always mentioned on the ample bills distributed from house to house, or printed in letters of enormous size on the bills stuck up in the streets, no more to be ignored than the open market-place is. After such a fine display if you hear that man preach, and listen for a while to what he says, you will find that in enumerating all his qualities, only one has been omitted, namely, that of being a wretched preacher.

(19.) The idleness of women, and the habit men have of frequenting the places they resort to, give a certain reputation to some dull orators, and for a while support the sinking credit of others.

(20.) Are greatness and power the only qualities which entitle a man to be praised at his funeral before the holy altar and from the pulpit, the seat of truth? Is there no other greatness but that derived from an official position or from birth? Why should it not be the custom publicly to bestow praise on a man who during his lifetime was pre-eminent for his kindness of heart, his love of justice, his gentleness, his fidelity, and his piety? What is called "a funeral sermon" is now-a-days but coldly received by the greater part of the audience, unless very different from a Christian discourse, or rather, unless very nearly resembling a secular panegyric.

(21.) An orator preaches to get a bishopric, an apostle to save souls; the latter deserves what the other aims at.

(22.) We see some of our clergymen[846] return from the country where they did not stay long, as proud of having made converts, who had already been made for them, as of those persons whom they could not convert, compare themselves to Saint Vincent de Paul and Saint Francis Xavier,[847] and fancy themselves apostles. For such onerous labours and such a fortunate result of their mission they would think themselves scarcely repaid by having an abbey given to them.

(23.) A man starts up on a sudden, and without any previous thoughts, takes pen, ink, and paper, and resolves within himself to write a book, but without any other talent for writing but the need he has of fifty *pistoles*.[848] In vain I say to him: "Dioscorus, take a saw, or else go to the lathe, make a spoke of a wheel, and you will be sure to earn your living."[849] "But I never served an apprenticeship to these

---

[846] In the original clercs, to which our author added a note in the first four editions to say that he meant "clergymen." The whole paragraph alludes to the missionaries sent into the provinces to convert the Protestants. Did La Bruyère, in speaking of the "converts who had already been made for these clergymen," hint at the dragonnades and at the other wretched and inhuman means employed to compel people to change their religion? I am afraid not, though he admits some persons could not be converted.

[847] Saint Vincent de Paul (1566-1660), a well-known philanthropical preacher, very successful in his missions; Saint Francis Xavier (1506-1553), a Jesuit missionary, who made many converts in the East Indies.

[848] See page 173, note 346.

[849] See the chapter "Of Works of the Mind," page 65, § 3.

trades." "Why then, copy, transcribe, become a reader for the press, but do not write." Yet Dioscorus will write and get it printed too. And because he must not send paper to the press with nothing written on it, he sets himself to scribble whatever he pleases, and likes to write such stuff as this: "That the Seine runs through the city of Paris; that a week has seven days; or that it threatens to rain,"[850] and as there is nothing in such phrases against religion or the government, and as they will only harm the public by vitiating their taste, and accustoming them to dull and insipid things, he obtains permission to get his book printed;[851] and to the shame of the age, and as a mortification to good authors, a second edition of it appears. Just so, another wiseacre resolves within himself that he will preach, and he preaches; he is without any talent, or has not the least vocation for it, but he wants a good living.

---

[850] Some scribbler of the time, a certain Gédéon Pontier, author of the Cabinet des Grands, is said to have written almost similar nonsense.

[851] In 1689, the same year this paragraph first appeared, seventy-nine royal censors had been appointed, and no book could be printed without their permission.

BOSSUET

(24.) A worldly and profane clergyman does but declaim when he preaches.

On the contrary, there are some holy men whose character carries persuasion with it; they make their appearance in the pulpit, and every one who comes to listen to them is already moved, and, as it were, carried away by their mère presence; the sermon afterwards completes their conversion.

(25.) The bishop of Meaux (Bossuet) and Father Bourdaloue recall to my mind Demosthenes and Cicero. As both of them are absolute masters of pulpit eloquence, they have had the fate of other great models; one of them has made many wretched cavillers, and the other many wretched imitators.

(26.) The eloquence of the pulpit, with respect to what is merely human and depending on the genius of the orator, is not easily perceptible, is known but to few, and attained with difficulty. It must be very difficult to please and to persuade at the same time; for a man is obliged to keep to beaten paths, to say what has been said, and what is foreseen he would say. The subjects he has to treat of are grand, but worn and trite; the principles are invariable, but every one of his audience perceives the inferences at the first glance. Some of the subjects are sublime; but who can treat of the sublime? There are mysteries to be explained, but they are better explained in a lecture at college than in a harangue. The morals, too, of the pulpit, though they comprehend matter as vast and diversified as the manners and morals of men, turn all upon the same pivot, exhibit the same imagery, and are restrained to much narrower limits than satire is; after the usual invective against honour, riches, and pleasures, there remains nothing more for the orator to do but to finish his discourse and dismiss his audience. There may sometimes be tears, and people may be moved; but let the calling and talent of the preacher be considered, and perhaps it will be found that the subject lends itself to a sermon, or that it is chiefly a feeling of self-interest which produces this agitation; and that it is not so much true eloquence as the strong lungs of the missionary which shake us and produce within us these emotions. In short, the preacher is not provided, as the lawyer is, with always fresh matters of fact, with various transactions and unheard-of adventures; his business is not to start doubtful questions, and improve probable conjectures—all subjects which elevate talent, give it force and breadth, and instead of putting a restraint on eloquence, only fix and direct it. The preacher, on the contrary, has to draw his discourse from a source known to all and used by everybody; if he deviates from these commonplaces, he ceases to be popular, becomes abstruse and a declaimer, and no longer preaches the Gospel. All he needs is a noble simplicity, which is difficult to attain, rarely found, and above the reach of ordinary men; their talent, imagination, learning, and memory, so far from assisting them, often prevent their acquiring it.

A barrister's profession is laborious, toilsome, and requires a vast amount of knowledge as well as great readiness of invention. A barrister is not, like a preacher, provided with a certain number of speeches, composed at leisure, learned by heart, uttered with authority, without any fear of contradiction, and which, with a few alterations, may serve more than once; his pleadings are grave, and delivered before judges who may silence him, and against adversaries who interrupt him; his replies have to be sharp and to the point; and in one and the same day he has to plead in several courts causes quite dissimilar. His house neither affords him shelter nor rest, nor protects him against his clients; it is open to all comers, who crowd upon him with their difficult or doubtful cases; he is not put to bed, nor is the perspiration wiped from his face, nor are refreshments offered to him; people of all qualities and sexes do not crowd his rooms to congratulate him upon the beauty and elegance of his style, or to remind him of a certain passage where he ran the risk of stopping short, or of some scruples he felt for having spoken with less warmth than usual; all the repose a barrister has after a long speech is immediately to set to work upon writings still longer; he only varies his labours and fatigues; I may venture to say he is in his profession what the first apostles were in theirs.

Having thus distinguished the eloquence of the bar from the profession of a barrister, and the eloquence of the pulpit from the calling of a preacher, it will appear, I believe, that it is easier to preach than to plead, but more difficult to preach well than to plead well.

(27.) What a vast advantage has a speech over a written composition. Men are imposed upon by voice and gesture, and by all that is conducive to enhance the performance. Any little prepossession in favour of the speaker raises their admiration, and then they do their best to comprehend him; they commend his performance before he has begun, but they soon fall off asleep, doze all the time he is preaching, and only wake to applaud him. An author has no such passionate admirers; his works are read at leisure in the country or in the solitude of the study; no public meetings are held to applaud him, nor do people intrigue to sacrifice all his rivals to him and to have him raised to the prelacy. However excellent his book may be, it is read with the intention of finding it but middling; it is perused, discussed, and compared to other works; a book is not composed of transient sounds lost in the air and forgotten; what is printed remains; sometimes it is expected a month or two before it is published, and people are impatient to damn it, whilst the greatest pleasure many will find in it will be their own criticisms; it vexes them to meet on each page passages which ought to please; often they are even afraid of being amused by it, and they throw the book away merely because it is good. Everybody does not pretend to be a preacher; the elocution, the figures of speech, the gift of memory, the gown or the calling of a preacher, are things people do not always venture on, or like to take on themselves, whilst every one imagines he thinks well and writes still better than he thinks, which renders him less indulgent to the person who thinks and writes as well as himself; in a word, the preacher of sermons will sooner obtain a bishopric than the most judicious writer a small living, and whilst new favours are still heaped on the first, the more deserving author may consider himself very fortunate if he gets some of the leavings of the preacher.

(28.) If it happens that the wicked hate and persecute you, good men advise you to humble yourself before God, and to beware of the pride you may feel in having displeased people of a similar character; so when certain men who admire everything middling, blame a work you have written, or a speech you have made in public, whether at the bar, in the pulpit, or elsewhere, humble yourself, for of all the temptations of pride there cannot be a greater and more enticing one.

(29.) A preacher, methinks, should select for every one of his sermons some capital truth, whether to terrify or to instruct, handle it thoroughly and analyse it, whilst omitting all fine-spun decisions so worn, trite, and different from one another; I would not have him suppose a thing which is notoriously false, namely, that great or fashionable people understand the religion they profess as well as its duties; so that he will be afraid of remonstrating with persons of their culture and subtle understandings. Let him employ the time others waste in composing a set, formal discourse, in making himself so completely master of his subject that his style and expressions may be original and natural; let him, after some necessary preparations, abandon himself to his own genius and to the emotions with which a great subject will inspire him; and then, he may be able to do without those excessive efforts of memory, which destroy all graceful gestures, and look more as if he had learned something by heart for a wager, than as if he were treating a matter of great importance; let him, on the contrary, kindled by a noble enthusiasm, persuade all minds, alarm all souls, and fill the heart of his hearers with another fear than that of seeing him stop short in the middle of his sermon.

(30.) A man who has not yet arrived to such perfection as to forget himself in the dispensation of Holy Writ, should not be discouraged by the austere rules which are prescribed, which may deprive him of the means of showing his intelligence and of attaining the honours to which he aspires. What more useful, more exalted talent can there be than preaching like an apostle; and who would better deserve a bishopric? Was Fénelon unworthy of that dignity, and could he have escaped his prince's choice but for another choice?[852]

[852] The last sentence of the above paragraph was added in the fifth edition of the "Characters," published in 1690, about one year after Fénelon had been appointed teacher of the Duke of Burgundy, the grandson of Louis XIV. Fénelon became archbishop of Cambrai in 1695.

BELIEF

XVI.

OF FREETHINKERS.[853]

(1.) DO freethinkers know that it is only ironically they are called strong-minded?[854] What greater proof of their weakness of mind can they give than their uncertainty about the very principles of their existence, life, senses, knowledge, and what will be their end? What can be more discouraging to a man than to doubt if his soul be material, like a stone or a reptile, and subject to corruption like the vilest creatures? And does it not prove much more strength of mind and grandeur to be able to conceive the idea of a Being superior to all other beings, by whom and for whom all things were made; of a Being absolutely perfect and

---

[853] See page 27, note 97. Several eminent divines had already written against "freethinkers," and about a year before the first edition of the "Characters" appeared, Fénelon preached a sermon against them. Those freethinkers were not deists nor atheists, but somewhat like those persons, at present called agnostics, who neither affirm nor deny anything, but simply state that they know nothing for certain. Among their sect might be reckoned at the time our author wrote the celebrated traveller Bernier, Saint Evremond, Bayle, Fontenelle, Chaulieu, La Fare, the Dukes de Nevers and de Bouillon, the Grand Prior de Vendôme, and many others.

[854] The French name for "freethinker" is esprit fort, literally "strong mind."

pure, without beginning or end, of whom our soul is the image, and of whom, if I may say so, it is a part, because it is spiritual and immortal?

(2.) The docile and the weak are susceptible of receiving impressions; the first receive good ones, for they are convinced and faithful, whilst the second receive bad ones, as they are stubborn and corrupted. A docile mind admits thus true religion, and a feeble mind either admits none or a false one. Now a freethinker either has no religion at all, or creates one for himself; therefore a strong-minded freethinker is in reality feeble-minded.[855]

(3.) I call those men worldly, earthly, or coarse, whose hearts and minds are wholly fixed on this earth, that small part of the universe they are placed in; who value and love nothing beyond it; whose minds are as cramped as that narrow spot of ground they call their estate, of which the extent is measured, the acres are numbered, and the limits well known. I am not astonished that men who lean, as it were, on an atom, should stumble at the smallest efforts they make for discovering the truth; that, being so short-sighted, they do not reach beyond the heavens and the stars, to contemplate God Himself; that, not being able to perceive the excellency of what is spiritual, or the dignity of the soul, they should be still less sensible of the difficulty of satisfying it; how very inferior the entire world is in comparison to it; how necessary is to it an all-perfect Being, which is God; and how absolutely it needs a religion to find out that God, and to be assured of His reality. I can easily understand that incredulity or indifference are but natural to such men, that they make use of God and religion only as a piece of policy, as far as they may be conducive to the order and decorum of this world, the only thing in their opinion worth thinking of.

(4.) Some men give the finishing-stroke to the spoiling of their judgment by their long travels, and thus lose the little religion which remained to them.[856] They meet daily new forms of worship, different manners and morals, and various ceremonies; they are not unlike those people who wander from shop to shop, and have not quite made up their mind what they are going to buy; the variety puzzles them, and as each thing pleases their fancy more or less, they are unable to come to a decision, and leave without buying anything.

(5.) There are some men who delay becoming religious and pious till the time everybody openly avows himself irreligious and a freethinker,[857] for, as this has then become vulgar, they will be distinguished from the crowd. In so serious and important a matter singularity pleases them; only in trifling things, of no consequence, they follow the fashion and do what others do; for all I know, they may consider it somewhat courageous and daring to run the risk of what may happen to them in the next world. Moreover, when men are of a certain rank, possess a certain freedom of thought, and have certain views, they should not dream of believing what learned men and the common people believe.

[855] Another play on words in the original on esprit fort and esprit faible.

[856] This is perhaps an allusion to the traveller F. Bernier, a pupil of Gassendi, who visited Assyria, Egypt, and India, and published a narrative of his travels in 1670.

[857] Libertin was another name for freethinker in French. See p. 161, note 319.

(6.) A man in health questions whether there is a God, and he also doubts whether it be a sin to have intercourse with a woman, who is at liberty to refuse;[858] but when he falls ill, or when his mistress is with child, she is discarded, and he believes in God.

(7.) People should examine themselves thoroughly before openly declaring themselves freethinkers, so that, according to their own principles, they at least may die as they have lived; or if they find they are not strong-minded enough to proceed so far, to resolve to live as they would wish to die.

(8.) Jesting in a dying man is out of place; and if it is on certain subjects, it is dreadful. To please our survivors with a jest at the expense of our own eternal happiness, is a very miserable business.

Whatever a man may think about a future state, dying is a very serious affair, and firmness is then more becoming than jesting.

(9.) In all ages there have been people with a certain amount of cleverness, and well read, who, servilely following men of high rank, embraced their loose principles, and all their lifetime groaned under their yoke, against their own knowledge and conscience. Some men only live for other men, and seem to consider themselves created for this purpose; they are ashamed to be seen bestowing a thought on their own salvation, and to appear outwardly such as they are perhaps in their hearts, and thus they ruin themselves out of deference or complacency. Are there then on this earth men of such high rank and so very powerful as to deserve that we should shape our beliefs and our lives according to their taste and fancy; nay, that we should carry our submission so far as at our death to leave this world not in the safest way for ourselves, but in the way most pleasing to them?

(10.) Men who run counter to all the world, and act against principles universally received, should know more than other men, be clear in their reasons and convincing in their arguments.

(11.) A sober-minded, cool-headed, chaste, and honourable man, who affirms there is no God, at least is dispassionate, but such a man is not to be found.

(12.) I admit I should very much like to see a man really persuaded there was no God; for then I should at least hear on what unanswerable arguments his unbelief is founded.

(13.) The impossibility I find myself under of proving there is no God, is to me a convincing argument for His existence.

(14.) God condemns and punishes those who offend Him, and He is the only judge in His own cause, which would shock all our ideas if He Himself were not Justice and Truth—that is, if He were not God.

(15.) I feel there is a God, and I do not feel there is none; this is sufficient for me, and all other arguments seem to me superfluous; I therefore conclude that He exists, and this conclusion is inherent to my nature. I acquired these principles readily in my childhood, and have kept them since too naturally in my riper years

---

[858] The original has une personne libre, to which our author adds in a note, une fille.

ever to suspect them of falsehood.—But there are some men who get rid of these principles.—I question whether there are any, but if there be, it only proves that monsters exist in this world.

(16.) There is no such thing as an atheist; the great men who are more or less suspected of being inclined that way, are too lazy to fatigue their minds with discussions whether there is a God or no; their indolence renders them careless and indifferent about such an important matter as well as about the nature of their own souls and the consequences of true religion; they neither deny nor grant any of these things; they never think of them.

(17.) All our health, all our strength, and our entire intellect are not more than sufficient in thinking of mankind or of our smallest interest; yet propriety and custom seem to require of us only to think of God when we are so situated that we have barely so much reason left as to enable us to say we are not totally without any.

(18.) A great man falls in a swoon, as it was thought, but is discovered to be dead,[859] another great man wastes away gradually, and daily loses something of himself before he expires; such lessons are dreadful, but useless. These circumstances, though so remarkable and so different from each other, are not noticed, affect nobody, and are no more heeded than the fall of a leaf, or the fading of a flower; people only want their posts vacant through their deaths, or they inquire if they have been filled up, and who are their successors.

(19.) Is there so much goodness, fidelity, and justice among men, that we should place unlimited confidence in them, and not, at least, wish for a God to exist to whom we might appeal from their injustice, and who might protect us against their persecutions and treacheries.

(20.) If freethinkers are dazzled and confounded by the grandeur and sublimity of religion, they are no longer freethinkers, but shallow geniuses and little minds;[860] if, on the contrary, they are repelled by its humbleness and simplicity, we must allow them to be real freethinkers, far stronger-minded than so many great men, enlightened and highly cultivated, who nevertheless were confirmed believers, such as the Leos, the Basils, the Jeromes, the Augustines.[861]

(21.) Certain people who have never read the fathers or doctors of the Church are frightened at their very names, and declare their writings dull, dry, pious, cold, and perhaps pedantic. But how astonished would all these people be who have formed such an untrue idea of the Fathers, if they found in their writings a better style, more delicacy, polish, and intelligence, a greater warmth of expression

---

[859] An allusion to some such men as the Duke de la Feuillade, the Minister de Louvois, and the Marquis de Seignelay, who have been mentioned before, and who almost all died after a very short illness.

[860] Whenever our author has an opportunity he always opposes esprits forts to esprits faibles, or faibles génies, as in the above paragraph.

[861] Leo I., bishop of Rome, called the Great, died 461; St. Jerome (331-420) was one of the fathers of the Latin Church. For Basil and Augustine (see page 446, note 837, and page 447, note 841.)

and strength of reasoning, sharper traits and more natural charms than are to be met with in most of the modern books read by connoisseurs, which increase the reputation and conceit of their authors. What a satisfaction to love religion and to see men of great talent and solid learning believe in it, assert its truth, and explain it! And whether you consider extent of knowledge, depth and penetration, the principles of pure philosophy, their application and development, the correctness of the conclusions arrived at, nobleness of expression, beauty of morals and sentiments, no profane author can be compared to Saint Augustine, except Plato and Cicero.

(22.) Man who is born a liar cannot relish the plainness and simplicity of truth; he is altogether hankering after appearance[862] and ornament. He has not made truth, for it comes from Heaven ready-made, as it were, in all its perfection, and man loves nothing but his own productions, Fable and Fiction. Observe the common people; they will invent a tale, add to it, and exaggerate it through coarseness or folly; ask even the most honest man if he always speaks the truth, if he does not sometimes discover that, either through vanity or levity, he has disguised the truth; and if to embellish a story he does not often add some circumstance to set it off? An accident happened to-day, and almost, as it were, under our eyes; a hundred people have seen it, and all relate it in as many different ways; and yet another person may come, and if you will only listen to him, he shall tell it in a way in which it has not yet been told. How then can I believe facts which are so old and took place several centuries ago? What reliance can I place on the gravest historians, and what becomes of history itself. Was Cæsar ever murdered in the midst of the senate? and has there ever been such a person as Cæsar? "Why do you draw such an inference?" you'll say; "why express such doubts and ask such questions?" You laugh, you do not think my question worthy of an answer, and I imagine you are quite right. But suppose the book which gives us an account of Cæsar was not a profane history, written by men who are liars, and had not been discovered by chance among certain manuscripts, some true, and others suspicious; but that, on the contrary, it had been inspired, and bore all the evidence of being holy and divine; that for nearly two thousand years it had been kept by a large society of men, who all this while would not allow the least alteration to be made in it, and held it as part of their creed to preserve it in all its purity; that these men, by their own principles, were indispensably compelled to believe religiously all the transactions related in this volume, whenever mention was made of Cæsar and his dictatorship; own it, Lucilius, would you then question whether there ever was such a man as Cæsar?

(23.) All kinds of music are not suited to praise God and to be heard in the sanctuary; all methods of philosophy are not fit for discoursing worthily of God, His power, the principles of His operations, and His mysteries. The more abstracted and ideal this philosophy is, the more vain and useless is it in explaining these things, which merely require common sense to be understood up to a certain point, and which cannot be explained farther. To pretend to give an account of the very essence of God, of His perfections, and, if I dare say so, of His actions, is

---

[862] Spécieux in the original, with the Latin meaning.

indeed going beyond the ancient philosophers, beyond the apostles themselves, and the first teachers of the Gospel, but it is not arguing so much to the point as they did; for people may dig for a long time, and deeply, without discovering the sources of truth. If once people set aside such words as goodness, mercy, justice, and omnipotence, which are apt to form in their minds such lovely and majestic ideas of the divinity, let them afterwards strain their imagination as much as possible, they will find nothing but dry, barren, and senseless expressions; they must admit wild and empty thoughts, contrary to all ordinary ideas, or, at least, subtle and ingenious thoughts, by which their religion will be weakened according as they improve in the knowledge of these new metaphysics.[863]

(24.) What excesses will a man not commit through his zeal for a religion, of the truth of which he is not entirely convinced, and which he practises so badly?

(25.) That same religion which men will defend so zealously and with so much warmth against those of a different persuasion, they themselves corrupt, by joining to it their own peculiar ideas; they add or take from it numberless things, which are often very material, according as it best suits their convenience, and remain steadfastly and firmly attached to the form they have given it themselves. So that, though it may be commonly said of a nation that it has but one manner of worship and one religion, it truly and really has many religions, for almost every individual has one of his own.

(26.) Two sorts of men flourish in courts and reign there by turns, freethinkers and hypocrites; the first gaily, openly, without art or disguise, the second cunningly and by intrigue. These latter arc a hundred times more enamoured of fortune than the first, and are excessively jealous of it; they wish to sway it, to be the sole possessors of it, share it among themselves, and exclude everybody else. Dignities, posts, offices, benefices, pensions, honours, everything belongs to them and to none but them; the rest of mankind are unworthy of these things, and they wonder how others, who are not their creatures, can be so impudent as to expect them. A company of persons in masks enter a ball-room; when it is their turn they dance, they dance with each other, dance again and continue to dance, but only among themselves and with no other person, however worthy of their regard; people grow annoyed and tired with looking on whilst these masked persons dance because they are not dancing themselves; some among them murmur, but the wisest make up their mind and go home.[864]

(27.) There are two sorts of freethinkers; those who are really so, or at least believe themselves so, and the hypocrites or pretended pious people, who are unwilling to be thought freethinkers; the latter are the best.

A man who pretends to be pious either does not believe there is a God, or makes a jest of Him; let us say of him politely, that he does not believe there is a God.

(28.) If every religion stands in respectful fear of God, what shall we think of

[863] This is perhaps a hit at Malebranche's Nouvelle Métaphysique.

[864] At the time our author wrote it was the custom to allow masked people to enter a ball-room.

those persons who dare affront Him in His representative on earth, the Prince?

(29.) Were we assured that the secret intention of the ambassadors who came lately from Siam was to persuade the most Christian king to renounce Christianity, and admit their Talapoins[865] into his kingdom to creep into our houses to convert to their religion our wives, our children, and ourselves, by their books as well as by their conversations, to allow them to erect pagodas in the midst of our towns to worship their brazen images, with what derision, what strange scorn, should we hear such an absurd story told? And yet we sail six thousand leagues to bring over to Christianity the Indies, the kingdoms of Siam, China, and Japan, and seriously to make to all these nations certain proposals, which, in their eyes, must appear as foolish and ridiculous. Yet they tolerate our friars and priests, and sometimes listen to them, allow them to build churches, and perform all their missionary duties. From whence proceeds such a behaviour, so different in them and us? May it not be caused by the force of truth?

(30.) It is not proper for all men to profess to give alms and to have the common beggars of the parish daily crowding at their doors, and not allow one to go home empty-handed. Who is not aware that there is a more concealed wretchedness, which may be relieved, either immediately and out of a man's own pocket, or at least by the intercession of others? In the same manner all persons are not qualified for the pulpit, nor fit to expound the Word of God in public, either as missionaries, or teachers; but what man does not, some time or other, meet a freethinker, whom he might attempt to reclaim and bring back to the fold by gentle and insinuating converse about the submission due to the teachings of the church? Should a man make but one convert in the whole course of his life, he cannot be said to have lived in vain, or to have been a useless burden on this earth.

(31.) There are two worlds: one we dwell in but a short time, and which we must leave never to return; another, to which we must shortly go, there to abide for ever. Interest, authority, friends, a great reputation, and riches are most useful in the first; an indifference to all these things is most useful for the next. It is a mere question of choice.

(32.) A man who lives a day lives an age; always the same sun, the same earth, the same world, the same sensations; to-day will precisely be like to-morrow; we ought to feel some curiosity to die, for then we are no longer a body, but only a spirit. However, man, though so impatiently hunting after novelties, is not anxious to die; restless and tired of everything, he is not tired of life, and would, perhaps, be satisfied to live for ever. What he sees of death makes a deeper impression on him than what he knows of it; sickness, pain, and the grave, make him dislike the knowledge of another world; and the strongest religious motives are needed to convert him.

---

[865] In "A New Historical Relation of Siam," by M. de la Loubère (see page 155, note 2), we find: "The priests are the Talapoins.... They have umbrellas in the form of a screen which they carry in their hand.... In Siamese they call them 'Talapat,' and it is probable that from hence comes the name of 'Talapir' or 'Talapoin,' which is in use among foreigners only." The embassy from the King of Siam to Louis XIV. took place in the year 1686. See page 338, note 624.

(33.) If Providence had left it to our choice to die or to live for ever, we should carefully consider how dismal it is for a man to see no end to his poverty, servitude, annoyance, or sickness; or, at best to enjoy riches, grandeur, pleasures, and health, only in time to behold them invariably change to their opposite conditions; and thus to be tossed to and fro between happiness and misery, and, therefore, we should be greatly perplexed; but Nature has settled it for us, and saves us the trouble of making a choice, as it has imposed on us the necessity of dying, which is, moreover, alleviated by religion.

(34.) If my religion be false, it is a snare which I must own is as well laid as can be imagined, so that it is impossible not to run into it and be caught. What dignity! what splendour in its mysteries! what a sequence and connection in all the several parts of its doctrine! how superb are its reasonings! how pure and innocent is its morality! how irresistible and overwhelming is the testimony of so many millions of the wisest and most thoughtful men then in existence, who during three centuries came one after another, and whom a feeling of the same truth so constantly supported in exiles, dungeons, torture, and even in death itself. Take any history, open it, and commence with the beginning of the world, with its creation; was there ever anything like it? Could the whole power of God Himself contrive anything better to deceive me? How can I avoid it? Whither should I run, or throw myself? I do not say to find anything better, but anything to be compared to it? If I must perish, it is in this way I will perish! I should feel more inclined to deny the existence of a God than to connect Him with such a plausible and complete deceit. But I have examined it thoroughly, and yet feel I cannot be an atheist; I am, therefore, forced back and irresistibly drawn to my religion, and this is my final resolution.

(35.) Religion is either true or false; if a fiction, a religious man, a Carthusian friar or a hermit, only lose three-score years, but run no other risk. But if based on truth itself, then a vicious man must feel most wretched; and I tremble at the very thought of the evils he prepares for himself; my mind cannot conceive them, and words fail me to express my feelings. Even if the truth of religion could be proved with less certainty than it can, man could not do better than be virtuous.

(36.) Those persons who dare deny the existence of a Supreme Being hardly deserve that a man should try and prove it to them; or, at least, that he should argue more seriously with them than I have done hitherto; they are so ignorant that they are unable to understand the clearest principles, and the truest and most natural inferences; yet I am willing to offer for their perusal the following lines, provided they do not imagine that it is all that can be said upon a subject of which the truth is so obvious.

Forty years ago I did not exist,[866] neither was it in my power ever to exist, any more than it is in my power to cease from existing, though I exist at present. My existence, therefore, had its beginning, and is now continued through the influence of something which exists without me, will subsist after me, and is better and more powerful than I am. Now, if that something is not God, I should like to

---

[866] In 1685, when this paragraph was first published, La Bruyère was forty years old.

know what it is.[867]

I exist; but perhaps this existence of mine proceeds from the power of a universal nature, which has been ever the same, such as we behold it, from all eternity.[868] But this nature is either only spiritual, and then it is God, or it is material, and, consequently, could not create that part of my being which is spiritual; or else it is composed of spirit and matter; and then, that part of nature which people say is spirit, is what I call God.

Again, perhaps you will add that what I call my spiritual being is nothing but a part of matter, subsisting through the force of a universal nature, which also is matter, which always was and ever will be such as we see it now, and which is not God.[869] But, at least, you must grant that what I call my spiritual being, let it be what it will, is something which thinks, and that if it is matter, it is cogitative matter; for no one will persuade me that, whilst I am thus arguing, there is not something within me which thinks. Now if this something owes its being and its preservation to a universal nature which always was and ever will be, and which it acknowledges as its primary cause, it necessarily follows that this universal nature either thinks, or is more noble and perfect than that which thinks; and if such a nature is matter, then we must come to the conclusion that it is a universal thinking matter, or one which is nobler and more perfect than that which does think.

I proceed further, and say, that such a supposed matter, if it be not chimerical but real, may be perceived by some of our senses, and that, if it cannot be discovered in itself, it may be known, at least, in the multiple arrangement of its different parts, through which all bodies are constituted, or differ. Therefore matter is itself all these different bodies; now since, according to our supposition, matter is a being which thinks, or is better than that which thinks, it follows that it is such in some of these bodies at least, and, consequently, that it thinks in stones, in minerals, in the earth, in the sea, in myself, who am but a body, as well as in all its other component parts; I am then beholden for this something, which thinks within me, and which I call my spiritual being, to all these gross, earthly, and corporeal parts, which all together make up this universal matter, or this visible world, which is an absurdity.

If, on the contrary, this universal nature, let it be what it will, is not all these bodies, nor any of these bodies, it follows that it is not matter, and cannot be perceived by any of our senses; and if, notwithstanding this, it possesses the faculty of thinking, or is more perfect than that which does think, I still conclude it is spiritual, or something better and more perfect than spiritual. Now if that which thinks within me, and which I call my spiritual being, not finding its principle within itself, and much less in matter, as has been just now demonstrated, is forced

[867] St. Augustin (see page 447, note 841) and Descartes (see page 150, § 56) had already made use of the above argument.

[868] Our author adds in a note: "An objection to the system of freethinkers." An allusion to the system of Spinosa, which Fénelon also attempted to refute in his Traité de l'existence de Dieu.

[869] "This is what freethinkers bring forward," says La Bruyère in a note. He means probably the disciples of Gassendi, and followers of the systems of Epicurus and Lucretius.

to acknowledge this universal nature to be the first cause, the only origin of its existence, then I will not dispute about words; but this first cause, the origin of all spiritual beings, which is itself spiritual, or better than spiritual, is what I call God.

In a word, I think, therefore, there is a God, for that which thinks within me is not derived from myself, since it was no more in my power to bestow it on myself at first as it is now to keep it for one single moment. I did not receive it from a material being superior to me, since it is impossible for matter to be superior to that which thinks; I must, therefore, have received it from a being superior to me, and consequently not material; and that superior being is God.

(37.) From the inconsistency of a cogitative universal nature with anything that is material, must necessarily be inferred, that any particular thinking being cannot admit within itself anything material; for though a universal thinking being does in its idea include infinitely more grandeur, power, independence, and capacity than a particular thinking being, yet it does not imply a greater inconsistency with matter, it being impossible for this inconsistency to be greater in the one case than in the other, because it is, as it were, infinite in both; and it is as impossible for the thinking principle within me to be matter, as it is to conceive that God should be matter; as God, therefore, is a spirit, so my soul is also a spirit.

(38.) I am not aware whether a dog has the faculties of selection, memory, love, fear, imagination, and thought. When, therefore, I am told that those actions in a dog are not the effect of either passion or sentiment, but proceed naturally and necessarily from a mechanical disposition caused by the multiple organization of the material parts of his body, I may, perhaps, acquiesce in this doctrine. But as for me, I think, and certainly know that I think.[870] Now, if we consider any organisation of material parts, namely, any space with all its dimensions, length, breadth, and depth, and which can be divided in all these directions, what proportion is there between such a space and cogitation?

(39.) If all things are matter, and if thought within me, as well as in other men, be no more than an effect of the arrangement of matter, how came any other idea, but that of material things into this world? Is matter able to produce so pure, so simple, so immaterial an idea as we have of spirit? How can matter be the origin of that which rejects and excludes such an idea from its very being? How can it be the cogitative principle in man, that is, that principle which convinces man he is not merely matter?

(40.) There are beings of short duration, because they are made up of things varying much in their nature, and destructive to one another; there are others more lasting, because they are simpler, but they perish at last, being made up of several parts, into which they are divisible. That which thinks within me must naturally be permanent, as it is a pure being, free from all mixture and composition; there is no reason why it should perish; for what can corrupt or divide a simple being, in which are no parts?

(41.) The soul sees colour through the organ of the eye, and hears sounds through the organ of the ear; but it may cease either from seeing or hearing when

[870] This is Descartes' doctrine.

those senses or those objects are absent, and yet not cease from existing, because it is not exactly the soul that sees or hears; it is only that which thinks. Now, how can it cease from being such? Not for want of organs, since it has been proved it is not matter; nor for want of objects, whilst there is a God and eternal truths; it is therefore incorruptible.

(42.) I cannot conceive the annihilation of a soul which God has filled with the idea of His infinite and all-perfect being.

(43.) Observe, Lucilius,[871] this spot of ground, which for neatness and ornament exceeds all other neighbouring estates; here are plots with the finest lakes and fountains, and endless hedge-rows of trees which shelter you against the north winds; on this side is a thick grove where the sun cannot penetrate; on the other side you have a beautiful view; a little lower, the Yvette or the Lignon,[872] which were running modestly between willows and poplars, have now become a canal quite bricked in; elsewhere long and cool avenues lead to the country, and foreshadow what the mansion will be, which is surrounded by water. Will you say, "This is an effect of chance," and suppose that all these admirable things met together accidentally? No, certainly; on the contrary, you observe that everything is well planned and arranged, and displays good taste and much intelligence. I agree with you, and take the liberty to add that I suppose it to be the residence of one of those men, who from the very minute they get into office, send for a Le Nôtre[873] to draw plans and take measurements. Yet what is this piece of ground so exquisitely laid out, on which a most skilful artist has employed all his science in order to embellish it, if the whole earth is but an atom suspended in the air, and if you will but listen to what I am going to say?

You are placed, Lucilius, on some part of this atom; you must needs be very little, since you take up so little room on it; yet you have eyes, like two imperceptible points; open them, however, and look up to the heavens; what do you sometimes perceive there? Is it the moon in its full? It is beautiful and very radiant at the time, though all its light be but the reflection of the light of the sun; it appears as large as the sun itself, larger than the other planets, than any of the stars, but do not be deceived by outward appearances. Nothing in the heavens is so small as the moon; its superficies exceeds not the thirteenth part, and its volume not the eight and fortieth part of the earth, whilst its diameter, which is two thousand two hundred and fifty miles, is but a fourth of the diameter of the earth. What makes it really appear so great is its proximity only; for its distance from us is no more than thirty times the diameter of the earth, or three hundred thousand miles.[874]

---

[871] Lucilius is supposed to have been the Duke of Bourbon, the pupil of La Bruyère, and the spot of ground, the park of Chantilly, the seat of the Condé family. (See page 25, § 48.)

[872] Instead of the Nonette and the Thève, two small rivers canalised by order of the Prince de Condé, our author names two other small streams, the Yvette, which has its source near Rambouillet, and the Lignon, an affluent of the Loire.

[873] André le Nôtre, a celebrated landscape-gardener, laid out the gardens of Versailles and Chantilly, and died in 1700.

[874] The calculations of La Bruyère were not always exact; thus the mass of the moon

Its motion is small in comparison to the prodigious long career of the sun through the spacious firmament;[875] for it is certain the moon does not move at the rate of above sixteen hundred and twenty thousand miles a day,[876] which is not above sixty-seven thousand five hundred miles per hour, or one thousand one hundred and twenty-five in a minute. And yet, to complete this course it must move five thousand six hundred times faster than a race-horse running twelve miles an hour; it must be eighty times swifter than sound—than the report, for example, of a gun or of thunder, which moves at the rate of eight hundred and thirty-one miles an hour.[877]

But if you will oppose the moon to the sun with respect to its size, its distance, and its course, you will find there is no comparison to be made between them.

Remember that the diameter of the earth is nine thousand miles, that of the sun a hundred times more,[878] which gives nine hundred thousand miles;[879] now, if this be its width in every direction, judge what its superficies and volume must be. Can you comprehend the vastness of this extent, and that a million of such globes as the earth, all together, would not exceed the sun in size?[880] You will ask, then, how far is the sun from the earth, if one can judge of it by its apparent small size? You are quite right, the distance can hardly be conceived; for it is proved that the sun's distance from the earth can be no less than ten thousand times the diameter of the earth, or, in other words, than ninety millions of miles; it may be four times, perhaps six times, perhaps ten times as much, for ought we know; there is no method discovered to determine this distance.[881]

Now, to assist you in understanding this, let us suppose a millstone falling from the sun upon the earth; let it come down with all swiftness imaginable, and even swifter than the heaviest bodies descend, falling from a very great height; let us also suppose that it always preserves the same swiftness, without increase or diminution; that it advances thirty yards every second, which is half the height of the highest steeple, and consequently, eighteen hundred yards in a minute; but to facilitate our computation, let us allow it two thousand six hundred and forty yards a minute, which is a mile and a half; its fall will then be three miles in two

---

is eighty-nine times less than the earth's; it is 2165 miles in diameter, and revolves at a mean distance of 238,800 miles round the earth.

[875] Our author argues as if he were no believer in the system of Copernicus (1473-1543), but he only states that the sun appears to move through the firmament, for on page 484 he distinctly mentions that "the earth is carried round the sun."

[876] If we suppose that the earth is immovable, the moon moves at a rate of more than eighteen hundred thousand miles a day, but in reality it moves at the rate of about sixty thousand miles during twenty-four hours.

[877] Sound travels at the rate of more than nine hundred miles per hour.

[878] It is in reality a hundred and ten times more.

[879] Its absolute diameter is 860,000 miles.

[880] The volume of the sun is equivalent to about one and a quarter million times the volume of our earth; but its mean density is only a quarter of that of the earth.

[881] The mean distance of the sun from the earth, is, according to the latest results, about 92,400,000 miles.

minutes, ninety miles in an hour, and two thousand one hundred and sixty miles in a day; now, it must fall ninety millions of miles before it comes down to the earth; so that it cannot be less than forty-one thousand six hundred and sixty-six days, which is more than one hundred and fourteen years before it can perform this journey. Let all this not frighten you, Lucilius; I will tell you more. The distance of Saturn from the earth is at least ten times as great as the sun's is; that is, no less than nine hundred millions of miles, and the stone would be above eleven hundred and forty years in falling down from Saturn to the earth.[882]

Now, by this altitude of Saturn, exert your imagination, if you can, and conceive the immensity of its daily course; the circle which Saturn describes is above eighteen hundred millions of miles diameter, and consequently above fifty-four hundred millions of miles in circumference; so that a race-horse, if supposed to run thirty miles an hour, must be twenty thousand five hundred and forty-eight years in going this round.

Lucilius, I have not said all that can be said on the miracles of this visible world; or, to use the expression you sometimes use, on the wonders of chance, which alone you affirm to be the primary cause of all things, and which is still more wonderful in its operations than you imagine. Learn what chance is, and allow yourself to become acquainted with all the power of your God.

Do you know that the distance of the sun from the earth, which is ninety millions of miles, and that of Saturn, which is nine hundred millions of miles, if compared to that of the other stars, is so inconsiderable, that comparison is an improper term when mentioning such distances; for, indeed, what proportion is there between anything that can be measured, whatever its extent may be, and that which is beyond all mensuration? The height of a star cannot be known; it is, if I may say so, immensurable;[883] all angles, sines, and paralaxes are of no use for this problem.[884] Should a man observe a fixed star at Paris, and another in Japan, the two lines which would reach from their eyes to that star, would make no angle at all, but be confounded together, and converge into one and the same line, so inconsiderable is the space of the whole earth in comparison to that distance; but the stars have this in common with Saturn and the sun; therefore I shall say something more. If two astronomers should stand, the one on the earth and the other on the sun, and from thence should observe a star at the same time, the two visual rays of these two astronomers would not form a sensible angle; but in order that you may conceive the same thing another way, imagine a man to be placed on one of these stars, and then this sun, this earth, and the ninety millions of miles that are between them would seem to him but as a dot. This has been proved.

----

[882] Saturn's volume is 686.7 that of the earth; it is the sixth planet in order of distance from the sun, and describes in 10,795,22 days, or twenty-nine years five months and fourteen days, an orbit whose semi-major axis is 872,137,000 miles. In our author's time Saturn was supposed to be the planet the farthest from the sun. See page 135, note 264.

[883] "Immensurable" is a word La Bruyère tried to naturalise in French, but he did not succeed, yet it exists in English; "incommensurable" is to be found in both languages.

[884] According to Arago's Leçons d'Astronomie the star nearest the earth is still 22,800,000,000,000 leagues distant from it.

Nor is the distance known between any two stars, however close they appear to one another. You would think, if you judge by mere ocular demonstration, that the Pleiades almost touch one another. There is a star which seems to rest on one of the stars forming the tail of the Great Bear; you can hardly, with the mere eye, discern that part of the heavens which divides them; they make together, as it were, but one double star; yet, if the most skilful astronomers cannot, with all their art, find out the distance between these stars, how far asunder must two stars be which appear remote from each other, and how much farther yet the two polar stars.[885] How prodigiously long must be that line which reaches from one to another! How immense the circle of which this line is the diameter! And how can we fathom what cannot be fathomed, and represent to ourselves the volume of the globe, of which this circle is but a section? Shall we still wonder that these stars, of such immensurable size, seem no larger to us than so many sparks? Shall we not rather admire that from such a height the least appearance of them should reach our eye, and that they can be discerned at all? And, indeed, the quantity of stars which escape our vision is countless. It is true, we limit the number of the stars, but that is only of stars visible to us, for how should we number those we cannot see; those, for example, which constitute the Milky Way,—that luminous tract, which, on a clear night, can be observed in the sky from north to south,—and which, by their immensurable height, cannot be distinguished individually by our optics, and at most produce but a white mark in that part of the heavens where they are placed?[886]

Behold, then, the earth on which we tread, suspended like a grain of sand in the air; an almost infinite number of fiery globes, the vastness of whose bulk confounds my imagination, and whose height exceeds the reach of my conceptions, all perpetually revolving round this grain of sand, have been for above six thousand years, and are still, daily crossing the wide, the immense space of the heavens. Do you desire another system no less amazing? The earth itself is carried round the sun, which is the centre of the universe, with inconceivable velocity.[887] Methinks I see the motion of all these globes, the orderly march of these prodigious bodies; no disorder, no deflection, no collision, ever happens; should but the smallest of them happen to deviate and meet the earth, what would become of this earth? But, on the contrary, all keep their respective positions, remain in the order prescribed for them; and this, with respect to us, is performed so silently, that no one's hearing is acute enough to hear them move, and that ordinary people know not that there are such bodies. How wonderfully are the works of chance! Could intelligence itself have surpassed this? Only one thing, Lucilius, troubles me. These vast bodies are all so constant and exact in their various courses and revolutions, and in their relations to each other, that a little animal, confined to a corner of that wide space which is called the world, from his observations on them,

[885] No south polar star exists.

[886] Though the number of stars visible to the naked eye is not more than five thousand, thousands of millions of stars are in existence of which only about a hundred thousand have been observed.

[887] See page 479, note 875. The sun is not the centre of the universe, but of our planetary system.

has contrived an exact and infallible method of foretelling in what degree of their respective courses every one of these stars will be two thousand, four thousand, nay, twenty thousand years hence. This is my scruple, Lucilius. If these stars by chance follow such invariable rules, what is order, what are rules?

Nay, I will ask you what is chance? Is it a body? Is it a spirit? Is it a being distinguished from all other beings, having a peculiar existence or dwelling in any place; or, rather, is it not a mode or fashion of being? When a ball rolls against a stone, we are apt to say it is a chance; but is it anything more than an accidental hitting of these bodies one against another? If, by this chance, or this knock, the ball changes its straight course into an oblique one; if its motion from direct becomes reflected; if it ceases to roll on its axis, but winds and whirls about like a top, shall I from thence infer that motion in general proceeds in this ball from this same chance? Shall I not rather apprehend that the ball owes it to itself, or to the impulse of the arm which delivered it? Or, because the circular motions of the wheels of a clock are determined one by the other, in their degrees of swiftness, shall I be less anxious to find out what may be the cause of these several motions; whether it lies in the wheels themselves, or is derived from the moving force of a weight which sets them in motion? But neither these wheels nor this ball could produce this motion in themselves, nor do they owe it to their own nature, if they can be deprived of it, without changing this very nature; it is, therefore, likely they are moved extraneously and by some power not inherent to them. And as for the celestial bodies, if they should be deprived of their motion, would their nature then be altered, and would they cease being bodies? I cannot believe they would. Yet they move, and as they move not of themselves, nor by their own nature, it behoves us, Lucilius, to examine whether there is not some principle, not inherent to them, which causes this motion. Whatever you may find it, I call it God.

If we should suppose these great bodies to be without motion, we should not then ask who moves them, but still the question would be pertinent as to who made these bodies, as I may ask who made these wheels or that ball? And though each of these bodies were supposed to be but a mass of atoms, fortuitously knit together through the shape and conformation of their parts, I should take one of these atoms, and ask: "Who created this atom: is it matter; is it spirit; and has it any idea of itself?" If so, then it existed a minute before it did exist; it was, and it was not at the same time; and if it be the author of its own being, and of its manner of being, why did it make itself a body rather than a spirit? Moreover, has this atom had a beginning, or is it eternal, infinite, and will you make a God of this atom?[888]

(44.) A mite has eyes; it turns aside if it meets objects that can hurt it; place it on a flat piece of ebony, so that people may see it better, and if, while it is walking, but the smallest piece of straw is put in its way, it will alter its course immediately. Do you think its crystalline fluid, its retina, and its optic nerve are the products of chance?

---

[888] The atomic system of philosophy started by Leucippus, and adopted by Epicurus, Democritus, and many other philosophers, was that the universe, material and mental, consisted of minute, indivisible, and impenetrable atoms, which atoms were assumed to be the ultimate ground of nature, whilst necessity was supposed to be the cause of all existence.

Let pepper lie in water a little time, and be well steeped in it; then view a single drop of it with a microscope, and an almost countless number of animalculæ will be perceived, moving about with incredible agility, like so many monsters in the vast ocean; each of these animalculæ is a thousand times smaller than a mite, and yet it is a living body, receiving nourishment, growing, having muscles, and even vessels performing the functions of veins, nerves, and arteries, and a brain for the distribution of its animal spirits.[889]

A speck of mould, though no bigger than a grain of sand, appears through a microscope like a collection of many distinct plants, of which some are plainly seen to bear flowers and other fruits; some have buds only, partly opened, and others are withered. How extremely small must be the roots and fibres through which these little plants receive their nourishment! And if a person considers that these little plants bear their own seed as well as oaks or pines, or that the animalculæ I was speaking of are multiplied by generation as well as elephants or whales, whither will not such observations lead? Who can have made things so fine and so exceedingly small as to be imperceptible to the naked eye, and which, like the heavens, border upon the infinite, though in the other extreme? Is it not the same Being who has created, and moves with so much facility, the heavens and the stars, those vast bodies so terrible in their dimensions, their altitude, celerity, and revolutions?

(45.) Man enjoys the sun, the stars, the heavens and their influences, as much as he does the air he breathes, and the earth on which he treads and by which he is supported. This is a matter of fact; and if every fact were to be illustrated by fitness and verisimilitude, they could be deduced from them, as the heavens and all they contain are not to be compared for grandeur and dignity to one of the meanest men on earth, there being the same proportion between them and him as there is between matter destitute of sensation, a mere space having three dimensions, and a spiritual, reasonable, and intelligent being.[890] If people argue that less would have served for the preservation of man, I reply that it is not too much to display the power, the goodness, and the magnificence of God, as He could do infinitely more than He has done, whatever we perceive He has done.

If the whole world were made for man, it is literally the smallest thing God has done for man, and this may be proved by religion. Man is therefore neither presumptuous nor vain, when he submits to the evidences of truth, and owns the advantages he has received; he might be accused of blindness and stupidity, did he refuse to yield to the multitude of proofs which religion lays before him, to show him the privileges he enjoys, his resources, his expectations, and to teach him what he is and what he may be.—But the moon is inhabited, at least we do

---

[889] According to Descartes' Discours de la Méthode, animal spirits, which are so often mentioned in the philosophical and moral works of his time, "are like a very subtle mind, or rather like a very pure and bright flame, which is continually and in great abundance ascending from the heart to the brain, proceeds from thence through the nerves into the muscles, and produces motion in all the members of the body."

[890] Pascal already in his Pensées (i. 6.) had called man "a thinking reed ... nobler than the universe, even if it were to crush him, because he knows he has to die."

not know but it may be.—Why do you mention the moon, Lucilius, and for what purpose? If you own there is a God, nothing, indeed, is impossible.

But do you mean to ask whether in the entire universe it is on us alone that God has bestowed such great blessings; whether there are not other men or other creatures in the moon, who have received such favours? What a vain curiosity and what a frivolous question, Lucilius! The earth is inhabited, we dwell there and we know we do; we have proofs, demonstrations, and convictions for everything we believe of God and of ourselves; let the nations who inhabit the celestial globes, whatever those nations may be, attend to their concerns; they have their troubles, and we have ours. You have observed the moon, Lucilius; you have seen its spots, depth, inequalities, altitude, extent, course, and its eclipses; and no astronomer has yet done more; now contrive some new instruments; observe it again, and see whether it is inhabited, and by what species of inhabitants, whether they are like men, or are really men. When you have done this, let me look, that we both may be convinced that there are men who inhabit the moon; and then, Lucilius, we will consider whether these men are Christians or no; and whether God has bestowed on them the same favours He has granted us.

(46.) Everything is great and wonderful in nature; there is nothing which does not bear the stamp of the artist;[891] the irregular and imperfect things we sometimes observe imply regularity and perfection. Vain and presumptuous man: make a worm which you trample under foot and despise; you are afraid of a toad; make a toad, if you can. What an excellent artist is He who makes those things which men not only admire but fear! I do not require you to go into your studio to create a man of sense, a well-shaped man, a handsome woman, for such an undertaking would be too hard and too difficult for you; only attempt to create a hunchback, a madman, a monster, and I will be satisfied.

Ye kings, monarchs, potentates, anointed majesties, have I given you all your pompous titles? Ye great men of this earth, high and mighty, and perhaps shortly almighty lords, we ordinary men, for the ripening of our harvests, stand in need of a little rain, or what is less, of a little dew; make some dew, or send down upon the surface of the earth one drop of water.

The order, the picturesqueness, and the effects of nature are commonly known, but its causes and principles are not so. Ask a woman what is the cause the eye sees as soon as it is opened, and ask a learned man the same question.

(47.) Many millions of years, nay, many thousand millions of years, in a word, as many as can be comprehended within the limits of time, are but an instant compared to the duration of God, who is eternal; the extent of the whole universe is but a point, an atom, compared to His immensity. If this be so, as I affirm it is, for what proportion can there be between the finite and infinite, I ask what is the length of man's life, or what the extent of that speck of dust which is called the earth, nay, of the small part of that earth man owns and inhabits?—The wicked prosper whilst they live.—Yes, some of them, I admit. Virtue is oppressed and vice remains unpunished on this earth.—This happens sometimes, I acknowledge

----

[891] In the original *ouvrier*. See page 159, note 314.

it.—This is unjust.—No, not at all. You should have proved, to warrant this inference, that the wicked are absolutely happy, that virtue is absolutely miserable, and that vice always remains unpunished; that the short time in which the good are oppressed and the wicked prosper is of some duration, and that what we call prosperity and good fortune is something more than a false appearance, a fleeting shadow; and that this atom, the earth, in which virtue and vice so seldom meet with their deserts, is the only spot of the world's stage where people receive rewards and punishments.[892]

I cannot more clearly infer that because I am thinking I am a spirit, than conclude from what I do or do not, according as I please, that I am free. Now freedom implies the power of choosing,[893] or, in other words, a voluntary determination for good or evil, so that virtue or vice consists in the doing a good or a bad action. If vice were to remain absolutely unpunished, it would be a real injustice, but for vice to remain unpunished on earth is merely a mystery. However, let us suppose, with the atheist, that it is an injustice; all injustice is a negation or privation of justice, and therefore every injustice presupposes justice. All justice is in conformity to a sovereign reason, and thus I ask, when was it against reason for crime to remain unpunished? At the time, I suppose, when a triangle had not three angles. Now, all conformity to reason is truth; this conformity, as I said just now, always subsisted, and is of the number of those truths we call eternal. But this truth either is not and cannot be, or else it is the object of an intelligence; this intelligence is therefore eternal, and is God.

The most secret crimes are discovered so simply and easily, notwithstanding the great care which the guilty take to prevent their being brought to light, that it seems God alone could have detected them. These discoveries are so frequent, that those who are pleased to attribute them to chance, must acknowledge, at least, that in all ages, chance seems to have been very regular in its operations.

(48.) If you suppose every man on earth, without exception, to be rich and to want nothing, I infer that every man on earth is extremely poor, and in want of everything. There are but two sorts of riches which comprehend all the rest, money and land; if all people were rich, who would cultivate land or toil in mines? Those who live away from any mines could not toil in them, and those who dwell on barren lands, where only minerals are found, could hardly gather any fruits from them. Trade is the expedient people would have recourse to, I suppose. But if riches should be abundant, and no man under the necessity of living by labour, who will transport your ingots, or anything that is bought and sold, from one place to another? Who will fit out your ships and sail them? Who would travel in caravans? Everything that is necessary and useful would then be wanting. If necessity no longer existed on this earth, we would need no longer arts, sciences, inventions,

---

[892] Similar ideas as those expressed in the above paragraph are to be found in a sermon "On Providence" preached by Bossuet at the Louvre in 1662, which was not printed until long after he and La Bruyère were dead. But as the two men were great friends, it is not unlikely that our author may have heard them expressed by the eloquent pulpit orator, either in private conversation or in a sermon.

[893] See the chapter "Of Opinions," page 364, § 104.

handicrafts. Besides, such an equality of riches and possessions would establish the same equality in all ranks and conditions of men; would banish all subordination, and reduce men to be their own servants and to receive no help nor succour from one another; it would make the laws idle and useless, bring in a universal anarchy, and produce violence, outrages, murders, and impunity.

If, on the other hand, you suppose all men to be poor and indigent, then the sun in vain rises on the horizon; in vain it warms and fructifies the earth; in vain the heavens shed their benign influence on it; in vain rivers water it with their streams; in vain the fields abound with fruits; in vain seas, rocks, and mountains are ransacked and rifled of their treasures. If you grant that, of all men who are scattered throughout the world, some have to be rich and others poor, then necessity must naturally unite and bind them together and reconcile them; some will have to serve and obey, invent, labour, cultivate the earth, and make improvements; others enjoy life, live well, assist, protect, and govern the masses. Order is restored, and Providence appears.

(49.) Suppose authority, pleasure, and idleness to be the share of some men, and subjection, care, and misery the lot of the rest, then either the malignity of men must have thrown things into this disorder, or else God is not God.

A certain inequality in the condition of men is conducive to the order and welfare of the whole, is the work of God, or presupposes a divine law; but too great a disproportion, and such as is generally seen amongst men, is their own work, or caused by the law of the strongest.

Extremes are faulty, and proceed from men; all compensation is just, and proceeds from God.

If these "CHARACTERS" are not liked, I shall be astonished; and if they are, my astonishment will not be less.

THE END.

Lector House believes that a society develops through a two-fold approach of continuous learning and adaptation, which is derived from the study of classic literary works spread across the historic timeline of literature records. Therefore, we aim at reviving, repairing and redeveloping all those inaccessible or damaged but historically as well as culturally important literature across subjects so that the future generations may have an opportunity to study and learn from past works to embark upon a journey of creating a better future.

This book is a result of an effort made by Lector House towards making a contribution to the preservation and repair of original ancient works which might hold historical significance to the approach of continuous learning across subjects.

HAPPY READING & LEARNING!

LECTOR HOUSE LLP
E-MAIL: lectorpublishing@gmail.com